CLIMATE CHANGE AND SOCIAL INEQUALITY

The year 2016 was the hottest year on record and the third consecutive record-breaking year in planet temperatures. The following year was the hottest in a non-El Niño year. Of the seventeen hottest years ever recorded, sixteen have occurred since 2000, indicating the trend in climate change is toward an ever warmer Earth. However, climate change does not occur in a social vacuum; it reflects relations between social groups and forces us to contemplate the ways in which we think about and engage with the environment and each other.

Employing the experience-near anthropological lens to consider human social life in an environmental context, this book examines the fateful global intersection of ongoing climate change and widening social inequality. Over the course of the volume, Singer argues that the social and economic precarity of poorer populations and communities—from villagers to the urban disadvantaged in both the global North and global South—is exacerbated by climate change, putting some people at considerably enhanced risk compared to their wealthier counterparts. Moreover, the book adopts and supports the argument that the key driver of global climatic and environmental change is the global economy controlled primarily by the world's upper class, which profits from a ceaseless engine of increased production for national middle classes who have been converted into constant consumers.

Drawing on case studies from Alaska, Ecuador, Bangladesh, Haiti and Mali, *Climate Change and Social Inequality* will be of great interest to students and scholars of climate change and climate science, environmental anthropology, medical ecology and the anthropology of global health.

Merrill Singer is Professor in the Departments of Anthropology and Community Medicine at the University of Connecticut, USA.

ROUTLEDGE ADVANCES IN CLIMATE CHANGE RESEARCH

For more information about this series, please visit: https://www.routledge.com/
Routledge-Advances-in-Climate-Change-Research/book-series/RACCR

CLIMATE CHANGE AND SOCIAL INEQUALITY

The Health and Social Costs of Global Warming

Merrill Singer

LONDON AND NEW YORK

First published 2019
by Routledge
2 Park Square, Milton Park, Abingdon, Oxon OX14 4RN

and by Routledge
711 Third Avenue, New York, NY 10017

Routledge is an imprint of the Taylor & Francis Group, an informa business

© 2019 Merrill Singer

The right of Merrill Singer to be identified as author of this work has been asserted by him in accordance with sections 77 and 78 of the Copyright, Designs and Patents Act 1988.

British Library Cataloguing in Publication Data
A catalogue record for this book is available from the British Library

Library of Congress Cataloging in Publication Data
A catalog record has been requested for this book

ISBN: 978-1-138-10290-3 (hbk)
ISBN: 978-1-138-10291-0 (pbk)
ISBN: 978-1-315-10335-8 (ebk)

Typeset in Bembo
by Taylor & Francis Books

CONTENTS

ACKNOWLEDGEMENT

I would like to thank Hans Baer, long-time friend and collaborator, for reading and providing comments on an earlier draft of this book.

INTRODUCTION

The year 2016 was the hottest year on record since measurement began 137 years ago and it was the third consecutive record-breaking year for planet temperatures. The following year was the hottest in a non-El Nino year. Of the 17 hottest years ever recorded, 16 occurred since 2000, indicating the trend in climate change is toward an ever-warmer Earth and most of this change is human-induced, estimated by some scientists to account for as high as 75 percent of rising temperatures. Additionally, in October 2017, the World Meteorological Organization announced that atmospheric concentrations of CO^2 increased at a record rate during 2016 and reached their highest point in 800,000 years. The last time there was this much CO^2 in the atmosphere, modern humans, like Cro-Magnons (who lived between 3,500 and 10,000 years ago) did not yet exist. The oceans were home to megatoothed sharks, sea levels were 100 feet higher than they are today. It is estimated by climate scientists that Earth's global average surface temperature was as much as 11°F warmer than it is now and there was comparatively little ice on the planet.

There are two key indicators of the extent of climate change in 2016: rising global surface temperatures and the shrinking extent of Arctic sea ice. Just a few years ago, 2014 was the hottest year on record, but then came 2015, which was hotter still. Now 2016 has broken the record, which for a three-year period is itself a record, an ominous sign of the climatic trend on Earth. In the words of the World Meteorological Organization's (WMO) World Climate Research Program Director, David Carlson, Earth has been pushed into "truly unchartered territory" (World Meteorological Organization 2017).

In addition to its overall record-breaking temperatures, it is not an overstatement to say that climate change caused disruption all over the world in 2016 according to the WMO. At least three times during the winter of 2016, the Arctic suffered a polar version of a heatwave, with sea ice coming close to the melting point when in the past it would be refreezing. Within the U.S., almost 12,000 local warm temperature records were broken or tied during the month of February. But new records were also being set in eastern Australia, suggesting the global nature of the transformations that are occurring. Oceans were also at or near record surface high temperatures, especially in the northern hemisphere. Global sea levels rose during the year, as glaciers and land ice melted. It appears that the Amazon Basin, home of the world's largest rainforest, was the driest on record. Extreme heatwaves occurred in southern Africa, South and South-East Asia, and parts of western and central Europe. Flooding was significant in the Yangtze basin of China, with some rivers achieving record flood levels. Conversely, the Slims River, a large flowing water-way that was almost 500 feet across at its widest point, filled with cold water from the Kaskawulsh glacier—one of Canada's largest—disappeared over a four-day period during the spring of 2016. The event was caused by intense glacier melting, a visible sign of how climate change is rearranging the geography of the world. Between 1956 and 2007, the Kaskawulsh glacier retreated by 2,100 feet. In 2016, there was a sudden intensification of this process further shrinking the glacier and causing the Slims to vanish. James Best, a geologist who was part of the team measuring the Slims River, reported:

> We went to the area intending to continue our measurements in the Slims river, but found the riverbed more or less dry. The delta top that we'd been sailing over in a small boat was now a dust storm. In terms of landscape change it was incredibly dramatic".
>
> *(Quoted in Devlin 2017)*

While the Slims, a popular site for whitewater rafting and a Unesco world heritage site, became a non-river, the Alsek River, which unlike the Slims empties into the Gulf of Alaska, grew in size as it received a massive influx of glacial melt. Researchers who have studied this dramatic shift believe that it can be attributed to anthropogenic climate change (Shugar et al. 2017). As Roe and colleagues (2016: 95) stress, given the highly visible and startling nature of the change, "The near-global retreat of glaciers over the last century provides some of the most iconic imagery for communicating the reality of anthropogenic climate change to the public."

The die-off of ocean corals also recorded new adverse milestones in 2016. Scientists studying the Great Barrier Reef off the coast of Queensland in northeast Australia reported the worst ever die-off they have ever seen (Hughes et al. 2017). Enormous stretches of the reef, extending for hundreds of miles, were found to be dead, cooked by the overheated ocean around it. The Great Barrier Reef is of vital importance not only because it is the largest coral reef in the world, or even because it is the world's largest living structure, but also because it is home to a vast array of fish and other sea organisms that are vital to ocean biodiversity. Death of two-thirds of the northern section of the reef is a tell-tale sign of the devastations being wrought by global climate change. The die-off represents the third global-scale event of its kind since the mass bleaching of the coral that comprises the reef was first documented in 1980.

Among the other noteworthy climate-related disruptions of 2016, there occurred the possible extinction of the Bramble Cy melonmy, a small rodent indigenous to a Torre Strait island off the coast of Australia. It is the first mammalian species suspected of falling victim to climate change but it will likely not be the last. Significantly, a number of primate species, such as the black and white colobine monkey, are currently in grave climate-related danger. In fact, research suggests that climate change is adversely affecting every primate species on Earth (Graham et al. 2016), including us.

But, of course, the dramatic climate story did not end in 2016. In early 2017, the amount of sea ice measured at both poles, Arctic and Antarctic, was found by NASA to be at their lowest points since U.S. satellites began the process of continuously monitoring sea ice in 1979. Total polar sea ice was found to be 790,000 square miles less than the average global minimum extent for the period 1981–2010. Lost was enough sea ice to cover the country of Mexico (Viñas 2017). These trends are expected to continue, year after year, although mitigation efforts can alter the nature of the future that lies ahead.

But climate change is not, as Michelle Williams, dean of Harvard's T. H. Chan School of Public Health, has observed, "a remote, abstract problem expressed in parts per million, in terms of temperature change of mere degrees, or in sea-level rises predicted decades into the future" (quoted in Feldscher 2017). Nor is it just a matter of thermal and environmental conditions, or even of disrupted weather patterns on every continent, or of the loss of species large and small. Although all of these are occurring, these changes do not speak to the fact that climate change does not occur in a social vacuum. Rather, in addition to all of its outward expressions in the atmosphere, on land, and in the sea, climate change reflects relations among human social groups expressed through the ways we think about and engage the environment and each other. Stresses Ribot (2014: 673), "environmental [h]azards and [community] vulnerabilities have social cause." Vulnerability is closely linked to the ability a group's ability to influence the political economy in which it is embedded. Vulnerability is produced in and by society, most notably by social inequality. Climate change and other ecocrises also have social causes, they are not merely products of nature. Climate change and social inequality not disparate factors, they are intimately linked.

Employing the experience-near anthropological lens on human social life in environmental context, in this book I examine the fateful global intersection of ongoing climate change and widening social inequality throughout the world. I argue that the social and economic precarity of poorer populations and communities, from villagers to the urban disadvantaged in both the global North and South, is exacerbated by climate change, putting some people at considerably enhanced climate-related risk and suffering compared to their wealthier counterparts. While there may not be winners and losers in climate change, as the progressive heating of Earth produces a wide array of climatic and environmental changes, some people are being disproportionately affected in conspicuously adverse and painful ways. Climate change produces or magnifies the already often perilous lives of the poor by eliminating potable water sources, causing desertification, reducing food production, increasing damaging weather events, promoting ocean rise, and causing the spread of disease, among other threats to life and well-being (Baer and Singer 2009). Precariousness is product of subjecting some people to far greater environmental threat than others, commonly as a consequence of policies and actions that favor elite advantage. The invisibility of the lives of the poor to those who most benefit from the continual expansion of greenhouse gas production and release helps to shield the elite from any sense of culpability. Yet, as discussed in this book, there are intimate causal connections between the lives of the rich and the lives of the poor. This nexus is the human face of climate change.

Although the poor are not influential in the decisions and actions that lead to most anthropogenic climate warming, they pay a colossal price for rising planet temperatures and related anthropogenic planetary changes, revealing the agonising and damaging nature of the contemporary social inequalities that characterize human societies and amplify social suffering. In this, the strategies and policies supported by social elites that increase the production and environmental discharge of greenhouse gases and black carbon—because of the economic benefits of unregulated production—constitute a form of structural violence that is taking a severe toll on the poor now and will increasingly do so in the future. Exposed by the examination of this often hidden form of violence are the ways the bodies, communities, and social environments of the poor are in intimate relationship with macroeconomic structures. The poor are treated as if they have "expendable bodies" and their deaths commonly are attributed to natural causes, poor habits, and inferior values rather than to the decisions and actions of wealthier, more powerful people. Climate change, in short, is not just a feature of a transforming environment, it is both an expression of social inequality and a force in the enhancement of social inequality with grave consequence for the lives of billions of people. In response to this inconvenient truth, social elites have engaged in a well-funded, multifaceted campaign of climate change denial or obfuscation, which joins the traditional strategy of blaming the poor for their own poverty as part of the culture of wealth embraced by social elites that is hegemonically disseminated and influential in the wider society. Rather than the ideology of a few scattered cranks and perpetuate doubters of science, climate change denial has become a strategic tool of elite polluters, their hired spokespersons, and conservative politicians who benefit from sizeable elite donations. Dissecting the climate change denial machine is therefore a critical task in the analysis of the intersection of global warming and social inequality.

While social inequality may be inscribed on their bodies by the diseases and damaging conditions of climate change and the polluting of their environments, the poor are not silent or docile. They develop local knowledge of their circumstances, adopt changes to cope with the risks they encounter, and band together to challenge the causes of their plight. Hearing their narratives, describing their coping strategies, and drawing attention to their social struggles are all within the wheel-house of anthropology, a discipline that finds the big stories of the world played out in the many small places of which is it composed. Consequently, this book focuses on the lives, thoughts, words, and actions of poor communities around the world as they encounter the effects of climate change while contextualizing downstream ethnographic accounts with upstream examination of the polluting elites primarily responsible for climate change and its incumbent impacts (Baer and Singer 2014).

This juxtaposing is framed by the theoretical perspective known as political ecology, a term coined by anthropologist Eric Wolf that expresses a union between ecologically rooted social science and the principles of political economy. Political ecological analysis begins with the holistic understanding that a tug on the strands of the global web of human–environment connections echoes throughout the system as a whole. As contrasted with other social scientific and physical science approaches to the biophysical environment, it emerged as an explicit alternative and corrective to apolitical ecological thinking. Unlike apolitical accounts of con-temporary environmental crises, political ecology does not ignore the significant influence of political economic factors—including issues of power, wealth, and the structure of social relationships—on population health and social well-being.

Moreover, with reference to health issues, political ecology asserts that in developing an understanding of modern global health it is insufficient to focus on either local cultural dynamics or international exchange relations; rather, these must be addressed in tandem. In sum, the political ecology of health is concerned with the impacts on environmental systems, human environmental health, and health-related experiences and behaviors of differential control over processes, resources and, especially, the products and by-products of production. Consequently, the political ecological approach seeks to denaturalize environmental and health con-ditions by revealing their historic manufacture in political economic context. For example, current global rates of cardiovascular health problems, such as progression in coronary calcification consistent with acceleration of atherosclerosis, cannot be understood independent of global air pollution and the role of the oil industry in promoting an oil-dependent global economy (Kaufman et al. 2016). The approach used in this book portrays anthropogenic climate and biophysical environmental change both as objective facts and human experiences.

There reasons for anthropologists to be involved with environmental issues, most notably the fact that there is a direct relationship between features of the local environment and the nature of society. Although climate change is a global pro-cess, it has significant but varying, consequences for communities studied anthro-pologically in local contexts around the globe.

Organizationally, this book begins in chapter 1 with a discussion of the anthro-pological approach taken in the book, the scientific sources of climate change knowledge and the multiple and diverse harmful impacts of the planet's changing climate patterns. The chapter also raises the issue of culpability for climate change, commonly described as a product of human activity. This way of thinking about climate change, which is challenged in the chapter, problematically generalizes it to a broad human problem, as if all people were equally at fault, from the energy corporation president in his expensively furnished office in New York, to the McDonald's worker driving her dated car to her low-wage job in Oklahoma City, to the manual laborer in a risky cottage industry in Manila, Philippines, who spends his day sitting on the ground breaking apart car batteries to extract components with recyclable value. The second chapter examines the production of climate change and its corporate and political denial or confusing complication intended to mislead the public. Chapter 2 also examines the tendency of social elites in the existing world economic system to treat the environment as a limitless resource and dumping ground for the by-products of manufacture and use, including CO_2, other greenhouse gases, and black carbon. Finally, the chapter engages the point that decreasing inequality of income will not diminish global climate change risk unless social equalization happens in a sustainable manner because otherwise it is unlikely that the overall consumption level of the human population will decrease. To clarify the importance of sustainable production and consumption as an alternative to elite strategies, I introduce the concept of "eco-equity," the notion that there can be no sustainable ecology without social equity and no social equity without sustainable human lifeways on the planet. Chapter 3 focuses on the ideology and election politics of climate change denial, while chapter 4 examines the socioeconomic roots and strategies of this quintessential expression of the social inequalities exposed by climate change. While both the U.S. National Academy of Sciences and the American Association for the Advancement of Science use the word "consensus" when describing the views of climate science on the existence and human-cause of climate change, some (primarily) non-climate scientists and paid policy commentators and their political allies dispute this. In other words, as examined in these two companion chapters, while we have overwhelming scientific agreement on climate change—with disagreements about the details not the primary patterns—we do not have social consensus on this issue. The debate about climate change, like almost all environmental issues, is of keen interest to anthropology because ultimately it is a debate about culture, worldviews, ideology, and, most importantly, the structure of society. As stressed in chapter 3, debates about climate change are as much about the distribution of wealth, power, and authority in society as they are about whether or not scientists have accurately depicted the extent and causes of climate change. Climate change denial is not an isolated perspective but rather part of a broad elite worldview. Thus, chapter 3 reviews the arguments of climate change deniers, assesses the ways social elites impose many of the uncalculated costs of climate change on poor and working people, and investigates the strategies used by social elites to blame the poor for their own suffering while seeking to silence their expressions of grievance by deploying tropes of personal responsibility, the innate goodness of development and economic grow, and the ever more vigilant needs of national security. Exemplary of this pattern are the remarks of Trump's appointee to secretary of the Department of Housing and Urban Development, Ben Carson, who believes that "poverty to a large extent is … a state of mind;" as a result, social programs to help the poor are ineffective because "You take somebody with the wrong mind-set, you can give them everything in the world [and] they'll work their way right back down to the bottom" (quoted in Fessler 2017). Chapter 4 peeks behind the curtain of the deceptive strategies used by the organized and well-funded deniers of climate change and follows the money trail back from them to the ultra-rich polluting elites who benefit financially from being allowed to befoul the environment with the toxic and disruptive by-products of ceaseless industrial production.

The subsequent five chapters draw on specific bodies of anthropological research on local weather/environmental effects, perceptions and experiences, and responses to climate change in societies in five regions of the world: Alaska (specifically the land of the indigenous Yupik and Iñupiat peoples), Ecuador, Bangladesh, Haiti, and Mali. Each of these case study chapters presents anthropological and related research on local weather/environmental effects of climate change, peoples' perceptions and experiences of the changes that are occurring, and the coping, vulnerability mitigating, and politically challenging responses they develop to the local impacts of climate change. The final chapter draws together the lines of argument developed in the previous chapters to highlight the consequential intersection of social inequality and climate change on everyday health, coping, and community organizing. As part of the discussion of the failure to fully consider the multidimensional aspects of climate change adversity, in this chapter I introduce the concept of "planetary health", a configuration spearheaded by the British medical journal *The Lancet* and which elsewhere I have suggested is the fifth stage in the historic evolution of the modern population health paradigm.

Overall, the book highlights the role anthropology can play in understanding climate change in human social and health contexts rather than an issue solely in terms of atmospheric, climatic, or ecological lens, while stressing the heightened costs of social inequality in a time of climate change. In doing so, it stresses that marginalized populations are not passive victims of the changes that are reshaping life on Earth, but rather are active, decision-making agents who strive to limit the harsh consequence of planetary warming. In writing this book, I have been motivated by the idea that "Society is positively transformed by showing, through [informed] criticism, what most needs changing and in which particular ways" (Peet and Hartwick 1990: 282).

References

Baer, H. and M. Singer. 2009. *Global Warming and the Political Ecology of Health: Emerging Crises and Systemic Solutions*. Walnut Creek, CA: Left Coast Press.

Baer, H. and M. Singer. 2014. *The Anthropology of Climate Change: An Integrated Critical Perspective*. Abingdon, Oxford, U.K.: Routledge, Earthscan.

Devlin, H. 2017. Receding glacier causes immense Canadian river to vanish in four days. *The Guardian*, April 17. www.theguardian.com/science/2017/apr/17/receding-glacier-ca uses-immense-canadian-river-to-vanish-in-four-days-climate-change.

Feldscher, K. 2017. Putting a human face on climate change. www.hsph.harvard.edu/news/features/climate-change-symposium/.

Fessler, P. 2017. Housing Secretary Ben Carson says poverty is a 'state of mind'. National Public Radio. www.npr.org/2017/05/25/530068988/ben-carson-says-poverty-is-a-state-of-mind.

Graham, T., H. Matthews, and S. Turner. 2016. A global-scale evaluation of primate exposure and vulnerability to climate change. *International Journal of Primatology* 37: 158.

Hughes, T., J. Kerry, M. Alvarez-Noriega, J. Alvarez-Romero, K. Anderson, A. Baird et al. 2017. Global warming and recurrent mass bleaching of corals. *Nature* 543: 373–377.

Kaufman, J., Adar, S., Barr, R., Budoff, M., Burke, G., Curl, C., M. Daviglus et al. 2016. Association between air pollution and coronary artery calcification within six metropolitan areas in the USA (the Multi-Ethnic Study of Atherosclerosis and Air Pollution): A longitudinal cohort study. *The Lancet* 388(10045): 696–704.

Peet, R. and E. Hartwick. 1990. *Theories of Development: Contentions, Arguments, Alternatives*, 2nd edition. London: Guilford Press.

Ribot, J. 2014. Cause and response: Vulnerability and climate in the Anthropocene. *Journal of Peasant Studies* 41(5): 667–705.

Roe, G., M. Baker, and F. Herla. 2016. Centennial glacier retreat as categorical evidence of regional climate change. *Nature Geoscience* 10: 95–99.

Shugar, D., J. Clague, J. Best, C. Schoof, M. Willis, L. Copland, and G. Roe. 2017. River piracy and drainage basin reorganization led by climate-driven glacier retreat. *Nature Geoscience* 10(5), 370–375.

Viñas, M.-J. 2017. Sea ice extent sinks to record lows at both poles. NASA's Global Climate Change: Vital Signs of the Planet. https://climate.nasa.gov/news/2569/sea-ice-extent-sinks-to-record-lows-at-both-poles/.

World Meteorological Organization2017. Climate breaks multiple records in 2016, with global impacts. https://public.wmo.int/en/media/press-release/climate-breaks-multiple-records-2016-global-impacts.

1

THE PHYSICAL AND SOCIAL DIMENSIONS OF CLIMATE CHANGE

Sources of the scientific evidence on climate change

The scientific evidence on climate change is the product of the work of countless scientists from around the world who have been trained in numerous different physical scientific disciples, including climatology, astrophysics, biology, archaeology, physics, oceanography, meteorology, geology, atmospheric chemistry, and glaciology. These researchers have published thousands of studies documenting increasing surface, atmospheric, and oceanic temperatures; melting land ice and glaciers; diminishing snow cover; shrinking sea ice; rising ocean levels; ocean acidification; and increasing atmospheric water vapor. The vast majority of scientists who study climate-related issues, approximately 97 percent, are in agreement that the world is heating up and human activity is the main driver of this change and the related environmental alterations noted above (Cook et al. 2016). Other individuals who claim to be climate scientists or climate experts do not share in this consensus, but, as discussed in chapters 3 and 4, their credentials are often suspect and/or they are heavily financed by the greenhouse gas-emitting energy industry. Nonetheless, because of the deep pockets of their backers they have succeeded in confusing the public about the incredible level of agreement about climate change among climate scientists.

Climate scientists comprise a diverse group of people, each having an area of research focus. Examining some of the work of individual climate scientists reveals details of how climate science has built a broad, integrated understanding of our changing world and the forces driving this change. Wenhong Li, for example, an atmospheric scientist at Duke University, studies the relationship between long-term climate change and weather variability. She became fascinated by weather as a child in China, and came to the U.S. to study climate science. Her research on precipitation patterns in the southeastern United States offers some of the clearest evidence available of how global warming can influence a regional weather pattern, often in surprising ways. In 2007, Georgia suffered the worst drought in a century, but two years later suffered late-summer flooding. Using data from rain gauges dating from 1948, Li and colleagues found that through time there was increasing variability in precipitation in the regions. Rain patterns were becoming more erratic, a pattern being seen around the globe, and one known to be tied to climate change.

From 1948 to 1977, Li found there were just two unusually wet and two unusually dry summers—("rainfall anomalies" that exceeded one standard deviation from the norm) in Georgia. By contrast, from 1978 to 2007, there were six unusually wet and five unusually dry summers. Using sophisticated statistical techniques to analyze the precipitation data, Li determined that both droughts and deluges had unquestionably increased in a statistically significant way. Further, Li and co-workers found a correlation of their data with data on the North Atlantic Subtropical High (NASH), an area of high pressure that forms each summer in the ocean near Bermuda, suggesting a direct tie to anthropogenic warming. In other words, human-induced climate change has caused a prevailing weather pattern to move closer in to North America. When that high-pressure area moves slightly to the north or south, the consequences are felt very acutely in the southeast's regional rainfall compared to six decades ago. Li's work predicts greater weather unpredictability as global warming continues.

Another climate scientist, Benjamin Santer, affiliated with the Lawrence Livermore National Laboratory, found that the various causes of climate change (known as "forcings") leave distinct signatures or patterns that climate scientists can identify and the signatures can tell us what is causing climate change. For example, if Earth's warming is caused by an increase in the sun's energy output scientists would expect to see warming from the top of the atmospheric column straight down to the surface. But if massive volcanic eruptions are a significant factor, dust from the volcano would cause cooling in the troposphere (the atmospheric layer closest to the surface) and heating in the stratosphere (the layer above the troposphere).

In fact, neither of those two profiles are found in Santar's and other researchers' data. Rather, what climate scientists find is a tell-tale warming of the troposphere and cooling of the stratosphere. This is the precise fingerprint that scientists since the 1960s predicted would occur from an intensified "greenhouse effect" as increasing amounts of heat-trapping CO^2 from fossil fuel emissions built up in the atmosphere.

Richard Seager, a climate scientist at Columbia University's Lamont-Doherty Earth Observatory, studies climate factors in southwestern U.S., an area he believes is soon likely to experience a condition of "permanent drought" that matches the Dust Bowl of the 1930s. In Seager's assessment, the southwest is dry because, like other parts of the so-called subtropics to the north and south of the equatorial tropics, the atmospheric flow tends to move far more moisture out of the region than the amount that storms bring back into it. With increasing concentrations of heat-trapping greenhouse gases, the planet's atmosphere will retain a growing level of moisture, in ever greater amounts as it warms. Evaporation from lakes and rivers will increase, soil is expected to become ever more arid, and plants will probably yield more moisture directly into the atmosphere.

Like people of the various science and social science disciplines, the climate scientists described above come from different national, regional, ethnic, and class backgrounds. What they share is a lifetime of research that has made it clear to each of them that Earth is warming because of human activity and that the climate and ecosystem changes this produces will have important and adverse impacts on human communities worldwide.

The human diseases of climate change

One of the adverse impacts of climate change that is already occurring is seen in an array of climate-influenced human diseases. The effects of weather (immediate) and climate (long-term trends) on human health are significant and multiple, and have a range of pathways, including heat, flooding, food availability, infectious disease, and geographic dislocation. Notably, climate change is not occurring at a time free of already heavy health burdens and significant vulnerabilities around the world. Climate change acts as a "stress multiplier" for many existing public health problems. In addition, as the planet warms, areas of the world will face new climate-related health threats, including new diseases. The impact of climate change on health varies by location and socioeconomic status; thus the existing social architectures of inequality mediate climate-related health problems. The poorest populations are the most vulnerable overall to the health effects of climate change, as are elders, children, and the ill. The more severe and rapid climate change occurs, the more unsettling to societies and burdensome to human health. Disruptions in social and infrastructural systems can increase overall health vulnerability. Exposure may not be to individual adverse effects of climate change but rather to serial or simultaneous multiple effects resulting in compounding or cascading health impacts.

One important way climate change threatens human health is through climate-sensitive infectious diseases. This occurs by: 1) potentially changing the spatial distributions infectious agents; 2) affecting their annual/seasonal cycles; and 3) altering disease incidence and severity. The climate sensitivity of pathogens is a key indicator that diseases might respond to climate change, but the proportion of pathogens that is climate-sensitive, and their characteristics, are not fully known. A study in Europe of a hundred human and 101 animal disease-causing pathogens found that 63 percent, at about equal levels of both groups, were climate sensitive (Morand et al. 2013). Also protozoa and helminths (worms), as well vector-borne, foodborne, soilborne, and waterborne pathogens were found to be associated with larger numbers of climate drivers, such as oscillations, extreme weather events, moisture, and wind. Zoonotic pathogens, those that infect humans and other species, were more climate sensitive than human- or animal-only pathogens. The pathogen with the highest sensitivity to climate factors was *Vibrio cholera*, the cause of the often deadly, diarrheal disease, cholera. Next most sensitive was the helminth, specifically a parasite known as the liver fluke, the source of liver disease. Third was, *Bacillus anthracic*—the pathogenic cause of anthrax—a bacteria that can prove fatal depending on infection type and available treatment. Fourth was *Borrelia burgdorferi*, the tick-borne bacteria that causes Lyme disease. This research predicts that with the increasing diverse impacts of climate change over time, these diseases and other pathogenic diseases like dengue and Zika will become increasing threats to human health.

Through its worsening of air quality and altered local and regional pollen production, climate change is also increasing the prevalence and severity of asthma and related allergic diseases. When exposed to warmer temperatures and higher levels of CO^2, plants grow more vigorously and produce more pollen than they otherwise would. Research suggests pollen counts could double by 2040. The burden from asthma and other allergic diseases is already significant. Globally, 300 million or more people have asthma, a quarter million people die from it annually. Other climate-sensitive respiratory allergies are even more prevalent, and diminish the quality of life of millions of people worldwide.

Fungus is a member of a large group of organisms that includes mushrooms and molds. Abundant worldwide, about 70,000 fungal species have been identified. The global food crisis is exacerbated by fungi infections that damage or kill crop plants, and, with climate change, the threat appears to be growing as seen in rising rates of potato blight, rice last, wheat stem rust, soybean rust, and corn smut.

Mold is a type of fungus that grows on plants and fibers and is most often associated with damp locations. Mold travels through the air as tiny spores. Mold is a common allergy trigger in which a person's immune system overreacts when breathing in mold spores. In some people, mold allergy is linked to asthma. All of this is relevant because of the role of climate change in: 1) increasing temperature; and 2) sparking violent storms and flooding. The extensive flooding in the aftermath of Hurricanes Katrina and Rita created conditions ideal for indoor mold growth. Studies evaluating the levels of indoor and outdoor molds in the months following the hurricanes found significant mold growth. Climate change-related flooding presents a major threat for mold-related health problems. There are other diseases of climate change but it is evident that human health, especially for some, is increasingly vulnerable.

Extreme weather

One of the fundamental consequences of climate change is an intensification of damaging extreme weather events, such as the growing intensity of hurricanes. By any standard, 2017 was an historic hurricane season in the Caribbean and Gulf of Mexico with the devastating arrival of back-to-back hurricanes Harvey, Irma, and Maria, as well as seven other storm events. The season recorded both the highest total accumulated cyclone energy—a measure used by the National Oceanic and Atmospheric Administration to index the activity of individual tropical cyclones/hurricanes and entire tropical cyclone seasons—as well as the greatest number of major hurricanes since 2005, the year of hurricanes Katrina and Rita. All ten of the season's hurricanes occurred consecutively, the greatest number of sequential hurricanes seen in the era of satellite observation. Moreover, 2017 achieved distinction as the costliest hurricane season on record, with losses of over $315, primarily wrought by Harvey, Irma, and Maria. Additionally, the season was one of only six years known to weather recording to produce multiple Category 5 hurricanes. Irma's treacherous landfalls on multiple Caribbean islands and Maria's landing on Dominica made 2017 the second season on record with two hurricanes making landfall at Category 5 intensity. These patterns indicate the rising risk of extreme weather in the time of global warming.

One of the places hardest hit during the season was the island of Puerto Rico. The 2017 hurricane season was particularly punishing for Puerto Rico. First, it was hit by Hurricane Irma when its eye passed just north of the island. The storm, which devastated several Caribbean islands, knocked out power for one million people in Puerto Rico. Then came Hurricane Maria. On September 20, this powerful Category 4 hurricane with 150 mph winds made direct landfall, bisecting the island. Tens of thousands of people were left without electricity. Maria followed a course directly over Puerto Rico, hit at its near peak intensity, developed a width of 50- to 60-miles across, and passed just 25 miles away from the historic capital of San Juan, home to approximately 400,000 people. Hurricane Maria lashed the island with damaging winds, caused extensive flooding, crippled communication systems, demolished buildings, and damaged a dam that threatened residents downstream. In many places, there was still no water to drink, bathe in, or flush toilets even months after the hurricane. Dozens of remote communities were completely cut off in the unfolding and prolonged humanitarian disaster. Moreover, help was slow to arrive in places where the devastation reached apocalyptic proportions. People were forced to find ways to survive without medicines, lights, refrigeration, gas, air conditioning, and jobs. Damages surpassed $90 billion and the mortality rate was devastating. Over 200,000 Puerto Ricans were forced to flee their island home which remained in tatters. Pointing to the failures of the federal government in responding to the crisis, Oxfam America President Abby Maxman (quoted in Holmes 2017) asserted:

> It's really quite shocking how long and slow it has been, and what it's taking to get back and move the recovery forward … . By any standard, three months where a majority of the population don't have access to clean water or electricity is a sign that it's been an exceptionally slow and really unacceptable level of response.

Also badly hit in 2017 was the U.S. Virgin Islands, which was struck by both Hurricanes Maria and Irma. St. John and St. Thomas were ravaged by Hurricane Irma. Fourteen days later, Maria hammered St. Croix, the largest of the U.S. Virgin Islands. The islands suffered vast ruin and deep desperation. Significantly adding to the brutal and long-enduring impact of the hurricane season was the damage to the tourism industry, which accounts for about three-quarters of the islands' economy. While many small and mid-size hotels reopened by February 2018, most of the hotel rooms on the islands were still out of commission because the large resorts suffered the worst damage. Full recovery is expected to take at least two years (Allen 2018).

During the 2017 season, the Gulf Coast of Texas faced extreme rains that inundated the Houston area during Hurricane Harvey. Harvey dumped an estimated 27 trillion gallons of water on Texas and Louisiana and was one of the most damaging "natural" disasters in U.S. history. The amount of rain that poured onto parts of southeast Texas set a new record of 51.88 inches, which broke the former record of 48 inches set in 1978. It is likely that the Texas flooding exceeds other such event in the continental U.S. over the past 1,000 years. Tens of thousands of people were forced to evacuate their homes, with many losing everything they owned and very few possessing flood insurance. This means that families with flooded basements, water-logged furniture, and water-damaged walls have to pay out of pocket or assume more debt to repair their homes. The economic devastation of Hurricane Harvey may even pass Hurricane Katrina's enormous cost.

There is evidence that the massive flooding caused by Harvey was made more likely by climate change. This is according to a study by Kerry Emmanuel (2017) of the Massachusetts Institute of Technology. Emmanuel's findings indicate that the kind of extreme flooding event seen with Harvey will become more frequent as the planet continues to warm. In the wake of Harvey, many researchers have pointed out that a warmer atmosphere holds more water vapor and that, as a result, a warmer planet should produce more extreme rains. But Emanuel's study goes beyond this general statement to support the idea that the specific risk of extreme rain events is increasing because of the ways humans have changed the planet, including the release of greenhouse gases. Based on climate modeling, Emanuel generated 3,700 computerized storms for each of three separate models that situated the storms in the climates seen during the years from 1980 to 2016. All of the storms were in the vicinity of Houston or other Texas areas. He examined how often, in his models, there would be about 20 inches of rainfall in one of these events. Harvey actually brought about 33 inches of rain to Houston. But in the tests performed under the conditions that prevailed 1980 to 2000, getting 20 inches of rain was an extremely rare occurrence. When Emanuel performed a similar analysis using projected climates for the years 2080 to 2100, the odds shifted toward a much greater likelihood of such events. Harvey's rains in Houston became a once-in-a-100-years event and for Texas as a whole, the odds increased from once in 100 years to once every five and a half years. This also means, according to Emmanuel's calculations, that Harvey was probably more likely in 2017 than in the era from 1981 to 2000 because of climate change. According to Noah Diffenbaugh, a climate scientist at Stanford University who has focused on the science of attributing extreme events to climate change, "Harvey was a complex event with lots of contributing ingredients. This study breaks new ground by isolating the role that global warming played in upping the odds that a storm like Harvey produces very heavy rainfall" (quoted in Mooney 2017).

Rising oceans

Another expression of the effects of a warming planet on which huge quantities of water are frozen in land-covering ice sheets and glaciers is ice melt and sea level rise. There is strong concern that before its 250th birthday Bangkok, the capital city of Thailand, will be below the ocean. The coastal city of Bangkok is only between 1.6 and 6.5 feet above sea level. The central metropolitan area was built precariously on what was once protective marshland. Below the city is layer of soft clay that is highly compressible. Besides the natural land subsidence, decades of excessive groundwater pumping and rapid development have put more pressure on this fragile foundation. As a result, every year the city sinks by 0.4–0.8 inches, in some areas even more (Weather Channel 2015). Remarks Thai architect Ponlawat Buasri (quoted in Promchertchoo 2017):

> the problem is slow and silent … . It won't be submerged all of a sudden but it will begin to malfunction little by little. One day, when we can't repair it anymore, we'll realise we have a problem but won't know how to deal with it … . One day Bangkok will be under water.

Exemplifying the problem, in 2011 Thailand was inundated by one of the worst floods in the country's history. It is estimated that more than 800 people were killed and 12 million others were adversely affected. Bangkok remained under-water for months. Then in 2017, Bangkok was hit by intense rains that flooded the city. The flooding caused damage in at least 20 districts across the city, including the central business district and the downtown area. Because of the heavy rain, the Yom River overflowed impacting 10,000 families.

The problems facing the city do not arise solely from changing climatic conditions. A report from Thailand's government says that Bangkok emphasized that immediate and admittedly costly solutions are need to deal with the over-pumping of underground aquifer water and the sheer number and weight of the many buildings (700 buildings with 20 floors or more and 4,000 buildings with 8–20 floors), roads, automobiles, and electric railways pressing on the underlying clay. In short, the city faces a two-headed anthropogenic problem that could lead to catastrophe in the not so distant future (Promchertchoo 2017).

On a smaller scale, there is the village of La Tirana, in the Bajo Lempa region of Western El Salvador. La Tirana is a poor community of just 22 families, with no electricity, running water, or sewerage. For their subsistence, residents rely on fishing and small-scale agriculture, growing corn, rice and vegetables, and rearing chickens and ducks. But the people of the village primarily depend on collecting punche, a local species of crab from the mangroves growing along the coastline, which they sell to buy cooking oil, clothing, and other necessities. However, a tiny rise in the sea level has resulted in 1,000 feet of the mangroves on which they depend vanishing beneath the ocean since 2005. Another 1,500 feet remains between the Pacific Ocean and the village of La Tirana. People in the community wonder just how long it will take for the waves reach their homes and flood the village permanently. McEvoy (2012) explains:

> La Tirana's problems all originate elsewhere, and with sea levels and temperatures expected to rise by far more than they already have in the next few decades, the community has more problems just around the corner … . In nearly a dozen community visits …, we've seen the extensive and varied problems faced by poor, struggling communities. The stories were all different, all gut-wrenchingly hard-hitting, and all traceable back to the same key factor: climate change.

El Salvador's Ministry of the Environment and Natural Resources believes that the country will lose somewhere between 10 percent and 28 percent of its coastal territories in the next century as a result of rising seas (Tigel 2012). Moreover, after decades of indiscriminate logging, only 2 percent of El Salvador's original forests remain. The result is that, when sudden heavy rains do occur, there are massive, sometimes catastrophic flash floods along the lower reaches of El Salvador's main river, the Lempa. Moreover, people complain they no longer know when it's winter or summer, as they used to sow their crops with the first rain, but now when they do that it may not rain again for a long time and the whole harvest is lost. Another problem caused by rising seas locally is contamination of well water for drinking. When people drill a new well, fresh water can only be drawn up for a short period of time before the water turns salty and makes them sick. Access to water is a growing problem because rising sea levels are slowly turning the water-bearing aquifers salty. In addition to rising seas, deforestation has left El Salvador very vulnerable to climate change and the storms it is increasingly bringing. Thus there was only one extreme storm in each of the 1960s and 1970s. In the 1980s there were two. But in the 1990s there were four. In the following decade, there were eight. Some have been massive. In 2015, there was Hurricane Sandra.

The immediate effects on people's lives of rising seas are also seen in the developing world. Tangiers Island, with a population of about 700 people, lies in Chesapeake Bay in Virginia. The island is populated by watermen, working-class people who make their livelihoods catching and selling crabs and oysters. One of the island's nicknames is "the soft-shell capital of the world." Long-time residents form a close-knit community where everyone knows everyone. While some residents own cars or trucks, bikes and golf carts are the primary modes of local transportation. In the summer months, tourism from the mainland, another source of income, brings in outside visitors.

The people of the island tend to be conservative, voting heavily for Trump in 2016, and concerned about disruptions to the community from less conservative outside influences. They also tend to embrace strong religious values, and a local ordinance prohibits the sale of alcohol. But the islanders face a daunting problem. Over the last 150 years, the size of the low-lying island has shrunk by 67 percent, with projections based on current rates of sea level rise of the island disappearing below the ocean by 2065 (Schulte et al. 2015). Already, areas that once were dry, places where people have built their homes, have become marsh-like because of saltwater intrusion. The island is slowly washing away. Tangiers is not unique; scientist estimate that as many as 500 Chesapeake Bay islands, at least 40 of them inhabited at one time, have disappeared below the waves over the last several hundred years.

Based on their conservative values, however, many of the islanders discount climate change and sea level rise, and explain their disappearing home as a result of erosion unrelated to any change caused by global warming. They do not have an explanation for the erosion, except to see it as part of God's world.

James Eskridge, whose father, grandfather, and great grandfather were also watermen, laments the fate of his island, "We've depended on the Chesapeake Bay for a couple hundred years or more, and now it's the Chesapeake Bay that's the greatest threat to our existence … . During the hurricane season we're just holding our breath and we're just praying that we don't get a storm" (quoted in Grey 2017). But they have had bad storms, including Hurricane Sandy. Still, Eskridge denies climate change and clings to the hope that Trump will help save the island.

The same threat is faced by Isle de Jean Charles, which is 80 miles from New Orleans on the Gulf coast. Most of the "island's" residents are members of the Biloxi-Chitimacha-Choctaw tribe, but some belong to the United Houma Nation. The state of Louisiana once considered the area as uninhabitable and a useless swamp. But Native Americans established a thriving community supported by trapping, fishing, and agriculture. Time moved more slowly on the island, and a person's sense of home, family, and community was more deep-rooted than often develops among urban dwellers. In 1953, a tiny road was constructed, but it became impassable during floods or when the wind shifted directions. Boats remained the primary means of transportation until the road was raised in the late 1990s. Although the residents think of Isle de Jean Charles as an island, it is actually a peninsula. Road or no road, in many ways the community remained isolated from the surrounding world.

Says tribal Chief Albert Naquin, "There's a lot of changes that happened on the island in my lifetime" (quoted in Northern Arizona University 2008). Most important in causing these changes initially was the decision of the oil and gas industry to dredge canals and built pipelines that allowed saltwater to encroach upon and destroy the freshwater wetlands that surrounded Isle de Jean Charles and made it a viable place to live. The wetlands had provided crucial habitat for many animal species as well as other ecological services. Moreover, the wetlands protected the coastal area from damaging storm surges, which, in turn, prevented land erosion. Wetlands act as natural buffers, slowing, absorbing, and storing significant amounts of floodwater. Eliminating wetlands and other natural barrier environments is a recognized recipe for damaging flooding, a danger made all the more riskier with global warming (Singer 2009).

During the twentieth and twenty-first centuries, land in southern Louisiana has been lost at a rapid rate, a process that threatens the sustainability of the entire coastal ecosystem. Varying degrees of loss are occurring at different costal locations, ranging from 0.1 square miles (64 acres) per year to 11.1 square miles (7,104 acres) per year. The causes of Louisiana's wetland loss have been researched and found to be the result of cumulative natural and human-induced impacts (Coastal Wetlands Planning, Protection and Act Program Reports 2008, Penland et al. 1996). Canals, dredged for navigation or in support of oil and gas extraction, have facilitated saltwater penetration into previously freshwater marshes. The placement of straight canals in areas that previously were drained by porous natural channels has accelerated the speed of tidal movements through the coastal marshes. High canal banks formed from placement of dredged material blocked both the drainage of water from the marsh and the input of washed-down sediment necessary to maintain wetlands. Most of the canals were dredged in the period from the 1950s to the 1970s. The damage they caused to the coastal ecosystem, however, continues to make local areas more susceptible to saltwater intrusion. Further, the construction of an extensive levee system along the Mississippi River to maintain navigation and reduce flooding of adjacent homes and businesses has resulted in the great river being confined to a small portion of its original flood plain. This prevented coastal wetlands from receiving the regular nourishment of upstream riverine water, nutrients, and sediment that are critical to coastal wetland survival. In addition, the declining sediment load in the Mississippi River, produced by the building of dams on the river and its tributaries, has caused less residue to flow downstream for coastal marsh maintenance. These anthropogenic impacts have been exacerbated by alterations that have modified the movement of freshwater and suspended sediment through the ecosystem.

If the current land loss rates continue unabated, by the year 2040 Louisiana will have lost more than one million acres of coastal wetlands, an area larger than the state of Rhode Island (Watzin and Gosselink 1992). Additionally, the Gulf of Mexico will continue to advance inland by as much as 33 miles through 2040, sinking previously productive wetlands below open water and leaving small communities like Isle de Jean Charles below sea level.

As levees were constructed north of Isle de Jean Charles, they cut the community off from the Mississippi River and the flow of sediment that had long replenished the local land base. An ongoing pattern of erosion, coupled with the intense storms and rising sea levels enhanced by climate change, threatens complete disaster for the people of the Isle de Jean Charles. The island was once 15,000 acres, but today the land has been whittled down to a tiny strip a quarter-mile wide by a half-mile long. Twenty-five houses and several fishing camps line the town's single street. Not long ago, the community comprised 63 homes. The rest have been swept away into the Gulf or abandoned. Sea water now covers the fields and forests where the community once raised families, carried out community activities, and sustained their livelihoods. There is no bright light at the end of the tunnel for this community. Their island is sinking fairly rapidly into the sea and the flooding is more damaging with each new storm season. Says Chief Naquin, "With each hurricane, there's less and less protection" (quoted in Northern Arizona University 2008).

The dilemma of this community certainly did not start with global warming. It is the result of a half-century of irresponsible oil and natural gas extraction practices, canal dredging, and a levee project that thrust people into the harm's way of severe storms. Yet like so many issues associated with climate change, anthropogenic ecological disasters are aggravated and hastened by a shifting climate. Residents of Isle de Jean Charles noticed a change, particularly after Hurricane Betsy hit in 1965. Since becoming chief in 1997, Naquin too thinks the storms have intensified. The tides, too, are changing. Naquin reports that water levels from high- to low-tide change "maybe two feet within an hour" (quoted in Northern Arizona University 2008) far more than when he was younger. Their island road, although it was elevated, is now cut in half during high tide. Says Naquin. "It's like you have a cancer and you don't do nothing about it, and then by the time you do something about it it's too late ..." (quoted in Northern Arizona University 2008).

For its inhabitants, the Isle de Jean Charles is not just a location, it is the meaningful setting of the tales of their elders, the resting place of the bones of their ancestors, the habitat where they know how to support their families, and the key to the fabric of their culture. The Biloxi-Chitimacha-Choctaw Indians and other residents of the Isle de Jean Charles are fishermen. Leaving the island for the mainland means leaving their world and their culture to vanish as strangers in to what for them is a strange land. Laments Naquin, "We're going to lose our heritage, all our culture ... . It's all going to be history" (quoted in Prescott 2018: 57).

Rising oceans put all coastal areas, including major global cities—especially port cities which have expanded greatly as sea trade doubled over the last 30 years—at increasing risk. Around the world large, densely populated cities like the following are particularly vulnerable: Mumbai (12 million people) and Kolkata (5 m), India; Guangzhou (11 m) and Shanghai China (18 m), Ho Chi Minh City (7 m), Vietnam, Osaka-Kobe (17 m), Japan, Bangkok (10 m), Thailand, and New York City (8 m). Together these cities have a total population of approximately 90 million people.

The 2012 heat dome over Greenland, which based on past climate history is an anomaly, was in fact the seventh year in a row of this occurring. In the center of Greenland, ice is up to 3,000 meters deep, but at the edges, the ice is much, much thinner and has been melting into the sea and raising the ocean. According to climatologist Thomas Mote:

> What we are seeing at the highest elevations may be a sort of sign of what is going on across the ice sheet. At lower elevation on the ice sheet, we are

seeing earlier melting, melting later in the season, and more frequent melting over the last 30 years and that is consistent of what you would expect with a warming climate.

(Quoted in Goldenberg 2012)

According to the IPCC (Church et al. 2013), the current ocean rise associated with this kind of melting comes after at least two millennia of roughly stable global sea levels. The rise is expected to speed up beyond 12 inches during the twenty-first century as climate change accelerates.

A report issued by the National Oceanic and Atmospheric Administration (2017), indicates that the global mean sea level has increased by about eight inches since 1880 because of global warming and the melting of land ice. The rise has been three inches since 1993. The rate of sea level rise since 1900 has been faster than during any comparable time over at least the last 2,800 years. This rise will continue, whatever we do at this point, because of global warming that has already occurred, and warming from new greenhouse gas emissions yet to come. In the U. S., millions of people live in coastal areas and are at risk of flooding, as are many of the nation's military, energy, and commercial assets which are located at or near the ocean. A sea level rise of three feet will permanently inundate areas that are home to two million people in the U.S., while a rise of six feet will permanently inundate areas home to six million. The impacts of ocean rise are intensified by a tide of urbanization along the shore globally putting increasing numbers at risk.

This change is the result of two phenomena produced by global warming: 1) thermal expansion as sea water increases in volume because of ocean temperature rises; and 2) flows of melt-water from the ice and snow of glaciers, ice sheets, and other land ice that is vanishing across the planet from Greenland to the Himalayas. Glaciers in many parts of the world are retreating with dramatic speed. In the context of oceans, thermal expansion is the increase in volume (or decrease in density) of ocean water as a result of increased temperature of the water. For example, according to NASA at one point during the summer of 2012, surface ice melt was found to be occurring across 97 percent of the Greenland ice sheet, something that has not been seen since the development of satellite measurement of ice sheets. This event so stunned NASA climate scientists they thought their instruments malfunctioned (but they were found to be working fine) (Goldberg 2012). Scientists attributed the sudden melt to a heat dome, or a burst of unusually warm air, which hovered over Greenland from July 8–16, 2012. This heat dome over Greenland, which based on past climate history is an anomaly, was in fact the seventh year in a row of this occurring. In the center of Greenland, ice is piled up to 3,000 meters deep, but on the edges, the ice is much, much thinner and has been melting into the sea and raising the ocean. According to the IPCC, the current ocean rise associated with this kind of melting comes after at least two millennia of roughly stable global sea levels. The rise is expected to speed up beyond 12 inches during the twenty-first century as climate change accelerates.

The critical state of coral reefs

A less well publicized but not less important impact of climate change involves coral reefs. Coral reefs are critical, in both senses of the word. On the one hand they are critical to the life of the oceans and are thus crucial to human subsistence. Between half a billion and a billion people are directly dependent for food on coral reefs and the marine life they attract. Coral reefs, which are symbiotic communities of plants and animals, are foundational to ocean life for several reasons. They serve as the nursery sites for tropical coastal fish stocks and, like rainforests, their counterpart on the land, they represent indispensable storehouses of biodiversity. Additionally, they are a vital bottom layer in a marine food chain that stretches across the seas, onto the shores, and into human communities. Moreover, they commonly function as barriers, protecting coasts from ocean flooding. On the other hand they are in a critical condition. Coral reefs are dying because of global warming, as well as ocean pollution and overfishing. A rise of 3.6°F in ocean temperature would kill all corals, aided by ocean acidification caused by CO^2 absorption from the atmosphere. At current rates of climate change we are headed in a dire direction: oceans without coral. Instead, where there were once magnificent built communities of living coral, which offered inviting homes and feeding sites for the manifold life of the oceans, there will only be algae and jellyfish. The scientific evidence for this chilling conclusion is both compelling and unequivocal.

Urban heat islands

While Earth is heating up generally, cities, home to an increasing share of the human population, in particular are growing warmer at a comparatively higher rate than elsewhere on the planet. A multicountry analysis found that in the years between 1950 and 2015, 27 percent of cities and 65 percent of urban populations warmed at more than one degree Fahrenheit above the overall planetary average (Estrada et al. 2017). This may not seem like a lot, but it is important to remember that the difference between water and ice is only one degree. Human bodies are not designed to handle heat above certain levels, especially if there is no cooling respite at night. The human body core, which includes the brain, lungs, and other organs, only functions within a narrow temperature range. A rise in core temperature of only a few degrees is extremely dangerous. A core body temperature of 103°F or above can be a sign of heat stroke.

For especially vulnerable groups like the elderly, the sick, the poor, pregnant women, and infants, one degree hotter on average may be enough to tip the scales toward illness or death. In a time of global warming and intensifying, longer summer heat waves, life in cities, especially for susceptible groups, is becoming more perilous. Researchers refer to this feature of cities as the urban heat island effect, a concept that dates to the 1830s when British chemist Luke Howard found that temperatures in London were consistently warmer than at sites outside the city. The annual mean air temperature of a city with a population of one million or more people can be 1.8 to 5.4°F warmer than its surrounding rural areas, and on clear, calm nights, the temperature difference can be as much as 22°F (Aniello et al. 1995, Oke 1982).

Heat islands develop when a large portion of the natural land cover in an area is replaced by built surfaces like roads, parking lots, and buildings. These structures trap incoming solar radiation during the daylight hours and release it at night. Cities, in effect, create their own climates. During recent decades, the largest urban heat islands in the U.S. experienced warming at twice the level of the "cooler sea" of smaller urban and nonurban areas. As the human population continues to urbanize and consume more fossil fuel, the health, social and economic impacts of summer urban overheating loom as major threats to the well-being of city dwellers worldwide. How bad might it get? One recent study estimates that about 30 percent of the world's population currently is exposed to deadly heat episodes for 20 days or more each year. By 2100, this figure is projected to climb as high as 74 percent unless there are reductions in greenhouse gas emissions (Mora et al. 2017). New York City could be subjected to 50 such days per year, while southern cities could see 100 deadly hot days each year.

Too hot for crops

All people must eat, but what they eat and how often, the nutrient value of their diets, and the security of their access to food varies widely. As reported by the IPCC, food production is directly affected by the rising temperatures of climatic conditions (Porter et al. 2014). Crop yields and harvest quality are susceptible to extreme weather events and changing precipitation and temperature. In places, over time, Earth may become too hot for the continuation of crop growth, with dramatic impact on local farmers. Observe Hallegatte et al. (2016: 51), "Climate change could even make agricultural areas unsuitable for cultivation of key crops, resulting in large economic impacts for poor economies that are highly dependent on a few agricultural commodities."

By 2080, the average yield declines estimated from all climate models could be as severe as 23 percent for South Asia, 17 percent for East Asia and the Pacific, 15 percent for Sub-Saharan Africa, and 14 percent for Latin America (Havlík et al. 2016). Andrew Challinor, professor of climate impacts at University of Leeds in the UK, has warned that climate change in Africa means that 60 percent of the acreage used to grow beans could become unworkable by 2100. Challinor is one of a team of scientists who tested the predicted impact of climate on global wheat yields using three independent methods to deliver much the same conclusion: with just 1 degree global temperature increase, wheat yields are expected to fall by 4.1–6.4 percent, a loss that will have severe consequences on human suffering (Challinor et al. 2014). Focusing on sub-Saharan Africa, researchers picked nine major crops that make up around half of all the food grown on the continent. Using computer crop models, they simulated whether those various fruits, vegetables, and cereals could still be grown as the planet warms. Their results suggest that if carbon emissions are not cut, large swathes of Africa will be unviable for growing such key crops as maize, beans, and bananas (Rippkke et al. 2016). An area is designated as unviable when its climate has changed so much that the crop fails to grow in ten out of 20 years. The computer simulations assume a business-as-usual scenario in which global greenhouse gas emissions are not curbed, which, given the last 50 years of rising emissions, does not seem unreasonable.

Lesser-known impacts of climate change

A 2017 report from the International Union for Conservation of Nature indicates that the number of natural world heritage sites being damaged and at risk from global warming has almost doubled to 62 over the past three years. A world heritage site is a landmark or area that has been selected by the United Nations Educational, Scientific and Cultural Organization because it is deemed to have cultural, historical, scientific or other significant value for humanity. To be selected, a site must be an already classified landmark, with unique geographically and historically identifiable features. Natural heritage sites are those that are not of human origin and reflect exceptional qualities. Sites now at high risk because of climate change include iconic spaces from the Galapagos Islands to the central Amazon Forest, as well as less well known but equally animated and unique sites such as the 712 karst caves on the border of Hungary and Slovakia and the monarch butterfly reserves in Mexico. Other historic ecosystems being damaged include the Everglades, where the rising ocean and saltwater are intruding. The Sundarbans mangrove forest on the delta of the Ganges, Brahmaputra and Meghna rivers on the Bay of Bengal, another of the natural wonders of the world at risk, was recognised as a world heritage site in 1997. The Sunderbans is both the largest river delta in the world and the largest estuarine mangrove forest in the world. But two islands in the delta already have been submerged below rising ocean water and at least a dozen more are threatened with a similar fate. Intense storms are contributing to increasing the risk of devastation facing the site. Elsewhere, increasing numbers and more intense wildfires are damaging the stunning Fynbos flowerscapes in the Cape region of South Africa. Warming temperature is melting the permafrost in the newly declared Qinghai Hoh Xil heritage site in the Qinghai-Tibetan Plateau. Australia is particularly exposed as it has ten natural heritage sites where climate change damage is rated as high or very high risk. While there are several threats to natural heritage sites, climate change is the fastest growing, with a 77 percent increase in sites where it is seen as a high or a very high threat. Climate change also is by far the largest potential threat. As this review indicates, the costs of climate change are not only multiple and diverse, they include losses that are rarely mentioned in discussions of the impacts of global warming.

Bramble Cay is a very small island with surrounding oval reef in the northeast Torres Strait. The island has a maximum elevation above high tide of only about ten feet. The island is the only known habitat of a terrestrial mammal, the Bramble

Cay melomys, *Melomys rubicola*. This small rodent possesses the most isolated and restricted distribution of all Australian mammals. It is also ecologically unique and considered to be the Great Barrier Reef's only endemic mammal species. However, researchers have now concluded that the melomys are gone, the first known case of anthropogenic climate change-caused extinction. According to Luke Leung who has studied the rodent, "The key factor responsible for the death of the Bramble Cay melomy is the almost certainly higher tides and surging seawater, which has travelled inland across the island …" (quoted in Innis 2016). While the melomy may be the first, it is not likely to be the last species to fall victim to climate change as environments change and become less stable. Many of our closest animal relatives, the primates, are at increasing climate change risk. Researchers have identified various critical hotspots of primate vulnerability due to climate changes. These areas have multiple primate species, high concentrations of endangered species, and are showing signs of large climate changes.

Conceiving the human role in a world in turmoil

Concepts like climate change and global warming have become familiar to people around the world in recent years, although studies suggest that detailed knowledge of their full implications for life on Earth is often limited. Even Americans, with their extensive access to world, national, scientific, and environmental news, exhibit important knowledge gaps in their knowledge. Research conducted through the Yale University Project on Climate Communication reveals that only 60 percent believe that the planet is warming, and even those who accept this significant change is occurring often do not understand why. The Yale Project translated popular knowledge on climate change into a letter score and found that only 8 percent of Americans have knowledge that would earn them an A or B if they were taking a college exam, 40 percent of study participants would receive a grade of a C or D, and a notable 52 percent would receive an F based on their answers to survey questions. The study found several key areas of knowledge insufficiency as well as a number of common misconceptions. Thus, 50 percent or fewer understood the concept of greenhouse gases, recognized that human activities are the primary driver of global warming, or were aware that our release of carbon dioxide into the atmosphere is resulting in ocean acidification and coral bleaching (Leiserowitz et al. 2010).

Perhaps part of the confusion people have about this issue stems from problems with the terms that are in use. Neither climate change nor global warming quite capture the entangled set of significant atmosphere and environmental changes now occurring on Earth that stem from the release of CO^2 and other gases. Certainly, Earth's climate is changing, but what is most important is not change itself— that has occurred throughout time—but rather the specific direction of the change that is now occurring: it keeps getting hotter (Chen and Tung 2014). This is important because for the past 10,000 years—the period of greatest growth and dispersal of the human population around the planet, Earth's overall temperature range has been remarkably mild and generally stable, not increasing or decreasing by more than about 0.9°F (Marcott et al. 2014). Our actions, however, have destabilized the environmental and climatic forces that produced Earth's moderate conditions. While generally accepted by climate scientists, the term climate change fails to capture the urgency of our current situation. Driven especially by the global social dependence on fossil fuels, the level of carbon dioxide in the atmosphere passed 400 parts per million (ppm), the highest level reached since the Pleistocene, and it continues to rise, as seen in the record increase of 1.4 percent to 31.6 giga-tons of CO^2 emissions in 2012. By 2016, atmospheric CO^2 remained above the 400 ppm level the entire year, marking the year as the likely time we moved a new and ever more precarious stage in our impact on the planet (Kahn 2016).

What is important in terms of how we label the planetary changes that are in process is that the transformations we are witnessing are not all directly about heat. Entwined with climate change are multiple other significant alterations, such as ocean acidification, the redistribution of plant and animal species, the modification of planet air patterns like the jet stream, and black carbon build-up, which are not obvious from the term climate change but are definitely components of the evolving hotter world of the Anthropocene. This latter concept gained traction in the year 2000 when the atmospheric chemist Paul J. Crutzen and ecologist Eugene F. Stoermer published an article on it in the newsletter of the International Geosphere-Biosphere Programme. These scholars proposed that the previous geological era had ended and Earth had entered a new period, the Anthropocene, a change intended to emphasize not the existence of humans but rather the central role they now played in shaping the geology and the ecology of the planet. The term, new to geochronology, unites two Greek root words: anthropo, meaning "human," and cene, meaning "new." Crutzen and Stoermer argued, in short, that for at least the last 150 years, especially since the rise of the Industrial Revolution, human activities have had the most significant impacts on the bio-geological environments of Earth and its climate and that the planet has entered the Age of People.

Humans, Crutzen and Stoermer believed, evolved from a local species adapted to some environments in Africa into a "geomorphic force" dispersed across the world (Yusoff 2013). The Anthropocene is of our own making, rather than a product of natural changes in the world (e.g. volcanic eruptions, asteroid collisions) to which we are merely adapting. Increasingly the biomass of Earth is human biomass, signifying the significance of our presence on the planet. In light of the numerous changes recorded by natural scientist in many dimensions of the planet, transformative changes stemming from our own activities, the idea of a human-shaped geological epoch found a ready audience among many geoscientists and social scientists as well.

The birth of the Anthropocene, suggest Crutzen and Stoermer (2000), can be identified through the analyses of air trapped in polar ice. Tiny air bubbles are buried as snow falls to the ground in frigid regions and never melts. Over time, the weight of the newer snow presses down and compacts the snowflakes below it, causing them to merge together and form ice. The air situated between the individual snowflakes gets pushed into long channels of ancient air. It is believed that air that dates as far back as 1.5 million years remains largely unchanged deep in the ice of Eastern Antarctica. Examination of the composition of air channels in Artic ice revealed to scientists that there was a growing global concentration of carbon dioxide and methane gases beginning about 200 years ago.

This date, supported by other signs of a durable human imprint registered in the geological record, suggests a start date for the Anthropocene, a time coincident with James Watt's design of the rotative steam engine during the last quarter of the eighteenth century (Crutzen 2002). The steam engine was one of the keystone developments of the Industrial Revolution because, in addition to pumping water from mines, it allowed mills and factories to be located anywhere, and not just close to the energy source of a river or stream. Its impact was dramatic. The steam engine required a source of heat to boil water and create steam, and the combustion of coal or wood became the fuel sources driving the Industrial Revolution. Burning coal soon became and remains a leading cause of smog, acid rain, and toxic air pollution, and of the ever-increasing levels of carbon dioxide in the trapped air of polar ice.

Human reshaping of the planet took a sizeable jump (known as the Great Acceleration) after the Second World War, when the population of our species doubled, going from three billion in 1950 to six billion in 50 years, and the scale of environmental resource extraction, industrial production, consumerism, urbanization, and globalism all accelerated rapidly. These socially driven changes, each dramatic in their own right, combined to physically transform Earth in dramatic ways, the precise nature of which we are still attempting to fully understand. One thing that is clear to environmental researchers is the rapid growth of human-dominated ecosystems across the planet. In these transformed arenas of the planet, ecological structure and function are being primarily determined by human social interactions, perceptions, and behaviors, making the nature of those interactions and the structures of social relationship that underlie them of vital importance. Through such rearranging Earth has been "anthroposized at high speed" (Crutzen and Schwägerl 2011).

As this discussion suggests, the term climate change is somewhat problematic because it is only part of the story; what is occurring is broader than climate per se and is social as well as physical in nature. Problems are also inherent in the companion term global warming. Certainly, as has been emphasized, the whole planet is warming and there are multiple indicators identified across various scientific disciplines of this consequential alteration. As discussed in the Introduction, 2016 was the world hottest year in the last 130 years based on accumulated weather data. Planetary heat levels in 2016 were been driven in large part by the rising temperatures of the upper layers of the world's oceans, which have absorbed much of the excess heat caused by the greenhouse blanket. Additionally, the land surface temperature achieved record warmth for the second year in a row, exceeding the previous record set just the year before by more than 0.2°F. This surpassed the average for the mid- to late

nineteenth century—which is commonly considered by scientists to be representative of pre-industrial conditions on the planet—by more than 1.8°F for
the first time. Moreover, average sea level around the globe rose to a new
record high during the year by about two and three-quarter inches over the
1993 average.

Even though it is the warming of the planet that is the force driving the array of
changes occurring around us, the everyday understanding of warming does not
really capture the erratic nature of what is occurring, nor does it quite describe the
sudden as well as ever more frequent occurrence of extreme weather events like
the megastorm Hurricane Sandy or the devastation of Hurricane Katrina. The
world is not just increasing in temperature, weather is becoming less stable, less
predictable, and more deadly in a variety of ways. Moreover, while human behaviors like the continually mounting release of greenhouse gases is at the heart of the
destabilization of climate patterns, there are multiple environmental feedback
mechanisms—outside of immediate human causation—that are also at play in what
is now happening on Earth. The melting of sea ice by rising planetary temperatures, for example, exposes dark water, which unlike ice absorbs rather than reflects
solar energy, leading to higher temperatures in the oceans. Warming that is
occurring in arctic areas accelerates the release of carbon dioxide from permafrost,
adding to the greenhouse blanket, which causes further permafrost melt. Also
released is methane, which is 25 times more powerful than CO^2 as a greenhouse
gas. Significant release of methane from thawing permafrost would be a powerful
driver of global warming.

Similarly, heatwaves, droughts, and storms impede plant growth, weakening a
major safeguard against increases in the level of CO^2 in the atmosphere, allowing
the upward spiral of planetary temperatures. Droughts and heatwaves, as well as
extreme storms that destroy forest biomass, further contribute to rising CO^2 levels
in the atmosphere, resulting in a worsening of droughts and heatwaves. Higher
amounts of atmospheric CO^2 also create turbulence. To get around growing
pockets of turbulence—and save passengers from the scary feeling that their plane is
going to crash—air craft are having to fly further, using more fuel and generating
more CO^2 in an ongoing upward trend. Many climatic feedback mechanisms are
of grave importance because once a threshold is passed triggering their activation
they can drive planetary heating without additional human inputs. As award-win-
ning writer Rebecca Solnit (2013) asserts, we now face a climate system that is

> thrashing out of control, so that it threatens to become too hot, too cold, too
> dry, too wet, too wild, too destructive, too erratic for many plants and animals
> that depend on reliable annual cycles. It affects the entire surface of the Earth
> and every living thing, from the highest peaks to the depths of the oceans, from
> one pole to the other, from the tropics to the tundra, likely for millennia—and
> it's not just coming like that wave, it's already here.

As Noam Chomsky (2014) points out, it is not all humans who are pushing the planet to another era of mass extinction:

> The entire socioeconomic system is based on production for profit and a growth imperative that cannot be sustained. There are also fundamental issues of value: What is a decent life? Should the master–servant relation be tolerated? Should one's goals really be maximization of commodities—Veblen's 'conspicuous consumption'? Surely there are higher and more fulfilling aspirations.
>
> *(Quoted in Polychroniou 2016)*

It is because of the interrelated complexity of human relations and social structures with the plant and human relations with each other that climate scientist Gavin Schmidt (2014) argues that it is necessary to understand the big picture of what is going on, because you cannot really appreciate what is happening by only studying the pieces: "It's the whole or it's nothing." The whole includes things operating on a range of scales from the microscopic particles that seed clouds to the planet itself. But terms that effectively cover all of the complexity involved are not readily available. In their attempt address this problem of encompassing the complexity of what contemporary anthropogenic climate change entails, the journalists and climate scientists that participate in Climate Central (2012), a nonpartisan science and journalism organization focused on research and communicating the impacts of a changing climate to general audiences, chose the unconventional title of Global Weirdness for their audiobook. This educational tool engages the complexities inherent in climate change in way that transcends scientific jargon and disciplinary expertise. In explaining this choice of title, the authors emphasize that it is not just warming that is going on in the world. As the climate is warming, this warming induces many other changes, including severe and damaging storms, taxing droughts, blistering heat waves, significant ocean level rise, and coral-killing ocean acidification, changes that cumulatively and in comparison with the past experience constitute climatic weirdness.

Alternately, the label of "climate turmoil" has been suggested by Hans Baer and me (2018) to encompass that dynamic interrelationships involved in increased global warming, including the more frequent occurrence of extreme and disruptive weather events, diverse and even contradictory environmental occurrences (such as drought, wildfires, windstorms, and flooding), and mounting weather erraticism and unpredictability. The use of the term turmoil in this way has its roots in the volume *Gaia in Turmoil*, an articulation of the Gaian theory (Crist and Rinker 2009). Turmoil imparts the idea that not only are many things changing at once but also the environment is becoming less dependable and more difficult to cope with successfully. As the American Association for the Advancement of Science (AAAS) has stated, we now face climate-related risks that are "abrupt, unpredictable and potentially irreversible" (American Association for the Advancement of Science 2014: 1). Further, the AAAS (2014: 1) stressed that "Earth's climate is on a path to warm beyond the range of what has been experienced over the past millions of years." The operative word in this quote is abrupt. Scientific research indicates that the crossing of climate tipping points can lead to major and rapid environmental changes over relatively short periods of time (National Research Council 2013). Now we have the capacity to trigger what the National Research Council (2002) called "inevitable surprizes" in the world we inhabit. There is growing recognitions that a progressively changing climate, driven by human action, can eventually push both natural and human systems across consequential and irreversible tipping points.

An example of abrupt historic change occurred at the end of the geographic age dating to 12,000 years ago known as the Younger Dryas, which as a period of very cold planetary conditions. When it ended, over 70 percent of the large mammals of North America, species adapted to cold weather, were extinct. In all periods of abrupt change, species face such risk. For humans, the architectural infrastructures of our societies are built with the expectation of long periods of stability and predictability. If the ocean rises above sea walls or other barriers and floods into cities, if permafrost melt destroys pipelines and roads, if heat waves endure for long periods and overuse of cooling appliances by those who can afford them cause breakdowns in the electrical grid, and a long list of other climate-triggered breakdowns occur, the result will be turmoil of historic proportions.

While I use the terms climate change and global warming interchangeably in this book, as they are now familiar to many people, it is with the understanding that what we are experiencing is more than climate change and not only global warming, that it is, in fact, anthropogenic climate and environmental turmoil with multiple entwined expressions. These changes are far-reaching and pose grave risks for human health and well-being, especially as they are mediated by environmental conditions and intersect with and magnify vulnerabilities created by structurally imposed social and economic inequalities in local and regional settings. As a result, climate change imposes undue stress on those with the most encumbered resilience and fewest means to respond effectively to mitigate harmful outcomes, making climate change an important driver of environmental and social injustice.

Anthropocentric or capitalocentric climate change

There is embedded in English common law the dictum that "an Englishman's home is his castle." This legal principle, dating to the seventeenth century and the writings of the jurist Sir Edward Coke (Sheppard 2005), but echoing ideas dating at least as far back as the Roman Empire, proposes that a man (and gender here is no accident) can do as he pleases within the confines of his own house. The linguist and progressive political analyst Noam Chomsky (2013) has raised some highly pertinent questions about behavior and ownership on a grander scale by enquiring "who owns the Earth [and who] owns the global atmosphere being polluted by the heat-trapping gases." His concern is informed by recognition that growing social inequalities have resulted in those most responsible for environmental disruption suffering the least consequences and those least responsible enduring the gravest penalties. Social elites, those with the greatest wealth and the most power, Chomsky argues, act as if they are the titleholders of our planet and hence free to do as they please, as if the whole planet was their castle—which cuts to the heart of the issues addressed in this book.

It has become standard usage to refer to contemporary global warming as a product of anthropocentric climate change. But it is not really the case that humans collectively (the "anthro" in anthropocentric) share anything near equal responsibility for the creation of the planet-heating blanket of greenhouse gases encircling Earth. As Frumhoff et al. (2015) point out, "[an] enormous quantity of emissions can be traced to a relatively small number of fossil fuel producers." Heede's (2014) analysis of the historic production records the 90 largest producers of coal, oil, and natural gas, as well as producers of cement, for the years 1854–2010, in terms of the carbon content of their products, found that they produced approximately two-thirds of the total industrial emissions of CO^2 and methane into Earth's atmosphere. Rather than being accurately described as anthropocentric, even though the release of greenhouse gases is driven by human activity, some people are far more responsible than others, and, especially, included in the latter group are a limited number of corporate manufacturers who not only produce fossil fuels but fight hard using all of their abundant financial resources to insure they will be unhindered by environmental or climatic policies now or in the future. As examined in chapter 3, an important component in the fossil fuel producer corporate agenda of defending its commitment to endless production is a no-holds barred war on climate science and its practitioners, a strategy that intimates there are only benefits and no significant social costs to a fossil fuel-based economy. In reality, limiting the regulation of industrially generated environmental and climatic pollution is a means of shifting the risk these create onto those least responsible for creating it. Wright and Nyberg (2015: 67) note that because of their deep financial pockets in defining risk, "businesses and other market entities … have a voice and enjoy the biggest say; others, such as local communities and [those] with limited political impact, have no voice, yet are left to face the greatest uncertainties." This pattern, which is based on a dangerous fallacy, has become one of "business as usual" over the last 100-plus years.

References

Allen, G. 2018. Visitors slowly returning to Virgin Islands after hurricanes' destruction. *National Public Radio.* www.npr.org/2018/02/02/580448399/visitors-slowly-returning-to-virgin-islands-after-hurricanes-destruction.

American Association for the Advancement of Science (AAAS). 2014. *What we know: The reality, risks and response to climate change.* Washington, DC: AAAS.

Aniello, C., K. Morgan, A. Busbey, and L. Newland. 1995. Mapping micro-urban heat islands using Landsat TM and a GIS. *Computers and Geosciences* 21(8): 965–969.

Atkin, E. 2015. Ted Cruz's bank account would soar if we increased oil and gas production. *Think Progress*. https://thinkprogress.org/ted-cruzs-bank-account-would-soar-if-we-increased-oil-and-gas-production-f3e744ad0e25.

Baer, H. and M. Singer 2018. *The Anthropology of Climate Change: An Integrated Critical Perspective*, 2nd ed. Abingdon, Oxford, U.K.: Routledge, Earthscan.

Challinor, A., J. Watson, D. Lobell, S. Howden, D. Smith and N. Chhetri. 2014. A meta-analysis of crop yield under climate change and adaptation. *Nature Climate Change* 4: 287–291.

Chen, X. and K.-K. Tung. 2014. Varying planetary heat sink led to global-warming slow-down and acceleration. *Science* 345(6199): 897–903.

Chomsky, N. 2013. Who owns the Earth? *TruthOut*. www.truth-out.org/news/item/17402-who-owns-the-earth.

Chomsky, N. 2014. The end of history? *In These Times*. http://inthesetimes.com/article/17137/the_end_of_history.

Church, J., P. Clark, A. Cazenave, J. Gregory, S. Jevrejeva, A. Levermann et al. 2013. Sea level change. In *Climate Change 2013: The Physical Science Basis. Contribution of Working Group 1 to the Fifth Assessment Report of the Intergovernmental Panel on Climate Change*. Cambridge and New York: Cambridge University Press.

Climate Central. 2012. *Global Weirdness: Severe Storms, Deadly Heat Waves, Relentless Drought, Rising Seas, and the Weather of the Future*. New York: Vintage Books.

Coastal Wetlands Planning, Protection and Act Program Reports. 2008. Wetland loss in Louisiana. www.lacoast.gov/reports/rtc/1997/5.htm.

Cook, J., N. Oreskes, P. Doran, W. Anderegg, B. Verheggen, E. Maibach, and D. Nuccitelli. 2016. Consensus on consensus: A synthesis of consensus estimates on human-caused global warming. *Environmental Research Letters*, 11(4): 048002.

Crist, E. and B. Rinker. 2009. *Gaia in Turmoil: Climate Change and Earth Ethics in an Age of Crisis*. Cambridge, MA: MIT Press.

Crutzen, P. 2002. Geology of mankind. *Nature* 415: 23.

Crutzen, P. and C. Schwägerl. 2011. Living in the Anthropocene: Toward a new global ethos. *Yale Environment 360*. http://e360.yale.edu/feature/living_in_the_anthropocene_toward_a_new_global_ethos/2363/.

Crutzen, P. and E. Stoermer. 2000. The Anthropocene. *Global Change Newsletter* 41: 17–18.

Emmanuel, K. 2017. Assessing the present and future probability of Hurricane Harvey's rainfall: Proceedings of the National Academy of Sciences of the United Sates of America. https://doi.org/10.1073/pnas.1716222114,

Estrada, E., W. Botzen, and R. Tol. 2017. A global economic assessment of city policies to reduce climate change impacts. *Nature Climate Change* 7(6): 403.

Frumhoff, P., R. Heede, and N. Oreskes. 2015. The climate responsibilities of industrial carbon producers. *Climate Change* 132: 157–171.

Goldenberg, S. 2012. Greenland ice sheet melted at unprecedented rate during July. *The Guardian*, July 24. www.theguardian.com/environment/2012/jul/24/greenland-ice-sheet-thaw-nasa.

Grey, J. 2017. Reporter's notebook: Visiting the disappearing Tangier Island. *CNN*. www.cnn.com/2017/06/09/us/weather-tangier-island/index.html.

Hallegatte, S. ,A. Vogt-Schilb, M. Bangalore, and J. Rozenberg. 2016. *Unbreakable: Building the Resilience of the Poor in the Face of Natural Disasters*. Washington, DC: International Bank for Reconstruction and Development/The World Bank.

Havlík, P., H. Valin, M. Gusti, E. Schmid, D. Leclère, N. Forsell et al. 2016. Climate change impacts and mitigation in the developing world: An integrated assessment of agriculture and forestry sectors. Policy Research Working Paper 7477. World Bank Group, New York.

Heede, R. 2014. Tracing anthropogenic carbon dioxide and methane emissions to fossil fuel and cement producers, 1854–2010. *Climate Change* 122(1–2): 229–249.

Holmes, J. 2017. Here's what life is like in Puerto Rico 3 months after Hurricane Maria. *Esquire*, December 21. www.esquire.com/news-politics/a14474788/puerto-rico-3-months-after-hurricane/.

Innis, M. 2016. Australian rodent is first mammal made extinct by human-driven climate change, scientists say. *New York Times*, June 15. www.nytimes.com/2016/06/15/world/australia/climate-change-bramble-cay-rodent.html?_r=0.

Kahn, B. 2016. The world passes 400 ppm threshold. Permanently. *Climate Central*. www.climatecentral.org/news/world-passes-400-ppm-threshold-permanently-20738.

Leiserowitz, A., N. Smith, and J. Marlon. 2010. *Americans' Knowledge of Climate Change*. New Haven, CT: Yale University.

Marcott, S., J. Shakun, P. Clark, and A. Mix. 2013. A reconstruction of regional and global temperature for the past 11,300 years. *Science* 339(6124): 1198–1201.

McEvoy, C. 2012. Dying mangroves and fading livelihoods in El Salvador. *Trócaire News*. www.trocaire.org/news/dying-mangroves-and-fading-livelihoods-el-salvador.

Mooney, C. 2017. Climate change upped the odds of Hurricane Harvey's extreme rains, study finds. *Washington Post*, November 13. www.washingtonpost.com/news/energy-environment/wp/2017/11/13/climate-change-upped-the-odds-of-harveys-extreme-rains-study-finds/?utm_term=.fafd8073f908.

Mora, C., B. Dousset, I. Caldwell, F. Powell, R. Geronimo, C. Bielecki et al. 2017. Global risk of deadly heat. *Nature Climate Change* 7: 501–506.

Morand, S., K. Owers, A. Waret-Szkuta, K. McIntyre, and M. Baylis. 2013. Climate variability and outbreaks of infectious diseases in Europe. *Scientific Reports* 3, Article number 1774.

National Oceanic and Atmospheric Administration. 2017. Global and Regional Sea Level Rise Scenarios for the United States. NOAA Technical Report NOS CO-OPS 083. Silver Spring, Maryland.

National Research Council. 2002. Abrupt climate change: Inevitable surprises. Washington, DC: National Academy Press.

National Research Council. 2013. Abrupt impacts of climate change: Anticipating surprises. Washington, DC: National Academies Press.

Northern Arizona University. 2008. Biloxi-Chitimacha-Choctaw Indians: Rising tides. www7.nau.edu/itep/main/tcc/Tribes/gc_choctaw.

Oke, T. 1982. The energetic basis of the urban heat island. *Quarterly Journal of the Royal Meteorological Society* 108: 1–24.

Penland, S., I. Mendelssohn, L. Wayne, and D. Britsch. 1996. Natural and human causes of coastal land loss in Louisiana. Workshop summary. Coastal Studies Institute, Wetland Biogeochemistry Institute, Louisiana State University, Baton Rouge.

Polychroniou, C. 2016. Global warming and the future of humanity: An interview with Noam Chomsky and Graciela Chichilnisky. *TruthOut*. www.truth-out.org/opinion/item/37631-global-warming-and-the-future-of-humanity-an-interview-with-noam-chomsky-and-graciela-chichilnisky.

Porter, J., L. Xie, A. Challinor, K. Cochrane, S. Howden, M. Iqbal et al. 2014. Food security and food production systems. In C. B. Field et al., *Climate Change 2014: Impacts, Adaptation, and Vulnerability: Intergovernmental Panel on Climate Change*. Cambridge: Cambridge University Press, pp. 485–533.

Prescott, M. 2018. *Food is the Solution*. New York: Flatiron Books.

Promchertchoo, P. 2017. Asia's Future Cities: Can Bangkok turn back the rising tide and stop sinking? *Channel News Asia*, March 1. www.channelnewsasia.com/news/asiapacific/a sia-s-future-cities-can-bangkok-turn-back-the-rising-tide-and-s-7612754.

Rippke, U., J. Ramirez-Villegas, A. Jarvis, S. Vermeulen, L. Parker, F. Mer et al. 2016. Timescales of transformational climate change adaptation in Sub-Saharan African agriculture. *Nature Climate Change* 6: 605–660.

Schmidt, G. 2014. The emergent patterns of climate change. *TED*. www.ted.com/talks/ga vin_schmidt_the_emergent_patterns_of_climate_change.

Schulte, D., K. Dridge and M. Hudgins. 2015. Climate change and the evolution and fate of the Tangier Islands of Chesapeake Bay, USA. *Scientific Reports* 5, Article number 17890.

Sheppard, S. (ed.). 2005. *The Selected Writings of Sir Edward Coke*. Indianapolis, IN: Liberty Fund.

Singer, M. 2009. Beyond global warming: Interacting ecocrises and the critical anthropology of health. *Anthropology Quarterly* 82(3): 795–820.

Solnit, R. 2013. Bigger than that: (The difficulty of) looking at climate change. *TomDispatch. com*. www.tomdispatch.com/blog/175756/tomgram%3A_rebecca_solnit,_the_age_of_ inhuman_scale.

Tigel, S. 2012. El Salvador in battle against tide of climate change. *Independent*. September 17. www.independent.co.uk/environment/climate-change/el-salvador-in-battle-against-ti de-of-climate-change-8145210.html.

Watzin, M. and J. Gosselink. 1992. The fragile fringe: Coastal wetlands of the continental United States. Louisiana Sea Grant College Program, Baton Rouge.

Weather Channel. 2015. Bangkok is sinking and may be underwater in 15 years, study says. https://weather.com/science/environment/news/bangkok-sinking-subsidence-wa rming-15-years.

Wright, C. and D. Nyberg. 2015. *Climate Change, Capitalism, and Corporations: processes of creative self-destruction*. Cambridge: Cambridge University Press.

Yusoff, K. 2013. Geologic life: Prehistory, climate, futures in the Anthropocene. *Environment and Planning D: Society and Space* 31: 779–795.

2

THE RISE AND ROLE OF SOCIAL INEQUALITY IN THE PRODUCTION OF CLIMATE CHANGE

Social inequity: stratification and the making of injustice

Social equality is a central concern in this book and yet it is not an easy term to define. Despite this problem, it is evident that there has been a surge of interest in this concept in recent years (Blofield 2010). In anthropology, concern with understanding the social and cultural context of production, exchange and consumption in society, and the relationship between economic activities and unequal social standing, has a long history. At the global level, anthropologist Eric Wolf (1982) addressed the historic drivers of inequality. He was able to demonstrate how the rise of European colonialism and emerging trade relationships like the fur and slave trades reshaped communities around the world as their members were pressed into subordinate positions in production processes organized to enrich Europe, especially its upper classes, and eventually some of its former colonies. Expansion of capitalist production units and markets into all corners of the world has further consolidated social structures built on marked social inequality, setting the foundation for the issues of concern to this book. Anthropologists have also focused on the lived and emotional experience of inequality and on the daily lives and subjectivities—thoughts, feelings, suffering, and anxieties—of people on the bottom rungs of social hierarchies, with their struggles to get by in worlds of precarity and uncertainty and with their hopes for their children. As they grapple with the unpredictability of life, including threats from the environment induced by global warming, the poor and marginalized must work very hard and call upon their networks of social relationships to meet their basic needs, something at which they do not necessarily succeed as challenges mount in a precarious world. As McGill (2016:1) stresses, "inequality matters."

As they look at societies across the globe, at the interpersonal relations that exist among people in diverse cultural systems, anthropologists see considerable heterogeneity and complexity. As has been emphasized, not only does inequality take on different forms and find multiple modes of expression, the historic pathways of development of inequality and its particular local manifestations are also manifold. Yet also visible are overarching global processes—such as the emergence and global reach of colonialism, the spread of capitalist economic systems with their labor and product markets and extraction of resources, and the imposition of neoliberal economic principles—in the emergence, historic consolidation, and continual promotion and entrenchment of social relations of inequality (Lesorogol 2015).

How are we to understand inequality in the world if we hold dear principles of fairness? We know that the U.S. Declaration of Independence asserts that "all men are created equal, that they are endowed by their Creator with certain unalienable Rights". Of course, at the time this document was written, these so-called natural rights were not seen as natural to everyone and were alienated from women, African slaves, Indians, and those who did not own property. This example underlines the importance of worthiness when it comes to rights, as some people may be deemed deserving of natural rights or even govern-ment-bestowed rights but others may be considered unworthy or even seen as exclusionable or even expendable. In short, some people count and others do not merit being counted. These conceptions of worthiness have often been built into the "social rules of the game" as formal laws, institutional practices, and everyday norms that profoundly structure social interactions. The rules of the game "appear to be neutral, non-ideological, natural, commonsensical," and it is these features that make them so effective in maintaining inequality (Žižek 2008: 36). By having control over and shaping the rules of the game, the rich are able to amass ever-greater wealth and keep control over labor and markets. Laws often most reflect the special interests of the elite rather than those of the middle and poor sectors of society (Goldín and Dowdall 2015). Inequality, in short, has become institutionalized and, to the degree that it garners attention, is rationalized and justified.

At least two alternative ways of thinking about social equality have been pro-posed by scholars (Fourie et al. 2015). One notion of equality emphasizes the issue of distribution. From this perspective, one that has been called "distributive egali-tarianism," equality is achieved when all people have access to equal amounts of things that are socially valued, be it opportunity, social prestige, wealth, material goods, or property. Certainly, one of the features of inequality in the con-temporary world, but with a history going back several thousand years, is the vast and out-of-control gap that separates the quality and material conditions of life for the very rich and the very poor. According to the 2016 Credit Suisse Global Wealth Databook, the richest five men in the world own over $400 billion in wealth, which means that each of them controls nearly as much wealth as 750 million people. While the poorest half of the global population possesses less than 1 percent of the total wealth in the world, the richest 10 percent holds 89 percent of it, and the top 1 percent owns half of all global assets. In short, the world "has a great number of people with little wealth" and a comparatively tiny number of people with massive wealth (Credit Suisse 2016: 119).

While there have been improvements in economic standing of segments of previously poor populations around the world in the last 50 years, as seen, for example in the falling percentage of Chinese found in the poorest 10 percent of the world's population during the twenty-first century, "tremendous socioeconomic inequalities have relegated a significant sector of the [global] population to economic and social deprivation" (Blofield 2010: 1–2). Existing socioeconomic inequalities, and social class divisions are often deeply entrenched in prevailing economic structures, including, in recent years, in the neoliberal economic development models that have been imposed on developing nations by development lender institutions and high-income nations. These models have dramatically undercut state protections from some of the harms of inequality (e.g. through subsidies to hold down the prices on basic food staple) in favor of market-based approaches that have diminished the economic standing of the poor.

Another conception of equality focuses less on possession of and more on issues of social domination, oppression, and exploitive social relationships or what has been termed "relational equality." The key element in social equality is power and the ability to enforce asymmetrical relationships that overwhelmingly benefit the dominant group while causing suffering for the subordinate one. Vastly unequal distribution of power in society ensures that the voice and concerns of the marginalized are rarely heard, including on issues of the environment. Subordinated groups are subject to social exclusion and much of their lives, including their struggles with social inequality, are rendered invisible (Márquez et al. 2008). Not surprisingly, wealth and power often go hand in hand, reinforcing each other and the prevailing unequal structures of society. Research indicates that economic inequalities, in fact, tend to be significantly correlated with social inequalities (Filgueira 2010, Crespo and Ferreira 2010). In their study of indigenous women in the central highlands of Guatemala employed under oppressive conditions in foreign-owned factories that produce clothing for export to the global market, for example, Goldín and Dowdall (2015) recognized that unequal social standing constituted a multi-dimensional arrangement that "extends beyond resource-based inequalities to include noneconomic forms, such as health and educational disparities, unequal opportunities for developing individual capabilities, ... and ...inequalities before systems of justice and the law."

Closely linked to the idea of relational equality are issues of social justice and injustice. Usually in discussions within political philosophy of these pivotal concepts is the treatment of injustice as the lack of justice. Defining injustice as the absence of justice leads to missing "[t]he sense of injustice, the difficulties of identifying both the unjust person and the victims of injustice, ... the many ways in which we learn to live with ... injustices ... [and] the relation of private injustice to public order" (Shklar 1990: 15). Shklar argues analysis of injustice must include not only its immediate causes but also society's refusal to prevent injustice or to mitigate the damage it causes, a form of inaction that she calls passive injustice. In her view, we must give the voice of the victim of injustice its full weight.

In examining the roll of inequality and its relationship to climate change in this book, the primary focus is on the social equality approach, although distributive equality is also important because a preponderance of wealth can be used to fund structures and promotional mechanisms of inequality, issues specifically addressed with regard to climate change in chapters 3 and 4. The goal of chapters 5–9 is to describe the lives and listen to the voice of the victims of climate injustice caught in asymmetrical relationships with social elites.

The history of stratification

A time of equalitarianism

Contrary to the often-expressed idea that there have always been poor people, social and distributive inequalities have a history. Anthropology has been particularly concerned with tracing this history and in understanding the birth and global spread of inequity and injustice. For this task, anthropologists have undertaken multiple studies of foraging societies with comparative simple technological toolkits in Africa, Asia, and South America like those the archeological record suggests were characteristic of all human communities until about 12,000 years ago. A note of caution is warranted here. Extrapolation of information from living societies to those of the past is not without great challenges, and even the living egalitarian societies described by anthropologists have been impacted by nation states and globalizing processes that have reshaped ways of life across the planet. These processes have continued so that many egalitarian societies described by anthropologists at one point in time have undergone considerable change afterward. These issues notwithstanding, in seeking to understand the rise of social inequality the ethnographic record is a valuable tool, which, if left unexamined could surely lead to the false conclusion that inequality is not only a constant feature of human society but also, as a result of its assumed ubiquity, somehow natural and unavoidable.

In fact, for most of the history of our genus Homo on Earth, a period stretching over three million years, the hallmark of human social life was equalitarianism. While there were always differences among people, in size, intelligence, skill, health, or other personal traits, humans and their immediate hominid ancestors did not dwell in hierarchical social worlds populated by haves and have nots. Rather, for the bulk of the human past, people lived in small, mobile foraging groups of no more than 25–50 people who knew each other well and maintained face-to-face relationships across the activities of daily life. Sharing of resources was the norm and distinct inequalities were not tolerated as they were seen as a threat to the fundamental resources of group solidarity and cooperation. Teamwork reduced the risk of extinction caused by the array of everyday threats to survival. People relied on their own labor power as hunters and gatherers of food and did not possess domesticated work animals as sources of labor. Their food sources were edible plants found in the environment and wild game, with the former comprising the largest share of the diet in most environments. Mobility was a necessary response to the movement of game animals and the eventual diminishment of local vegetable food sources due to foraging. Such societies must be highly attuned to shifting opportunities and constraints in the environment around them. Lack of domestic animals and the demands of mobility held in check the quantity of material goods people possessed. However, the private accumulation of items of value, what economist and sociologist Thorstein Veblen (1899) called "conspicuous consumption," was not practiced and possession was not linked to social status (Marshall 1961), making these societies highly contrastive with those that now dominate. Collective, consensual decision-making among adults and individual autonomy in foraging societies were components of the dominant political ethos. There were no powerful leaders, those with the ability to impose their will on the behavior of others, although individual skills and experience were relied upon. However, as Kaplan and Hill (1985) indicate, based on their ethnographic research among the Aché of eastern Paraguay, the most skilled hunters receive no material benefit from their superior subsistence abilities. Food is shared in a manner that insures everyone in the group is fed. The central political value of groups like the Aché is counter-dominance behavior that diminishes individual concentration of authority, which anthropologists conclude was a routine feature of human foraging cultures since their evolution.

Wolf (1982) has labeled the social approach to the acquisition and preparing of food and the creation of tools, clothing, decorations, shelters, and other products of human labor in foraging societies as the "kin-ordered mode of production." By this, he means, with specific reference to foraging societies, that productive inter-action with resources available in nature are organized by various types of kinship connections. It is kinship, including consanquinity (culturally recognized descent from a common ancestor), marriage, and even fictive or socially assumed familial ties, around which social labor is organized in such societies. Alternately, the mode of production in these societies has been labeled "communal" as property (the land and the resources it holds) are held in common by members of the community (Nassaney 1992). Transformations in the nature of modes of production, away from kinship to other systems for organizing and deploying labor and distributing its products is critical to the original of social inequality.

One issue of debate is the status of women in egalitarian society. Assertion of female subservience in these societies can certainly be found in the early literature on foragers. Certainly a gendered division of labor is found in egalitarian societies described by ethnographers, with men filling the primary roles in hunting and women in the gathering of edible plants, as well as in childcare. But in such societies, the separation of the domestic and public spheres of life are narrow, and women can call on their kinship connection to avoid oppressive relationships with their husbands. Moreover, ethnographic accounts make it clear that women exer-cised control over their personal lives and daily activities (Leacock (1992).

How is a level social playing field maintained in egalitarian societies? Anthropologists have identified a number of cultural leveling mechanisms used to diminish the potential for social inequality in wealth or power. One of these, a practice known as "shaming the meat," was explained to anthropologist Richard Lee (1969: 34) by a member of the foraging San people of the Kalahari area in Southern Africa: "When a young man kills much meat, he comes to think of himself as a big man, and he thinks of the rest of us as his inferiors. We can't accept this … . So we always speak of his meat as worthless." Some leveling mechanisms, like the restrictions on the accumulation of property imposed by the need for mobility, are automatic, they are built into the foraging way of life. Others, however, like the example cited by Lee are intentional. Boehm (1993) identified a number of intentional mechanisms used by foragers. One of these was the controlling effects of public opinion. Often this operates informally when people gather to discuss plans and make subsistence or other decisions. Individuals who are deemed to be too assertive may face negative response from the group. For people who have lived their whole lives in a small-scale moral community, "negative opinion can be psychologically troubling even when unaccompanied by other sanctions simply because socialization makes them highly sensitive to group disapproval" (Boehm 1993: 230). Turnbull (1965), for example, reported that among the Mbuti of the Democratic Republic of the Congo, the best hunters tend to keep a low profile in group meetings to avoid public derision. If these measures do not work, progressively harsher strategies may be invoked to avoid asymmetrical relationships from forming.

Foragers, in sum, tend to be fiercely egalitarian (Lee 1988), and this pattern is probably not a recent development. Note Erdal and Whiten 1994: 176), "the universality of egalitarianism in hunter-gatherers suggests that is it an ancient, evolved human pattern."

Many popular conceptions of our ancestors or modern foraging societies—such as the ideas that in these societies life was lived on the edge of starvation with scarce resources at hand, there was an incessant quest for food with limited time for leisure activities, and foraging technologies could not produce anything but a minimal level of existence—have proven to be false. As Sahlins (1972) argues, a large body of ethnographic work has shown that in foraging societies, people have considerable leisure time, their lives are not brutish or unelaborated, people's needs are readily met through their skilful use of even relatively simple technologies coupled with their considerable store of local environmental knowledge, and access to productive resources is not hindered by private property rules. Within the confines of their limited wants and needs for material possessions, life under most circumstances allowed for prosperity, or what Sahlin's humorously called a Zen road to affluence. In fact, Sahlin's maintains, it is the market-industrial society that is currently dominant in the world that institutes scarcity for it is in this kind of society that private ownership and the market create a differential access to resources and stand between processes of production and access to things of value. Insufficiency and the experienced need to have more, buy more, and spend more in a producer promoted treadmill of consumption of an endless and always evolving array of must-have products. In this game of consumerism, "every acquisition is simultaneously a deprivation, for every purchase of something is a foregoing of something else," and hence is born the experience of scarcity (Sahlins 1972: 4). A significant cost of market-industrial economy, a cost that is non-existent in egalitarian foraging societies, is the entrenchment of inequality. It is in these societies that contrasts of wealth and relations of dominance flourish. Moreover, while egalitarian societies leave a very shallow footprint on their local environments, market-industrial society wreaked havoc with the global environment while driving global warming.

A people's history of political centralization and the rise of inequality and global warming

In 1980, historian and political scientist Howard Zinn (2009) published his landmark book, *A People's History of the United States*. Rather than take a top-down approach that focused on the country as a place created by great leaders with human frailties but pure ideals, Zinn reversed the lens and told the story of the U.S. from the eyes and based on the actions of poor and working people who had to struggle every step along the way because of the self-aggrandizing activities of the wealthy and powerful. Mainstream writers did not ignore the book as unimportant but attacked it with frequency and a vehemence suggesting that Zinn had hit a raw nerve. Telling is the nature of the criticism of Oscar Handlin (1980), a professor of history at Harvard University for over 50 years, who, while claiming the book had "the deranged quality of [a] fairy tale," curiously asserted: "It would be a mistake … to regard Zinn as merely Anti-American. Brendan Behan once observed that whoever hated America hated mankind, and hatred of mankind is the dominant tone of Zinn's book." Such a clear expression of elite ideology and hubris has rarely been articulated. It has echoes today in a core, often-repeated message of Donald Trump noted by journalist David Leonhardt (2017), that "people who support him are fully American, and people who don't are something less." In this light, the following sections present the global emergence of inequality and its role in the making of climatic and environmental crises.

The climatic context of emergent inequality

The rise of systematic inequality historically was tied to the emergence of political centralization and the institutionalization of power. These transitions from egalitarian kin-ordered society occurred when some sectors of society were able to gain control of social mechanisms that allowed them to acquire some level of power over productive resources. Such control, in turn, appears to have become the foundation for the implementations of hierarchical divisions within society. A question of historic importance is what were the drivers of this reordering of social relationship. Explanations like the development of technologies such as the domestication of plants and animals previously foraged as wild species, that allowed the growth of a surplus of food and other goods, have been suggested. Domestication requires some degree of settlement that diminishes mobility as a check on property and on the ability of some people in society to gain some control over property and the labor of others. Explanations of these far-reaching developments are often phrased as internal occurrences, a working out of human potential, reflecting an advance of knowledge and of society, commonly portrayed as a process of moral progress.

An alternative perspective concerns the effects on society and on production of a changing climate. Climate change this early in the human story was not, of course, of anthropogenic origin but rather was part of the long sweep of natural environmental changes that comprises the chapters of Earth's history. One hypothesis is that a drying climate created pressure on people to find new subsistence strategies, but such explanations have not been supported by the archeological record. Of greater plausibility is the importance of the amelioration of the colder climate characteristic of the Pleistocene and the warmer, wetter, and stabilizing trends of the Holocene. This climatic change is reflected in the rising CO^2 levels found in ice and ocean-core samples in the transition between these two geographic ages of human presence on the planet. Notably, "amelioration of the climate was followed immediately by the beginnings of plant-intensive resource-use strategies in some areas" and "eventually agriculture became the dominant strategy in all but marginal environments: (Richardson et al. 2001: 387). The process of species domestication appears to have occurred independently at somewhat different times in at least seven different sites in the ancient world, each with their own assemblage of domesticated plants and animals, and spread from them to other areas at the expense of local foragers. In this interpretation of a wide array of archeological finding, the increase in the CO^2 content of the atmosphere and increases in rainfall rather abruptly changed Earth from a regime where agriculture was impossible everywhere to one where it was possible in various places. Since groups that use effective, plant-rich subsistence systems tend to out-compete groups that make less efficient use of land, "the Holocene has been characterized by a persistent, but regionally highly variable, tendency toward subsistence intensification" (Richardson et al. 2001: 404). Hand in hand with climate-influenced technology and subsistence changes were changes in the mode of production that laid the groundwork for the rise of social inequality.

Rise of elite status and the birth of the tributary mode of production

A notable step to the institutionalization of inequality was the rise of social ranking among sedentary horticulturalists involving an institutionalization of status differences within the body of society. The appearance of elite social status can develop with the consolidation of advantage across arenas of social life and production. Thus, would-be elites "may try to manipulate the organization of technology to accumulate resources or intensify production" (Nassaney 1992: 116). Additionally, aspirants to elite status may seek to control the distribution of the surpluses of finished products made possible by domestication. Surpluses may be used to garner degrees of power through the acquisition of "paid" henchmen who do their bidding. To mark their special status, elites may display symbols of authority proclaiming their exalted rank. Separation of aristocratic families from those of commoners in varying forms of status hierarchies can be read as an incipient transition away from egalitarianism toward class formation.

These initial breaks with egalitarianism were fully consolidated with the emergence of the tributary mode of production (Amin 1976). This mode existed in early state level societies and involved the extraction of surplus goods from the immediate producers to political or military rulers that was paid in the form of tribute. Underlying such payment is significant unequal power and a political system organized around social domination. Commonly, rulers in such systems controlled important means of production, such as watering systems for agriculture and standing armies provisioned by extracted surplus and trained to enforce the will of the elite. An example of a tributary state was the Hindu Tai-Ahom kingdom located in the fertile Brahmaputra river valley in northeastern India from 1220 to 1826 (Borah 1994). The ruler, known as the Gohains, a member of the royal family, was supported by a political hierarchy composed of three hereditary lineages of priests and an array of henchmen, soldiers, and servants. Various social rules, such as the stipulation that only the king could wear shoes made of leather and certain types of silk, symbolically reinforced social inequality. Tribute was paid in labor to the elite by those who worked the land or engaged in other direct production processes, in a complex organization of labor, enabling a society of considerable economic inequality based on militarily and symbolically enforced social relationships of domination, oppression, and exploitation. In social systems like this, the long history of egalitarianism in human societies was cast aside for the significant benefit of the elite minority. Domination was not passively accepted in Tai-Ahom, as the suppressed peasantry mounted a series of rebellions over time to gain control of the state. No doubt, other less overt, everyday forms of resistance were enacted as part of "the prosaic but constant struggle" carried out by peasants to "avoid claims on their surplus and assert their rights to the means of production" (Scott 1985: xvi). Among the best known and biggest of the tributary states, and in various ways the model for modern Western nations, was the Roman Empire. Within the empire, inequality of power over lives and freedom, in which some people were converted into property claimed by others, was built into the dominant religious-based belief system and accepted by Romans as natural.

Of much debate among historians is the cause of the fall of the mighty Roman Empire. Various drivers, alone or in combination, including the demands of being in a constant state of war, the outbreak of epidemics, rebellion among subordinated populations, invasions by emergent outside rival groups, a declining population, and excessive urbanization, have been cited (Tainter 2006). An alternative climate-based perspective has been offered by paleoclimatologists based on an analysis of tree rings from over almost 9,000 pieces of wood to establish a record of weather in France and Germany dating from the present back to some 2,500 years ago (Büntgen et al. 2011). Their findings show that the rise of the Roman Empire between 350 BCE and 200 CE coincided with a period of warm, wet summers that favored agricultural production. By contrast, the period of collapse of Rome was characterized by extended droughts. Rapid climate change may have, in fact, been a driver of some of the other calamities that contributed to the fall of Rome, particularly in western parts. This research points to "climate forcing as one agent of distinct episodes of societal crisis" (Büntgen et al. 2011: 578).

The collapse of Rome was not an even process. Although the empire fell in West Europe, it continued, as Byzantium, also known as the Eastern Roman Empire, under different eco-climatic and social conditions for almost another thousand years in the eastern part of the Mediterranean. But disruptions to and the ultimate collapse of Byzantium may also have been influenced by climatic factors (Büntgen et al. 2016).

In Western Europe, the downfall of the political and military infrastructure imposed by Rome led to fragmentation and a period of local tributary production and smaller scale fiefdoms organized around inequality known in historic analysis as feudalism. While the actual structures varied across localities and there has been considerable debate on the matter (Brown 1974; Reynolds 1994), the basic ideal model of the feudal expression of the tributary mode of production involved claimed ownership of arable land by a local noble that was then farmed by commoners who had to pay homage to the crown in labor, including military service, and a share of their produce, in exchange for protection from the incursions of rival fiefdoms. Over time, these local tributary entities began to fuse into larger, militarily consolidated polities. Wolf (1982) identifies three factors compelling geopolitical expansion and unification: 1) the growth of seaports on the Italian peninsula shifted long-distance trade with southwest Asia to the advantage of the West; 2) favorable climatic conditions allowed an agricultural intensification and extension of cultivation, which produced surpluses that could be claimed by emergent kings to fund predatory ventures and the political amalgamation of larger areas; and 3) rebellions by oppressed peasants protesting rising kingly demands for tribute—known to historians as "the crisis of feudalism"—triggered a search for new sources of wealth beyond the frontiers of Europe. The latter dynamic sparked the era of European global trade and military-enforced colonialism, overseen by a collaboration between political rulers and emergent global merchants seeking wealth and power at home and in the wider world. During the resulting era of colonialism, inequality became embedded in a global structure of oppressive social relationships, and an emergent capitalist mode of production in Europe became a world system. As accurately asserted by Wolf (1982), we cannot understand the world of the present, including the role of humans in reshaping the climate and environments around us, which in turn, directly impact our well-being, without tracing the development and nature of the capitalist world system.

The global impress of colonialism

Merchant capitalism was born as a system involving control of labor and trade to produce profit comprised of extracted wealth from other lands while allowing "Europe to live above its means, to invest beyond its savings," particularly the ruling class of European countries (Braudel 1974: 268). The people of the colonies came to have a very different experience as their bodies became racialized units of labor for colonial administrators and their social worlds and interior lives were shaken and re-ordered in often jarring and abusive ways.

Colonial extraction varied in form by location and colonial power but it had dramatic impact around the globe. Most egregious was the slave trade that ripped people from their homes in Africa, transported them—if they survived the middle passage—across the ocean in chains to the New World, turned them and their children, with state sanction, into sellable commodities, and forcibly extracted their labor to produce wealth for their owners, while they dwelled their lives in poverty. Ideologically, the slave trade was justified as a reasonable and fair playing out of alleged innate differences between whites and Africans, a part of the racist legacy of colonial inequality that remains part of the structural violence of everyday life in the twenty-first century.

In colonial India, the British introduced a form of debt bondage that they used to send over three million Indian workers to toil on British lands in Mauritius, Guyana, Trinidad, Jamaica, Fiji, and elsewhere. Resistance to British colonial rule could lead to mass slaughter, as occurred in the Rebellion of 1857. The "drain of wealth" (Naoroji 1901) from India to England was based on oppressive land revenue policies, monopolistic control over Indian markets, taxation, and a range of fees and charges to pay British expenses. For most Indians, the bottom 90 percent of the population, colonialism meant trying to eke out a living from the soil, worrying about burdensome taxes and debt, and fearing starvation and disease. In the words of John Sullivan who served in the British colonial structure in Madras, India, "Our system acts very much like a sponge, drawing up all of the good things from the banks of the Ganges, and squeezing them down on the banks of the Thames …" (quoted in Dutt (1908: 140).

In Southeast Asia, France dominated Vietnam, Laos, and Cambodia, a colony it referred to as Indochine Francais (French Indochina). The colony became one of France's most lucrative possessions. The French justified their presence as a civilizing mission to bring Western enlightenment and technologies to backward and impoverished peoples. But this "was a facade: the real motive for French colonialism was profit and economic exploitation. French imperialism was driven by a demand for resources, raw materials and cheap labour" (Llewellyn et al. 2016). France seized vast tracks of land from small landholders and restructured them into large plantations. The former owners were given the choice of laboring for the French on these plantations or getting out. When additional labor was needed, small farmers were brought in from outlying villages, sometimes at the point of a gun. Rice and rubber were the primary plantation cash crops. Plantation workers, who were derogatively called "coolies," toiled long hours on pitifully low wages. To extract further wealth, the French imposed an elaborate taxation system that included an income tax, a poll tax, stamp duties on publications and documents, and compulsory payments during the weighing and measuring of agricultural goods. In 1881, French government officials and colonial merchants took control of the poppy crop, introduced European equipment to improve the yield, and began to sell locally as well as export the addictive narcotic opium. By 1914, opium was one of the largest sources of income for French colonial coffers producing 37 percent of all revenues. During this period, France's annual sale of rice wine, salt, and opium was earning the colonial power the equivalent of $5 billion (Llewellyn et al. 2016).

In the interandean region of South America, in countries like Ecuador, during the first century Spanish colonial rule, most of the indigenous population was wiped out by introduced diseases, military conquest, the expropriation of lands, labor and production, and the ruthless conditions of slavery. Mecham (2001) notes:

> The *conquistadores* dedicated their first years to sacking the impressive wealth of the Inca Empire, whose precious metals were to subsidize the rapid expansion of the newly-emerging capitalist economy in Europe. The Spanish colonial economy was organized around the large estates, mines and textile mills worked by the indigenous and African slave populations which produced the wealth for the Crown and colonial elites.

Colonialism, a social system whose mission was to create a new world order to the advantage of Europe (Mitchell 1988), left an indelible legacy of inequality around the globe. In part this is a product of the wealth extracted from the colonies that furthered the technological and institutional development of colonial powers. It is also a consequence of the ideological assertions colonial rulers called on to represent Western culture and distinguish themselves morally, intellectually, and physically from those they colonized (Bernal 1997). Embedded in this distinction was the unquestioned assumption within Europe of the right of the colonists to reconfigure other lands and other lives, an assemblage of actions seen as the positive imposition of colonial order on pre-colonial irrationality. The global social relations of colonialism reflected in the culture of justified dominance continue to echo into the present, as "colonialism's living consciousness" (Simpson 2000: 115) and in various expressions of colonial nostalgia, and can be heard in contemporary narratives about global warming.

The instatement of the capitalist mode of production

The full transition into the capitalist mode of production, which remains the globally dominant economic system, was the conversion of the mercantile wealth garnered through colonial expansion into workable capital. Critical sites for this transition were the textile factories that developed in England during the eighteenth century. Factory owners used colonial wealth to acquire land, build facilities, purchase machinery, and hire labor. Some of the consequent surplus, gained by selling factory products, was used to enrich the material lives of factory owners and invested as capital in ongoing expansion and, when necessary, the social control of a rebellious working class outraged by intensifying social inequality. Under emergent industrial capitalism, people of lesser means, those who did not own factories or other means of production, were increasingly forced to sell their labor if they were to survive. But individuals who previously had worked the land or as artisans resisted the harsh conditions of the privately owned factory with its unrelenting demands for long hours of labor, often prison-like working environment, and the disciplining presence of profit-conscious supervisors. In Marx's (1990) analysis, the transformation of immediate producers in the early factories, those who performed labor within the factory walls, was an alienating process. Workers were alienated from the productive process, which they engaged in for a wage but the work was not as inherently meaningful. They were alienated from the products of their labor, which were owned by the factory owners. They were alienated from their fellow humans, who were competitors for jobs or work advantages. And they were alienated from themselves as autonomous individuals empowered to meet their needs through the direct engagement with nature.

Marx's discussion of alienation and oppression of the working poor in the early days of industrial capitalism were informed by the observations of his collaborator, Frederick Engels, in the textile producing city of Manchester, England in the mid-1800s. In the book he wrote based on his fieldwork in Manchester, *The Conditions of the Working-Class in England*, he wrote:

> During my residence in England, at least twenty or thirty persons have died of simple starvation under the most revolting circumstances … . The bourgeoisie dare not speak the truth in these cases, for it would speak its own condemnation. But indirectly, far more than directly, many have died of starvation, where long-continued want of proper nourishment has … brought on severe illness and death. The English working-men call this 'social murder', and accuse our whole society of perpetrating this crime perpetually. Are they wrong?
>
> *(Engels 2015: 25)*

In his discussion, Engels appears to recognize the importance of multiple intersecting environmental threats to health in light of the structure of social relationships responsible for creating life-threatening living conditions. He commented (Engels 2015: 17–18): "if life in large cities is, in itself, injurious to health, how great must be the harmful influence of an abnormal atmosphere in the working-people's quarters, where … everything combines to poison the air … ."

Prior to the Industrial Revolution, textiles, which were primarily made from wool, were made by hand. In the early years of capitalism, the machinery of the new industrial age, especially the spinning wheel and loom, led to a focus on otton in textile manufacture, because its shorter production time increased the profits of factory owners. Water power, with the help of giant water wheels, energized the new machinery. However, as noted in chapter 1 in relation to its critical role in driving global warming, as the nineteenth century unfolded, the fuel-burning and pollution and emission-releasing steam engine increasingly took over as the energy source of industrialization. As historian Stanley Chapman (2013: 19) indicates, by 1835 the steam engine "had become the predominant form of power in [almost] every cotton town in the North of England." Coal came to be of ever-greater value as the dominant energy source for the steam engine. The transition from water to steam did not occur because steam was cheaper or more powerful. Rather, steam gave factory owners better access to a labor force and more opportunity to exploit their workers. While water-driven machines had to be located near fast-flowing rivers or waterfalls, adequate numbers of potential factory workers did not necessarily live near where these were found, especially in rural areas. Housing, at some cost to the owner, had to be built, and when workers protested against unfair conditions they were hard to replace. Coal, by contrast, was a mobile energy source. It allowed the owner to locate his factory in an expanding urban area. Such a location was also a source of potential replacement workers hungry for jobs should there a strike at the factory, and the town was likely to have a police force and hireable thugs to further limit worker unrest. The cost of paying for coal was offset by the benefit of power over workers. Coal rapidly became the fuel driving capitalist economic growth and expansion into new areas of production, triggering the full economic conversion to industrial fossil fuel production. At the heart of this transition was not a natural evolution of ever-improving human technology but rather issues of power, injustice, and inequality.

Given that the textile factories of England received a high percentage of their cotton from the American South, during a period when slavery provided the labor power for the cotton plantations, the global nature of the inequality at the birth of capitalism is notable. Moreover, the inequality built in to the capitalist mode of production arrived hand in hand with the pivotal turn toward massive greenhouse gas emissions and distinct global warming. In fact, one of the grievances of early British industrial workers, especially those who lived in densely crowded areas with a concentration of factories, was the horrible air quality caused by coal smoke (Akatsu 2015). These workers and their families had to contend with noxious clouds of industrial pollutants that caused extensive respiratory disease and rising death rates. Unknown to them at the time, the factory smoke stacks were also emitting greenhouse gases that were heating the planet. Nowadays, the science of emissions and climate change linking fossil fuel use to adverse environmental changes is clear. But the processes of emission and dangerous environmental destruction nevertheless continue today, and for the same reasons.

The capitalist world system

The complex development of the capitalist mode of productions, and the social and economic relationships it brought into being, forged a world system that ultimately connected all parts of the globe into a single if geographically and structurally differentiated economy. One of the first articulations of the nature of the capitalist world economy was published in 1974 in the journal *Comparative Studies in Society & History* by historical social scientist Immanuel Wallerstein (1974), followed by a four-volume set, *The Modern World-System*. Wallerstein's perspective was influenced by Fernand Braudel's notion of *la longue durée*, which referred to the need for a long term of the history of society. From Marx, Wallerstein adopted a recognition of the social conflicts and inequalities of materially based human groups. Wallerstein (1976: 229) argues that "a world-system is a social system, one that has boundaries, structures, member groups, rules of legitimation, and coherence." Capitalism allowed "constant economic expansion of the world-system, albeit a very skewed distribution of its rewards" (Wallerstein 1976: 230). While the tributary mode of production supported political empires that covered wide regions under a governmental institutional structure, capitalism subsumed a multiplicity of formally independent political entities—indeed, today, all nations of the world—within a single economic system, the global market. Nations, and other political entities (e.g. cities, states) and hence their resident taxpayers, commonly absorb the losses of capitalism, from the federal bailout of the automobile industry from 2009–2013 to the clean-up of hazardous substances and contaminated areas left behind by polluting industries. By contrast, the economic gains of capitalism across the world system are retained in private hands.

Across the world system there is a complex division of labor and a hierarchy of occupational tasks entwined with varying local traditions, cultural arrangements, and pre-existing social hierarchies. Consequently, numerous scholarly analyses have challenged the notion that "capitalism enacts itself monolithically" across the world (Freeman 2007: 252). From an anthropological perspective, it is thus critical to balance a broad view of global history with the focused, on-the-ground view produced by local and multisited ethnography. This enables understanding of "the particulars hidden by … sameness" (Trouillot 2003: 122).

At the economic hub of the system are the technologically developed "core" societies with varying but relatively stable state structures, places like the U.S. or Japan, that control the market and use it to dominate and exploit underdeveloped "peripheral" societies with weak or even failed state structures and widespread and often severe poverty. Standing between these two ends of the economic structure are "semiperipheral" societies, currently nations like Mexico, Brazil, or India, which have more developed economies than peripheral societies and may even have rapidly expanding economic sectors, but also are characterized by steep social inequalities and significant levels of poverty. Over the long sweep of history, a region of the world may change its structural role in the world-economy, moving for example from core to semiperiphery or from the periphery to the semiperiphery, although the basic pattern of disparities within the world-economy remains.

The world system is characterized by unequal exchange, a systematic flow of wealth from the periphery and semiperiphery to the core. This allows capital accumulation in the core, some of which, as discussed in chapters 3 and 4, is used to influence political campaigns and state policies, including those that involve the regulation of greenhouse gases and related issues. As this suggests, in terms of environmental hazards, there is a counter-flow to the primary movement of surplus. This entails movement from the core to the periphery, such as the dumping of garbage, radioactive substances, and used and worn out electronic goods, "e-waste," from the core onto the periphery. Unequal access to the conditions that foster health across the core, semiperiphery, and periphery is another feature of the world system (Baer et al. 2013, Singer and Erickson 2013).

The term "development gap" has been introduced to describe the ever-widening separation between the richest and most developed nations at the core of the world system and the poorest, and least developed nations in the periphery (Fukuyama 2008). There are various measures of this gap, such as the Gini coefficient, a statistical measure of the degree of inequality in a country or even in the world, using measures like income distribution. Based on such assessment, it became clear that a line could be drawn on a global map that generally separated the wealthy countries of the Northern Hemisphere from poorer countries in the Southern Hemisphere, except for Australia and New Zealand, producing a visual cartography of the development gap. The concept drew attention to the fact that "in countries throughout the world the expansion of prosperity for some, [has been] accompanied by an expansion of unspeakable poverty for others" (World Summit for Social Development 1995). It is not only wealth that is unevenly distributed across this line—so too are key indicators of human development and quality of life, like health, life expectancy, and literacy. The development gap reflects the fact that whether we notice or not, a variable heavily influenced by our geography of residence and social standing, "[w]e live in a world of extreme inequality" (McGill 2016: 27).

The business of development

Officially, it is the position of core nations that they and several globally active institutions they created are trying to help poorer nations develop into technologically advanced, social and politically stable places with a good quality of life for their respective citizens. To achieve these goals, wealthy countries provide and insure development loans and grants, suggesting a flow of wealth from the core to the periphery. Ultimately, development has been said by its advocates to be about human rights, especially expanding freedoms, addressing pressing human needs, and improving the quality of life. Yet, as Escobar (2011: 13) indicates, development as a social process "has relied exclusively on one knowledge system, namely, the modern Western one. The dominance of this knowledge system has dictated the marginalization and disqualification of non-Western knowledge systems." Development has been portrayed as the transformation of traditional, backward-facing societies into modern, forward-facing ones, as if such framing was based on an objective assessment rather than a privileged cultural construct (Morandé 1984). Development, in short, has been about Western ways of knowing the world, and, in light of the hegemony of capitalist assumptions, concepts, and values, with the class-interested construction of a global reality by the wealthy.

Development initiatives by core nations appeared on the global landscape in the period following the Second World War, a Euro-driven global conflict that both inflicted tremendous suffering on poorer nations and simultaneously toppled remaining structures of colonial social domination. In the analysis of Frank (1991), development thinking in core nations, as an approach to dealing with new conditions in the world, "was the child of neo-imperialism and neo-colonialism." The older colonial powers of Europe were weakened by the war, while the U.S. had come out of the conflict largely unscathed and in possession of unparalleled levels of economic and military might. The economic elite of the U.S. saw in this an opportunity to act aggressively on global designs. So much of the world's physical resources, markets, and laboring masses were now situated in emergent nations rather than historically divided colonial territories. Consequently, they appeared ripe for the taking by the world's new powerhouse. Henry Luce, publisher of *Time Magazine*, described the period as the beginning of an "American Century" during which the U.S. rather than Europe would shape events and the structure of relations to meet its economic aspirations.

This moment of gleeful anticipation did not last long. In 1949, the Chinese revolution occurred, sweeping a quarter of the world's population outside of the global capitalist economy, an event that sent a shockwave through the American elite. Other anti-capitalist revolutionary struggles broke out, intensified concern about the prospects for unencumbered access to global wealth. There was a keen interest in thwarting this threat, by war if necessary but by other means if possible. Frank (1991) observed, "Developing a more harmless alternative became a matter of the greatest urgency, especially in the newly hegemonic United States." Herein was born the idea for Western support of peripheral development and the conceptual understandings of the nature of underdevelopment needed to support this globalizing initiative. Ultimately, the primary goal of development was not the elimination of the intertwined plagues of poverty, inequality, and injustice but rather making the world safe for making a profit. In his inaugural address to the nation on January 20, 1949, President Harry Truman plainly stated:

> More than half the people of the world are living in conditions approaching misery. Their food is inadequate. They are victims of disease. Their economic life is primitive and stagnant. Their poverty is a handicap and a threat both to them and to more prosperous areas.
>
> *(Avalon Project 1997)*

Underdevelopment was a threat to prosperous areas because nations of the periphery might embrace socialism and reject participation in the Western-dominated, global economy.

It was against this background, at a moment of doubt in core nations, that development was born. The strength of concern among the social elite in the core of the world system soon resulted in the formation of several powerful institutions, including the International Monetary Fund (IMF), the World Bank, and the World Trade Organization, to advance development. Each of these had a specific order-maintaining mission on the global scene, but the overriding objectives, according to Eric Helleiner (2014), were the maintenance of global stability, opening up the markets of the world for cheap imports, and the creation of new markets for development country exports. Also driving development was an approach that depoliticized social problems as technical issues and deepened Western influence over the direction of what was often called "modernization" (Ferguson 1994).

Both the IMF and the World Bank have been disparaged for helping "lock developing countries into carbon-intensive development" (Orenstein 2010) that contributes to climate change. By 2010, the Bank, for example, had become one of the world's premier multilateral fossil fuel financiers. The Bank's $3 billion loan that year to South Africa's state utility Eskom to develop a 4,800-megawatt coal-fired plant drew particular opposition because of the high greenhouse gas emission levels of such plants (Reuters 2010). Notably, some of the criticism came from Western governments that supported their own coal-fired plants while opposing their construction in developing countries. However, opposition also came from citizen and environmental groups, faith-based organizations, students, and trade unions in South Africa that pointed out that the main beneficiaries of profits from the plant were multinational corporations, like the Anglo American Corporation. In a number of poor countries, "local communities began to protest development that threatened forests, fisheries, and agricultural lands on which they depended" (Rich 2013: 17). Eventually, Barber Conable, a former U.S. Congressman who served as president of the Bank from 1986 to 1991, admitted "the World Bank has been part of the problem" and promised changes (quoted in Shabecoff 1987).

Despite the heartening words and lofty goals that ushered in the era of development, the contradiction of development borrowing and wealth extraction came to a head in the Debt Crisis of the late 1970s to mid-1980s, a period during which many peripheral and semiperipheral countries that had been the recipients of significant development loans from the World Bank and the IMF, or directly from core nations (e.g. the United States Agency for International Development), were too poor to make payments on their debts. Economists within and beyond the big development lenders concluded that the primary barrier to development and, hence to loan repayment, was that in the developing world "the state played too great a role in the economy, inhibiting markets and firms from operating in a manner that would raise overall welfare" (Gershman and Irwin 2002: 22). Thus began a new period in the character of relations within the world-economy, an era of so-called "neoliberalism."

The term neoliberalism, which reflected a new consensus among leaders in the developed world, especially the Thatcher government in the U.K., the Reagan administration in the U.S., and the Kohl regime in Germany, that the capitalist market, if left unfettered by government intervention in economic and social issues, would, among other accomplishments, solve the problem of global poverty. As an economic philosophy, embraced generally by the corporate capitalist class. Its adoption lead to a shake-up in top economic positions at the World Bank and IMF. The neoliberal solution to the Debt Crisis and to most other problems of poorer countries, known as structural adjustment, consisted of several components. These basic pillars of neoliberalism are of special relevance to task of this book as they find repeated expression as accepted reality among the deniers and obfuscators of climate change, as discussed in chapters 3 and 4.

First of the components of neoliberalism is an often sweeping privatization and out-sourcing of state services (e.g., health care for families in need) leading to deluge of often competing international nongovernment organizations that undermined successful development assistance and fragmented access to needed services for the poor (Kim et al. 2000, Pfeiffer 2003). In a developing country like Mexico, the first nation to default on its development loans, foreign debt soared from $6.8 billion to $58 billion between 1972 and 1982 (Mason 2013). The neoliberal restructuring of the Mexican economy illustrates the impact on the Third World of the new era of lending policies:

> Privatization and deregulation … contributed to a steep concentration of income and wealth … . In what analysts term a 'trickle up' process, there has been in Mexico a massive transfer of resources from the salaried population to owners of capital, and from public control to a few private hands.
>
> *(Heredia and Purcell 1994)*

Second is liberalization, which involved both the removal of government protections for the products of local industries (e.g. tariffs) in peripheral nations—allowing an opening up to the free flow of trade from other nations—and the removal of government subsidies that kept the purchase of basic goods affordable. Already pressed poorer populations were further squeezed by a loss of assisted access to the basic staples of life in local contexts. Representative of the impact, the population of Mexico suffered around a 25 percent loss of their standard of living 1982–1986 as per capita income fell. Between 1980 and 1992, infant deaths due to nutritional deficiencies almost tripled to rates higher than those in the 1970s (Salinas de Gortari 1992).

The final component of the neoliberal solution is deregulation. It was based on a view of government as a hindrance to the naturally beneficial effects of a free market. Deregulation entailed restricting the role of governments in the flow of investment capital, commodities, and labor markets. Except for the military and other social control functions, this often has entailed a hollowed-out and reshaped state structure that does not even attempt to provide "adequate safety nets for its population, especially those who are young, poor, or marginalized" as "private interests trump social needs, and economic growth becomes more important than social justice" (Giroux 2008: 113). Neoliberal cuts imposed on governments by lender institutions, as a condition of new loans, have systematically targeted government social expenditures for healthcare, education, and environmental protection (Weaver et al. 2012). Thus, UNICEF reported in the late 1980s that the neoliberal structural adjustment programs of the World Bank had been responsible for "reduced health, nutritional and educational levels for tens of millions of children in Asia, Latin America, and Africa" (Cornia et al. 1987).

In short, the neoliberal diagnosis of the inability of debtor nations to repay their development loans focused on and found fault with internal features of developing nations. Not considered were the relations of poorer with richer nations or the effects of the location of debtor countries in the capitalist world system. In other words, and contrary to a long history of unequal relations dating to colonialism, neoliberalism ignored interconnectedness and treated debtor nations as autonomous spaces rather than locations caught up with wealthy nations in a "topography of power" (Gupta and Ferguson 1992: 8). This blinkered view does not consider the fact that the core countries did not develop and become wealthy because of their superior internal and ultimately cultural characteristics (e.g. having a disciplined attitude toward work, respecting entrepreneurship), but rather gained advantage through their hierarchical relations with and "at the expense of their poorest counterparts" (McGill 2016: 36).

In its impact on the world, neoliberalism undercut the life of the poor as well as many middle social groupings around the world. During the twenty-first century, thus far, there have been signs of renewed dramatic increases in distributive inequality, especially inequality of wealth (Berman et al. 2015). These have gained notice as the damaging effects of climate change have become more evident. Driving these developments as entwined threats are the actions of a group of very wealthy people who have been called "the polluting elites," those who "direct leading sectors of their economies and exercise disproportionate control over national and foreign environmental policies" and practices (Roberts and Parks 2007: 118).

The industrial capitalist class: the polluting elite

Examination of the polluting elites draws attention to the ways the political economy of the capitalist system "promoted ecologically destructive behavior by profit-driven corporations, exploits nature and human labor, generated ecological destruction/disorganization, and furthers the unequal distribution of wealth and ecological resources" (Lynch et al. 2017). This destruction, carried out by wealthy and often lauded banner corporations, occurs within a framing of reality that diminishes their role in pollution while highlighting their contributions to society, from the creation of jobs to protecting the environment, as well as their close adherence to standards of corporate responsibility. It is for this reason that companies with poor environmental records might adopt the use of recycled paper in their offices or other minimal changes compared to the environmental damage they cause, and publicize such actions as a sign of deep environmental concern. Alternatively, they might donate to an environmental group or support an environmental project, and cite these expressions of their generosity in their public relations materials. Even changes imposed by government or court action may be scripted as expressions of commitment to the environment (Beder 1997). In addition, the framing of reality by the polluting elites commonly construct poor people, especially those in developing countries where natural resources are desired, as "a collection of individuals who are simply deficient competitors in an otherwise fair" (Greenbaum 2015: 13) and morally sound capitalist economic system. In this understanding, the poor suffer from defective character traits, lack temperance and self-discipline, and as a result have a dearth of virtuous morality. These are the reasons they are poor and endure the ignominies of marginal existence. In blaming the poor for their own plight, the role of unfair structural inequalities and the contributions of the elite to creating the living conditions of poverty, including shaping of environmental factors that burden the lives of the poor, are obscured. The influence of the "blame the poor" narrative on policy and on the actions of the elite, and those they employ to promote their interests, is a recurrent theme in dominant announcements about the nature of social and environmental problems.

Who are the polluting elites?

An examination by the Center for Public Integrity (Hopkins 2016), using several U.S. federal datasets, found that in 2014 a third of the toxic air releases from power plants, factories and other entities originated in just 100 complexes of the 20,000-plus facilities reporting release data to the Environmental Protection Agency. These top 100 polluters vented more than 270 million pounds of chemicals in 2014, most of which are known to create health risks A third of the greenhouse-gas emissions also are reported as coming from around a hundred industrial sites, while 21 sites appear on both lists. These sites are super polluters of the environment and the atmosphere and they are headed by the polluting elites.

A site that appears on both lists is ExxonMobil's huge refinery and petrochemical complex in Baytown, Texas, the largest such facility in the U.S. While ExxonMobil officials claim on their Baytown website that they "control emissions, enhance energy efficiency and maintain the highest standards for safety, security, health and environmental care" (ExxonMobil 2018), in 2017 a federal judge ordered the company to pay almost $20 million for pumping millions of pounds of excess pollution into the air (Collier 2017). The region in which the plant is located is among the most ozone-polluted urban area in the U.S. Another ExxonMobil site included in the report is the company's refinery and chemical plant in Baton Rouge, Louisiana. The latter is noteworthy because of the people most immediately affected by the plant's releases; almost 90 percent of those living within three miles of the facility are African American, and about a third live below the federal poverty line. The complex vented more than 2.6 million pounds of chemicals to the air in 2014 through its giant smoke stacks, including hydrogen cyanide—which is linked to headaches, confusion and nausea—and benezine, a known carcinogen (Hopkins 2016).

With a value at over $350 billion, ExxonMobil is the leading publically traded, multinational oil and gas company in the world. At the close of 2015, the largest holders of the company's stock were Rex Tillerson, Stephen Pryor, and Michael Dolan. Appointed by Trump as secretary of state, in 2015 Tillerson held 2.4 million shares of ExxonMobil stock, with a value of almost $200 million. At the time he left the company to join the Trump administration, Tillerson's annual compensation from ExxonMobil was over $25 million (Salary.com 2016). At his departure, ExxonMobil gave Tillerson a $180 million severance package. Forbes Magazine estimates Tillerson's total net worth at $330 million (Alexander 2017). In 2015, Tillerson was named as the 24th most powerful person on the planet by Forbes Magazine (2016). Tillerson resides in Bartonville, Texas, an area known for its exclusive horse farms. On an 18-acre parcel, the Tillersons have a luxurious 4,200 sq ft home. Following his appointment as Secretary of State, Tillerson also bought a five bedroom, five full and a two half bathroom colonial revival home in the upscale and secluded Kalorama neighborhood in the northwest quadrant of Washington D.C. for $5.6 million. The comfortable, five level, brick exterior home has three fireplaces and central air conditioning (Freed 2017, Washington Fine Properties 2017). The Tillersons also own a vacation home, valued at around $3.25 million, in the almost all white town of Horseshoe Bay, Texas. The couple owns other property in Texas as well, including a two-story house overlooking River Crest Country Club in Fort Worth (Strum 2017, Heinkel-Wolfe 2016).

Exxonmobil is not alone as a superpolluter. What has been described as the biggest single emitter of greenhouse gases is a facility located in the rolling hills of north-central Alabama (Hernandez 2017). The site, known as the James H. Miller Jr. Electric Generating Plant, is a subsidiary of the Southern Company, which owns 11 utilities spread across 18 states and is the second largest generator and provider of home energy in the U.S. based on the size of its customer base of about nine million. The Miller plant released over 19 million metric tons of greenhouse gases in 2015. This is about the amount pumped out by four million passenger cars over the course of one year. U.S. Environmental Protection Agency data indicate that Miller has been among the top three greenhouse gas-producing U.S. facilities since federal tracking began in 2010. In 2006, following EPA allegations of violations at Miller of the Clean Air Act, Southern agreed to install new pollution controls and to pay a fine of $100,000 (Environmental Protection Agency 2006).

Significant greenhouse gas emissions from the plant continued however. But for the head of Southern Company, chairman and CEO, Thomas Fanning, there is no convincing scientific evidence that this release of CO^2 causes global warming. When asked during a CNBC interview if he believes it has been proven that CO^2 is the primary cause of climate change, Fanning ignored the preponderance of scientific evidence and replied, "No, certainly not. Is climate change happening? Certainly. It's been happening for millennia" (video recording in Belvedere 2017).

While constrained in his comments on climate change during the Obama administration, the election of Donald Trump appears to have convinced Fanning that it is okay to say in public what his company's lobbying efforts and funding of global warming denial organizations has expressed through its deeds behind closed doors.

The Southern Company (2017) on its website, under the heading of Environmental Responsibility—which is rather devoid of much information on that topic—proclaims that it uses "outside firms to assist our efforts and support coalitions and trade organizations that engage in lobbying activities. Expenses associated with operating our Washington office in 2015 were about $12.86 million." Washington has increasingly become a focus of Southern lobbying as climate change came to the fore during the Obama administration. In 2009, as climate legislation was moving forward in the House of Representatives, the company spent over $6 million more than the nearest competitor to try to win opposition to greenhouse gas regulation. Southern had 63 climate lobbyists working for them in Washington during the first quarter of 2009. Afterward, Southern emphasized efforts to strip the EPA of its authority to regulate greenhouse gas emissions. In Georgia, Southern successfully lobbied for several laws that limited the ability of customers to install and use solar energy (Edwards and Larsen 2011).

During 2016, Southern Company made political donations in the amount of almost half a million dollar, mostly to Republican committees and associations. The company uses its donations and other activities to maintain friendly ties with state regulators in the states where it operates to insure the passage of favorable laws and to restrict the regulation of the energy industry. Haley Barbour, governor of Mississippi from 2004 to 2012, served as a lobbyist for Southern before and after his stint living in the governor's mansion. While in office, Barbour signed a corporate-friendly law that allowed companies to pass on the cost of building new power plants to ratepayers. While Fanning maintains that "taking responsibility for the enterprise" (quoted in Dormann 2012) is a core feature of Southern's corporate culture, he blames others when things go wrong, such as the failed "clean coal" Kemper power plant the company built near Meridan, Mississippi. The facility, which was supposed to be in service by May 2014, at a cost of $2.4 billion, was still not operational by May 2017, while project costs had ballooned to $7.3 billion (Maloney 2017), making it one of the most expensive power plants ever built. By December 2017, Kemper shut down the failed coal initiation and turned to burning natural gas. Rather than shoulder responsibility for the failure, Fanning launched a public relations campaign to assert the culpability on state energy regulators. Fanning asserted that the plant was started because the Mississippi Public Service Commission wanted a coal plant as a way to protect the state from rising gas prices. However, documents obtained through a Freedom of Information Act request filed by the U.S. Department of Energy, which has provided over $400 million in grants for Kemper, contradict Fanning's assertion (Zegart 2017).

As discussed in detail in chapters 3 and 4, ExxonMobil and Southern Company are not only superpolluters, controlled by polluting elites, they also have long histories of climate change denial and the funding of a broad network of denial promoting organizations. In this doubly adverse global role, they are joined by the Koch brothers and other extremely wealthy fossil fuel industry figures. In fact, the number of superpolluters appears to be growing. Analysis by Oxfam International (2018) of data provided on the Forbes world billionaire list for the years 2010 and 2015, found that the number of billionaires with economic interests in fossil fuels rose from 54 to 88, while the size of their combined personal fortunes grew by about 50 percent, going from over $200 billion to more than $300 billion. Expressive of the social gap this disparity of wealth suggests, as Robinson (2004) observes, whatever their country of origin and residence global elites increasingly share similar lifestyles and have more in common with each other than they do with their fellow citizens.

On a global scale, wealthy people are, by far, the biggest greenhouse gas emitters. The study by Oxfam International (2015a), affirmed that the poorest 50 percent of the global population, or about 3.5 billion people, are responsible for only about 10 percent of global carbon emissions, with the wealthiest 10 percent of people in the world being responsible for about half of global carbon emissions. Oxfam (2015b) sees its study as helping to dispel

> the myth that citizens in rapidly developing countries are somehow most to blame for climate change. While emissions are rising fastest in developing countries, much of this is for the production of goods consumed in other countries, meaning that the emissions associated with the lifestyle of the vast majority of their citizens are still far lower than their counterparts in developed countries.

There is a locational link within nations between income inequality and greenhouse gas emissions. A study in the U.S. for the years 1997–2012, for example, found that state-level carbon emissions were positively associated with that share of the wealth within a state controlled by the richest 10 percent of the state's population (Jorgenson et al. 2015). Also of interest is the relationship between consumption-based emission of CO^2 and domestic inequality within nations. Several questions have been raised about the relationship between inequality and greenhouse gas emissions: are nations with greater levels of inequality higher emitters? Conversely, does greater income equality, associated with the growth of a middle class living carbon-intensive lifestyles lead to higher emission levels? In addressing these questions, a study of 67 nations during the years 1991–2008 (Jorgenson et al. 2016) found variation among high-, middle-, and low-income countries. Among high-income nations, growing income inequality was associated with increases carbon emissions during the target years. In middle-income and low-income nations, the researchers could find no significant directional association between emissions and degree of inequality. What is critical, in short, is the growing wealth and social inequality within core nations and relations between the core and peripheral and semiperipheral nations in the making of a warming plant, affirming the link between climate change and injustice.

Environmental crime and punishment

In concluding this chapter, it merits re-asking a critical query that has been raised by international climate mitigation advocates: are climate polluters, and their political allies, prosecutable for committing environmental crimes against humanity? The Rome Statute, which established the International Criminal Court (ICC) as part of the U.N. structure in 2002, defines "crimes against humanity" as "inhumane acts … intentionally causing great suffering, or serious injury to body or to mental or physical health" (United Nations 2002: 4). Such acts must be "committed as part of a widespread or systematic attack directed against any civilian population, with knowledge of the attack" (United Nations 2002: 3). The statue established the legal foundation for the creation of the International Criminal Court with the power to exercise jurisdiction for serious crimes against humanity. This power, however, did not enable the ICC to directly prosecute and try climate crimes per se and legal experts often have drawn the conclusion that proving in a court of law the relationship between the acts of a corporation and specific climate damages is an overwhelming task.

In 2016, however, the ICC Office of the Prosecutor released a policy paper that indicated it would include within its selection criteria and prioritize crimes involving the environment, including "the destruction of the environment [and] the illegal exploitation of natural resources" (Office of the Prosecutor 2016: 14). Alice Harrison, an adviser at Global Witness, a group that investigates and exposes environmental and human rights abuses, responded to the ICC policy statement by saying that it "should send a warning shot to company executives and investors that the environment is no longer their playground" (quoted in Vidal and Bowcott 2016). The Center for Climate Crime Analysis (CCCA) (2017), a non-profit organization set up to support the ICC prioritization of environmental crimes, defines "climate crimes" as

> criminal activities that result in, or are associated with, the emission of significant amounts of greenhouse gases (GHG). The CCCA does not aim to criminalize GHG emissions per se. Most emissions are legal. However, a significant share of GHG emissions results from, or is associated with, conduct that violates existing criminal law.

Moreover,

> if there is a concrete causal link between a specific source of GHG emissions and a harmful consequence – such as serious injury to body or physical health or the destruction of property – this may constitute a crime both under national and international law.

A question that will be answered by the legal precedents it sets is whether the ICC would prosecute a corporation that knowingly hid knowledge from the public of the dangers of climate change its practices were causing, which occurred in the case of ExxonMobil (Cousins 2016), as discussed in chapter 4.

Eco-equity: climate change and social inequality

There are identifiable harsh consequences for the lives of the poor of the practice of polluter elites in the existing world economic system treating the environment as a limitless resource and dumping ground for the by-products of production and use, including CO^2, other greenhouse gases, and black carbon—a pattern that creates conditions of eco-inequity. Eco-inequity refers to the formation, operationalization, and enforcement of environmental policies and practices that result in some people having to endure a disproportionate share of the harmful effects of pollution, environmental hazards, and global warming because they do not have sufficient power and economic resources to resist environmental injustice (Business Dictionary 2017). It is the argument of this book that a reversal of eco-inequity and a movement toward environmental justice is needed to achieve sustainable ways of life. As Stone and Athanasiou (2017) point out, eco-equity is the missing piece of the puzzle in most designs for achieving net-zero CO^2 emissions and limiting global warming below the dangerous threshold of a 2°C increase (e.g. Rockström et al. 2017).

There is a critical need for "eco-equity," based on the recognition that there can be no sustainable ecology without social equity and no social equity without sustainable human lifeways on the planet.

References

Akatsu, M. 2015. The problem of air pollution during the Industrial Revolution: A reconsideration of the enactment of the Smoke Nuisance Abatement Act of 1821. In S. Sugiyama (ed.), *Economic History of Energy and Environment*. Tokyo: Springer, pp. 85–112.

Alexander, D. 2017. Secretary of State appointee Rex Tillerson reaches $180 million severance deal with Exxon. *Forbes*. www.forbes.com/sites/danalexander/2017/01/04/secretary-of-state-appointee-rex-tillerson-reaches-180-million-severance-deal-with-exxon/#574c4cef4d3a.

Amin, S. 1976. *Unequal Development*. London: Monthly Review Press.

Avalon Project. 1997. Inaugural address of Harry S. Truman. Yale School of Law. www.yale.edu/lawweb/avalon/presiden/inaug/truman.htm.

Baer, H., M. Singer, and I. Susser. 2013. *Medical Anthropology and the World System: A Critical Perspective*. Santa Barbara, CA: Praeger.

Beder, S. 1997. *Global Spin: The Corporate Assault on Environmentalism*. Totnes, UK: Green Books.

Belvedere, M. 2017. CEOs face a 'false choice' on whether or not to stick with Trump, says Southern Company CEO. *CNBC*. www.cnbc.com/2017/08/16/ceos-face-a-false-choice-on-whether-or-not-to-stick-with-trump-says-southern-company-ceo.html.

Berman, Y., Y. Shapira, and E. Ben-Jacob. 2015. Modeling the origin and possible control of the wealth inequality surge. *PLoS ONE* 10(6): e0130181.

Bernal, V. 1997Colonial moral economy and the discipline of development: The Gezira scheme and "modern" Sudan. *Cultural Anthropology* 12(4): 447–479.

Blofield, M. 2010. Introduction: Inequality and politics in Latin America. In M. Blofield (ed.), *The Great Gap: Inequality and the Politics of Redistribution in Latin America*, pp. 1–20. University Park, PA: The Pennsylvania State University Press.

Boehm, C. 1993. Egalitarian behavior and reverse dominance hierarchy. *Current Anthropology* 34(3): 227–254.

Borah, G. 1994. A study of the Asiatic mode of production with the Tai-Ahom state as a test case. PhD dissertation. Temple University, Philadelphia, PA.

Braudel, F. 1974. *Capitalism and Material Life, 1400–1800.* New York: Harper Torchbooks.

Brown, E. 1974. The tyranny of a construct: Feudalism and historians of Medieval Europe. *American Historical Review* 79(4): 1063–1088.

Büntgen, U., W. Tegel, K. Nicolussi, M. McCormick, D. Frank, V. Trouet et al. 2011. 2500 years of European climate variability and human susceptibility. *Science* 331(6017): 578–582.

Büntgen, U., V. Myglan, F.Ljungqvist, M.McCormick, N.Di Cosmos, M.Sigl et al. 2016. Cooling and societal change during the Late Antique Little Ice Age from 536 to around 660 AD. *Nature Geoscience* 9: 231–236.

Dictionary. 2017. Environmental equity. www.businessdictionary.com/definition/environm ental-equity.html.

Center for Climate Crime Analysis. 2017. Climate crimes. www.climatecrimeanalysis.org/ crimes.html.

Chapman, S. 2013. The cost of power in the industrial revolution in Britain: The case of the textile industry. *Midland History* 1(2): 1–24.

Collier, K. 2017. ExxonMobil ordered to pay $20 million for air pollution at Houston plants. *Texas Tribune*, April 27. www.texastribune.org/2017/04/27/exxonmobil-order ed-pay-20-million-excess-air-pollution/.

Cornia, G., R. Jolly, and F. Stewart. 1987. *Adjustment with a Human Face: Protecting the Vulnerable and Promoting Growth.* New York: Oxford University Press.

Cousins, F. 2016. House Science Committee leader says climate scientists are trying to control people's lives. www.desmogblog.com/2017/04/07/house-science-committee-lamar-smith-says-climate-scientists-trying-control-people-lives.

Credit Suisse. 2016. *Global Wealth Databook.* Zurich: Credit Suisse Research Institute.

Crespo, A. and F. Ferreira. 2010. Inequality of opportunity in Latin America: Economic well-being, education, and health. In M. Blofield (ed.), *The Great Gap: Inequality and the Politics of Redistribution in Latin America.* University Park, PA: Pennsylvania State University Press, pp. 58–88.

Dormann, H. 2012. An interview with Thomas A. Fanning. *Leaders Magazine.* www.leadersma g.com/issues/2012.4_Oct/ROB/LEADERS-Thomas-Fanning-Southern-Company.html.

Dutt, R. 1908. *The Economic History of India under Early British Rule.* London: Kessinger Publishing.

Edwards, J. and T. Larsen. 2011. *Leadership We Can Live Without: The Real Corporate Social Responsibility Report for Southern Company.* Washington, DC: Green America.

Engels, F. 2015. *The Conditions of the Working-class in England.* Oxford: Oxford University Press,

Environmental Protection Agency. 2006. Alabama power company Clean Air Act settlement. www.epa.gov/enforcement/alabama-power-company-clean-air-act-settlement.

Erdal, D. and A. Whiten. 1994. On human egalitarianism: An evolutionary product of Machiavellian status escalation? *Current Anthropology* 35(2): 175–183.

Escobar, A. 2011. *Encountering Development: The Making and Unmaking of the Third World*. Princeton: Princeton University Press.

ExxonMobil. 2018. Baytown area operations. http://corporate.exxonmobil.com/en/compa ny/worldwide-operations/locations/united-states/baytown-area-operations.

Ferguson, J. 1994. The anti-politics machine: "development" and bureaucratic power in Lesotho. Minneapolis: University of Minnesota Press.

Filgueira, F. 2010. Fault lines in Latin American social development and welfare regime challenges. In M. Blofield (ed.), *The Great Gap: Inequality and the Politics of Redistribution in Latin America*. University Park, PA: Pennsylvania State University Press, pp. 21–57.

Forbes Magazine. 2016. The world's most powerful people. www.forbes.com/powerful-peop le/list/#tab:overall.

Fourie, C., F. Schppert, and I. Wallimann-Helmer. 2015. *Social Equality: On What it Means to be Equals*. Oxford: Oxford University Press.

Frank, A. 1991. The underdevelopment of development: From a personal preface to the author's intentions. www.druckversion.studien-von-zeitfragen.net/The%20Under development%20of%20Development.htm.

Freed, B. 2017. Rex Tillerson buys $5.6 million Kalorama home. *Washingtonian*. www.wa shingtonian.com/2017/02/22/rex-tillerson-buys-5-6-million-kalorama-home/.

Freeman, C. 2007. The "reputation" of neoliberalism. *American Ethnologist* 34(2): 252–267.

Fukuyama, F. 2008. *Falling Behind: Explaining the Development Gap between Latin America and the United States*. Oxford: Oxford University Press.

Gershman, J., and A. Irwin. 2002. Getting a grip on the global economy. In J. Kim, J. Millen, A. Irwin, and J. Gershman (eds). *Dying for Growth: Global Inequality and the Health of the Poor*, pp. 11–43. Monroe, MA: Common Courage Press.

Giroux, H. 2008. *Against the Terror of Neoliberalism: Politics beyond the Age of Greed*. Abingdon, UK: Routledge.

Goldín, L. and C. Dowdall. 2015. Inequality of rights: Rural industrial workers' access to the law in Guatemala. *Economic Anthropology* 2(2): 278–294.

Greenbaum, S. 2015. *Blaming the Poor: The Long Shadow of the Moynihan Report on Cruel Images of Poverty*. New Brunswick, NJ: Rutgers University Press.

Gupta, A. and J. Ferguson. 1992. Beyond 'culture': Space, identity and the politics of dif-ference. *Cultural Anthropology* 7(1): 6–23.

Handlin, O. 1980. Review: Arawaks: a people's history of the United States by Howard Zinn. *American Scholar* 49(4): 546, 548, 550.

Heinkel-Wolfe, P. 2016. Tillerson family is right at home in Denton County. *Denton Record-Chronicle*, December 13.

Helleiner, E. 2014. Forgotten foundations of Bretton Woods: International development and the making of the postwar order. Cornell, NY: Cornell University Press.

Heredia, C. and M. Purcell. 1994. *The Polarization of Mexican Society: A Grassroots View of World Bank Economic Adjustment Policies*. Mexico City: Equipo Pueblo.

Hernandez, E. 2017. America's biggest greenhouse-gas polluter, and the place that relies on it. Center for Public Integrity. www.publicintegrity.org/2017/06/05/20897/america s-biggest-greenhouse-gas-polluter-and-place-relies-it.

Hopkins, J. 2016. Meet America's super polluters. *USA Today*, September 29. www.usa today.com/story/news/2016/09/29/toxic-air-pollution-concentrated-small-number-sites/ 90846584/.

Jorgenson, A., J. Schor, and X. Huang. 2015. Income inequality and carbon emissions in the United States: A state-level analysis 1997–2012. *Ecological Economics* 134: 40–48.

Jorgenson, A., Schor, J., Knight, K. and X. Huang. 2016. Domestic inequality and carbon emissions in comparative perspective. *Sociological Forum* 31(51): 770–786.

Kaplan, H. and K. Hill. 1985. Food sharing among Ache foragers: Tests of explanatory hypotheses. *Current Anthropology* 26: 223–245.

Kim, J., A. Shakow, J. Bayona, J. Rhatigam, and E. de Celis. 2000. Sickness amidst recovery: public debt and private suffering in Peru. In J. Kim, J. Millen, A. Irwin, and J. Gershman (eds), *Dying for Growth: Global Inequality and the Health of the Poor*. Monroe, MA: Common Courage Press, pp. 127–153.

Leacock, E. 1992. Women's status in egalitarian society: Implications for social evolution. *Current Anthropology* 33(1): 225–259.

Lee, R. 1969. Eating Christmas in the Kalahari. *Natural History* (December): 60–64.

Lee, R. 1988. Reflections on primitive communism. In T. Ingold, D. Riches, and J. Woodburn (eds), *Hunters and Gatherers*. Oxford: Berg, pp. 252–268.

Leonhardt, D. 2017. The lawless presidency. *New York Times*, June 6. www.nytimes.com/2017/06/06/opinion/the-lawless-presidency.html?src=me&ref=general.

Lesorogol, C. 2015. Inequality in our midst. *Economic Anthropology* 2(2): 241–249.

Llewellyn, J., J. Southey, and S. Thompson. 2016. French colonialism in Vietnam. *Alpha History*. http://alphahistory.com/vietnamwar/french-colonialism-in-vietnam/.

Lynch, M., P. Stretesky, M. Long, and K. Barrett. 2017. Social justice, environmental destruction, and the Trump presidency: A criminological perspective. *Social Justice: A Journal of Crime, Conflict, and World Order* 44(1): 8–12.

Maloney, P. 2017. Mississippi Power fails to reach PSC settlement over Kemper costs again. *Utility Dive*. www.utilitydive.com/news/mississippi-power-fails-to-reach-psc-settlement-over-kemper-costs-again/504689/.

Márquez, G., A. Chong, A. Duryea, J. Mazza, and H. Ñopo. 2008. Outsiders? The challenging patterns of exclusion in Latin America and the Caribbean. Washington, DC: Inter-American Development Bank.

Marshall, L. 1961. Sharing, talking, and giving: relief of social tensions among !Kung Bushmen. *Africa* 31: 231–249.

Marx, K. 1990. *Capital*, vol. I. Translated by B. Fowkes. London: Penguin.

Mason, M. 2013. *Global Shift: Asia, Africa, and Latin America, 1945–2007*. Montreal: McGill-Queen's University Press.

McGill, K. 2016. *Global Inequality*. Toronto: University of Toronto Press.

Mecham, J. 2001. Causes and consequences of deforestation in Ecuador. Centro de Investigacion de los Bosques Tropicales. www.rainforestinfo.org.au/projects/jefferson.htm.

Mitchell, T. 1988. *Colonising Egypt*. Cambridge: Cambridge University Press.

Morandé, P. 1984. *Cultura y modernización en America Latina*. Santiago, Chile: Centro de Estudios Públicos, no. 16.

Naoroji, D. 1901. *Poverty and Un-British Rule in India*. London: Swan Sonnenschein.

Nassaney, M. 1992. Communal societies and the emergence of elites in the prehistoric American Southeast. *Archeological Papers of the American Anthropological Association* 3(1): 111–143.

Office of the Prosecutor. 2016. Policy paper on case selection criteria and prioritization. International Criminal Court. www.icc-cpi.int/itemsDocuments/20160915_OTP-Policy_Case-Selection_Eng.pdf.

Orenstein, K. 2010. Capitalizing on climate: The World Bank's role in climate change and international climate finance. Friends of the Earth, U.S. www.un-ngls.org/IMG/pdf/FOE_-_Capitalizing_on_Climate.pdf.

OxfamInternational. 2015a. Extreme carbon inequality. www.oxfam.org/sites/www.oxfam.org/files/file_attachments/mb-extreme-carbon-inequality-021215-en.pdf.

OxfamInternational. 2015b. World's richest 10% produce half of carbon emissions while poorest 3.5 billion account for just a tenth. www.oxfam.org/en/pressroom/pressreleases/2015-12-02/worlds-richest-10-produce-half-carbon-emissions-while-poorest-35.

OxfamInternational. 2018. Forbes billionaires list shows economies reward wealth, not work. www.oxfam.org/en/tags/forbes.

Pfeiffer, J. 2003. International NGOs and primary health care in Mozambique: The need for a new model of collaboration. *Social Science and Medicine* 56: 725–738.

Reuters. 2010. World Bank approves loan for coal-fired power plant in South Africa. *Washington Post*, April 4. www.washingtonpost.com/wp-dyn/content/article/2010/04/08/AR2010040805407.html.

Reynolds, S. 1994. *Fiefs and Vassals: The Medieval Evidence Reinterpreted*. Oxford: Oxford University Press.

Rich, B. 2013. *Foreclosing the Future: The World Bank and the Politics of Environmental Destruction*. Washington, DC: Island Press.

Richardson, P., R. Boyd, and R. Bettinger. 2001. Was agriculture impossible during the Pleistocene but mandatory during the Holocene? A climate change hypothesis. *American Antiquity* 66(3): 387–411.

Roberts, T. and B. Parks. 2007. *A Climate of Injustice: Global Inequality, North-South Politics, and Climate Policy*. Cambridge, MA: MIT Press.

Robinson, W. 2004. *A Theory of Global Capitalism: Production, Class, and State in a Transnational World*. Baltimore: Johns Hopkin Press.

Rockström, J., O. Gaffney, J. Rogelj, M. Meinshausen, and J. Nakiceno. 2017. A roadmap for rapid decarbonisation. *Science* 365(6331): 1269–1271. www.usatoday.com/story/news/2016/09/29/toxic-air-pollution-concentrated-small-number-sites/90846584/.

Sahlins, M. 1972. *Stone Age Economics*. Chicago: Aldine.

Salary.com. 2016. R. W. Tillerson. www1.salary.com/R-W-Tillerson-Salary-Bonus-Stock-Options-for-EXXON-MOBIL-CORP.html.

Salinas de Gortari, C. 1992. *Cuarto informe de gobierno*. Mexico City: National Statistics Institute.

Scott, J. 1985. *Weapons of the Weak: Everyday Forms of Peasant Resistance*. New Haven, CT: Yale University Press.

Shabecoff, P. 1987. World Bank offers environmental projects. *New York Times*, May 6. www.nytimes.com/1987/05/06/world/world-bank-offers-environmental-projects.html.

Shklar, J. 1990. *The Faces of Injustice*. New Haven, CT: Yale University Press.

Simpson, A. 2000. Paths toward a Mohawk nation: Narratives of citizenship and nationhood in Kahnawake. In D. Ivison, P. Patton, and W. Sanders (eds), *Political Theory and the Rights of Indigenous Peoples*. Cambridge: Cambridge University Press, pp. 113–136.

Singer, M. and P. Erickson. 2013. *Global Health: An Anthropological Perspective*. Long Grove, IL: Waveland Press.

Southern Company. 2017. Environmental responsibility. www.southerncompany.com/corporate-responsibility/environmental-responsibility.html.

Stone, K. and T. Athanasiou. 2017. Equity is the missing key for climate roadmaps. *Huffington Post*, April 17. www.huffingtonpost.com/entry/58f4e75ce4b0156697225134.

Strum, B. 2017. Rex Tillerson drops $5.5 million on new DC digs. *Fox News*. www.foxnews.com/real-estate/2017/03/02/rex-tillerson-drops-5-5-million-on-new-dc-digs.html.

Tainter, J. 2006. Archeology of overshoot and collapse. *Annual Review of Anthropology* 35: 59–74. *Science* 331: 578–582.

Trouillot, M.-R. 2003. *Global Transformations: Anthropology and the Modern World*. New York: Palgrave.

Turnbull, C. 1965. The Mbuti pygmies: An ethnographic survey. *American Museum of Natural History Anthropological Papers* 50(3): 139–282.

United Nations. 2002. Rome statute of the international criminal court. www.icc-cpi.int/nr/rdonlyres/ea9aeff7-5752-4f84-be94-0a655eb30e16/0/rome_statute_english.pdf.

Veblen, T. 1899. *The Theory of the Leisure Class*. New York: MacMillan.

Vidal, J. and Bowcott, O. 2016. ICC widens remit to include environmental destruction cases. *The Guardian*, September 15. www.theguardian.com/global/2016/sep/15/hague-court-widens-remit-to-include-environmental-destruction-cases.

Wallerstein, I. 1974. The rise and future demise of the world capitalist system: concepts for comparative analysis. *Comparative Studies in Society & History* 6(4): 384–387l5.

Wallerstein, I. 1976. *The Modern World-system: Capitalist Agriculture and the Origins of the European World-economy in the Sixteenth Century*. New York: Academic Press.

Washington Fine Properties. 2017. 1832 24th St NW, Washington, DC 20008. www.wfp.com/listing-showcase/sold-property-details.asp?mlsID=DC7570026.

Weaver, T., J. Greenberg, W. Alexander, and A. Browning-Aiken. 2012. *Neoliberalism and CommodityPproduction in Mexico*. Boulder, CO: University of Colorado Press.

Wolf, E. 1982. *Europe and the People without History*. Berkeley, CA: University of California Press.

World Summit for Social Development. 1995. Copenhagen declaration on social development. UN Documents. www.un-documents.net/cope-dec.htm.

Zegart, D. 2017. Southern Company says Kemper not viable as coal plant, blames the PSC. Climate Investigations Center. http://climateinvestigations.nationbuilder.com/southern_company_kemper_not_viable_as_coal_plant_and_it_s_the_psc_s_fault.

Zinn, H. 2009. *A People's History of the United States*. New York: HarperCollins.

Žižek, S. 2008. *Violence*. New York: Picador Books.

3

MAINTAINING INEQUALITY

The ideology of denial and the creation of climate change uncertainty

The state of the scientific knowledge about the extent and nature of climate change, as well as its causes and already mounting adverse consequences, would seem to make it untenable now to deny the reality of a warming planet, and yet denial continues to have a noticeable and influential presence in the social land-scape, particularly in the U.S. In fact, with the election of Donald Trump and Republican control of both the Senate and House of Representatives in 2016, it has gained vast ground and the full power of the American government behind it. With regard to the issue of social inequality, climate change denial and its goal of obfuscation of the facts known to science is of importance because it is very much a product of the elite effort to maintain the existence of the reigning system for the production and massively unequal distribution of wealth to the detriment of the world generally and the most vulnerable in particular. This is why what has been called the climate change denial machine—the interlocked network of organiza-tions and individuals committed to bashing climate science and its findings on cli-mate change—has been bought and paid for by very wealthy people who overwhelmingly benefit not only from enormous wealth inequality but also from the increasingly growing gap between the super-rich and everyone else. Main-taining such social inequality in a world of mass access to information requires considerable ideological work, and climate change denial is part of that profitable conceptual and political labor. One victim of this heavily financed crusade is the credibility of science in the eyes of a sector of the public, a loss that holds grave potential costs. In the assessment of famed astrophysicist Neil deGrasse Tyson,

> science is a fundamental part of the country that we are. But in this the 21st century, when it comes time to make decisions about science, it seems to me that people have lost the ability to judge what is true and what is not … . And when you have people who do not know much about science standing in

denial of it, and rising to power, that is a recipe for the complete dismantling of our informed democracy.

(Quoted in Chow 2017)

It has become evident from studying climate science denial the astonishing lengths that extremely wealthy corporations and individuals are willing to go to ensure a maximization of profits and income. Climate change denial is not a tangential issue in the calculation of the relationship between climate change and social inequality, it is a foundational component of the ideological and instrumental machinery that has allowed the continuation of the growing climate crisis that now most threatens the global poor but ultimately all people and life forms. Knowing in some detail how climate change denial emerged, its political allies and their motivations, its key players individually and organizationally, its ideological assertions, and the threat it presents provides an illuminating window on the ways that both climate change and inequality are driven by the ultra-wealthy as by-products of their unceasing effort to maintain and expand their vast fortunes. These are the issues, set against the backdrop of the election of Donald Trump as president, addressed in this chapter.

Science at risk

Writing in 1999, Adger, an environmental scientist, could assert: "At present there is agreement, in principle, by the world's governments that the human impacts on the global climate system are significant." Eighteen years later, however, despite the voluminous growth in climate change knowledge and the accumulation of overwhelming scientific evidence, Adger could no longer conclude that there is agreement in the world's governments about the threat of climate change. Throughout this period, while the leading scientific associations in the U.S., like the U.S. National Academy of Sciences and the American Association for the Advancement of Science, could comfortably use the word "consensus" when describing the views of climate scientists on the existence and human cause of climate change, some (primarily) non-climate scientists disputed this claim and their words found a receptive audience among conservative politicians. In other words, while there has developed an overwhelming scientific agreement on climate change, with disagreements emerging primarily about the details not the primary patterns of what is happening on the planet, there has not developed a social consensus on this issue. More importantly, with the election of Donald Trump as the 45th president of the United States, agreement among world governments on climate change has been shattered. Instead, in 2017, we have people like Earth scientist Peter Kalmus (2017) of the Jet Propulsion Laboratory at Caltech writing about the reality of climate change: "I'm afraid to publish this article. Why? Because I'm a climate scientist who speaks out about climate change, and in speaking out I may be risking my career." Kalmus underlined the contradictions of the current moment by citing the comments of Kim Cobb, a paleoclimatologist from Georgia Tech given at a rally against climate change denial that 2016 was a tough year for him personally. As a scuba diver on a coral reef in the tropical Pacific Ocean, he had watched

> 85 percent of that reef die between one of my trips and the next in six months … . We have for too long, as scientists, rested on the assumption that by providing indisputable facts and great data that we are providing enough … and obviously that strategy has failed miserably.
>
> *(Quoted in Kalmus 2017)*

Cobb is not alone. The frustration of having their carefully collected data indicating that the consequences of climate change is alarming be ignored or being personally vilified by people in positions of political power has been part of the past experience of many climate scientists. Camille Parmesan, a Nobel Prize winning professor in the School of Biological & Marine Sciences at Plymouth University, reports:

> I felt like here was this huge signal I was finding and no one was paying attention to it … . I was really thinking, 'Why am I doing this?' In the U.S., [climate change] isn't well-supported by the funding system, and when I give public talks in the U.S., I have to devote the first half of the talk to [affirming] that climate change is really happening.
>
> *(Quoted in Thomas 2014)*

While it was not a central issue during the campaign generally and rarely a news topic on the major U.S. television news programs during the entire year of 2016, both of which are remarkable given the climate urgency at hand, Donald Trump's election to the U.S. presidency was undeniably a triumph of climate change denial. Climate was not of much concern to Trump voters, and his election was a clear sign that, for many Americans, failing to acknowledge that climate change is occurring or denying the warnings of multiple scientists about the severe consequences of ignoring this fact do not disqualify a presidential candidate in the early years of the twenty-first century. In an affirmation of an old adage, if 2016 were given a motto a leading candidate would be "ignorance is bliss." That bliss, however, will melt away as we move deeper into the century and global warming and its punishing effects continue to mount, especially for the poor.

As early as 2014, Donald Trump made his evolving thoughts on the issue of climate change clear in a bluntly worded Tweet: "This very expensive GLOBAL WARMING bullshit has got to stop. Our planet is freezing, record low temps, and our GW scientists are stuck in ice" (cited in D'Angelo 2017). In November of 2012, he remarked: "The concept of global warming was created by and for the Chinese in order to make U.S. manufacturing non-competitive" (quoted in Schulman 2017). The following year he embraced the denial mantra that climate change science is a hoax: "Ice storm rolls from Texas to Tennessee - I'm in Los

Angeles and its freezing. Global warming is a total, and very expensive, hoax!," an assertion he repeated many times afterward (quoted in Schulman 2017).

Upon assuming the office of president, Trump translated these views into his selection of climate change deniers to fill open positions in his administration. He selected Myron Ebell, a climate contrarian who directs environmental and energy policy at the Competitive Enterprise Institute, a libertarian advocacy group in Washington, DC. supported by the coal and oil industries, to lead the transition at the Environmental Protection Agency (EPA). The Competitive Enterprise Institute does not openly disclose the sources of its $7 million annual budget, but the *Washington Post* (Eilperin 2013) was able reveal some of the contributors to the organization by examining a list of donors to its annual dinner in 2013. Donors included the energy companies Marathon Petroleum, Koch Industries, Devon Energy, American Coalition for Clean Coal Electricity, and American Fuel and Petrochemical Manufacturers. Reflecting the interests of this funding base, Ebell has said about the EPA:

> There are still some local problems, but the EPA's mission has been basically been accomplished. The fact is, you say that oil, coal, and gas are polluting, but no. All of those pollutants have been cleaned up… By and large, the air is clean, the water is pure … .
>
> *(Quoted in E&E TV 2017)*

Calling himself an enemy of environmentalism, as far back as 1998, Ebell was a member of the American Petroleum Institute's Global Climate Science Communications Team, which worked on a plan to create doubt in the public about climate science and the consensus about the reality of global warming. From the perspective of the deniers on the Team: "it's not known for sure whether (a) climate change actually is occurring, or (b) if it is, whether humans really have any influence on it" (Walker 1998). Ebell gained particular media attention as a climate denier who dispenses catchy sound bites on cable news shows and at conservative gatherings. Typical of his statements, he called Pope Francis's 2015 encyclical on climate change "scientifically ill informed, economically illiterate, intellectually incoherent and morally obtuse" (quoted in Fountain 2016). Although he has been a frequent critic of climate science, he studied philosophy and political theory in college and has never done climate change research. Nonetheless, contrary to available science, he argues:

> There hasn't been much warming for the last 20 years, or statistically no warming for the last 20 years, but it is going to happen because we keep pumping more carbon dioxide into the atmosphere … . In all of this discussion of the impacts of global warming, the benefits of higher carbon dioxide levels and of warming … are completely minimised by the alarmist community.
>
> *(Quoted Griffin 2017)*

A primary goal of Ebell and other climate change deniers is to force the EPA to rescind its finding that greenhouse gas emissions are a direct danger to human health. The endangerment finding, which was compelled by the Supreme Court in the landmark 2007 Massachusetts v. EPA case, is the scientific foundation for the EPA's regulation of greenhouse gas emissions. In December 2009, the EPA completed a review of the scientific research on the issue and determined that greenhouse gas emissions endanger the public health and welfare of current and future generations. Climate change deniers have not hidden the fact that their top priority during the presidency of Trump is to rescind the finding, which would automatically cripple the EPA's rationale for working on climate change issues. Doing this requires further advancing the effort to delegitimize any scientific research that is deemed ideologically unacceptable.

As a general pattern, Trump packed his initial cabinet with people who question the science of climate change and remain publically skeptical of the impact of human society on global warming or insist that mitigation should not hurt the environment and are not likely to be pro-active on the issue, including the secretary of state, secretary of the interior, secretary of energy, and secretary of agriculture. All of these appointees made statements that downplayed established understandings among climate scientists. The man he selected to head the EPA, Scott Pruitt, a former Oklahoma attorney general, for example, shares Ebell's perspective on climate change, asserting during a television interview:

> I think that measuring with precision human activity on the climate is something very challenging to do and there's tremendous disagreement about the degree of impact, so no, I would not agree that it's a primary contributor to the global warming that we see. We need to continue the debate and continue the review and the analysis.
>
> *(Quoted in Satlin 2017).*

Pruitt is known to have close ties to the oil and gas industries, electric utilities, and political groups funded by wealthy advocates of climate change denial. A large set of emails exchanged Pruitt and energy companies made public in February 2017 (Davenport and Lipton 2017a) revealed that the industry provided Pruitt with draft letters that he reproduced and sent his signature as attorney general for Oklahoma to federal regulators in an effort to block regulations on greenhouse gas emissions from oil and gas wells, contributions to ozone air pollution by fracturing companies, and other aspects of the environmentally damaging use of hydraulic fracking. Pruitt also sued the EPA more than a dozen times over its efforts to regulate the release of toxic and heat-driving industrial chemicals. After taking the reins at EPA, Pruitt's politics on the environment were quickly in evidence in a silencing of climate science. The EPA suddenly took down its climate change website, including pages titled Basic Info, Causes of Climate Change, Future of Climate Change, Science, Impacts, Extreme Weather, Adapting, Reducing Emissions, What EPA is Doing, and What You Can Do, that had provided the public with science-based information about climate change. This out of sight, out of mind approach has been shaping up in the Trump administration as the institutional expression of climate change denial.

Early in 2018, Pruitt (quoted in Bacon 2018) asserted a new perspective that recognized global warming:

> No one disputes the climate changes … . We obviously contribute to it … our activity contributes to it … . We know humans have most flourished during times of what? Warming trends … . I think there are assumptions made that because the climate is warming, that it necessarily is a bad thing.

Asserting that global warming may be a good thing for humanity, Pruitt ignored all of the known harm it has already caused, especially to those subject to oppressive social inequality.

Even more bluntly than Pruitt, Mick Mulvaney, the Office of Management and Budget director appointed by Trump, has stated "As to climate change, I think the president was fairly straightforward saying we're not spending money on that any-more. We consider that to be a waste of your money" (quoted in Buxton 2017).

Anthony Leiserowitz, the director of Yale University's Program on Climate Change Communication, observed after the election, "If the Trump administration continues to push the false claim that global warming is a hoax, not happening, not human caused, or not a serious problem, I'd expect many conservative Republican voters to follow their lead" (quoted in Foran 2016). The pattern here is clear: the deniers of climate change have gained the upper hand in American policy forma-tion and federal action and climate scientists—indeed, scientists focused on a mul-titude of environmental, social, and other issues—are worried.

Underlining his hostility toward the scientific evidence affirming the pressing reality of climate change, on June 1, 2017 Trump announced that the U.S was withdrawing from the 2015 Paris Climate Agreement, significantly weakening global efforts to combat global warming. The accord, signed by 194 other nations, which only called for voluntary cuts in greenhouse gas emissions, was sharply opposed by EPA director Scott Pruitt and Trump's initial chief strategist Stephen Bannon. At his White House Rose Garden announcement of the U.S. withdrawal, Pruitt was called up to the podium to share victory remarks. Pruitt had spent months rallying conservative support in opposition to the Paris accord. In ending the U.S. involvement in the international agreement, the U.S. joined Syria (which was heavily focused on trying to put down a popular uprising during the original signing) and Nicaragua (which did not sign because it wanted stronger, mandatory controls on emissions). In his announcement speech (transcript in Sweet 2017), Trump justified his decision by making a number of claims that were immediately cited as false by fact checkers, including Trump's adoption of several fully debunked conservative talking points as well as referencing studies issued by cli-mate change denier think tanks with ties to the fossil fuel industry. Exemplary was Trump's assertion that by staying in, the U.S. would be subject to "massive legal liability." Being a voluntary program, however, there was no liability enforcement built into the Paris accord, the very reason Nicaragua stayed out. Trump also inaccurately said that China and India were the biggest emitters of greenhouse gases, but in fact the U.S. follows China as the second biggest leader in emissions globally. Moreover, measured on a per capita basis, the U.S. in 2015 produced more than double the CO^2 emissions of China and eight times more than India (Oliver et al. 2016).

Trump additionally asserted that "the onerous energy restrictions it has placed on the United States could cost America as much as 2.7 million lost jobs by 2025 according to the National Economic Research Associates" (NERA) (Sweet 2017). However, Trump failed to mention what this organization is. A conservative economic consulting firm with ties to the coal industry, NERA was founded by Irwin Stelzer, a senior fellow at the climate change denying Hudson Institute (Horn 2012). NERA has a long history of claiming sky-high job loss numbers for regulations designed to curb the environmental harm of energy producers. The NERA study was commissioned by the American Council for Capital Formation with support from the U.S. Chamber of Commerce Institute for 21st Century Energy, both long-term opponents of regulations designed to combat climate change. The American Council for Capital Formation has received significant funding from energy industry sources including ExxonMobil, the American Petroleum Institute, and Charles G. Koch Charitable (DeSmog 2017).

Trump falsely claimed that the accord bars the U.S. from building new coal plants but allows China and India to do so. But, as the agreement is nonbinding, the U.S. was free to set its own targets and methods of emission reduction. There is no language in the accord giving China and India the right to build coal plants or stopping the U.S. from doing so. The demand for coal and hence the availability for jobs in the coal industry in the U.S. has dropped, not because of government regulations or due to the Paris accord but because the price of natural gas has fallen dramatically, as discussed in chapter 4 (Kessler and Lee 2017).

Trump also contended that the Paris accord would not reduce temperatures enough to make any impact and cited research from the Massachusetts Institute of Technology to argue that full global compliance would only produce a two-tenths of 0.36°F reduction in global temperature by 2100, which Trump called a very tiny amount. This assertion is misleading according to the MIT researchers who authored the study Trump mentioned and who support the Paris accord. Without the pact, which had as its intention to continue to lower allowable emission levels over time (and not impose a one-time reduction), global temperatures could rise by a catastrophic 7.2°F by 2100 according to the MIT scientists (Wang 2017). The whole point of the Paris deal was to begin to reverse the direction of emissions and commence a downward trend that would be achieved by a series of enhanced reductions in acceptable emissions levels over time.

In response to Trump's decision, John Reilly, lead author of the MIT study commented: "The logic that, 'This isn't making much progress on a serious problem, therefore we're going to do nothing,' just doesn't make sense to me" (quoted in Kessler and Lee 2017). Noted climate scientist Michael Mann added, Trump's statics were

> off by a factor of 10, because it will shave at least a degree Celsius. And with proper ratcheting up, it will literally cut the projected warming in half, getting us onto a path where we could see stabilizing the warming below 2 degrees Celsius, [above which] most scientists who study the impacts of climate change will tell you constitutes sort of the level of dangerous interference with the climate.
>
> *(Quoted in Democracy Now 2017)*

Alarm about the U.S. withdrawing also was voiced by UN secretary general, António Guterres: "climate change is a multiplier of many other threats" (quoted in Holpuch 2017), including poverty, displacement and conflict, and those hit "first and worst" by climate change.

Trump's action on the Paris climate agreement, which reflected a "campaign carefully crafted by fossil fuel industry players" (Davenport and Lipton 2017b), sent the political message that the extensive scientific evidence on the existence and threat of climate change, including its enhanced risk to the global poor, will not influence U.S. policy; only wealth-enhancing factors will be considered by the administration, in particular the wealth of America's richest corporations and individuals and its polluting elites. In addition, as a result of the 2016 national election, the political environment in the U.S. grew increasingly threatening to climate scientists, as witnessed by the list of questions issued by the Trump transition team as it was taking over the Department of Energy. The transition team asked the department to identify the names of those employees and contractors who have worked on international climate agreements or on domestic efforts to cut carbon production in the country. The team also wanted to know which programs that it operated were part of meeting President Obama's Climate Change Action plan. The response to these requests, which many felt might be the beginning of a witch hunt targeting climate scientists, was that thousands of scientists quickly signed petitions calling on Trump and his transition team to respect scientific integrity and end efforts to single out individual researchers whose work might not match the new administration's policy goals (Mufson and Ellperin 2016).

As the Trump presidency moved on from its first days, the overall trend became avoiding the discussion of climate change altogether. Typical was a May 2017 press release announcing a new study by the U.S. Geological Survey that highlighted the connection between sea-level rise and global warming. Three of the authors of the study reported that the Department of the Interior deleted a line that read: "Global climate change drives sea-level rise, increasing the frequency of coastal flooding" (quoted in Grandoni 2017). Neil Frazer, a geophysics professor at University of Hawaii at Manoa and one of the study's co-authors, responded to the deletion by saying: "The suppression of this information is a scandal" (quoted in Grandoni 2017). Similarly, in the June 2017 White House announcement of National

Oceans Month, there was no mention of the changing condition of the oceans because of climate change.

Mounting concern among climate scientists and their supporters, including K-12 science teachers, triggered a massive and historically unprecedented March for Science in Washington, DC, in April 2017. Other marches and teach-ins on science involving tens of thousands of people took place around the country as well as in Europe and Asia in what organizers felt was an effort to speak truth to power. Naomi Oreskes, professor of the history of science at Harvard University, who has written about climate change denial, observed before the march, "I can't think of a time where scientists felt the enterprise of science was being threatened in the way scientists feel now" (quoted in Fluer 2017). A speaker at the DC rally, engineer Bill Nye, known as 'the science guy" through his frequent television appearances, and an honorary co-chair of the march, told the audience: "Today we have a great many lawmakers—not just here but around the world—deliberately ignoring and actively suppressing science … . Their inclination is misguided and in no one's best interest" (quoted in Smith-Spark and Hanna 2017).

The battle Hayes referenced continued as the pro-science marchers returned to their homes, jobs, and the routines of their lives. In the Trump administration, there was a steady drum beat of hostility toward inconvenient science. As the Union of Concerned Scientists noted,

> The Trump administration is attempting to delegitimize science, it is giving industries more ability to influence how and what science is used in policy-making, and it is creating a hostile environment for federal agency scientists who serve the public. This is a new era in which political interference in science is more likely and more frequent and will present serious risks to the health and safety of the American people.
>
> *(Carter et al. 2017: 1)*

The pattern of attempting to delegitimizing science could be seen in Trump's appointment of officials who have strong ties to polluting industries and a consistent track record of misrepresenting scientific information, delaying or undercutting science-based rules intended to safeguard workers from toxic work environments, hindering government efforts to help communities prepare for the adverse effects of climate change, weakening science-informed pollution standards, reducing public access to scientific data collected by government scientists, dismissing independent science advisors, leaving high-level science positions in the government unfilled, restricting communication among government-employed scientists, and generally creating a hostile environment for scientists working for federal government.

The attack on climate science and science generally reflects a dimension of conservative thinking written about disparagingly more than 50 years ago by noted conservative Austrian economist and philosopher Friedrich Hayek (2011: 526):

> Personally, I find that the most objectionable feature of the conservative atti-
> tude is its propensity to reject well-substantiated new knowledge because it
> dislikes some of the consequences which seem to follow from it—or, to put it
> bluntly, its obscurantism.

Championed by mainstream conservative politicians like Margaret Thatcher and
Ronald Reagan for his views on government's inability to address economic
issues, Hayek has long troubled thinkers on the right who have struggled to
explain away his charge of conservative obscurantism (e.g. Bloom 2013). This
effort notwithstanding, with climate change denialism, conservative obscurantism has once more raised its objectionable propensity to hide and hide from
established facts.

Trust in science

Research suggests that polarization over the issue of climate change is the product of a
coordinated and well-funded disinformation campaign in which conservative media
outlets have played a fundamental role in building a level of popular distrust of the
science on climate change (McCright and Dunlap 2011, Hamilton 2011). Among
conservatives in the U.S., there has been a steady decline in confidence in scientists
over the last several decades (Gauchat 2012), with a particularly steep decay in trust in
scientists as a credible source of information on climate change (Leiserowitz et al.
2010). A similar drop in trust of science has not occurred among Democrats or liberals
generally (Brewer and Ley 2012).

   The role of conservative media in the creation of a rejection of the reality of
climate change has been described in a number of studies. Examinations of the
content of climate-related news stories that air on Fox News, for example, find a
consistent pattern of questioning the scientific consensus on planet warming and
the adoption of a more dismissive tone on the topic of climate change than major
news program on other networks (Feldman et al. 2012). This approach has been
supported directly by the Fox News' management. For example, in December
2009, managing editor Bill Sammon sent an email to Fox reporters instructing
them to always follow news reports on climate change by mentioning that theories about planetary warming are based on data that have consistently been
called into question (Dimiero 2010). Studies of environmental news communication indicate that how stories are framed and whether sources are credible
and legitimate is of fundamental importance in reviewer response. Framing shapes
the way the world is presented, but frames tend to be embedded and accepted as
self-evident and factual rather than something to be scrutinized. As Anderson
(2015: 179) comments,

> Framing involves selecting certain truth claims over others, and, in the process,
> denying or silencing rival versions of reality. The wealthiest and most powerful in
> society are in a position to be prominent framers of environmental reality and are

positioned through their wealth and ownership to exert pressure on the reporting of environmental affairs.

(Anderson 2015: 191)

This strategy appears to work in moderating public awareness of and concerns about the fact that industrial pollution is occurring on a vast and ominous scale around the planet.

With regard to global warming, research on Fox News' frequent viewers shows that they are more likely to say that Earth's temperature has not been rising, that any temperature increase is not due to human activities, and that addressing climate change would have deleterious effects on the economy (Krosnick and MacInnis 2010). The research concluded that a likely interpretation of their findings is that they reflect a combination of two factors: 1) selective exposure of climate change contrarians to get their news from Fox because it confirms beliefs they already hold; and 2) persuasion of some viewers that climate science is not trustworthy or is unsettled on the occurrence of global warming. Fox also tends to feature climate change deniers as climate experts in their programming (Malka et al. 2009).

The intensifying clash over climate change, like the human dimensions of almost all environmental issues, is of keen interest to anthropology because ultimately it is a contestation over culture, worldviews, ideology, and, most importantly, the structure and equitable nature of society. Debates about climate change are as much about the distribution of wealth, power, and authority in society as they are about whether or not scientists have accurately depicted the extent and causes of climate change. The contemporary rigid partisan divide on climate change in the U.S. was not the case in the 1990s. It is a recent phenomenon, following in the wake of the 1997 Kyoto Treaty that threatened the material interests of powerful economic and political sectors, particularly those linked to the fossil fuel industry. The perspective found in this small but powerful and highly influential segment of society and circulated by it through the media and political structures is that Earth's temperature has not been rising dramatically, that any temperature increase is not due to human activities, and that addressing climate change would have deleterious effects on the economy. A close look at arguments expressing so-called climate "scepticism" indicates that one of its key tactics is cherry-picking small pieces of evidence while rejecting any data that don't fit the desired picture. Ultimately, rather than skepticism, it ignores inconvenient facts.

All of the arguments made by global warming deniers, including those made by politicians, media commentators, and conservative policy groups—many of which have ties to the corporate energy industry—have been thoroughly debunked by multiple climate scientists, and yet they persist because they are useful as tools of obfuscation for power and economic elites (Oreskes and Conway 2010). The origins, functioning, and goals of climate change obfuscation as a mechanism for sustaining the unjust status quo are examined in this chapter.

Culture and what we believe

As an Earthling, when you look up in the sky at night and see a large, round, shiny disk, most of us identify it as the moon, and we have certain information about the moon; it orbits Earth, it is much smaller than our planet, it is not inhabited, it affects ocean waves across our world, its view is eclipsed when it passes behind Earth and direct sunlight cannot illuminate the moon because of our planet's shadow. Yet only a handful of Earthlings have been to the moon or perhaps even studied much existing science about the moon and its physical characteristics. The moon, as we know it, is part of our cultural knowledge about our world that we learn growing up and that is reinforced throughout our lives in society. In their day-to-day experiences, people use cultural filters in their experience of the world, paying particular attention to some things ignoring others. Thus we group some natural objects together and call them palm trees or clouds and ignore the many ways each member of a cultural category like palm trees is different from every other member (e.g. height, angle, color, circumference, number of fronds).

In complex societies, which are divided into various subgroups (by ethnicity, region, social class, employment, etc.), it is also possible to talk about subcultural filters. These are strongly influenced by group values, and we generally endorse the position that most directly reinforces the connection we have with others in our referent group (the group we identify with, an affiliation that helps define our sense of self). This tendency is driven by an innate desire to maintain a consistency in beliefs by giving greater weight to evidence and arguments that support pre-existing beliefs, and by expending disproportionate energy trying to refute views or arguments that are contrary to those beliefs. Instead of investigating a complex issue, we often simply learn what our referent group believes and seek to integrate those beliefs with our own views.

The result of this cultural processing and group cohesion dynamics, in the view of Andrew Hoffman (2015), professor of sustainable enterprise at the University of Michigan, leads to two overriding conclusions about the climate change debate. First, climate change is not really a "pollution" issue per se. The reduction of greenhouse gases is not the same as the reduction of pollutants like sulphur oxides, nitrogen oxides, carbon monoxide, or particulate matter. All of these forms of pollution are human-made, harmful to us, and the unintended waste products of industrial production. But the chief greenhouse gas, carbon dioxide, is both man-made and natural. It is not inherently harmful; it is a natural part of the natural systems; and we do not desire to completely eliminate its production. It is not a toxic waste or a strictly technical problem to be solved. Rather, it is an endemic part of our society and who we are.

In a way, it is a highly desirable output, as its rise correlates with rising standards of living: greenhouse gas emissions rise with an increase in a nation's wealth, something all people want (although, as emphasized in this book, wealth is not equitably distributed nor does its unending production lacking serious environmental and human costs). To reduce carbon dioxide requires an alteration in nearly every facet of the economy, and therefore nearly every facet of our culture. To recognize greenhouse gases as a problem requires us to change a great deal about how we view the world and ourselves within it. Most Americans want clean air to breathe and they want their children to be raised in toxic-free environments. This does not mean, however, that they cannot be convinced that polluting industries are over-regulated by the government by ideological appeals to preserving the "American way of life" through permanently expanding economic production and consumption (Stimson 2009). Nor does it mean that they cannot come—through well-funded influence campaigns—to believe that environment-preservation laws like the Clean Air Act of 1963, the Clean Water Act of 1972, or the Endangered Species Act of 1973 are not in their best interest. Similarly, Americans enjoy numerous benefits of government programs, from bridge inspections to national parks, and from Medicaid to cancer research. Again, this does not mean they cannot be sold on the idea that a significantly smaller federal government, which will result in the loss of many programs from which they directly benefit, is in their best interest. That all of these changes, would be, in fact, in the narrow self-interest of giant polluting corporations and the mega-rich people who benefit from the enormous profits they reap, is a missing piece in the social inequality puzzle of climate change denial.

Second, climate change is an existential challenge to our contemporary cultural worldviews in three ways. For one thing, we have to think of a formerly benign, even beneficial, material in a new way—as a relative, not absolute, hazard. Not only do we have to change our view of the ecosystem, we also have to change our view of our place within it. Have we as a species grown to such numbers, and has our technology grown to such power, that we can alter a planetary scale? Some people have difficulty answering this in the affirmative but science suggests we are now the primary drivers of planetary conditions.

Finally, there is an issue of ethics. While every individual has an incentive to emit greenhouse gases to improve his/her standard of living, the costs of this activity are not equitably distributed. Rather, the distribution of costs is asymmetrical, with vulnerable populations in poor countries bearing the larger burden. Does mowing the lawn in St Louis or driving a fuel-inefficient car in Los Angeles, California, have ethical implications for the people living in low-lying areas of Bangladesh? If you accept that anthropogenic climate change is primary driven by human emission of greenhouse gases, then the answer to this question is yes, and this raises fundamental issues about living together on Earth and equity among human populations. Indeed, it raises fundamental questions about global ethics and governance on a scale that our species have never encountered before, affecting virtually every economic activity on the globe and requiring the most complicated and intrusive global agreements ever negotiated.

As climate change policy researcher Mike Hulme (2009) discussed in his book *Why We Disagree About Climate Change*, the issue of climate change provokes a violent debate among cultural communities on one side who perceive their values to be threatened by change and cultural communities on the other side who perceive their values to be threatened by the status quo. The nature of this kind of sentiment was reflected in one of the key motivators that won Don Trump many votes in the 2016 election: large numbers of voters felt their values and their well-being were not issues of national political priority and they turned to Donald Trump to champion their cause while embracing or ignoring many components of his message.

Climate change fell into the cultural debate for two reasons: 1) it is a problem of massive proportions that fits the urban social planning concept of "wickedness," meaning problems of such enormous complexity that they provoke "contradictory certitude" and consequently defy graceful, consensual solutions and hence are resistant to resolution; 2) it is the focus of an organized and vocal denial movement composed of moneyed interests, conservative think tanks, and conservative mass media. Wicked problems, which are dependent on the information needed to understand them, require a great number of people to change their minds and their behaviors (Horst and Webber 1973). Many of the large problems (e.g. poverty, pollution, inequality) engaged by applied anthropology, in fact, fit this definition of wickedness. They are problems that are not easily solved, they are entwined with many other issues, and, while ignoring them is a grave decision, addressing them is costly. In the short run, ignoring climate change has been the way many people have responded. Even if they think climate change is happening they tend to view it as a problem of the future or of distant lands far from where they live.

Ultimately, the climate change denial messages to which people are exposed through the media have, according to history professor Naomi Oreskes, two primary drivers: 1) economic self-interest—for example, the fossil fuel industry has an obvious self-interest in the continued and even expanded use of fossil fuels that motivates opposition to anything that would undercut its ability to reap massive profits; and 2) ideological conviction—some people are willing to overlook the evidence on climate change because they claim that if we allow the government to intervene in the marketplace to stop climate change, it will lead to further expansion of government power that they believe will threaten our rights and freedoms. This latter view, however, does not necessarily extend to concern about the role of corporations in limiting people's rights and freedoms through environmental injustice and disease-causing environmental pollution or government infringement on the rights and freedoms of people who might vote for more liberal candidates (e.g. voter suppression strategies). Additionally, the message of climate scientists that it is human action itself that has created the growing climate crises is seen as an affront to the embedded cultural celebration of human ingenuity and its elevation as our most cherished capacity.

In a blog entry entitled "As a Conservative, Evangelical Republican, Why Climate Change Can't be True (Even Though It Is)," Scott Rodin (2014), a theologian and organizational development consultant, identifies the cultural knowledge he learned about environmentalism and its adherents growing up in a religious Republican household: people who care about and are focused on saving the environment: 1) are socially undesirable individuals who have no jobs and hate people who do have jobs; 2) favor big government, crushing regulations, and higher taxes and only want to ruin the economy; 3) are scare-mongering alarmists who always think the world is coming to an end; 4) want people to feel guilty about their standard of living; and 5) are atheists who worship nature, hate Christians, and believe humans are intruders on Earth. Although he ultimately came to realize that all of these views were simplistic, and that deep concern about the environment including global warming did not contradict his religious beliefs, his earlier dismissive views of environmentalists are deeply embedded in the attitudes of climate change deniers.

Taking climate change denial to school

One place that climate change deniers hope to have influence on popular attitudes about the environment is in the classroom, a site where future scientists begin to form foundational understandings of the world and all students acquire their view of the nature of science. To reach and try and influence science teachers about climate change, the Heart Institute developed a booklet authored by three climate change deniers, Craig Idso, Robert M. Carter, and S. Fred Singer, entitled "Why Scientists Disagree About Global Warming" and sent it and a companion DVD out to 300,000 K-12 and college science teachers around the U.S., hoping to put the booklet in the hands of every science teacher in the country. While these authors are well known in the intertwined climate denial world, Fred Singer, a physicist, has gained the most notoriety as a fixture on the denial roster. He freely admits he has received funding from an array of oil companies including ExxonMobile, Shell Oil Company, ARCO, Union Oil Company of California (Unocal), and Sunoco (Gelbspan 2004). He claims, however, that his view of climate change science is not influenced by this funding.

In a glaring statement of bravado and wilful ignorance, the president of Heartland asserted that most scientists

> don't believe computer models can predict future weather patterns or tell us whether global warming is a threat. Real peer-reviewed science shows the human impact on climate is probably too small to measure and not worth trying to prevent or undo … . The Heartland Institute has exposed the 'consensus' fallacy by publishing Climate Change Reconsidered, a series of volumes summarizing the vast scientific scholarship that refutes global warming alarmism. Our most recent book, Why Scientists Disagree About Global Warming, zeroes in on the false 'consensus' claim and utterly demolishes it.
>
> (Bast 2017a)

The demolition Bast imagines did not occur among the vast majority of climate scientists, who tend to find Heartland documents to be political ideology not science, but the piece was no doubt well received among the climate-denying faithful because it confirmed yet again what they "knew" to be true.

Heartland does not just issue documents, it gained notoriety and considerable criticism in 2012 when it sponsored a billboard that read, "I still believe in Global Warming. Do you?" next to a picture of Ted Kaczynski, the infamous Unabomber who killed three people and injured 23 others in a bombing campaign. The organization is also known for its rigorous and completely failed attempt to deny that tobacco use has any harmful health effects. As a pattern, the Heartland Institute opposes the regulation of industry while attacking scientists whose research indicates the industrial pollution and industrial products can be a cause of human illness and death. Based on their publications, the mission of Heartland is to prevent environmental and health safeguards that might limit corporate profit, especially, currently, the profits of the fossil-fuel industry, which is a primary funder of Heartland.

Accompanying the mailed Heartland booklet for educators was a cover letter written by Lennie Jarratt, project manager of Heartland's Center for Transforming Education. Jarratt asked teachers to "consider the possibility" that the science on climate change is not settled and then asks, "If that's the case, then students would be better served by letting them know a vibrant debate is taking place among scientists " (quoted in Worth 2017). The letter also invites teachers to review an online guide for using Heartland materials in their classrooms.

The arguments of the booklet are: 1) there is no proof that almost all climate scientists agree that climate change is occurring; 2) the Intergovernmental Panel on Climate Change (IPCC) is not a credible source of climate knowledge and may be corrupt; and 3) climate scientists, like all people, can be biased, and they are driven to accept climate change by careerism, as a way to get grants, and by their political views. The first of these is patently false, the second is little more than an ideologically driven attempt to malign a reputable and highly cautious organization whose job is merely to track and summarize current science reporting on climate change, and the last is aspersive and hypocritical and fails to consider the biases of the Heartland's book authors, people who get paid to question climate science. In the assessment of Ann Reid, executive director of the National Center for Science Education (NCSE), the booklet is "not science, but it's dressed up to look like science. It's clearly intended to confuse teachers" (quoted in Worth 2017). In other words, reflecting a common pattern in denier materials, it is an intentional mirage.

Brandie Freeman (2017), an experienced science teacher in Georgia, who served on the Board of Georgia Science Teachers Association, received and carefully read the Heartland booklet, and then posted on her blog some of the most glaring shortcomings and contradictions of the booklet: 1) it is issued by an organization that has publically set as its goal winning "the global warm war" during Trump's administration, as if science was merely propaganda that could be defeated; 2) the references in the booklet are frequently to other Heartland publications underlying the echo chamber nature of much climate change denial literature; 3) the notion that there is no evidence supporting the high level of agreement among climate scientists about global warming directly contradicts assessments of published peer-reviewed professional journal articles on the topic, such as the significant (but noticeably overlooked by Heartland) finding that during 2013/14, only four of 69,406 (0.0058%) of such articles published by climate scientists questioned the veracity of the ongoing process of anthropogenic global warming (Powell 2016), as well as the findings of multiple other surveys and literature reviews that drew the same conclusion about broad climate science consensus (e.g. Bray and von Storch 2016; Verheggen et al. 2014); 4) the booklet praises the Global Warming Petition Project that urged rejection of the Kyoto Protocol on carbon emission control and allegedly was signed by over 31,000 U.S. scientists, although only 12 percent of signatories were found to hold any kind of earth, environmental, or atmospheric science degree at any college level, with the largest group of signatories only having BA degrees, an unlikely final degree for a working scientist (Kasprak 2016); 5). In its attack on bias among scientists, the booklet fails to consider the nature of science publication, which is based on peer review, a process that results in articles submitted to journal undergoing careful blind evaluation by people who work in the same or related fields and are qualified to assess the arguments, methods, and findings of papers under review, a process that never happens with denial political tracts like the Heritage booklet; 6) the booklet relies on outdated information and ignores more recent publications if their findings run counter to the Heartland position on climate change.

In response to criticism that its booklet is propaganda not science, Heartland's president (Bast 2017b) marshalled a defense asserting that the document was not propaganda because: 1) it was written by three "distinguished climate scientists"; 2) it is part of a Heartland book series that is "so highly regarded by the scientific community it has been cited more than 100 times in peer-reviewed articles"; and 3) the book series was translated into Chinese and published by the Chinese Academy of Science (CAS).

None of Bast's responses holds water. First, not one of the authors has actually produced widely respected climate science research and all of them have connections to energy industry's climate change denial campaigns. What they have done, instead, is write in house books about climate for climate change denial organizations. Dunlap and Jacques (2013), who have analysed 108 books published through 2010 that deny the reality and importance of global warming, found that the authors of 72 percent of the books had direct linkages to conservative think tanks, and most of those for which a linkage could not be established were self-published books. Publishing a book functions socially as a mechanism for claiming expertise. Books bestow a mantle of validity and authority. Rather than appearing between the covers of scholarly journals that are rarely read by the general public, as is the case with most scientific literature affirming climate change, books have the potential to reach a general readership and even policy makers. As a result, authors of some climate denier books have gained questionable status as climate experts— including being called to testify at government hearings or being interviewed as authoritative individuals by journalists—irrespective of their unrelated academic backgrounds or lack of scientific credentials. Second, Bast does not provide any of the claimed citations in the scientific literature of Heritage book. Indeed, he offers no evidence that the citations are not merely part of refutations of the climate denial literature, as are the citations of Heartland publications in this book. Finally, while the Chinese Academy of Science did publish an abridged version of two Heartland books in a single volume, the intention was to share with Chinese scientists the range of views that exist on the topic, not to endorse the Heartland position. Consequently, given the continued Heartland claims of endorsement, the CAS issued a statement that read:

> the Heartland Institute published the news titled 'Chinese Academy of Sciences publishes Heartland Institute research skeptical of Global Warming' in a strongly misleading way on its website, implying that the Chinese Academy of Sciences … supports their views, [is] contrary to what is clearly stated in the Translators' Note in the Chinese translation. The claim of the Heartland Institute about CAS' endorsement of its report is completely false … .
>
> *(Cook 2017)*

Ignoring the Chinese refutation, based on his three points, the Heartland's president then asks rhetorically: "Does that sound like 'propaganda' to you?" In fact, the appeals to authority and use of unsubstantiated or blatantly false assertions, and other Heartland and denier tactics like demonizing opponents, endless repetitions of the same arguments such as the supposed lack of consensus among climate scientists, big lie assertions of a global hoax, cherry-picking appealing climate evidence and ignoring evidence that contradicts denier beliefs, flag-waving appeals about the risk of climate mitigation to the American way of life, use of half-truths from the scientific record, and the employment of glittering generalities range of issues, sound very much like propaganda. Intended to reduce public understanding of climate change, climate change denialists routinely engage in "nitpicking existing science and promoting conspiracy theories about fraud that routinely get pants on fire level ratings [from fact checkers]. It's a clever tactic, but totally bogus … . [T]he tactics are indefensible. It's pseudoskepticism, and pseudoscience, and the key from distinguishing it from actual science is to point out that no actual science is being" by almost all climate change deniers (Hoofnagle 2015).

Another tactic adopted by Heartland and its denier collaborators is the claim of neutrality. In this curious worldview, climate scientists have been unduly influenced by government agencies because they receive research grants from the government, and because the International Panel on Climate Change which reviews and synthesizes the findings of climate scientists is a United Nations body representative of member nation governments, the scientific evidence indicating the planet is warming is tainted by government influence. The implication is that governments and their agencies are prejudiced in favor of a global warming scenario. This is a curious assertion—given that governments, including the government of the U.S., have hardly been rushing to take dramatic action on global warming—but to push it Heartland has banded together with the Center for the Study of Carbon Dioxide and Global Change and the Science and Environment

Policy Project to form the Nongovernmental International Panel on Climate Change (NIPCC). The goal of NIPCC is to counter the fantasized deep-seated government bias through a more even-handed and impartial approach to climate information. Thus, its founders describe NIPCC as

> an international panel of nongovernment scientists and scholars who have come together to present a comprehensive, authoritative, and realistic assessment of the science and economics of global warming. Because it is not a government agency, and because its members are not predisposed to believe climate change is caused by human greenhouse gas emissions, NIPCC is able to offer an independent 'second opinion' of the evidence reviewed—or not reviewed—by the Intergovernmental Panel on Climate Change (IPCC) on the issue of global warming.
>
> *(Nongovernmental International Panel on Climate Change 2016).*

The NIPCC's assertion of neutrality unravels quickly however upon inspection.

While the ties of Heartland to the energy industry-driven denier movement have been discussed, their two partner agencies are no less mired in industry funding. The Center for the Study of Carbon Dioxide and Global Change is a family operation involving Sherwood Idso and his two sons, Craig and Keith, that denies the need to reveal its sources of funding. To try and justify this stance they maintain: "we believe that ideas about the way the world of nature operates should stand or fall on their own merits, irrespective of the source of support for the person or organization that produces them" (Idso 2017). When it was revealed that the Center received ExxonMobil funding, Sherwood Idso (2017) begrudgingly admitted it was true. Craig Idso, who now runs the Center, was previously the director of environmental science at Peabody Energy, the world's largest privately owned coal company and a funder of the climate change denier machine. Peabody too has donated funds to the Center (Harkinson 2009).

The second NIPCC partner organization, the Science and Environment Policy Project (SEPP), was founded in 1990 by Fred Singer, whose personal ties to the energy industry have been discussed. John Mashey (2012), who investigated SEPP's finances including its IRS filings, concluded that "SEPP paid no salaries, even for Singer's 60-hour workweeks. Money flowed oddly. Asset trades often exceeded normal income and they accumulated to $1.5M, tax-free. Then one money trail led to Heartland."

Far from being neutral, the sponsors of the NIPCC are ideologically committed climate change deniers, all of which have been funded by the very industries that most benefit from continued government inaction on the damaging emission of greenhouse gases.

The knowledge of climate change deniers and of science

From the standpoint of science, it is possible to assess existing climate change knowledge, but what of the knowledge of climate change deniers? It is clear that they embrace a number of established positions that are routinely articulated in debates and critiques, spoken at conferences, and expressed in denier-issued documents. These talking points constitute a stock set of fixed responses to any assertions that the climate is trending in a dangerous direction or that humans are now a primary force driving this pattern. In the view of well-known climate scientist Michael Mann (2013), "A good rule of thumb is that the more insistent climate-change deniers are about any particular talking point, the greater the likelihood is that the opposite of what they are claiming actually holds." It is possible to examine denier positions and compare them with the available science on every issue, as shown below.

1. "Even before the introduction of sport utility vehicles and other greenhouse-gas spewing modern technologies, Earth's climate was changing, so humans can't be responsible for today's global warming." However, in the assessment of climate scientists: climate changes in the past suggest that our climate reacts to energy input and output, such that if the planet accumulates more heat than it gives off global temperatures will rise. It is the driver of this heat imbalance that differs. Currently, CO^2 of our manufacture is the primary driver.

2. "The planet can't be warming if heavy snow is falling on my front yard. This winter has been one of the coldest I can remember, how is that possible in a warming world?" Before he was president, in 2010, Donald Trump (Schulman 2017) voiced a version of this argument, telling an audience at one of his golf clubs, "With the coldest winter ever recorded, with snow setting record levels up and down the coast, the Nobel committee should take the Nobel Prize back from Al Gore … . Gore wants us to clean up our factories and plants in order to protect us from global warming, when China and other countries couldn't care less." Indeed, the occurrence of large winter storms or a period of abnormally chilly weather often raises the question: how can global warming be occurring when it's snowing outside? But general patterns of global warming are compatible with the local occurrence of blizzards or unexpected cold weather. In assessing climate change, it is the long-term trends that are important, those that are measured over decades or more, and consistently long-term trends show that the globe is still, unfortunately, steadily warming. High and low temperature data from recent decades shows that new record highs occur nearly twice as often as new record lows (Meehl et al. 2009).

3. "If it ever was occurring, global warming has stopped and the Earth even has begun to cool." This idea grew out of climate change research findings suggesting what came to be called "a pause" or "hiatus" in global warming ensued during the first 15 years or so of the twenty-first century (1998–2013). In 2013, the Intergovernment Panel on Climate Change Fifth Assessment Report stated that the global surface temperature that "the rate of warming over the past 15 years … is smaller than the rate calculated since 1951"

(Hartmann et al. 2013). But this interpretation of the existing data was brought into question by a number of studies, of which two papers by the U.S. National Oceanic and Atmospheric Administration (NOAA) published in the journal *Science* in 2015 and *Earth's Future* in 2016 were the most influential (Karl et al. 2015, Yan et al. 2016). In the first paper, NOAA researchers reported that ocean temperatures were being regularly underestimated by the most frequently used global climate computer models. The problem these researchers discovered was that special ocean buoys that scientists used to monitor ocean temperatures tended to report slightly cooler surface temperatures than ship-based measures carried out during the 1990s. Reanalysis of the data with this insight in hand and the integration of information on ocean temperatures from three sources (buoys, satellites, and robotic floats) led to the conclusion that, in fact, a pause had not occurred and that the warming the planet experienced during the first 15 years of the twenty-first century was "virtually indistinguishable" from the rate during the period from 1950–1999" (Karl et al. 2015: 1472).

4. The second paper concluded that the global mean surface temperature of Earth is a surface characteristic that does not represent a slowdown in warming of the climate system but rather reflects energy redistribution within the oceans. In other words, heat build-up in the oceans that is not measured by surface monitoring technology could mask continued heating of the planet (Yan et al. 2016). Not surprisingly, climate change deniers were outraged by the NOAA publications and conservative members of the U.S. House of Representatives, assuming a conspiracy, demanded that the agency turn over all emails from the scientists who authored the paper or the scientists involved would face prosecution. Also demanded were the methods used in the study and the data they produced, a curious emphasis given the public nature of this information in the already published paper. NOAA refused the demand, however, asserting that the procedure for questioning scientific studies was peer review and replication of research by other scientists (as occurred with the publications in question), not subjecting scientists to personal investigation when their findings do not match preconceived ideas about the world. It is the nature of science, and a fundamental aspect of its approach to knowledge creation, that specific findings are subject to reconsideration in light of subsequent research. This does not mean that all climate science conclusions are invalid, especially not understandings about the overall nature of global warming, because these are not based on one or two studies within a particular discipline at one point in time but on literally hundreds of studies across diverse environmental, climatic, and social science disciplines with differing methodologies and areas of research over decades. All science, ultimately, is contingent, but degrees of confidence mount considerably when a wide array of studies draw a common conclusion. Politicians who embrace the denial position have had trouble grasping this point and prefer to only mention findings they believe supports their position.

5. In 2017, on the Seth Meyers' Late Night TV program, Senator Ted Cruz (R-Texas) told the viewing audience, "Many of the alarmists on global warming, they got a problem because the science doesn't back them up. And in particular, satellite data demonstrates for the last 17 years, there's been zero warming. None whatsoever" (quoted in *Media Matters* 2017). In a subsequent appearance on the program, climate scientist Benjamin Santer responded:

    Listen to what he said. Satellite data. So satellite measurements of atmospheric temperature show no significant warming over the last 17 years, and we tested it. We looked at all of the satellite data in the world, from all groups, and wanted to see, was he right or not? And he was wrong. Even if you focus on a small segment of the now 38-year satellite temperature record—the last 17 years—he was demonstrably wrong. More importantly, if you look at the entire record it shows strong evidence of a human effect on climate. Warming of the lower atmosphere. Cooling of the upper atmosphere. And that's the fingerprint of human-caused changes in heat trapping greenhouse gases. So the bizarre thing is, Senator Cruz is a lawyer. He's got to look at all of the evidence when he's trying a case, when he's involved in a case, not just one tiny segment of the evidence.

    (Quoted in Media Matters *2017)*

6. In the words of sociologist and U.S. Senator Daniel Patrick Moynihan, "Everyone is entitled to his own opinion, but not his own facts" (quoted in Will 2010). Or, according to well-known Canadian zoologist and geneticist, science broadcaster, and environmental activist David Suzuki (2017):

    There's nothing wrong with challenging research, developing competing hypotheses and looking for flaws in studies. That's how science works. But rejecting, eliminating, covering up or attacking evidence that might call into question government or industry priorities—evidence that might show how those priorities could lead to widespread harm—is unconscionable.

    "Changes on the sun are to blame for global warming. Over the past few hundred years, the sun's activity, including the number of sunspots, has increased, causing the world to get warmer." In fact, over the last 35 years of global warming, the sun has shown a slight cooling trend, while the climate has been heating up, scientists say. In the past century, solar activity—which includes the sun's magnetic field and includes magnetic field-powered sunspots and solar flares—can explain some of the increase in global temperatures, but a relatively small amount. A study published in the journal *Atmospheric Chemistry and Physics* in December 2011 revealed that even during a prolonged lull in the sun's activity, Earth still continued to warm (Hansen 2011).

7. "Carbon dioxide (CO^2) is not a pollutant!" Rick Santorum (quoted in Gentilviso 2012), as a GOP presidential candidate in 2012, summed up this argument when he stated to Associated Press: "The dangers of carbon dioxide? Tell that to a plant, how dangerous carbon dioxide is." Similarly, according to Congresswomen Michele Bachmann (quoted in Johnson 2009): "Carbon dioxide is natural. It occurs in Earth. It is a part of the regular life-cycle of Earth … . [T]here isn't even one study that can be produced that shows that carbon dioxide is a harmful gas." The link here between natural and not harmful is specious. Radon, for example, is a natural substance on Earth released during the normal decay of the elements uranium, thorium, and radium found in rocks and soil. Yet, as a radioactive substance, radon exposure causes cancer.

    While it is true that plants photosynthesize and therefore take up carbon dioxide as a way of forming energy with the help of the sun and water, this gas is both a direct pollutant (as seen in acidification of oceans) and more importantly is directly linked to the greenhouse effect. When heat energy gets released from Earth's surface, some of that radiation is trapped by greenhouse gases like CO^2; the effect is what makes our planet comfy temperature-wise, but too much and you get global warming. Thus, while greenhouse gas may not be a pollutant in the conventional sense, the global toll of greenhouse gas build up may be as many as 20,000 related deaths per year per 1.8° Farenheit (Darby et al. 2001). The problem is not CO^2 per se, which is indeed needed by plants, but too much CO^2, and this is the growing problem we are facing. By way of analogy, water is absolutely necessary for life, but too much water in the form of massive and increasingly frequent flooding and water-related storms like hurricanes tend to take the greatest toll on human lives among the various kinds of natural disasters (Borden and Cutter 2008).

8. "Climate scientists are conspiring to push global warming. Thousands of emails between climate scientists leaked in November 2009 (dubbed Climategate) revealed a cover-up of data that conflicted with research showing the Earth is warming." Indeed, a hacker did access and release 1,079 emails and 72 other documents produced by leading climatologists concerned with human-caused warming from the University of East Anglia server, and for climate deniers the so-called Climategate incident soon became "the worst scientific scandal of our generation" (Booker 2009). But there was no cover-up; a number of investigations were launched, including two independent reviews set up by the university. The investigations cleared the researchers involved with the emails of scientific misconduct and found no evidence of a cover-up (the emails were about advancing personal careers, not the falsification of climate change evidence). In August 2011, the National Science Foundation (2011: 5) concluded: "Finding no research misconduct or other matter raised by the various regulations and laws discussed above, this case is closed."

9. "Don't worry, it's not that bad." Indeed, some deniers have pointed to human history as evidence that warm periods are good for people, while the cold, unstable stints have been catastrophic. Climate scientists say any positives are far outweighed by the negative impacts of global warming on agriculture, human health, the economy, and the environment. For instance, a warming planet has produced an increased growing season in Greenland, the largest island in the world. As a result in 2007, potatoes and radishes were produced at bumper levels and further north than has been the case in the past—only 185 miles from the Arctic Circle. For the first time, Greenlanders were able to grow broccoli. But the positive effects are universally shared by the island nation (Michael and Masters 2013).

For indigenous people who depend on the country's ice sheet for transportation and as an environment for subsistence hunting and fishing, the trend toward warmer weather is not seen as a blessing. The appearance of longer summers has meant that there is a less time when sea ice is constant enough to allow passage by sled dog or snowmobile. Many of the Inuit communities of Greenland lack roads that connect them to the rest of the island. Instead, they are dependent upon being able to travel over the ice. There is also a growing fear in these communities that increased access for boats allowed by melting sea ice will overload local fisheries that are not able to handle the pressure of increased harvesting. Beyond Greenland, climate change is producing deadly water shortages, more frequent and more intense and damaging wildfires, and expanding deserts that encroach on the livelihoods of growing numbers of poor farmers. In coastal areas of the planet, the rapidly melting glaciers of Greenland are contributing to sea level rise and inland flood. Consequently, it is critical to consider all of the effects of global warming, locally and throughout the planet, and their distribution among various populations.

10. "Antarctica is gaining ice. Ice covering much of Antarctica is expanding, contrary to the belief that the ice cap is melting due to global warming." The argument that ice is expanding on Antarctica omits the fact that there is an important difference between land ice and sea ice, climate scientists emphasize. "If you are talking about the Antarctic ice sheet, we expect some gain in accumulation in the interior due to warmer, more moisture-laden air, but increased calving/ice loss at the periphery, primarily due to warming southern oceans," according to climate scientist Michael Mann (quoted in Bryner 2012). The net change in ice mass is the difference between this accumulation and peripheral loss. According to Mann: "Models traditionally have projected that this difference doesn't become negative (i.e., net loss of Antarctic ice sheet mass) for several decades." Detailed gravimetric measurements, which looks at changes in Earth's gravity over spots to estimate, among other things, ice mass, suggest that the Antarctic ice sheet is already losing mass and contributing to sea level rise.

11. "Climate models are unreliable; models are full of 'fudge factors' or assumptions that make them fit with data collected in today's climate; there's no way

to know if those same assumption can be made in a world with increased carbon dioxide." In fact, models have successfully reproduced global temperatures since 1900, for land, the air, and the oceans. Models are simply a formalization of our best understanding of the processes that govern the atmosphere, the oceans, the ice sheets. They are simplifications of reality, not distortions of it. Certain processes, such as how clouds, will respond to changes in the atmosphere and the warming or cooling effect of clouds, are uncertain and different modeling groups make different assumptions about how to represent these processes. Even so, certain predictions are based on physics and chemistry that are so fundamental, such as the atmospheric greenhouse effect, that the resulting predictions—that surface temperatures should warm, ice should melt, and sea level should rise—are robust no matter what the assumptions.

12. "Not everyone agrees. There's no consensus among climate scientists on whether the planet is actually warming." This is a central and often repeated assertion of the denier camp, although it has no convincing evidentiary support. In truth, it is possible to find some level of disagreement among scientist about all topics of scientific concern.

In fact, contrary to the denialists, what is remarkable about the climate science of global warming is that almost all involved researchers agree that human-made global warming is happening, based on their own work and their awareness of the overwhelming body of evidence that supports this conclusion. There have been several studies that have attempted to measure the degree of scientific consensus on climate change (e.g. Naomi Oreskes in 2004; Doran and Zimmerman in 2009; Anderegg et al. in 2010; and the Vision Prize in 2012). All found convincing evidence for a very high level of consensus among climate scientists for the idea that recent climate change can mostly be attributed to human activities. In the words of famed anthropologist and conservationist Jane Goodall, Many scientists have spent years collecting information about the effect of human actions on the climate. There's no question that the climate is changing, I've seen it all over the world. And the fact that people can deny that humans have influenced this change in climate is quite frankly absurd.

(Quoted in D'Angelo 2017)

In the next chapter, the politics and economics driving climate change denial are addressed, as are the patterns of deception and personal attacks unleased by deniers on climate scientists.

References

Anderson, A. 2015. News organisation(s) and the production of environmental news. In A. Hansen and R. Cox (eds), *The Routledge Handbook ofEenvironment and Communication*, pp. 176–184. Oxon, UK: Routledge.

Bacon, J. 2018. Scientists rebuff EPA chief's claim that global warming may be good. *USA Today*. www.usatoday.com/story/news/nation/2018/02/08/epa-chief-scott-pruitt-global-warming-may-good-thing/318850002/.

Bast, J. 2017a. Winning the global warming war. The Heartland Institute. www.heartland.org/news-opinion/news/winning-the-global-warming-war.

Bast, J. 2017b. The Heartland Institute replies to the national science teachers association. The Heartland Institute. www.heartland.org/news-opinion/news/heartland-institute-replies-to-the-national-science-teachers-association.

Bloom, A. 2013. Why Hayak is a conservative. *The American Conservative*. www.theamericanconservative.com/2013/05/08/why-hayek-is-a-conservative/.

Bray, D. and von Storch. 2016. The Bray and von Storch 5th international survey of climate scientist 2015/2016. www.hzg.de/imperia/md/content/hzg/zentrale_einrichtungen/bibliothek/berichte/hzg_reports_2016/hzg_report_2016_2.pdf.

Brewer, P. and B. Ley. 2012. Whose science do you believe? Predicting trust in sources of scientific information about the environment. *Science Communication* 35: 115–137.

Brock, D. 2014 .The Koch brother from another mother. *Politico Magazine*. www.politico.com/magazine/story/2014/07/the-koch-brother-from-another-mother-108709.

Buxton, N. 2017. The military is resisting Trump's denialism, but it's still not a force for climate justice. *Truth Out*. www.truth-out.org/news/item/40082-the-military-is-resisting-trumps-denialism-but-its-still-not-a-force-for-climate-justice.

Chow, L. 2017. Neil deGrasse Tyson slams science deniers for "dismantling of our informed democracy." *EcoWatch*. www.ecowatch.com/neil-degrasse-tysons-science-video-2371964033.html.

Cook, J. 2017. Heartland's Chinese Academy of Sciences fantasy. *Skeptical Science*. www.skepticalscience.com/heartland-cas-fantasy.html.

D'Angelo, C. 2017. Jane Goodall wants you to stand up to those who belittle science. *Huffington Post*. www.huffingtonpost.com/entry/jane-goodall-march-for-science_us_58dfa6c7e4b0b3918c83e5ba.

Davenport, C. and E. Lipton. 2017a. The Pruitt emails: E.P.A. chief was arm in arm with industry. *New York Times*, February 22. www.nytimes.com/2017/02/22/us/politics/scott-pruitt-environmental-protection-agency.html.

Davenport, C. and E. Lipton. 2017b. How G.O.P. leaders came to view climate change as fake science. *New York Times*. June 3. www.nytimes.com/2017/06/03/us/politics/republican-leaders-climate-change.html?_r=0.

Democracy Now. 2017. Top climate scientist, journalist & activists blast Trump's withdrawal from Paris accord. www.democracynow.org/2017/6/2/top_climate_scientist_journalist_activists_blast?utm_source=Democracy+Now%21&utm_campaign=f022bc7176-Daily_Digest&utm_medium=email&utm_term=0_fa2346a853-f022bc7176-191277585.

DeSmog. 2017. American Council for Capital Formation. www.desmogblog.com/american-council-for-capital-formation.

Dimiero, B. 2010. Fox boss ordered staff to cast doubt on climate science. *Media Matters*, December 15. www.mediamatters.org/blog/2010/12/15/foxleaks-fox-boss-ordered-staff-to-cast-doubt-o/174317.

Dunlap, R. and P. Jacques. 2013. Climate change denial books and conservative think tanks. *American Behavioral Scientist* 57(6): 699–731.

E & E TV. 2017. Ebell, Pica, Bravender and Lehmann on the Trump regulatory climate agenda. www.eenews.net/tv/2017/03/01.

Eilperin, J. 2013. Anatomy of a Washington dinner: Who funds the Competitive Enterprise Institute? *Washington Post*, June 20. www.washingtonpost.com/news/the-fix/wp/2013/

06/20/anatomy-of-a-washington-dinner-who-funds-the-competitive-enterprise-institute/?utm_term=.15723847644f.

Feldman, L., E. Maibach, C. Roser-Renouf, and A. Leiserowitz. 2012. Climate on cable: The nature and impact of global warming on Fox News, CNN, and MSNBC. *International Journal of Press/Politics* 17(1): 3–31.

Fluer, N. 2017. Scientists, feeling under siege, march against Trump policies. *New York Times*, April 22. www.nytimes.com/2017/04/22/science/march-for-science.html.

Foran, C. 2016. Donald Trump and the triumph of climate-change denial. *The Atlantic*. Retrieved from www.theatlantic.com/politics/archive/2016/12/donald-trump-climate-change-skeptic-denial/510359/.

Fountain, H. 2016. Trump's climate contrarian: Myron Ebell takes on the E.P.A. *New York Times*, November 12. www.nytimes.com/2016/11/12/science/myron-ebell-trump-epa.html?_r=0.

Freeman, B. 2017. *The Sustainable Schoolteacher Blog*. http://sustainableschoolteacher.blogspot.com/search?q=climate+denial.

Gauchat, G. 2012Politicization of science in the public sphere: A study of public trust in the United States, 1974 to 2010. *American Sociological Review* 77(2): 167–187.

Gelbspan, R. 2004. *Boiling Point: How Politicians, Big Oil, and Coal, Journalists, and Activists are Fueling the Climate Crisis—and What We Can Do to Avert Disaster*. New York: Basic Books.

Grandoni, D. 2017Interior Department agency removes climate change language from news release. *Washington Post*, May 22. www.washingtonpost.com/powerpost/interior-department-agency-removes-climate-change-language-from-news-release/2017/05/22/774c122a-3f23-11e7-adba-394ee67a7582_story.html?utm_term=.6528bfa781c3.

Griffin, A. 2017. Donald Trump advisor and climate change denier Myron Ebell goes to Number 10. *Independent*, January 31. www.independent.co.uk/environment/donald-trump-myron-ebell-theresa-may-climate-change-global-warming-environment-a7555371.html.

Hamilton, L. 2011. Education, politics and opinions about climate change evidence for interaction effects. *Climatic Change* 104: 231–242.

Harkinson, J. 2009. No. 8: Center for the Study of Carbon Dioxide and Global Change (a.k.a. the Idso family). *Mother Jones*, December 5. www.motherjones.com/environment/2009/12/dirty-dozen-climate-change-denial-11-idso-family%20%20.

Hayek, F. 2011. *The Constitution of Liberty: The Definitive Edition*. Oxford: Routledge.

Hoffman, A. 2015. *How Culture Shapes the Climate Change Debate*. Palo Alto, CA: Stanford University Press.

Holpuch, A. 2017. Quitting Paris climate deal would threaten US security, UN chief warns. *The Guardian*, May 30. www.theguardian.com/environment/2017/may/30/paris-climate-deal-un-us-donald-trump.

Hoofnagle, M. 2015. Bill Maher, the moronic Food Babe, and the NYT discuss what to call climate change denialists. *Denialim Blog*. http://scienceblogs.com/denialism/2015/02/14/bill-maher-the-moronic-food-babe-and-the-nyt-discusses-what-to-call-climate-change-denialists/.

Horn, S. 2012. Revealed: NERA economic consulting is third party contractor for DOE LNG export study. *DeSmog*. www.desmogblog.com/2012/11/19/revealed-reuters-ids-nera-economic-consulting-third-party-contractor-doe-lng-export-study.

Horst, R. and M. Webber. 1973. Dilemmas in a general theory of planning. *Policy Sciences* 4: 155–169.

Hulme, M. 2009. *Why We Disagree about Climate Change: Understanding Controversy, Inaction and Opportunity*. Cambridge: Cambridge University Press.

Idso, S. 2017. What motivates the Center for the Study of Carbon Dioxide and Global Change? *CO2 Science*. www.co2science.org/about/position/funding.php.

Kalmus, P. 2017. To my fellow climate scientists: Be human, be brave, speak truth. *Yes! Magazine*, February 7. www.yesmagazine.org/issues/science/to-my-fellow-climate-scien tists-be-human-be-brave-tell-the-truth-20170207.

Kasprak, A. 2016. 30,000 scientists have signed a petition arguing that there is no convincing scientific evidence for anthropogenic climate change. Snopes Fact Checker. www.snopes. com/30000-scientists-reject-climate-change/.

Kessler, G. and M. Lee. 2017. Fact-checking President Trump's claims on the Paris climate change deal. *Washington Post*, June 1. www.washingtonpost.com/news/fact-checker/wp/ 2017/06/01/fact-checking-president-trumps-claims-on-the-paris-climate-change-deal/? utm_term=.1c5b31e067db.

Krosnick, J. and B. MacInnis. 2010. Frequent viewer of Fox News are less likely to accept scientists' views of global warming. Stanford University. https://woods.stanford.edu/sites/ default/files/files/Global-Warming-Fox-News.pdf.

Leierowitz, A., E. Mailbach, C. Roser-Renouf, and J. Hmielowski. 2011. *Politics and Global Warming: Democrats, Republicans, Independents, and the Tea Party*. New Haven, CT: Yale University.

Malka, A., J. Krosnick, M. Debell, J. Pasek, and D. Schneider. 2009. *Featuring Skeptics in News Media Stories about Global Warming Reduces Public Beliefs in the Seriousness of Global Warming*. Technical Paper. Stanford, CA: Stanford University Press.

Mashey, J. 2012. Fake science, fakexperts, funny finances, free of taxes. *Desmog*. www.desm ogblog.com/fake-science-fakexperts-funny-finances-free-tax.

McCright, A. and R. Dunlap. 2011. Defeating Kyoto: The conservative movement's impact on U.S. climate change policy. Social Problems50(3): 348–373.

Mufson, S. and J. Warrick. 2015. Obama urges world action on climate change: No nation 'immune' to global warming. *Washington Post*, November 30. www.washing tonpost.com/business/economy/obama-urges-world-action-on-climate-change-hour- is-almost-upon-us/2015/11/30/2765bac4-975c-11e5-8917-653b65c809eb_story.htm l?utm_term=.984f3d210a5f.

Nongovernmental International Panel on Climate Change. 2016. About the NIPCC. http://climatechangereconsidered.org/about-nipcc/.

Oliver, J., G. Janssens-Maenhout, M. Muntean, and A. Peters. 2016. Trends in global CO2 emissions: 2016 Report. Netherlands Environmental Assessment Agency, The Hague. http://edgar.jrc.ec.europa.eu/news_docs/jrc-2016-trends-in-global-co2-emissions-2016-rep ort-103425.pdf.

Oreskes, N. and M. Conway. 2010. *Merchants of Doubt: How a Handful of Scientists Obscured the Truth on Issues from Tobacco Smoke to Global Warming*. New York: Bloomsbury Press.

Powell, L. 2016. Climate scientists virtually unanimous: Anthropogenic global warming is true. Bulletin of Science, Technology & Society35(5–6).

Rodin, S. 2014. As a conservative, evangelical Republican, why climate change can't be true (even though it is). *The Steward's Journey*. http://thestewardsjourney.com/as-a-con servative-evangelical-republican-why-climate-change-cant-be-true-even-though-it-is/.

Satlin, A. 2017. EPA Chief Scott Pruitt disagrees with science on another major climate change issue. *Hufffington Post*, September 3. www.huffingtonpost.co.uk/entry/scott-p ruitt-carbon-dioxide_us_58c16401e4b0d1078ca48714.

Schulman, D. 2014. *Sons of Wichita: How the Koch brothers Became America's Most Powerful and Private Dynasty*. New York: Grand Central Publishing.

Smith-Spark, L. and J. Hanna. 2017. March for Science: Protesters gather worldwide to support 'evidence.' CNN. www.cnn.com/2017/04/22/health/global-march-for-science/

Stimson, J. 2009. *Tides of Consent: How Public Opinion Shapes American Politics*. Cambridge: Cambridge University Press.

Sweet, L. 2017. Transcript: President Donald Trump's Paris Climate Accord exit speech. *Chicago Sun Times*, June 2. http://chicago.suntimes.com/politics/transcript-trump-paris-climate-accord-exit-speech/.

Thomas, M. 2014. Climate depression is for real: Just ask a scientist. *Grist.* http://grist.org/climate-energy/climate-depression-is-for-real-just-ask-a-scientist/.

Verheggen, B., Strengers, B., Cook, J., van Dorland, K.Vringer, J.Peters et al. 2014. Scientists' views about attribution of global warming. *Environmental Science and Technonology* 48: 8063–8971.

Walker, J. 1998. Memo: Draft global climate science communication plan. www.euronet.nl/users/e_wesker/ew@shell/API-prop.html.

Wang, A. 2017. MIT says Donald Trump totally misunderstood its climate science. *Quartz Media.* https://qz.com/997757/paris-climate-agreement-donald-trump-misunderstood-climate-change-research-says-the-mit-professors-who-conducted-it/.

Worth, K. 2017. Climate change skeptic group seeks to influence 200,000 teachers. CPTV. www.pbs.org/wgbh/frontline/article/climate-change-skeptic-group-seeks-to-influence-200000-teachers/.

4

THE POLLUTING ELITE AND THE POLITICAL ECONOMY OF CLIMATE CHANGE DENIAL

Climate change denial has become ensnared in the American political process as a point of tension between Republicans and Democrats. Complete polarization and a left/right divide on climate change is not necessarily the case in other developed countries. An analysis of the party platforms of nine conservative parties—the U.K., Norway, Sweden, Spain, Germany, Australia, New Zealand, Canada, and the U.S.—found that it is only in the U.S. that the dominant conservative party openly denies climate change, while in the other countries the conservative parties tend to promote technological solutions that allow a lowering of emissions without significant societal or economic change (Båtstrand 2015). The study also found that in countries with major reserves of fossil fuels conservative parties do not challenge national fossil fuel industries. This finding is affirmed for Australia by Baer's examination (2016) of the close relationship between the coal mining industry and the federal and various state governments, constituting a state/coal industry nexus across both Coalition and Australian Labor Party governments.

In the U.S., which has considerable oil, gas, and coal reserves, conservatives views in recent years have been particularly impacted by organized efforts guided by enormously affluent individuals and highly prosperous corporations, particularly those involved in the energy sector, that benefit from favorable government policies. For example, in the years 2013 and 2014, the oil, gas, and coal industries spent a total of $350 million lobbying Congress on issues of concern to energy corporations. During these same two years, fossil fuel companies were awarded $41.8 billion in federal production and exploration subsidies. This amounts to a return of $119 for every dollar spent on trying to insure the passage of favorable legislation (Oil Change International 2017a). A comprehensive study issued by the Stockholm Environment Institute (Davis 2017) that assessed the impacts of U.S. government subsidies on both oil production and CO_2 emissions concluded that almost half of new oil fields depend on government subsidies to be brought online. The report estimated that subsidies shift about 20 billion barrels of still-undeveloped oil reserves from being unprofitable to drill to becoming profitable to go after. Once burned, this amount oil would emit around eight billion tons of CO^2, which is about 1 percent of the world's remaining carbon budget under the Paris climate agreement. Profits from these new fields further widen social inequality, with government assistance, while speeding along climate change.

While climate change deniers commonly rail against big government, the giant corporations that contribute most to greenhouse gas emissions are often the biggest benefactors of government actions. There are multiple kinds of government subsidy that fossil fuel companies receive, including direct funding, tax giveaways, loans and guarantees at highly favorable rates, price controls, government provision of land and water at below market rates, and research and development funding. This pattern of subsidizing wealthy corporations, which has been labeled corporate welfare, is a critical factor that has helped to shift the tax burden onto middle class earners even in years of booming fossil fuel profits.

At a time of global warming, energy companies are being assisted by the government to lower the cost of developing fossil fuels so that "not only are their true costs being shifted onto the poor via climate and health impacts, but the fossil fuel industry is actually being paid for this privilege" (Oil Change International 2017b). Spoiled by the largess of this sweet corporate/government partnership and used to getting their way, the fossil fuel-based social elite has fought hard to undercut any threat to their favored and highly lucrative position, including the creation and underwriting of climate change denial. The history of the entwinement of the industry, climate change denial, and the American political system is examined in this chapter, followed by a closer look at the deceitful game plan of deniers and the deep-pocket sources of their funding.

Denial from George W. Bush to the Tea Party

While the accusation of climate change hoax has grown considerably over the years, there was a brief time in 2008 when it appeared that the scales of American political action might finally be tipping toward a serious regard of the considerable body of scientific findings affirming the dramatic environmental changes underway and the human role in the reshaping of the planet. The time came at the end of the George W. Bush administration, after what people with strong environmental concerns viewed as eight years of turning a blind eye on climate change. That dark period began in 2001 when the Bush administration announced that it would not implement the relatively modest Kyoto Protocol, an international treaty that would have required participating countries to diminish their release of greenhouse gases by 5.2 percent of 1990 levels by 2012. As Christie Todd Whiteman, director of the EPA affirmed at the time, despite her own recognition that global warming was occurring: "We have no interest in implementing that treaty" (quoted in Kirby 2001). As an alternative, the Bush administration—with considerable influential input from the ExxonMobil corporation and Global Climate Coalition, a pro-business lobbying organization (Vidal 2005)—developed an alternative plan that would allow the release of greenhouse gases to grow, but at a slower pace. Overall, the Bush approach to climate change has been called a charade. In the view of American political correspondent Tim Dickinson (2007),

> Bush's do-nothing policy on global warming began almost as soon as he took office. By pursuing a carefully orchestrated policy of delay, the White House … blocked even the most modest reforms and replaced them with token investments in futuristic solutions like hydrogen cars.

Particularly influential on the Bush response to climate change and other issues within the administration was Vice President Dick Cheney, the former CEO of Halliburton Company, one of the country's largest oil industry service corporations. Cheney embraced the common denier belief that anthropogenic climate change was an unresolved issue and hence should not be the basis of national policy. Even Christine Todd Whitman found the vice president's assertions untenable given the available scientific evidence: "I don't see how he can say that with a straight face anymore" (quoted in Dickinson 2007). Nonetheless, Cheney spearheaded an effort to pressure government-employed scientists to silence their discussion of new findings indicating global warming. As reported by the Associate Press (Roberts 2007): "Climate scientists at seven government agencies say they have been subjected to political pressure aimed at downplaying the threat of global warming." Many of these scientists reported that at some point they were told to remove reference to either "global warming" or "climate change" from government reports in an effort to censor information reaching the public. This same pattern was seen in the Bush administration's efforts to bury the 600-page 2001 National Assessment of the Potential Consequences of Climate Variability and Change, a report required by law that provides updates on scientific findings on the national threats posed by global warming (Piltz 2007). This entire effort was driven by a desire to slow popular demand for climate change action that would control climate polluters and potentially diminish profits in the energy industry.

Within this context, the election of Barack Obama as president in 2008 was welcomed with considerable enthusiasm by scientists and citizens alike who feared that eight years of opportunity to do something meaningful about climate change had been wasted during the Bush administration. After all, Obama not only viewed climate change as the gravest long-term threat facing the world, but one that was already taking a toll through its various manifestations of drought, heat waves, and flooding. Addressing a climate change summit in 2015, Obama made his views clear; even if it was hard for him to win legislative support from the Republican controlled House of Representatives, he still asserted that "The growing threat of climate change could define the contours of this century more dramatically than any other … . What should give us hope at this is a turning point, that this is the moment we finally determined we would save our planet" (quoted in Mufson and Warrick 2015). Despite opposition, Obama found ways to act on limiting the threat of climate change. For his pushing through of the Clean Power Plan that was designed to create standards for limiting power plant carbon pollution, his investments in wind, solar and other clean energy sources, and his work on reducing federal government greenhouse gas emissions, some have called Obama the first climate president (Abraham 2016a).

This positive view of Obama, or appreciation of his perception of climate change as a mounting threat, however, was not a universally shared view, and one place it was not supported was in the Tea Party. As a result, only two years after Obama was first elected, "the prospects for climate change legislation began to deteriorate" (Layzer 2012). The Tea Party can be traced to 1984, when ultra-wealthy conservatives David and Charles Koch founded Citizens for a Sound Economy (CSE) as a conservative political group dedicated to fighting for a smaller federal government, lower taxes, and less government regulation. The early work of the CSE was lobbying for policies that favored major corporations, like those run by the Koch brothers. It was also very active in climate change denial, providing training and funding for individuals like Andrea Saul (Mitt Romney's former press secretary) and Bob Paduchik of the American Coalition for Clean Coal Electricity, who would go on to become outspoken critics of climate science and scientists alike (Coleman 2013). In 2002, the CSE launched the Tea Party's first website at U.S. Tea Party.com (Wayback Machine 2016).

While not initially creating much of a stir, key figures involved in the effort, including Dick Armey of Freedom Works (an offshoot of CSE) and David Koch as chair of the Americans for Prosperity Action (another CSE offshoot), continued to embrace the Tea Party strategy. With the election of Obama, these pro-business advocates finally found an audience among people who for various reasons hated Obama. Research by Hochschild (2016) and Skocpol and Williamson (2013) indicates that many Tea Party advocates were afraid of losing their middle-class status which made them hostile to those they perceived as receiving tax-funded government benefits including their own family members and neighbors. Increasingly, this led to an opposition us vs. them social understanding in which President Obama was perceived as a social Other, as not a real American, and as most likely a Muslim, attitudes Donald Trump publically pushed for five years as a leading spokesman of the "birther" movement. Hochschild (2016) found that Tea Party members came to feel like "strangers in their own land," but never linked their angst to the ever-greater proportion of wealth in the U.S. controlled by the wealthiest people (Walley 2017). The first anti-Obama Tea Party protest occurred in February of 2009, followed by a national rally that was actively promoted by Fox News in April. Various local groups formed and jumped onboard, often without knowledge of the deep-pocket funders driving the Tea Party agenda. Like Koch Industries, ExxonMobil was another fossil-fuel corporation that was a CSE contributor (Pilkington 2009). The considerable wealth behind the Tea Party paid for group rallies, promotional materials, and regional and national conventions, all designed to build the organization as a political force with asserted grassroots credentials but largely secreted funders and coordinators (Coleman 2013). Using loaded buzzwords like freedom, patriotism, and liberty to attract followers, the Tea Party built a large, relatively homogenous constituent base of voters and ultimately, in 2010, a set of ultra-conservative candidates for public office.

In the 2010 mid-term elections, Republicans gained 63 seats in the House of Representatives, and added six seats in the Senate, six governorships, and about 700 seats in state legislatures. This victory gave a major boost to lavishly funded arch-conservative advocacy organizations, including denier-supporting outfits like Freedom Works and Americans for Prosperity Action. These sought to coordinate and direct local Tea Party efforts, provide the Tea Party with spokespersons, while latching onto the Tea Party's populist mantle. Based on their ethnographic study of the Tea Party, Skocpol and Williamson (2012: 11) ask, "What kind of mass rebellion is funded by corporate billionaires, like the Koch brothers, led by over-the-hill former GOP kingpins like Dick Armey, and are ceaselessly promoted by millionaire media celebrities like Glenn Beck and Sean Hannity." Adds David Axelrod, "this is a grassroots citizen's movement brought to you by a bunch oil billionaires" (quoted in Mayer 2010). Given the curious nature of funding and leadership in a supposedly grassroots movement, critics have described the Tea Party as more astroturf (artificially developed) than authentically grassroots.

While the Tea Party emerged with a real base among disaffected people with conservative views and an activist bent, the direction of their movement was quietly steered by members of the social class whose economic activities most contributed to the disaffection of those who became Tea Party members. The thinning-out of the American middle class was caused not by the poor or the actually shrinking government benefits paid out in welfare but by the ever-larger portion of the total wealth of the nation held by the super-rich. Over the past quarter century, the U.S. economy has grown significantly but the same has not been true of the average family's income. During this time,

> corporate profits doubled as a share of the economy. Workers today produce nearly twice as many goods and services per hour on the job as they did in 1989, but as a group, they get less of the nation's economic pie … . In this new reality, a smaller share of Americans enjoy the fruits of an expanding economy.
>
> *(Tankeraley 2017)*

In other words, the real threat to the lives and livelihoods of many Tea Party faithful are the very corporations that have underwritten their organized anger and their self-defeating demand for the deregulation of corporations.

Critical to the shaping of the worldviews of Tea Party members were Fox News and right-wing radio personalities like Rush Limbaugh. These media sources "put out a steady diet of information and misinformation—including highly emotional claims—that keep Tea Party people in a constant state of anger and fear about the direction of the country and the doings of government officials" (Skocpol and Williamson 2012: 13), including the effort by Obama to address environmental issues and global warming. Given its distrustful view of the government and anti-regulatory perspective, the Tea Party effortlessly incorporated a general anti-environmentalist stance and the denial of global warming into its political agenda. Noted Mayer, the wealthy funders of the Tea Party "succeeded to a remarkable extent in channeling the populist anger into the climate fight" (Mayer 2016: 216).

Research by the Yale Center for Climate Change Communication found that the majority of individuals who identified with the Tea Party denied that climate change was happening (Leiserowitz et al. 2011), a finding also reflected in a *New York Times* poll (Eilperin and Clement 2013). They also voiced strong mistrust of scientists who have called attention to the dangers of climate change. Additionally, most such respondents stated that they were already very informed about climate change and needed no additional information on the topic. As the *New York Times* reported during an election in Indiana in 2010, "Skepticism and outright denial of global warming are among the articles of faith of the Tea Party movement …" (Broder 2010). Opposition to the idea of global warming became a litmus test for Tea Party-backed candidates in the election, producing a House of Representatives that was vehement in its opposition to Obama's plan to begin controling green-house gas emissions (McCright and Dunlap 2011).

It was during this period that there emerged what anthropological linguist, Adam Hodges (2015), refers to as the 'paranoid style of climate change denial'. This term labels a populist theme latter embraced by Donald Trump asserting that there exists a self-serving super elite that cares little for the needs of the common people. Included in this privileged group are grant-hungry climate scientists, left-leaning political leaders, and a "deep state" of government officials who promote the hoax of climate change. For the most part, the actual members of the climate change elite are left nameless as an amorphous but powerful threat to American society. Among the sources of the shadowy elite's power, claim climate change deniers, is the mainstream media of the sort that Trump would later come to label fake news. Also included are scientific journals that publish articles supporting the climate change lie and "fake weather reporting" that links extreme weather events like hurricanes to warming oceans.

Strategies of climate deception

A common charge of climate change deniers is that the effort to convince people that human activity is causing significant and lasting change to the planet is deception on a global scale. In the words of Timothy Ball (quoted in Morano 2016), a former professor of geology at the University of Winnipeg, "It is the greatest deception in history and it affects everything." The charge of deception against climate scientists is ironic in light of the identifiable pattern of deception that is the usual approach of organized climate change denial. An example of this pattern is seen by considering the author of the words quoted above. Ball, a consistent critic of the science of climate change, has worked closely with both Friends of Science and the Natural Resources Stewardship Project, entities with funding from big energy firms (Gorrie 2007, Pilkington 2008). In 2006, Ball published an opinion column in the *Calgary Herald* entitled "Aussies' Suzuki Heavier on Rhetoric than on Science." In the op-ed piece, Ball unleashed a scathing character assassination of Australian mammologist and paleontologist Tim Flannery and his bestselling book on climate change *The Weather Makers*. According to Ball, Australian scientists had already debunked Flannery's book, arguing that its author had "no professional credentials in the field" and someone who "blunders regularly" (Hoggan and Littlemore 2009: 141). In fact, Flannery is a celebrated scholar and environmental advocate who was named Australian of the Year in 2007. His book, noted above, was honored as Book of the Year in 2006 at the New South Wales Premier's Literary Awards. In a biographical note at the end of his vitriolic editorial column, Ball described himself as "a Victoria-based environmental consultant" who "was the first climatology Ph.D. in Canada and worked as a professor of climatology at the University of Winnipeg for 28 years" (Hoggan and Littlemore 2009: 141). Ball's claims about his own credentials were soon questioned and Ball subsequently conceded that he had inflated his biography.

In 2007, along with several co-authors, including frequent climate change deniers Willie Soon, David Legates, and Sallie Baliunas, all of whom have been regularly funded by fossil-fuel interests (but caught up in ethics controversies because they did not always reveal this source of their funding), Ball published a commentary in the journal *Ecological Complexity*. The paper argued that spring air temperatures around the Hudson Bay basin for the period 1932–2002 show no significant sign of a warming trend. As a result, the authors assert "that the extrapolation of polar bear disappearance [due to global warming] is highly premature" (Dyck et al. 2007: 73). The paper, funded by Charles G. Koch Charitable Foundation, American Petroleum Institute, and ExxonMobil Corporation, was an opinion piece that was not subject to scientific peer-review. Its assertions were soon contradicted by researchers at the U.S. Geological Survey and the National Snow and Ice Data Center, and other scientists who maintained that

> Long-term trends in the population ecology of polar bears in western Hudson Bay in relation to climate change … continues to be consistent with the thesis that climate warming in western Hudson Bay is the major factor causing the sea ice to breakup at progressively earlier dates, resulting in polar bears coming ashore to fast for several months in progressively poorer condition, resulting in negative effects on survival of young, subadult, and older (but not prime) adults and reproduction.
>
> *(Stirling et al. 2008: 193)*

One of Ball's co-authors on the polar bear paper, Willie Soon, of the Harvard-Smithsonian Center for Astrophysics and a frequent voice on the denial circuit, has been well funded by the oil industry, although not openly despite his employment at a public institution. A series of documents and emails obtained through the Freedom of Information Act by GreenPeace and the Climate Investigation Center show Soon was the recipient of $1.2 million in research funding—covering all of his salary and research costs—from fossil fuel companies between 2001 and 2012. Unlike his colleagues at the Center for Astrophysics, Soon did not receive any grants from NASA, the National Science Foundation, or other mainstream science research funders (Goldberg 2015). Soon's corporate funders retained the right to review any papers he wrote prior to publication. As part of agreements signed by the Smithsonian, Soon's funders had to grant him permission to reveal their role in funding his work before he could report it in his publications as part of standard scholarly transparency procedures (Smithsonian Institution 2008). The documents made public by Green Peace and the Climate Investigation Center "clearly show a corporate intent to deceive" and a willingness of a hired gun scientist to maintain the deception about his conflicts of interest (Union of Concerned Scientists 2015).

Another form of climate denier deception involves using covers on denier reports that give them the appearance of official government documents. For example, every four years, federal and other institutions are supposed to issue a report to Congress on the state of understanding of climate change and its potential impacts. The 2009 report (Karl and Melillo 2009), entitled Global Change Impacts in the United States, warned that widespread climate effects are occurring now and are expected to increase. Climate change, it concluded, will "stress water resources" and challenge crop and livestock production. Afterwards, in 2012, a document titled Addendum: Global Climate Change Impacts in the United States (Cato Institute 2012), with a cover that largely replicated the government report was circulated by the Cato Institute, a conservative Washington, DC, policy think tank that received over a million dollars in donations from climate change-denying Koch-owned foundations during the period before the addendum was issued. Cato was co-founded by Ed Crane and Charles Koch, and Charles Koch's brother, David, is on the Cato board of directors. Cato's consistent track record of denying global warming is seen in the 7th edition of its Handbook for Policymakers (Michaels 2009), which argues that Congress should "pass no legislation restricting emissions of carbon dioxide." The subsequent 8th edition of this in-house publication urged a rejection of taxes on the emission of carbon dioxide, a phase-out of all large-scale computer modeling of climate change, and a termination of research funding on the environmental and social impacts of climate change that are based on computer modeling (Michaels and Knappenberger 2017). But, as Gavin Schmidt (2007), a climatologist and Director of the NASA Goddard Institute for Space Studies, pointed out,

> Climate models are unmatched in their ability to quantify otherwise qualitative hypotheses and generate new ideas that can be tested against observations. The models are far from perfect, but they have successfully captured fundamental aspects of air, ocean, and sea-ice circulations and their variability.

According to John Abraham, an associate professor at the University of Saint Thomas in Minnesota who studies clean power sources, the Cato's Addendum:

Global Climate Change Impacts in the United States is "not an addendum. It's a counterfeit" (quoted in Fischer 2012). Michael MacCracken, chief scientist for climate change programs at the Climate Institute, who helped review the 2009 report, adds: "They made it look really similar. Why would they do that unless they're trying to mislead?" (quoted in Fischer 2012).

Mimicry of scientific publications by climate change deniers also occurred in 1998 with a bulk mailing to U.S. scientists by Frederick Seitz, a former president of the National Academy of Sciences. The mailing urged scientists to sign what became known as the Oregon Petition against the U.S. becoming a party to the Kyoto climate treaty. The petition was initiated by Arthur Robinson, president of what he calls the Oregon Institute of Science and Medicine, which is housed on the 350-acre sheep ranch Robinson owns in Cave Junction, Oregon. The mailing, stirred contempt among some recipients, who pointed out that it containing an eight-page article entitled "Environmental Effects of Increased Atmospheric Carbon Dioxide" by four climate deniers that appeared to replicate the format of articles printed in the *Proceedings of the National Academy of Sciences*. One of the recipients, Raymond Pierrehumbert, an atmospheric chemist at the University of Chicago, complained that "The mailing is clearly designed to be deceptive by giving people the impression that the article, which is full of half-truth, is a reprint and has passed peer review" (quoted in Malakoff 1998). Arthur Robinson, the lead author on the questionable document, responded to critics saying, "I used the Proceedings as a model but only to put the information in a format that scientists like to read, not to fool people into thinking it is from a journal" (quoted in Malakoff 1998). Scientists, who are by nature true skeptics and read many academic journals with varying formats, might find this assertion unpersuasive. The concept about deception was sufficient for the National Association for the Advancement of Science (1998) to issue a statement affirming that Oregon Petition "has nothing to do with the National Academy of Sciences and that the manuscript was not published in the Proceedings of the National Academy of Sciences." Rather, available scientific information on greenhouse warming, the scientific body affirmed, "poses a potential threat sufficient to merit prompt responses."

These example highlights the denial effort to treat climate science as an opposable ideology rather than an evidence-based and rigorously engaged search for truth as best we can know it (Oreskes and Conway 2010). In its effort to undercut the legitimacy science of climate change, deception appears to be treated by deniers as an available tactic in a "by any means necessary" ideological war.

Another way that climate change deniers mimic climate science is in the hosting of conferences that are dressed up to look like standard academic gatherings at which researchers present their findings to peers, opening up their ideas and methods to immediate peer review and potential questioning by fellow researchers. Papers first presented at real scientific conferences are commonly revised in light of peer criticisms and suggestions and submitted for consideration of publication by scholarly professional journals, where they must once more undergo generally intensive peer review. The process is not a walk in the park for the authors of scientific papers. Reviewers tend to be most closely attuned to find weakness in scholarly manuscripts rather than strengths. Consider two top scientific journals that have published research articles on climate change, *Nature* and *Science*, both of which show up in the studies cited in this book. Between 2009 and 2013, *Nature* (2017) received 53,631 manuscripts written by science researchers but only accepted four, 139 (7.7%) for publication. The acceptance rate at *Science* (2017) is even lower at under 7 percent. The criteria for publication in science journals is that submissions are original, of considerable scientific importance, and pass the peer review process that is designed to identify any technical failings of the paper under review. The same intensive process of peer review is also part of the process for receiving federal research funding.

Presentations at climate change denial conferences, by contrast, tend not to be submitted to peer-reviewed scientific journals; they may, however, wind up as in-house publications by denier policy organizations, creating the illusion of scholarly publication. In this way, they never undergo peer review, nor does their funding.

In the process of deceptively pulling the trappings of science around the denial movement without taking on the actual rigor of science, there is exposed another mission of the conservative astroturf organizations: the de-legitimation of science and academia generally. This effort is furthered by the frequent labeling of inconvenient science as "junk science" or attacks on the peer review process as being inherently biased. Sometimes it involved deniers falsely claiming their own in-house publications, op-ed opinion pieces, and blog posts are peer reviewed and hence the equal of climate science publications (DeSmog 2017).

Also of note in the pattern of climate change denial deception is what has come to be known as the "Exon knew" story about how studies by Exxon's scientists accurately predicted rising temperatures and melting ice in the Artic but the changing environment of the north was consistently denied or hidden by company spokespersons. As the *Los Angeles Times* reported, "The gulf between Exxon's internal and external approach to climate change from the 1980s through the early 2000s was evident in a review of hundreds of internal documents, decades of peer-reviewed published material and dozens of interviews conducted by Columbia University's Energy & Environmental Reporting Project and the Los Angeles Times" (Jerving et al. 2015). The company's public position was that the facts about future Artic melting are unclear and not something the Exxon would act on. The general strategy was to downplay the significance and certainty of global warming. Exxon's plan, along the American Petroleum Institute and Chevron, included a multimillion-dollar, multi-year effort to instill uncertainty about climate change in the public policy arena. Target audiences were identified for this message of doubt, including the media, policy makers, and science teachers. This plan found expression in, for example, a speech by Lee Raymond (ClimateFiles 2017), head of Exxon, at the World Petroleum Congress, China, in 1997. During his talk, Raymond addressed three climate-related questions: is the Earth really warming? Does burning fossil fuels cause global warming? And do we now have a reasonable scientific basis for predicting future temperatures? Contrary to all evidence, including that produced by Exxon scientists, the first of these questions he answered by saying that Earth was experiencing a cooling spell. The second question was addressed by arguing that almost all greenhouse gases are caused by nature. In response to the final question, he denied the scientific basis for predicting future temperatures.

In fact, during the same period, researchers and engineers who worked for Exxon were taking their findings on melting and projections about future melting into their planning for drilling in the Artic. As a senior researcher at an Exxon Canadian subsidiary, Ken Croasdale, reported at an engineering conference in 1991,

> Certainly any major development with a life span of say 30–40 years will need to assess the impacts of potential global warming … . This is particularly true of Arctic and offshore projects in Canada, where warming will clearly affect sea ice, icebergs, permafrost and sea levels.
>
> *(Quoted in Jerving et al. 2015)*

Croasdale noted the hazards of warming in the Artic, including higher seas and bigger waves that could damage the company's existing and planned coastal and offshore drilling platforms, artificial islands, processing plants, pumping stations, and pipelines. Projections by Croasdale have proved to be accurate, with large losses of sea ice occurring just as the models he used indicating they would. A geographer, Stephen Lonergan, of McMaster University, who Exxon hired to examine climate change in the Mackenzie River Delta, also came to conclusions that the company did not make public. Using NASA climate models, Lonergan concluded that the area would get considerably warmer and this fact should not be ignored as it will sizably increase the cost of maintaining roads, pipelines, and engineering structures. Melting permafrost, he reported to the company, would damage buildings, processing plants, and pipelines. This was not the story Exxon presented to the public as Exxon-funded organizations helped to manufacture doubt about the nature and causes of climate change for decades afterward their own research contradicted such doubt.

In fact, the actual risky state of climate change well known to ExxonMobil-employed scientists extended to issues far beyond the Artic. This conclusion is supported by an empirical study involving document-by-document textual content analysis of peer-reviewed and non-peer-reviewed scholarly publications by company scientists, internal company documents, and paid, editorial-style advertisements (called advertorials) ExxonMobil published in the *New York Times* for the period 1977–2014 (Supran and Oreskes 2017). The researchers examined the thematic consistency of these communications concerning the state of climate science and its implications for human communities. Specifically, they compared the positions taking in the communications on whether climate change was real, whether it was human-caused, whether it should be taken as a serious threat, and whether it was a solvable problem. Analysis revealed that the clear and undeniable thrust of both peer-reviewed publications by ExxonMobil scientists and internal, non-public documents was that climate change was both real and caused by human activities, conclusions reached generally among climate scientists around the world. However, despite this internal knowledge, when ExxonMobil communicated with the public through its editorial-style paid advertisements the company conveyed a message of uncertainty and doubt about climate change.

Strategies of climate war

In its Quarterly Performance Report for the first quarter of 2017, Joseph Bast (2017), the president and CEO of The Heartland Institute, announced, "What to do about global warming, or 'climate change,' is the most consequential political war of our era. The Heartland Institute's primary goal over the next four years is to win the global warming war." Bast chose his words carefully: his goal as the head of a key denier organization had been elevated by the election of Donald Trump from sowing confusion to winning a political war.

Denier attacks on climate scientists have often been phrased as if the speaker had the technical expertise to fairly evaluate the field from an informed perspective. Typical is the statement of Congressman Lamar Smith (R-Texas), a lawyer by training, during a committee hearing on climate change. After explaining the scientific method, Smith stated: "Much of climate science today appears to be based more on exaggeration, personal agendas, and questionable predictions than on the scientific method. Those who engage in such action do a disservice to the American people and to their own profession … . Alarmist predictions amount to nothing more than wild guesses" (Smith 2017). Smith did not indicate how he knew climate scientists were not following the scientific method, although had they not been their papers would have had a hard time passing peer review and never been published and Smith would have never known about them. The implication of his statement was that climate scientists whose work supports the occurrence of global warming must be doing bad science, how else could they reach conclusions he found unpalatable, which is a form of circular reasoning known as begging the question, a fallacy that scientists seek to avoid. Smith's response has been to attempt to discredit climate scientists, as well as to use the power of his office to try and intimidate them. What motivates the nefarious assertions of climate scientists about the dangers of global warming? According to Smith, "It is all posturing for their own purposes, including a desire to control people's lives or get another government grant or an academic promotion" (quoted in Cousins 2016).

With more of his campaign contributions coming from the fossil fuel industry than any other source. Smith has actively gone after specific climate scientists. A common strategy he has used as chair of the House Committee on Science, Space and Technology is issuing subpoenas for the records and communications of scientists who published papers become important landmarks of climate change research. As a result, Smith's crusade has been described as a witch-hunt against climate scientists (Abraham 2015). In a letter to Smith, the American Meteorological Society stressed: "The advancement of science depends on investigators having the freedom to carry out research objectively and without the fear of threats or intimidation whether or not their results are expedient or popular."

The campaign conducted by Smith is not a unique event (McCright and Dunlap 2003). A similar approach has been used by Joe Barton (R-Texas), a Tea Party member, as chair of the House Energy and Commerce Committee. In 2005, Barton sent letters to a number of climate scientists and the University of Virginia demanding information on what he claimed were methodological flaws and data errors in published papers on global warming. Recipients were told they had to supply information on all financial support they received for their research, the location of the data archives for all of their published studies, and any agreements relating to grants or other funding. Barton was motivated by a paper that used tree ring, glacial ice, and coral layer data to show that there had been a significant rise in global temperatures during the twentieth century. With a master's degree in industrial administration, it is far from clear how Barton would identify methodological flaws and data errors in an analysis of the sort he was attacking. But, as is common among climate change deniers, actual training and experience in climate science is not considered important in being an expert on the topic. In his widely cast demand for information from climate scientists, Barton was hoping "to find something, anything" (Mann 2017) with which to discredit climate science and its practitioners. Highly motivated to find wrongdoing, searches of this kind often find what they are looking for, even if it is based on misinterpretation, misattribution, or misunderstanding. Nonetheless, if the dogma of denial is right then climate scientists must be wrong and proof of their chicanery should be easy to find. Except, of course, that the track record of deniers in finding actual climate science malpractice has been dismal. This is certainly true of Joe Barton.

A supportive and well-funded friend of Big Oil, who was a consultant to Atlantic Richfield Oil and Gas prior to being elected, Barton gained public notoriety for apologizing to BP after President Obama got the multinational company to commit $20 billion to pay for damages caused by a deadly explosion and massive oil leakage at its Deepwater Horizon drilling rig in the Gulf of Mexico. Apparently not believing that massively wealthy corporations should be responsible for the environmental (as well as human) damage they cause, Barton said, "I'm ashamed of what happened in the White House … . I think it is a tragedy of the first proportion that a private corporation can be subjected to what I would characterize as a shakedown, in this case, a $20 billion shakedown." In its response, the White House replied, "What is shameful is that Joe Barton seems to have more concern for big corporations that caused this disaster than the fishermen, small business owners and communities whose lives have been devastated by the destruction" (quoted in Montopoli 2010).

One of the strategies of the war on climate scientists has been ad hominem attacks on individual climate scientists including personal threats and efforts to get them fired or their research de-funded. A leading recipient of these kind of attacks is Michael Mann of Pennsylvania State University. Reports Mann: "I've faced hostile investigations by politicians, demands for me to be fired from my job, threats against my life and even threats against my family" (Mann 2016).

Mann watched all of these things happen in 2010 because deniers did not like that his research affirmed global warming. He realized then that many of the attacks on his work could be traced back to organizations with ties to the Scaife Foundation. Supported by oil baron Richard Mellon Scaife, these organizations have had aggressive climate denial agendas. One such Scaife-funded outfit, the National Center for Public Policy Research (NCPPR), tried to pressure the National Science Foundation to revoke Mann's research grants on global warming. The unsupported and easily refuted assertion made by NCPPR was that Mann was pocketing research funding. The issue of research funding for climate science and the alleged unethical and perhaps illegal nature of grant writing by climate scientists is an old saw for NCPPR (McCright and Dunlap 2003). The organization does not seem to understand (or want to understand) that federal grants go to universities or research centers, not individual scientists, and that spending for research costs is closely monitored and reported to the government. Another Scaife funded entity, the Commonwealth Foundation, tried to convince Pennsylvania State University to fire Mann in the aftermath of the faux climategate scandal. Commonwealth failed in this effort but did get the sympathetic ear of the Republican chair of the Pennsylvania state senate education committee. He threatened to freeze Penn State's funding hostage until "appropriate action is taken by the university against associate professor [sic, he is actually a full professor] Michael Mann" (quoted in Mann 2016). The Commonwealth campaign against Mann pushed the controversy-sensitive university to launch an inquiry against Mann in December 2009. To keep the pressure on, Commonwealth held a series of press conferences and issued numerous press releases slamming Mann personally and criticizing the university for an alleged 'whitewash" of Mann's many asserted offenses. The organization purchased daily ads for a week criticizing Mann in *The Collegian*, the university's campus newspaper. The university's initial inquiry and subsequent formal investigation, however found no evidence of misconduct by Mann.

Perhaps most outrageous in the litany of offenses directed at Mann occurred in 2010. He had received a letter in his university mailbox that he carried back to his office to read. As he tore open the hand-addressed letter, white powder spilled from it, sending Mann on a mad dash to scrub his hands. He then called the FBI, which ultimately determined that the powder was cornstarch, not anthrax spores.

Mann is not alone as a target of hostility by climate deniers. One of his colleagues, Kevin Trenberth of the National Center for Atmospheric Research in Colorado, received 91 pages of attack emails in the aftermath of the Climategate hysteria. Naively seeking to have a meaningful exchange with his attackers, Trenberth initially responded to some of the authors, only to find that he had already been tried, found guilty, and was in need of punishment in their skewed view. Trenberth "tried not to take it personally, but [found] sometimes it's a bit difficult when some of these attacks occur the way they do" (quoted in Pappas 2011).

In an investigation into the dirty tactics of climate change deniers, Inside Climate News (ICN) interviewed about ten climate scientists and reported:

> For them, death threats, sexist remarks, claims of fraud, bomb threats, letters laced with powdery substances, references to rape and Nazis have become almost standard. According to emails shared with ICN, messages range from derisive ("I hope your mental illness gets better") to downright threatening ("YOU ARE GOING TO HANG SOON!").
>
> *(Bagley and Sadasivam 2015)*

Katherine Hayhoe, director of the Climate Science Center at Texas Tech, whose work focuses on developing high-resolution climate projections that are used to evaluate the future impacts of climate change on human society and the natural environment, has attempted to bring climate science knowledge to public audiences, including evangelical Christians. She told Inside Climate News that after a public speaking event she can receive as many as 200 emails and letters telling her she is a fraud and a liar, threatening her family, and questioning her religious views. People have also shown up at her university office to angrily confront her about her scientific views. She recalled,

> One email I got said something like, "I hope your child sees your head in a basket after you've been guillotined for all the fraud you climate scientists have been committing." There are people who become dedicated to following you, who have Google alerts set up on your name, who stalk your Twitter and Facebook accounts, who essentially make a career out of ridiculing and vilifying you.
>
> *(Quoted in Bagley and Sadasivam 2015)*

Because they have faced unbridled vitriol, many climate scientists have had to hide their home addresses, unlist their phone numbers, or have their mail delivered to a P.O. box. Some have suffered emotionally because of the unrelenting and personal nature of many denier broadsides (Bagley 2015). What the harassment of climate scientists has not done is stop scientific progress in figuring out the nature, expressions, and causes of climate change. In fact, denier attacks have spurred climate scientists to publish a significant number of papers in peer-reviewed scientific journals to fully explain their findings on climate change (Lewandowsky et al. 2015) and to counter what Freudenberg et al. (2008) have labeled the Scientific Certainty Argumentation Methods (SCAMs) of climate change deniers.

In response to the repugnant nature and extent of personal attacks on climate scientists, the American Association for the Advancement of Science (2011), the largest general scientific association in the world, issued a statement in 2011, noting that the anti-science campaign has

> created a hostile environment that inhibits the free exchange of scientific findings and ideas and makes it difficult for factual information and scientific

analyses to reach policymakers and the public. This both impedes the progress of science and interferes with the application of science to the solution of global problems.

As descriptions of the tactics used in the war on climate science suggest, for some deniers opposing climate science is not mere skepticism, it reflects "true believer" commitment. Philosopher Eric Hoffer introduced the term true believer to label the psychology of fanaticism. True believers elevate faith over reason and tightly embrace doctrines that serve as "fact-proof screens between the faithful and the realities of the world" (Hoffer 1951: 79). What unites true believers, he observes, is hatred.

Climate denial hate is often extended to journalists who report on new scientific findings on global warming. Journalist Seth Borenstein, who writes about climate science for the Associated Press, reported to Inside Climate News that he is frequently the target of harassment on social media. One Twitter user tagged Borenstein in a post that read: "Why can't we put these dangerous eco-terrorists in prison, or better yet, just execute them" (quoted in Bagley and Sadasivam 2015).

While one might at first dismiss such a malicious Tweet, or even powder-filled letters, as the work of delusional individuals, the overall pattern of climate denier personal threat, the active promotion of climate scientist demonization by organized and corporately funded policy groups, and the repeated statements from politicians, including Donald Trump, implying nefarious activities among climate scientists make it clear that Joseph Bast of the Heartland Institute actually did mean a war needed to be fought to defeat and silence climate science. It is rather remarkable that in the twenty-first century such a war would be waged, suggesting the lengths to which those who economically benefit from being able to freely pollute the environment and fill the atmosphere with greenhouse gases will go to keep the profits rolling in.

Funding climate change denial

There is an old catchphrase in investigative reporting that says to get to the heart of a story you have to "follow the money." This recommendation is a useful guide to the examination of the origin and motivation for climate change denial. In the period just after World War II, some of the wealthiest people in the U.S. began to fund the creation of think tanks to promote their narrow economic interests. Styled as if they were independent scholarly organizations that dispassionately searched for truth related to key public policy issues, they have in fact operated like an incestuous branch of the highly influential corporate lobbying effort. Following the money in climate change denial means deconstructing the climate change denial industry by tracing the relationship of various ultra-conservative billionaires, the corporations they run, and the foundations they set up to support the network of think tanks involved in promoting the denial stock of well-worn contrarian ideas and assertions, as well as, as discussed above, the mobilizing of forces in the war on climate scientists and their unwelcome message of climate reality. The goal of this well-oiled and oil-funded machine is "denigrating scientists and studies whose findings do not serve the corporate cause" (Michaels 2008: 57).

In 2013, in an eye-opening investigative journalism report (Fischer 2013), the *Guardian*, a British newspaper, revealed the existence of two secret and related funding routes, called Donors Trust and Donors Capital Fund, for very conservative and very wealthy individuals to funnel money into the bank accounts of over 100 denier organizations in the U.S. This secretive system was geared to serve clients prepared to make large donations—the average account size at both Donors Trust and Donors Capital Fund was about half a million dollars (Donors Trust 2017)—but who preferred to retain complete anonymity, leading the *Guardian* to label their donations "dark money." Both of these entities are spin-offs of the Philanthropy Roundtable, a coordinating body for conservative foundations formerly headed by Whitney Ball, who also served as director of development at the Cato Institute, and was the co-founder, president and CEO of Donors Trust prior to her death in 2015. Ball believed that Donors Trust "needed to play a central role in expanding the financial resources available to the libertarian and conservative movement" (Donors Trust 2017).

The current president and CEO of both fund organizations is Lawson Bader, who was the former president of the energy industry-funded policy organization the Competitive Enterprise Institute. In September 2014, Bader, an avowed evangelical Christian, signed a declaration developed by the Cornwall Alliance (2017)—an evangelical climate change denier organization—that called on politicians to "abandon fruitless and harmful policies to control global temperature." Such policies were unnecessary, the declaration claimed, because "God's wise design and faithful sustaining" of Earth would "suppress and correct" any damage done by humans, including to the climate. Consequently, rising levels of CO^2 in the atmosphere will have "a relatively small and benign rather than large and dangerous warming effect." The declaration, which voiced a common denier set of inaccurate statements about the impacts of burning fossil fuels on the world's climate, claimed that their real concern about acceptance of the reality of climate change is that it would lead to policies that hurt the poor. In fact, in one of its most disingenuous and egregious assertions that whitewashes the role of Big Oil in Third World poverty, the declaration stated the reason for opposing mitigating CO^2 emissions is because "[t]o demand [the poor] forgo the use of inexpensive fossil fuels and depend on expensive wind, solar, and other 'Green' fuels to meet [their needs] is to condemn them to more generations of poverty and the high rates of disease and premature death that accompany it." In an impressive bit of legerdemain, it is not the very wealthy who most benefit from unhindered dependence on fossil fuel but the very poor. To further its evangelical campaign to deny global warming, Cornwell developed a 12-part video series titled "Resisting the Green Dragon." Promoted as "a Biblical response to one of the greatest deceptions of our day," the programs claims that the effort to call attention to the dangers of climate change is a "false religion" and grave threat to the church that is intended to empower eugenicists and create a "global government." The environmental movement from this conspiratorial perspective is not really concerned with protecting the planet, it is rather about power and controlling people.

Examination of the funding of the Cornwall Alliance suggests that it has deep ties to the oil industry through the network of astroturf organizations that orchestrate the climate science denial machine (Think Progress 2010), although it refutes that it has direct industry funding (Hickman 2011).

Before his hiring at the Competitive Enterprise Institute, Bader worked for 16 years at the Mercatus Center, a conservative think tank based at George Mason University in Virginia (Readfearn 2015). According to Greenpeace (2016), during Bader's time at Mercatus the Center received more than $9 million in funding from foundations linked to the oil billionaire brothers Charles and David Koch. Both Charles Koch and Koch Industries director Richard Fink have served as board members of Mercatus.

Donors Trust, under both Bader and Ball's tenures, have referred clients to its affiliate the Donors Capital Fund for specialized treatment if they intend to maintain a balance of $1 million or more in their accounts (Donors Capital Fund 2013). The goal for some wealthy contributors to these grant-giving entities is to bankroll opposition to action on climate change mitigation policy. According to journalist Suzanne Goldberg (2013), these funds helped to build up a broad network of think tanks and media activist organizations focused on redefining "climate change from neutral scientific fact to a highly polarising 'wedge issue' for hard core conservatives."

On its website, Donors Trust (2017) describes itself as "the only fund committed to supporting and promoting the principles of liberty. We make grants to charities that do not rely on government funding but do promote the foundations of civil society: limited government, personal responsibility, and free enterprise … ." Also of expressed concern to Donors Trust is the fact that the offspring and grandchildren of their donors may make their own, more liberal decisions about where family charitable contributions will go after a donor dies. While right-wing billionaires may spend millions of dollars on lobbying and otherwise advocating for conservative solutions to policy issues, staunchly oppose campaign-finance disclosure laws, support the 2010 Supreme Court decision to remove limits on the total amount of money donors can give to all candidates, political action committees and political parties, and scoff at blatant conflicts between self-interest and regulation policy, their offspring do not necessarily share their views. West (2014), vice president of Governance Studies at the Brookings Institution, observes:

> When large wealth passes to the next generation … conservatives will start to understand the threat posed by big money in American politics. They may rue the day they encouraged wealthy benefactors to enter the political arena without required disclosure or transparency.

Consequently, one service offered by the Donors Trust is "safeguarding the charitable intentions of donors" from the values of future generations (Donors Trust 2017).

Since it was founded in 1999, Donors Trust reports it has received over $1 billion from over 200 donors and distributed over $900 million to grant recipient organizations. Donors, who are promised their identities will be kept private—as donations are made to grant recipients in the name of either Donor Trust or Donor Capital Fund rather than in the name of the actual individual who provided the funding—are informed on the website that they can contribute cash to lower their income taxes or appreciated stock to avoid capital gains taxes. Entities active in climate change denial that have been recipients of Donor Trust and Donor Capital Fund money include the American Enterprise Institute, the Federalist Society, Americans for Prosperity Foundation, the Cato Institute, the Commonwealth Foundation, the Competitive Enterprise Institute, the Heartland Institute, the Heritage Foundation, the Hoover Institute, the Hudson Institute, and the Pacific Research Institute (Donors Trust 2017, Donors Capital Fund 2013). The relative scale and wide distribution of these two hidden funding mechanisms suggests how fundamental they have been to sustaining the deceptive campaign to block action on climate change. To assess the scale of donor contributions to individual denier groups, the *Guardian* (Goldenberg and Bengtsson 2016) obtained annual tax filings made to the IRS by Donor's Trust and Donor's Capital Fund for the period 2011–2013 and cross-checked recipients with a list of organisations associated climate change denial. In 2011, 42 percent of their dark money funding, or $35.7 million, went to climate denial groups and organizations opposed to regulations designed to protect the environment. In 2012, the percentage jumped to 51 percent of Donors Trust and Donors Capital Fund donations, for a total of just over $49 million. In 2013, 46 percent or $41 million from the two funds went to denier outfits allowing them, in the words of sociologist Riley Dunlap, to become "an immense megaphone that amplifies very, very minority voices" (quoted in Goldenberg and Bengtsson 2016).

While the identities of donors to the two funds are almost always hidden, sometimes they are revealed in tax filings. A case in point is the Dick and Betsey DeVos Family Foundation, which is known to have donated $2.5 million in 2009–2010 (Kroll 2013). In 2016, Forbes listed the DeVos family as the 88th richest in the U.S.—and hence comfortably in the uppermost 1 percent of the superrich. Rewarding her conservative education activism, Betsy DeVos was appointed by Donald Trump as secretary of education. In a 1997 op-ed she wrote for the Washington newspaper *Roll Call*, Betsy DeVos acknowledged that she expects results from her political contributions: "My family is the largest single contributor of soft money to the national Republican Party. I have decided to stop taking offense at the suggestion that we are buying influence … . Now I simply concede the point. They are right" (quoted in Gordon 2005).

Energy industry corporations have been another important source of denier funding. As suggested above, ExxonMobil for a number of years played a lead role in this initiative. The oil giant got into the denial funding business in the period after 1988 when the United Nations Intergovernment Panel on Climate Change (IPCC) was launched. ExxonMobile's own scientists had predicted that the point would come that carbon-related global warming would eventually reach a point that governments around the world would seek to control release of greenhouse gases into the atmosphere. Establishment of the IPCC was a sign that that moment had arrived and the subsequent release of ever more certain IPCC assessments of global warming and the human role in this planetary change affirmed this was the case. In response, ExxonMobil set up the Global Climate Coalition (GCC), a lobbying program backed by other Big Oil and Big Auto corporations intent on blocking government controls on carbon release. As Frumhoff et al. (2015: 162) explain, "[f]rom 1989 to 2002, the GCC led an aggressive lobbying and advertising campaign aimed at achieving these goals by sowing doubt about the integrity of the IPCC and the scientific evidence that heat-trapping emissions from burning fossil fuels drive global warming." Between 1988 and 2005, ExxonMobil poured over $16 million into the eager-to-please network of climate change denier groups that were already established or emerging during this period (Frumhoff et al. 2015). As exposures of the role of ExxonMobil in denial funding began to multiply, the company reduced its contributions to the denier machine organizations and was reported to have ceased such funding by 2007 (Brulle 2013). In a corporate responsibility report, under the leadership of Rex Tillerson, the man Donald Trump appointed as secretary of state, ExxonMobil (2008: 39) stated: "In 2008, we will discontinue contributions to several public policy groups whose position on climate change could divert attention from the important discussion on how the world will secure energy required for economic growth in an environmentally responsible manner." However, in 2015 ExxonMobile was still funding the American Enterprise Institute to the tune of $325,000 as it launched a campaign to undercut the United Nations Climate Change Conference in Paris. The oil giant was also funding American Legislative Exchange Council (ALEC) and the Manhattan Institute for Policy Research, both of which have been active in climate change denial and other efforts to protect the environment from corporate despoilment (Readfearn 2016). ExxonMobil's commitment to corporate responsibility appears to remain what it always has been: staying responsible to its big shareholders to make enormous profits in part by offloading significant production costs on the world in the form of carbon release and environmental pollution. ExxonMobil has also donated $1.8 million in campaign contributions since 2007 to more than 100 members of Congress who deny climate change, such as Texas senators Ted Cruz and John Cornyn (Banerjee 2016). Cruz is noteworthy as a politician because the oil and gas industries have been his biggest corporate financial supporters since he campaigned for the Senate in 2012. Moreover, at least a quarter of his personal wealth is composed of investments in fossil fuel company stock. As an elected official, Cruz has strongly supported policies that benefit the oil and gas sector, while opposing policies intended to develop renewable energy (Atkin 2015).

Tillerson himself has walked a crooked line on the issue of climate change, sometimes admitting the planet is warming, sometimes, as at the 2013 company shareholders meeting, incorrectly asserting that science really does not understand how climate conditions are changing and that for the previous ten years planet temperatures have been relatively unchanged (Bradley 2013). Meanwhile, under Tillerson, the company did not change its pattern of contributing mightily to greenhouse gas emission.

In May of 2016, the denier group Competitive Enterprise Institute ran a costly full-page ad in the *New York Times* expressing outrage that several state attorney generals were harassing and attempting to silence organizations and individuals who did not accept that global warming was real and were investigating their relationship with ExxonMobil. Davies (2016) reports that the signers of the ad—including Myron Ebell, Craig Idso, Jim DeMint, president of the Heritage Foundation, and Joseph Best of the Heartland Institute—were the recipients of $10.1 million from Exxon, ExxonMobil, and the ExxonMobil Foundation in the years 1997–2014, and that many were key players in the ExxonMobil effort to deceive the public and its shareholders about what its researchers had established concerning the causal role of carbon emissions in climate change.

Another highly committed set of energy industry funders of climate change denial is Koch Industries, one of the largest privately held corporations in the U.S., with annual revenues over $100 billion, and its associated Koch family foundations (Forbes 2016a). In 2010, Greenpeace issued a report that identifying Koch Industries as a "kingpin of climate science denial." The report showed that from 2005 to 2008, the Koch brothers, Charles and David, vastly outspent ExxonMobil in giving money to organizations fighting legislation related to climate change and in underwriting a huge network of foundations, think tanks, and political front groups that deny global warming (Greenpeace 2010). In 2016, Greenpeace updated its financial report on Koch funding of climate change denier groups revealing a significant increase.

The Koch brothers are sons of Fred Koch, an MIT graduate and chemical engineer who amassed a fortune building oil refineries (Schulman 2014). Blocked by the hegemonic strategies of the big oil companies from expanding his small company in the U.S., Koch entered into contracts to build petroleum distillation capacities in the Soviet Union, helping the Stalin regime to set up modern oil facilities. Also at issue in the move to the Soviet Union was whether Fred Koch had stolen or perhaps merely re-invented the methodology of Universal Oil Products for breaking down heavy crude into useable gasoline (Dickinson 2014). Ultimately, Stalin's purges of intellectuals turned Koch against the Soviet Union and long influenced his political thinking. Koch also partnered with American Nazi sympathizer William Rhodes David to build a massive oil refinery for Adolf Hitler's Germany, a vital cog in the Nazi war effort (Mayer 2016). These deals made Koch a very wealthy man. This was his ticket to marrying the wealthy belle of an old-money family, Mary Clementine Robinson. Their honeymoon lasted seven months and spanned four continents, including trips to Tanzania and Kenya, where Fred shot two leopards and had their fur made into a coat for Mary. Upon their return to the U.S., Fred had a Tudor-style mansion built for the couple. Fred used his treasure to become a big game hunter and build a trophy room in this home that he filled over the years with elephant tusks, polar bear pelts, water buffalo heads, and assorted other stuffed animal hides and horned heads. Mary returned from their trip pregnant with their first son, the first of four.

The Koch children were raised somewhat sternly, even miserly, but ultimately with immense social privilege in luxurious surroundings. For weekend getaways, the family would regularly go to their 10,000-acre ranch (the first of multiple Koch-owned ranches), a site of tall grass, ponds, and flowing creeks in eastern Kansas. Later in his life, Fred got involved with and rose to the top ranks of the John Birch Society, an ultra-conservative group that vehemently opposed the Civil Rights movement and equated the Kennedy administration with a national descent into communism. According to Daniel Schulman (2014), Koch "saw evidence for communist infiltration everywhere" in America and this issue "was regular table talk for the Koch boys" as they were growing up. Included in his perspective on the world was seeing a positive aspect to the rise of fascism in Germany because, he believed, it improved the life of working people.

When his father died in 1967 while on a hunting trip in Utah, Charles assumed the head of the family enterprises, which in 1968 he renamed Koch Industries. By this point, Charles was a committed listener to the radio program of Robert LeFevre, founder of the Freedom School, a training center that asserted that "natural law" is more important than the law of the state and that for American society to flourish economically it must be ruled by a fully free market unrestricted by government regulation. Charles internalized this perspective and came to see government regulation as totalitarianism (Schulman 2014).

The Koch company has grown enormously with Charles at its helm and David at his side, with expansion into natural gas, petrochemicals, oil pipelines, and other products. According to Forbes (2016b), the estimated annual revenues of Koch Industries are $115 billion. Under its wholly owned subsidiary, Flint Hills Resources, the corporation owns a chain of refineries capable of processing more than 600,000 barrels of crude oil a day, and another subsidiary, Koch Pipeline, that owns or operates 4,000 miles of pipelines that transport crude oil, refined petroleum products, natural gas liquids and chemicals (Davenport and Lipton 2017). Additionally, Koch Industries owns Brawny paper towels, Dixie cups, Georgia-Pacific lumber, Stainmaster carpet, and Lycra (clothing), among other products. The Koch approach to expansion into new areas of production reflects its long-term plan for unending growth:

> While it began as an oil company, Koch today operates more like a giant private equity fund. It is essentially a massive pool of cash that is looking to invest wherever it sees the potential for long-term profits. When the company moves into a new industry, it does so strategically and patiently.
>
> *(Leonard 2013)*

In recent years, Koch turned its sights on the information technology industry with its $7.2 billion purchase of Molex, a global electronics components manufacturer. At the hub of the company's expanding economic empire, under Charles's direct supervision, is Koch Equity Development, which operates like a high-level economic think tank, assessing reports from the various company divisions that constantly monitor the landscape for potential acquisitions.

The combined fortune of the two Koch brothers at the head of the company is $35 billion, which is exceeded only by the fortunes of Jeff Bezos, Bill Gates, and Warren Buffett in terms of wealthiest Americans. Maximal company growth and expansion have been the heart of Charles' business plan. But the road has not been without some major bumps. Under him, the previously obscure company has suffered a string of problems with federal agencies, including the Department of Energy (which began an investigation of Koch Industries for violating price controls on oil) and the Internal Revenue Service (over their taxes). In 1980, Koch Industries pleaded guilty to five felonies in federal court, including conspiracy to commit fraud in a deceptive effort to buy up cheap oil exploration tracts from the government using front men who were actually working for Koch (Dickinson 2014).

In recent years the company has also significantly expanded and become somewhat more visible in its contributions to conservative causes and the organizations that fostered them. In particular, Charles and David Koch have espoused a deep disdain for government while nonetheless lobbying government officials to vote in ways that benefit their companies and donating extensively to the campaign coffers of conservative candidates. As part of this alignment, Charles Koch co-founded the Cato Institute to serve as a breeding ground for libertarian ideas and a training site for conservative libertarian advocates. Together, Charles and David have risen to become conservative linchpins, loaded with cash for donation to politicians running for office who tout restrictions on government and are committed to denying climate change. Through these strategies, "they helped win acceptance for anti-government and anti-tax policies that would protect their businesses and personal fortunes, all under the guise of promoting the public interest" (Confessore 2016).

Koch Industries has a noteworthy track record as an environmental polluter. When a poorly maintained company pipeline exploded in 1994, it spilled more than 90,000 gallons of crude oil into Gum Hollow Creek in south Texas, polluting surrounding marshlands and both Nueces and Corpus Christi bays with a large oil slick. The following year, the EPA sued Koch for violation of the Clean Water Act. Internal Koch records show that its pipelines were in poor condition. Koch Industries was fined $30 million—which at the time was the largest such penalty in the history of U.S. environmental law—because of 312 oil spills in six different states. Carol Browner, a former EPA administrator, said of Koch, "They simply did not believe the law applied to them" (quoted in Dickinson 2014). In late 2000, the company was charged with covering up the illegal release of 91 tons of the known carcinogen benzene from its refinery in Corpus Christi. Initially facing a 97-count indictment and potential fines of $350 million, Koch cut a deal with the then attorney general John Ashcroft to drop all major charges in exchange for a guilty plea for falsifying documents, a $20 million settlement, and the successful completion of a five-year term of probation including adherence to a strict environmental compliance program (U.S. Department of Justice 2001). Externalizing the cost of pollution onto the communities around its facilities, for Koch Industries, like other big industrial polluters, "amounts to a perverse, hidden subsidy" Dickinson (2014). In addition to their other business holdings, the Koch's own Frac-Chem, a top supplier of hydraulic fracturing chemicals to driller operations. During the George Bush administration, the chemical cocktails that are injected underground, where they can threaten vital aquafers, are almost entirely exempt from the Safe Drinking Water Act. Koch representatives had a hand in crafting this anti-regulatory legislation as part of further building their license to pollute into the law (Dickinson 2014).

While Charles Koch has traditionally been reluctant to be viewed as a public figure, in the several years before and during the 2016 presidential campaign he began to move a bit more into the spotlight. In a soft-spoken, folksy interview with *Fortune Magazine* (2016), he explained that his company had grown big enough and "gained enough notoriety" to compel him to step forward; in addition, he was motivated by a desire to promote his book, *The Science of Success*. Also during the interview, Koch admitted that greenhouse gases were contributing to warming but used the fact that ultimately the science on any topic is never permanently settled—as new knowledge may lead to new understandings or broader formulations of the nature of reality—to confuse the overwhelming direction of the evidence base indicating the growing adverse impacts of climate change. By way of analogy, when Koch Industries is scanning a new area for expansion, it gathers up as much information as possible and reaches a conclusion about taking action. Of course, Koch can never know everything about an industry or even a single company, but at a certain point the preponderance of available evidence is deemed adequate to make a confident decision. So too climate science on global warming and its very definite negative consequences. Science cannot say with complete certainty that an specific ocean will rise 12 versus 14 inches over the next 50–75 years, but it is undeniable that ocean levels are rising in measurable if variable amounts over time and place, low-lying islands and coast areas are being flooded, and rates of coast erosion are mounting. Waiting for absolute certainty about the specific number of inches an ocean will rise within a given timeframe before acting means never acting to curb climate change. Such a stance is not motivated by a concern about getting the science precisely right, it is about intentionally portraying science wrongly for political and economic reasons.

Linked to the Koch brothers in both political philosophy and willingness to use vast personal wealth to advance conservative causes like climate change denial, as well as in funding attacks on opponents, was reclusive billionaire Richard Mellon Scaife, a man that has been called "the Charles and David Koch of the 1990s" (West 2014). Scaife was the primary heir to the Mellon fortune that was amassed in banking, oil, newspaper ownership, and aluminum. In 1957, when Forbes launched its first list of the wealthiest people in the U.S., it estimated that Sarah Mellon Scaife (Richard's mother), her brother, and two of her cousins were among the ten richest people in the country, each with holdings in the amount of $400–$700 million (DeSmog 2015). By 2013, the year before Richard died, Forbes listed him as having a personal fortune of $1.4 billion (Durgy 2013). His lifestyle reflected his wealth, and was intertwined with elite families in several parts of the counting, using his private DC-9 to travel between his homes in Pittsburgh, Nantucket, Pebble Beach, and a resort home in Ligonier, PA.

Scaife gained public attention and notoriety during the 1990s for funding the Arkansas Project with $2.4 million in grants to the conservative *American Spectator* magazine from two foundations he controlled (Lewis 1998). The money paid to the magazine to produce a concocted series of alleged investigative press reports was intended to take down Bill and Hillary Clinton using an ever more frequently seen strategy that has come to be known as "the politics of personal destruction." In many respects, Scaife's efforts targeted at the Clintons "were precursors of the highly polarizing attack-oriented politics that we see today" (West 2014), such as those that have been launched against individual climate scientists. Indeed, as noted above, Scaife funded such campaigns against climate scientist Michael Mann. These personalized attacks by Scaife seem to reflect his reported tendency to develop intense distain for some people and to long hold a grudge. His particular political bent was shaped by his introduction while still a boy to conservative Republican politics by his sister's boyfriend, Robert Duggan, who was later indicted for tax fraud, and by his mother's support of the failed Barry Goldwater campaign for president in 1964 (Kaiser 1999). David Brock (2014), who worked on the *American Spectator* attack pieces but later had a change of heart about what he had been engaged in with Scaife's backing, was astonished to discover "the existence of Scaife's vast, relentless and systematically funded enterprise, and its fueling of a doctrinaire, Manichean right-wing movement willing to do just about anything to establish its political hegemony … ."

Of the several Scaife foundations, the largest is the Sarah Scaife Foundation, named after Richard's mother, which had a market value of $700 million in 2015 (Sarah Scaife Foundation 2015). Originally, her foundation focused on educational institutions, such as funding the university laboratory where Jonas Salk developed his first polio vaccine. Sarah Scaife died in 1965, however, giving Richard the opportunity to begin turning the family foundations into the ATM of conservative politics. This was fully achieved by 1980 when conservative groups received 72 percent of the $18 million in donations it awarded that year (Kaiser and Chinoy 1999). When global warming became a core political issue for the right, this cause also attracted Scaife funding. Scaife financing enabled the Heartland Institute to launch their initial climate change-denying International Conferences on Climate Change, get-togethers of climate science opponents that continue to be held annually. Scaife donated well over $100 million to the co-sponsors of the second, fourth, sixth, and seventh Heartland conferences (DeSmog 2015). The foundation has served as a major means of support, often bankrolling core organizational operation costs and public activities of the conservative organization-based denier machine.

In April of 2016, Peabody Energy Corp, the largest U.S. coal producer, filed for bankruptcy protection follow a sharp drop in coal prices that left the company unable to make payments on its debt of $10.1 billion. A year later, St. Louis-based Peabody emerged from the Chapter 11 protections afforded by going bankrupt and its stock soon began to be traded again on the New York Stock Exchange (Reuters 2017). The re-emergence of Peabody, which owns prime assets in coal-rich Wyoming and Australia that are mined for metallurgical coal used in steelmaking and to generate electricity, was aided by "anticipation of eased regulation under U.S. President Donald Trump that has fueled investor enthusiasm for coal" (Rucinski 2017). However, when it filed for bankruptcy, the 130-year old Peabody company said that the primary forces driving the decision were an economic slowdown in the Chinese economy, and the resultant drop in the demand for coal, and the shale-gas boom in the U.S. that has flooded the market with cheap natural gas (Mooney and Mufson 2016). Still, it is hard to untether coal production from concern about climate change. With the highest carbon content of all the fossil fuels, CO_2 emissions from coal combustion accounted for 24.5 percent of total U.S. greenhouse gas emissions in 2012, although coal was the source of only 18 percent of all energy consumed that year. It is also estimated that coal contributed between 8–10 percent of human-made methane emissions worldwide in 2012. Coal is also an important source of a number of other pollutants including nitrogen oxides, particulate matter, mercury, other heavy metals, and coal ash (Center for Climate and Energy Solutions 2015).

In 2015, in an effort to address the role of coal in global warming, the Obama administration unveiled a new set of EPA rules intended to curb the amount of CO_2 allowed to be emitted by coal-fired power plant smokestacks by 32 percent by the year 2030. Even before the regulations were finalized, they were condemned by various opponents, including the U.S. Chamber of Commerce, the Heritage Foundation, Robert Murray, the chief executive of the largest privately held coal mining company in the U.S., and Speaker of the House of Representatives, John Boehner. Fact checking of criticisms made of Obama's Clean Power Plan regulations found them to be largely groundless exaggerations and misstatements of fact (Contorno 2014). Far from being an outright enemy of coal, as Trump's interior secretary, Ryan Zinke, indicated in saying with Trump "the war on coal is over" (quoted in Connelly 2017), the U.S. government under Obama provided billions of dollars in subsidies to the coal industry (The Center for Media and Democracy 2014). Ultimately, what the actions of the coal industry and the fossil fuel industry generally suggest they want is not smaller government per se but government that better serves their special interests.

To promote its financial interests, Peabody has funded at least two-dozen groups engaged in climate change denial and opposition to environmental regulation. This funding pattern came to light when Peabody sought bankruptcy protection from its creditors. In the experience of Kert Davies, who has spent 20 years tracking the funding of climate change denial at the Climate Investigation Center, "It's the broadest list I have seen of one company funding so many nodes in the denial machine" (quoted in Goldenberg and Bengtsson 2016). Beyond Peabody, bankruptcy filings by a number of other coal companies in recent years have revealed a previously hidden pattern of funding components of the denier machine by the coal industry.

During 2016, Peabody and other energy producers called on some of the leading voices in climate denial as expert witnesses in a Minnesota legal case involving where to set the appropriate social cost of carbon release. The case was a response to a filing by several environmental activist groups that the price placed on carbon and nitrogen oxide release were too low. The backdrop for the filing was that in 1993 the Minnesota legislature had enacted a statute that required the quantification of environmental costs generated by all methods of electricity generation. A central underlying issue in the case from the perspective of the environmental activists was that those who argue that the costs of solar and other renewable forms of energy are too high fail to factor in the full costs of fossil fuel production, such the cost of the release of carbon emissions in terms of climate change and global warming. Consequently, the idea of the "social cost of carbon" was developed to allow an estimation of the direct effects of carbon release on the economy in terms of the damages it causes—to human health, agricultural productivity, property from flooding or violent storms, and ecosystem services like destruction of recreational areas—and to put a monetized value on it per metric ton of CO^2 (Johnson and Hope 2012). The denier scientists hired by Peabody, William Happer, Roy Spencer, and Richard Lindzen, asserted that Earth is not warming, focused their attention on high-altitude temperatures rather than those at the planet's surface or in the oceans, misassembled data from different sources, and were highly selective in their presentation of data. All of these problems were pointed out by the two unpaid climate scientists who testified on behalf of the environmental groups who filed the case (Abraham 2016b). The judge sided with science against the denier junk science and ruled in favor of increase valuation of the social costs of carbon release (Abraham 2016c).

Not all of the wealthy deniers of climate change are rooted in the fossil fuel industry. Important examples of funders of denial whose riches comes from other sources are Robert Mercer, a reclusive tycoon closely linked to Donald Trump, and his daughter, Rebekah Mercer, head of the Mercer Family Foundation and a board member of the Heritage Foundation. The Mercer fortune was made in the hedge fund industry, specifically when, in 2009, Robert, who holds a PhD in computer science, assumed the role of co-C.E.O. of Renaissance Technologies. A New York-based investment management firm, Renaissance is one of the most profitable hedge funds companies in the country (Copeland 2015). Ironically, in light of the climate denier full-bore attack on the use of predictive modeling by climate scientists, Renaissance employs complex computer-based mathematical models—trading algorithms—to analyze and execute stock trades. These models analyze as much data as can be gathered on stock trading, seeking to identify nonrandom patterns and use this information to make predictions about which stocks to buy or sell.

While retaining a middle-class discomfort with the super rich, Mercer used his vast new income to step into the lifestyle of the rich. The Mercers left their modest home and purchased a waterfront estate with a value of $18 million—which they dubbed the Owl's Nest—in Head of the Harbor Village, an almost all-white sea-side community on Long Island. In 2013, he purchased a 203-foot, multideck superyacht with a crew of 18 and an estimated value of $75 million (Super Yacht Fan 2017).

Robert Mercer has been described as "an enigmatic figure who has a reputation for rarely speaking publicly" (Grey 2017). He has also been described as both brilliant and eccentric. Consequently, the development of Robert Mercer's political views are not known publically, although it is evident that he has connections with both the ultra-conservative and libertarian arms of the Republican Party as well as with those like the rebellious alt-right (alternative right) who distain both mainstream conservatism and the reality of multicultural America. A core figure in the alt-right is outspoken nationalist Steve Bannon, who formerly headed the alt-right media outlet Breitbart News and went on to become the White House chief strategist in the Trump administration for seven months. Mercer donated heavily to Breitbart and developed a close relationship with Bannon (Bowers 2016) until a public falling out in early 2018. Since gaining great wealth, Mercer has been using his money, "as billionaires are wont, trying to reshape the world according to his personal beliefs" (Cadwalladr 2017).

Like Scaife, the Mercers have long been part of the conspiracy-embracing, anti-Clinton cottage industry. Mercer was a principle funder, to the amount of $1.7 million, of the book *Clinton Cash*. Authored by Peter Schweizer (2014), a senior editor at Breitbart, the book was harshly critical of the large fees Hillary Clinton received for speaking engagements and the sources of donations to the Clinton charitable foundation. The book was produced by a non-profit organization called the Government Accountability Institute, which was founded by Steven Bannon. A film adaptation of the book was produced by Steve Bannon, Rebekah Mercer, and Peter Schweier. The tone and content of these sources provided much of the fodder for Trump's campaign criticisms of Hillary Clinton in 2016.

Among Mercer's views is a firm denial of global warming, a belief he has tried to advance through the significant financing of a number of aggressive denier organizations. According to a 2013 study by sociologist Robert Brulle (2013), the Mercer Family Foundation donated almost $4 million between 2003 and 2010 to groups that oppose climate change action, including the Oregon Institute of Science and Medicine. The latter entity, referred to above with reference to an often-brandished denier document known as the Oregon Petition, is headed by Arthur Robinson, a biochemist and, until 1972, a faculty member of the University of California. Robinson has given himself the title of professor of chemistry at the Oregon Institute of Science and Medicine, although the institute rarely has staff beyond Robinson's own children. From his ranch he publishes a monthly newsletter called Access to Energy which has carried articles attacking Rachel Carson (1962) and her groundbreaking book, *Silent Spring*, on the dangers of DDT as "a book filled with deliberate falsehoods and blatantly marketed unreasoning and unjustified fear;" the Environmental Protection Agency as "riddled with the worst politicos in our country," (Robinson 2012a); and the tax-financed public education system as filled with "socialist schools" (Robinson 2012b) that are "are uninterested in ability" (Robinson 2012c). He also uses the newsletter to complain about "soaking the rich" with taxes, which he views as a form of theft (Robinson 2012c); to call for a resumption of nuclear weapons testing based on his belief that the threat of radiation to health has been overblown by those he calls the "enviros," people he believes "don't have much for brains" (quoted in Bethell 2001); and to bemoan the alleged fabrications of climate science. Although he has never actually worked on climate-related issues as a scientist, he developed strong views on the issue and on the motives of climate scientists that echo timeworn denier dogma. He has justified his speaking out on issues beyond his arena of expertise by asserting, "An enemy is not beaten … unless he is, in fact, beaten. It is best to win, even if this requires actions outside one's field of specialization" (quoted in Bethell 2001).

Robinson's libertarian political views about the environment first began to come to light in 1978 when he gave a speech at the Cato Institute in which he deprecated government funding of science research as harmful to the independence of scientific inquiry (Bethell 2001). Climate scientists will only get government grants, he maintains, if their research affirms the conclusions the funders want, namely providing findings that global warming is occurring. Why the federal government, which, as indicated, provides massive subsidies to the fossil fuel industry, would be biased in favor or such conclusions is a conundrum never explained by Robinson or other climate change deniers.

While Robinson grumbles about the corrupting effects of government funding, he does not seem to worry about the pernicious effects of receiving at least $1.6 million in funding for his projects from an ideologically motivated tycoon like Robert Mercer. Yet Robinson's attempts to make a case against on climate change and to discount the IPCC have been sharply critiqued by other scientists for their manipulation, if not outright fabrication, of data, and for their incorporation of many scientific misstatements (MacCracken 2008).

Mercer has not only bankrolled Robinson's institute, he also has underwritten his series of failed runs for political office with several million dollars in campaign donations over the years (Mapes 2014), including money for attack ads. His opponent in repeated runs for office, Democratic Congressman Peter DeFazio has charged that if he were elected Robinson would push to significantly lower taxes on billionaires like Mercer, something Mercer also knows is on the agenda of the recipient of his largest donations in the 2016 election cycle, Donald Trump. Paradoxically, although Mercer, Trump's biggest funder, and Trump himself are both billionaires, during the campaign they relied on computer analysis to tract the public's resentment against elites and used this information to sculpt the campaign message. Ultimately, during and after the campaign Trump surrounded himself with Mercer affiliates like Steve Bannon, and Mercer's point of view on many issues, including climate change, became agenda items for the new administration.

There are, of course, additional deep-pocket funders of climate change denial, including some of the biggest European corporate emitters of CO^2, such as BP, BASF, Bayer, and Solvay (Goldberg 2010). These groups have donated to the political campaigns individuals running for office in the U.S. who reject the reality of global warming. Through such donations and the various strategies described above and in chapter 3, all heavily funded by individuals and corporations with massive wealth but seeking additional financial gain as well as ideological victory, the organized campaign for climate change denial has contributed to slowing down meaningful response to the grave threat posed by global warming, especially for the poor of the developing world; a growing danger examined in sites around the world address in the following five chapters based on individual case studies.

References

Abraham, J. 2015. Lamar Smith, climate scientist witch hunter. *The Guardian*, November 11. www.theguardian.com/environment/climate-consensus-97-per-cent/2015/nov/11/lamar-smith-climate-scientist-witch-hunter

Abraham, J. 2016a. Barack Obama is the first climate president. *The Guardian*, November 2. www.theguardian.com/environment/climate-consensus-97-per-cent/2016/nov/02/barack-obama-is-the-first-climate-president.

Abraham, J. 2016b. A striking resemblance between testimony for Peabody Coal and for Ted Cruz. *The Guardian*, January 20. www.theguardian.com/environment/climate-consensus-97-per-cent/2016/jan/20/a-striking-resemblance-between-testimony-for-peabody-coal-and-for-ted-cruz.

Abraham, J. 2016c. Peabody coal's contrarian scientist witnesses lose their court case. *The Guardian*, May 2. www.theguardian.com/environment/climate-consensus-97-per-cent/2016/may/02/peabody-coals-contrarian-scientist-witnesses-lose-their-court-case.

American Association for the Advancement of Science. 2011. Statement regarding personal attacks on climate scientists. AAAS. www.aaas.org/news/statement-regarding-personal-attacks-climate-scientists.

Atkin, E. 2015. Ted Cruz's bank account would soar if we increased oil and gas production. *Think Progress*. https://thinkprogress.org/ted-cruzs-bank-account-would-soar-if-we-increased-oil-and-gas-production-f3e744ad0e25.

Baer, H. 2016. The nexus of the coal industry and the state in Australia: Historical dimensions and contemporary challenges. *Energy Policy* 99: 194–202.

Bagley, K. 2015. Climate denial takes a toll on scientists—and science. *InsideClimate News*. https://insideclimatenews.org/news/11052015/climate-denial-takes-toll-scientists%E2%80%94and-science.

Bagley, K. and N. Sadasivam, 2015. Climate denial's ugly side: Hate mail to scientists. *InsideClimate News*. https://insideclimatenews.org/news/11122015/climate-change-global-warming-denial-ugly-side-scientists-hate-mail-hayhoe-mann.

Banerjee, N. 2016. Rex Tillerson's record on climate change: rhetoric vs. reality. *InsideClimate News*. https://insideclimatenews.org/news/22122016/rex-tillerson-exxon-climate-change-secretary-state-donald-trump.

Bast, J. 2017. Winning the global warming war. The Heartland Institute. www.heartland. org/news-opinion/news/winning-the-global-warming-war.

Båtstrand, S. 2015. More than markets: a comparative study of nine conservative parties on climate change. *Politics and Policy* 43(4): 538–561.

Bethell, T. 2001. A scientist finds independence: Art Robinson fights aging with his home-schooled lab rats. *American Spectator* (February). www.independentscientist.com/.

Bowers, J. 2016. A hedge fund house divided: Renaissance Technologies. Center for Reponsive Politics. www.opensecrets.org/news/2016/06/a-hedge-fund-house-divided-renaissance-technologies/.

Bradley, R. 2013. Rex Tillerson (Exxon Mobil) on climate change (energy/climate realism trumps alarmism). *Master Resource*. www.masterresource.org/exxon-mobil/exxon-mobil-trumps-alarmists/.

Brock, D. 2014. The Koch brother from another mother. *Politico Magazine*. www.politico.com/magazine/story/2014/07/the-koch-brother-from-another-mother-108709.

Broder, J. 2010. Climate change doubt is Tea Party article of faith. *New York Times*. http://chemconnections.org/general/chem120/Global%20Warming%20Party%20-%20NYT.pdf.

Brulle, R. 2013. Institutionalizing delay: Foundation funding and the creation of U.S. climate change counter-movement organizations. *Climate Change* 122: 681–694.

Cadwalladr, C. 2017. Robert Mercer: The big data billionaire waging war on mainstream media. *The Guardian*, February 26. www.theguardian.com/politics/2017/feb/26/robert-mercer-breitbart-war-on-media-steve-bannon-donald-trump-nigel-farage.

Carson, R. 1962. *Silent Spring*. New York: Houghton Mifflin.

Cato Institute. 2012. Addendum: Global climate change impacts in the United States. Washington, DC.

Center for Climate and Energy Solutions. 2015. Coal. www.c2es.org/energy/source/coal.

ClimateFiles. 2017. October 13, 1997 Exxon's Lee Raymond speech at World Petroleum Congress. www.climatefiles.com/exxonmobil/october-13-1997-exxon-lee-raymond-speech-at-world-petroleum-congress/.

Coleman, J. 2013. Mercenary Admen: 5 ways one PR group has hijacked politics for corporate gain. Greenpeace. www.greenpeace.org/usa/mercenary-admen-5-ways-one-pr-group-has-hijacked-politics-for-corporate-gain/.

Confessore, N. 2016. Father of Koch brothers helped build Nazi oil refinery, book says. New york Times, January 11. www.nytimes.com/2016/01/12/us/politics/father-of-koch-brothers-helped-build-nazi-oil-refinery-book-says.html.

Connelly, J. 2017. Trump's interior secretary: The "war on coal is over." *Seattle Post-Intelligencer*, March 29. www.seattlepi.com/local/politics/article/Trump-administration-lifts-coal-leasing-11036876.php.

Contorno, S. 2014. Fact-checking Obama's rules on carbon and coal plants. *PolitiFact*, August 14. www.politifact.com/truth-o-meter/article/2014/aug/14/fact-checks-obama-coal-rules-carbon-politics/.

Copeland, R. 2015. Renaissance Technologies to close $1 billion hedge fund". *Wall Street Journal*, October 13. www.wsj.com/articles/renaissance-technologies-to-close-1-billion-hedge-fund-1444768099.

Cornwall Alliance. 2017. Protecting the poor: ten reasons to oppose harmful climate change policies. http://cornwallalliance.org/landmark-documents/protect-the-poor-ten-reasons-to-oppose-harmful-climate-change-policies/.

Cousins, F. 2016. Could the International Criminal Court start prosecuting climate crimes? *DeSmog*, October 1. www.desmogblog.com/2016/10/01/could-international-criminal-court-prosecute-climate-crimes.

Davenport, C. and E. Lipton. 2017. How G.O.P. leaders came to view climate change as fake science. *New York Times*, May 3. www.nytimes.com/2017/06/03/us/politics/rep ublican-leaders-climate-change.html?_r=0.

Davies, K. 2016. Competitive Enterprise Institute NYT ad signatories got $10 million from Exxon. Climate Investigations Center. http://climateinvestigations.nationbuilder.com/ nyt_ad_signatories_got_10_million_from_exxon.

Davis, M. 2017. Nearly half of discovered U.S. oil resources are subsidy-dependent. Stockholm Environmental Institute. www.sci-international.org/-news-archive/3612.

DeSmog. 2015. Scaife family foundations. www.desmogblog.com/scaife-family-founda tions/.

DeSmog. 2017. American Council for Capital Formation. *DeSmog*. www.desmogblog. com/american-council-for-capital-formation.

Dickinson, T. 2007. Six years of deceit: Inside the Bush administration's secret campaign to deny global warming and let polluters shape America's climate policy. *Rolling Stone*. www.rollingstone.com/politics/news/six-years-of-deceit-20070628.

Dickinson, T. 2014. Inside the Koch Brothers' toxic empire. *Rolling Stone*. www.roll ingstone.com/politics/news/inside-the-koch-brothers-toxic-empire-20140924.

Donor's Capital Fund. 2013What is Donors Capital Fund. http://donorscapitalfund.org/ AboutUs/Overview.aspx.

Donors Trust2017. Mission & principles. www.donorstrust.org/who-we-are/mission-princip les/.

Durgy, E. 2013. The complete list of the Forbes 400 members 2013. Forbes. www.forbes. com/sites/edwindurgy/2013/09/16/the-complete-list-of-the-forbes-400-members/12/# 388bfa436c37

Dyck, M., W. Soon, R., Baydack, D. Legates, S. Baliunas, T. Ball, and L. Hancock. 2007. Polar bears of western Hudson Bay and climate change: Are warming spring air temperatures the "ultimate" survival control factor? *Ecological Complexity* 4(3): 73–84.

Eilperin, J. and S. Clement. 2013. Tea party Republicans are biggest climate change deniers, new Pew poll finds. *Washington Post*, November 1. www.washingtonpost.com/news/ the-fix/wp/2013/11/01/only-tea-party-members-believe-climate-change-is-not-happ ening-new-pew-poll-finds/?utm_term=.1fcfd849ad14.

ExxonMobil. 2008. Corporate citizenship report (2007). www.socialfunds.com/shared/rep orts/1211896380_ExxonMobil_2007_Corporate_Citizenship_Report.pdf.

Fischer, D. 2012. Fake addendum by contrarian group tries to undo U.S. government climate report. *Scientific American*. www.scientificamerican.com/article/fake-addendum-by-contrari/.

Fischer, D. 2013. "Dark money" funds climate change denial effort. *Scientific American*. www.scientificamerican.com/article/dark-money-funds-climate-change-denial-effort/.

Forbes. 2016a. America's largest private companies. #2 Koch Industries. www.forbes.com/ companies/koch-industries/.

Forbes. 2016b. The world's most powerful people. www.forbes.com/powerful-people/ list/#tab:overall.

Fortune Magazine. 2016. Full transcript of Charles Koch's interview with Fortune. http:// fortune.com/2016/07/12/transcript-charles-koch-fortune/.

Freudenberg, W., R. Gramling, and D. Davidson. 2008. Scientific certainty argumentation methods (SCAMs): Science and the politics of doubt. *Sociological Inquiry* 78: 2–38.

Frumhoff, P., R. Heede, and N. Oreskes. 2015. The climate responsibilities of industrial carbon producers. *Climate Change* 132(2): 157–171.

Goldberg, S. 2010. Tea Party climate change deniers funded by BP and other major polluters. *The Guardian*, October 24. www.theguardian.com/world/2010/oct/24/tea-party-climate-change-deniers.

Goldberg, S. 2013. Secret funding helped build vast network of climate denial thinktanks. *The Guardian*, February 14. www.theguardian.com/environment/2013/feb/14/funding-climate-change-denial-thinktanks-network.

Goldberg, S. 2015. Work of prominent change denier was funded by energy industry. *The Guardian*, February 21. www.theguardian.com/environment/2015/feb/21/climate-change-denier-willie-soon-funded-energy-industry.

Goldenberg, S. and H. Bengtsson. 2016. Biggest US coal company funded dozens of groups questioning climate change. *The Guardian*, June 13. www.theguardian.com/environment/2016/jun/13/peabody-energy-coal-mining-climate-change-denial-funding.

Gordon, N. 2005. Organizational donors. www.publicintegrity.org/2005/05/26/5838/organizational-donors.

Gorrie, P. 2007. Who's still cool on global warming? *Toronto Star*, January 1. www.thestar.com/news/2007/01/28/whos_still_cool_on_global_warming.html.

Greenpeace. 2010. Koch Industries: secretly funding the climate denial machine. www.greenpeace.org/usa/wp-content/uploads/legacy/Global/usa/report/2010/3/koch-industries-secretly-fund.pdf?9e7084/.

Greenpeace. 2016. Mercatus Center Koch Industries climate denial front group. www.greenpeace.org/usa/global-warming/climate-deniers/front-groups/mercatus-center/.

Grey, J. 2017. Reporter's notebook: Visiting the disappearing Tangier Island. CNN. www.cnn.com/2017/06/09/us/weather-tangier-island/index.html.

Hickman, L. 2011. The US evangelicals who believe environmentalism is a 'native evil.' *The Guardian*, May 5. www.theguardian.com/environment/blog/2011/may/05/evangelical-christian-environmentalism-green-dragon.

Hochschild, A. 2016. *Strangers in Their Own Land: Anger and Mourning on the American Right*. New York: New Press.

Hodges, A. 2015. The paranoid style in politics: Ideological underpinnings of the discourse of Second Amendment absolutism. *Journal of Language Aggression and Conflict* 3(1): 87–106.

Hoffer, E. 1951. *The True Believer: Thoughts on the Nature of Mass Movements*. New York: Harper.

Hoggan, J. and R. Littlemore. 2009. *Climate Cover-up: The Crusade to Deny Global Warming*. Vancouver: Greystone Books.

Jerving, S., K. Jennings, M. Hirsch, and S. Rust. 2015. What Exxon knew about the Earth's melting Arctic. *Los Angeles Times*. http://graphics.latimes.com/exxon-arctic/.

Johnson, L. and C. Hope. 2012. The social cost of carbon in U.S. regulatory impact analyses: An introduction and critique. *Journal of Environmental Studies* 2(3): 205–221.

Kaiser, R. 1999. Money, family name shaped Scaife. *Washington Post*, October 9. www.washingtonpost.com/wp-srv/politics/special/clinton/stories/scaifemain050399.htm.

Kaiser, R. and I. Chinoy. 1999. Scaife: Funding father of the right. *Washington Post*, May 2. www.washingtonpost.com/wp-srv/politics/special/clinton/stories/scaifemain050299.htm.

Karl, T. and J. Melillo. 2009. *Global Change Impacts in the United States*. Cambridge: Cambridge University Press.

Kirby, A. 2001. US blow to Kyoto hopes. BBC News. http://news.bbc.co.uk/2/hi/science/nature/1247518.stm.

Kroll, A. 2013. Exposed: The dark-money ATM of the conservative movement. *Mother Jones*. www.motherjones.com/politics/2013/02/donors-trust-donor-capital-fund-dark-money-koch-bradley-devos.

Layzer, J. 2012. *Open for Business: Conservatives' Opposition to Environmental Regulation*. Cambridge, MA: MIT Press.

Leiserowitz, A., N. Smith, and J. Marlon. 2011. *Americans' Knowledge of Climate Change*. New Haven, CT: Yale Project on Climate Change Communication. environment.yale.edu/climate/files/ClimateChangeKnowledge2010.pdf.

Leonard, C. 2013. The new Koch. *Fortune Magazine*, December 19. http://fortune.com/2013/12/19/david-charles-koch/.

Lewandowsky, S., N. Oreskes, J. Risbey, B. Newell, and M. Smithson. 2015. Seepage: Climate change denial and its effects on the scientific community. *Global Environmental Change* 33: 1–13.

Lewis, N. 1998. Almost $2 million spent in magazine's anti-Clinton project, but on what? *New York Times*, April 15. www.nytimes.com/1998/04/15/us/almost-2-million-spent-in-magazine-s-anti-clinton-project-but-on-what.html.

MacCracken, M. 2008. Analysis by Michael MacCracken of the paper "Environmental effects of increased atmospheric carbon dioxide" by Arthur B. Robinson, Noah E. Robinson, and Willie Soon. Climate Science and Policy Watch. www.climatesciencewatch.org/file-uploads/Comment_on_Robinson_et_al-2007R.pdf.

Malakoff, D. 1998. Advocacy mailing draws fire. *Science* 280(5361): 195.

Mann, M. 2016. I'm a scientist who has gotten death threats: I fear what may happen under Trump. *Washington Post*, December 16. www.washingtonpost.com/opinions/this-is-what-the-coming-attack-on-climate-science-could-look-like/2016/12/16/e015cc24-bd8c-11e6-94ac-3d324840106c_story.html?utm_term=.42714c67d44e.

Mann, M. 2017. Testimony of Dr. Michael E. Mann before the House Committee on Science, Space, and Technology. https://science.house.gov/sites/republicans.science.house.gov/files/documents/HHRG-115-SY-WState-MMann-20170329.pdf.

Mapes, J. 2014. New York billionaire spends big yet again to aid Art Robinson in race against Peter DeFazio. *The Oregonian*. www.oregonlive.com/mapes/index.ssf/2014/10/new_york_billionaire_spends_bi.htm.

Mayer, J. 2010. Covert operations. *The New Yorker*, August 30. www.newyorker.com/magazine/2010/08/30/covert-operations.

Mayer, J. 2016. *Dark Money*. New York: Doubleday.

McCright, A. and R. Dunlap. 2003. Defeating Kyoto: the conservative movement's impact on U.S. climate change policy. *Social Problems* 50(3): 348–373.

McCright, A. and R. Dunlap. 2011. The politicization of climate change and polarization in the American public's views of global warming. 2001–2010. *Sociological Quarterly* 52: 155–194.

Michaels, D. 2008. *Doubt is Their Product: How Industry's Assault on Science Threatens Your Health.* Oxford: Oxford University Press.

Michaels, P. 2009. Global warming and climate change. In D. Boaz (ed.), *Cato Handbook for Policymakers*, 7th edition. Washington, DC: Cato Institute, pp. 475–484

Michaels, P. and P. C. Knappenberger. 2017. Global warming and climate change. In *Cato Handbook for Policymakers*, 9th edition. Washington, DC: Cato Institute, pp. 627–636

Montopoli, B. 2010. Rep; Joe Barton apologizes to BP's Tony Hayward for White House "shakedown." CBS. www.cbsnews.com/news/rep-joe-barton-apologizes-to-bps-tony-hayward-for-white-house-shakedown-video/.

Mooney, C. and S. Mufson. 2016. How coal titan Peabody, the world's largest, fell into bankruptcy. *Washington Post*, April 13. www.washingtonpost.com/news/energy-environment/wp/2016/04/13/coal-titan-peabody-energy-files-for-bankruptcy/?utm_term=.75fbc7d7c423.

Morano, M. 2016. Climatologist Dr. Tim Ball: Global warming is the greatest deception in history. *Climate Depot*, December 13. www.climatedepot.com/2016/12/13/climatologist-dr-tim-ball-global-warming-is-the-greatest-deception-in-history/.

Mufson, S. and J. Warrick. 2015. Obama urges world action on climate change: no nation 'immune' to global warming. *Washington Post*, November 30. www.washingtonpost.com/business/economy/obama-urges-world-action-on-climate-change-hour-is-almost-up

on-us/2015/11/30/2765bac4-975c-11e5-8917-653b65c809eb_story.html?utm_term=.
984f3d210a5f.

National Association for the Advancement of Science. 1998. Regarding global change petition. www8.nationalacademies.org/onpinews/newsitem.aspx?RecordID=s04201998.

Nelson, L. 2001. The Roman Empire at its height. Lectures in Medieval History. University
of Kansas. www.vlib.us/medieval/lectures/roman_empire.html.

Oil Change International. 2017a. Fossil fuel funding to congress: industry influence in the
U.S. http://priceofoil.org/fossil-fuel-industry-influence-in-the-u-s/.

Oil Change International2017b. Fossil fuel subsidies: overview. http://priceofoil.org/fossil-
fuel-subsidies/.

Oreskes, N. and M. Conway. 2010. *Merchants of Doubt: How a Handful of Scientists Obscured
the Truth on Issues from Tobacco Smoke to Global Warming*. New York: Bloomsbury Press.

Pappas, S. 2011. How scientists cope as climate debate gets personal. *Live Science*. www.
livescience.com/17257-scientists-cope-personal-climate-debate.html.

Pilkington, E. 2008. Palin fought safeguards for polar bears with studies by climate change
sceptics. *The Guardian*, September 30. www.theguardian.com/world/2008/sep/30/uselec
tions2008.sarahpalin1.

Pilkington, E. 2009. Republicans steal Barack Obama's internet campaigning tricks. *The
Guardian*, September 18. www.theguardian.com/world/2009/sep/18/republicans-inter
net-barack-obama.

Piltz, R. 2007. Testimony of Rick Piltz, director, Climate Science Watch, Government
Accountability Project, U.S House of Representatives. https://democrats-oversight.
house.gov/sites/democrats.oversight.house.gov/files/migrated/20070130113813-92288.
pdf.

Readfearn, G. 2015. Climate science denier Lawson Bader named CEO at conservative
funding arm Donors Trust. *Desmog*, September 28. www.desmogblog.com/2015/09/28/
climate-science-denier-lawson-bader-ceo-donors-trust.

Readfearn, G. 2016. ExxonMobil: new disclosures show oil giant still funding climate science denial groups. *Desmog*, July 8. www.desmogblog.com/2016/07/08/exxonmobil-
new-disclosures-show-oil-giant-still-funding-climate-science-denial-groups.

Reuters. 2017. Peabody Energy emerges from bankruptcy protection. www.reuters.com/a
rticle/us-peabody-energy-bankruptcy-idUSKBN1752EZ.

Reuters. 2010. World Bank approves loan for coal-fired power plant in South Africa.
Washington Post, April 8. www.washingtonpost.com/wp-dyn/content/article/2010/04/
08/AR2010040805407.html.

Roberts, J. 2007. Groups say scientists pressured on warming. CBS/AP. www.cbsnews.com/
news/groups-say-scientists-pressured-on-warming/.

Robinson, A. 2012a. USNAS estimates DDT saved 500 million lives before it was banned.
Access to Energy. www.accesstoenergy.com/2012/01/29/ddt-and-malaria/.

Robinson, A. 2012b. Comparing models to facts: an acquired skill. *Access to Energy*, January
26. www.accesstoenergy.com/2012/01/26/comparing-models-to-facts/.

Robinson, A. 2012c. Model building: far more important than memorizing facts and pro-
cedures. *Access to Energy*, January 1. www.accesstoenergy.com/2012/01/27/model-buil
ding-far-more-important-than-memorizing-facts-and-procedures/.

Rucinski, T. 2017. Top U.S. coal miner Peabody eyes bankruptcy exit in April. Reuters.
www.reuters.com/article/us-peabody-energy-bankruptcy-idUSKBN16N2GR.

Sarah Scaife Foundation. 2015. Annual report. www.scaife.com/sarah15.pdf.

Schmidt, G. 2007. The physics of climate modeling. National Aeronautics and Space
Administration. www.giss.nasa.gov/research/briefs/schmidt_04/.

Schulman, D. 2014. *Sons of Wichita: How the Koch Brothers Became America's Most Powerful and Private Dynasty*. New York: Grand Central Publishing.

Schweizer, P. 2014. *Clinton Cash: The Untold Story of How and Why Foreign Governments and Businesses Helped Make Bill and Hillary Rich*. New York: Harper.

Science. 2017. The science contributors FAQs. www.sciencemag.org/site/feature/contribinfo/faq/#pct_faq.

Skocpol, T. and V. Williamson. 2013. *The Tea Party and the Remaking of Republican Conservatism*. Oxford: Oxford University Press.

Smith, L. 2017. Statement of Chairman Lamar Smithe (R-Texas): Climate science: Assumptions, policy implications, and the scientific method. Committee on Science, Space and Technology. https://science.house.gov/sites/republicans.science.house.gov/files/documents/HHRG-115-SY-WState-S000583-20170329_0.pdf.

Smithsonian Institution. 2008. Agreement between Smithsonian Astrophysical Observatory and Southern Company Services, Inc. https://s3.amazonaws.com/ucs-documents/global-warming/Climate-Deception-Dossier-1_Willie-Soon.pdf

Stirling, I., A. Derocher, W. Gough, and K. Rode. 2008. Response to Dyck et al. (2007) on polar bears and climate change in western Hudson Bay. *Ecological Complexity* 5(3): 193–201.

Super Yacht Fan. 2017. Yacht Sea Owl. www.superyachtfan.com/superyacht/superyacht_sea_owl.html.

Supran, G. and N. Oreskes. 2017. Assessing ExxonMobil's climate change communications (1977–2014). *Environmental Research Letters* 12: 1–18.

Tankeraley, J. 2017. Why America's middle class is lost. *Washington Post*, December 12. www.washingtonpost.com/sf/business/2014/12/12/why-americas-middle-class-is-lost/?utm_term=.1d8b7aea911d.

The Center for Media and Democracy. 2014. Federal coal subsidies. www.sourcewatch.org/index.php/Federal_coal_subsidies.

Think Progress. 2010. The oily operators behind the religious climate change disinformation front group, Cornwall Alliance. https://thinkprogress.org/the-oily-operators-behind-the-religious-climate-change-disinformation-front-group-cornwall-alliance-536175fe5e04.

U.S. Department of Justice. 2001. Koch pleads guilty to covering up environmental violations at Texas oil plant. www.justice.gov/archive/opa/pr/2001/April/153enrd.htm

Union of Concerned Scientists. 2015. The climate deception dossiers. www.ucsusa.org/global-warming/fight-misinformation/climate-deception-dossiers-fossil-fuel-industry-memos#.WP-412d1rm4.

Vidal, J. 2005. Revealed: How oil giant influenced Bush. *The Guardian*, June 8. www.theguardian.com/news/2005/jun/08/usnews.climatechange.

Walley, C. 2017. Trump's election and the "white working class": What we missed. *American Ethnologist* 44(2): 231–236.

Wayback Machine, Internet Archives. 2016. U.S. Tea Party. http://web.archive.org/web/20020821185019/http://www.cse.org:80/tea/about.php.

West, D. 2014. Republican big bucks backfire. *USA Today*, August 11. www.usatoday.com/story/opinion/2014/08/11/millionaire-inheritance-wealth-heirs-democrats-republicans-liberal-children-column/13910613/.

5

ANTHROPOLOGICAL LENS ON CLIMATE CHANGE

Anthropological lens

The anthropology of climate change extends from historic cases deep in humanity's past to contemporary cases tied to anthropogenic greenhouse gas emissions (Dove 2014). A distinctive feature of anthropology is its focus on fine-grained studies of big social issues in small places. Certainly climate change is a big issue with implications for all of humanity. But impact, expression, experience, and response to climate change occur in diverse local settings, with varying geophysical environments and sociocultural systems. As a result, the experience of climate change varies, as do the severity of its costs on human social life and well-being. Location as a factor in climate change effects does not just include geographic place but socioeconomic position in hierarchies of wealth, power, and control of resources.

Hearing the narratives of the poor, describing their coping strategies, and drawing attention to their social struggles are all within the wheelhouse of anthropology, a discipline that finds the big stories of the world playing out differently in the many small places of which is it composed. This chapter frames the importance of focusing not solely on macrostructures or the actions of elites but also on the lives, perceptions, thoughts, and actions of poor communities around the world as they encounter the effects of climate change. It provides the conceptual tools for integrating into a single model the downstream ethnographic accounts of everyday lives around the world with the upstream activities of the polluting elites primarily responsible for climate change. The chapter is framed by political ecology theory that posits a conceptual union between ecologically rooted social science and the principles of political economy. Unlike apolitical accounts of contemporary environmental crises, political ecology does not ignore the significant influence of social inequality on population health and social well-being. Moreover, with reference to these issues, political ecology asserts that it is insufficient to focus on either local cultural dynamics or international exchange relations; rather, these must be addressed in tandem. Consequently, the political ecological approach seeks to denaturalize environmental and social conditions by revealing their historic creation in political economic context. Further, unlike natural science understandings of ecological features and systems (which, with reference to climate factors, are referred to as "natural forcing mechanisms"), the approach developed in this chapter portrays anthropogenic climate and biophysical environmental change with a distinctly human face.

There are many good reasons for anthropologists to be concerned with environmental issues, including the ability of people to make a livelihood, achieve social justice, and be healthy. While climate change is a global process, it has profound, and varying, shorter and longer-term consequences for the local populations being studied anthropologically in local settings, populations that collectively comprise a large sector of humanity, as illustrated in the next five chapters on low-income populations of Alaska, Ecuador, Bangladesh, Haiti, and Mali. This approach highlights the lived experience of anthropogenic climate change as it intersects with and reflects social inequality around the world, both within and between countries.

In the contemporary world of interconnection and the rapid flow of people, objects, ideas, commodities, and corporate activity, local worlds, those of people's immediate perception and experience, are not made only at the local level, but rather are embedded in historic and ongoing connections and impacts that occur across levels and as a result of cross-cutting processes including climate change (Wolf 1982). Modern anthropological investigation focuses its research lens at various scales and especially at nixes of intersection and flow between the local and the global. It is in this context that an anthropology of environmental change has emerged with an emphasis on "the importance of inserting anthropological arguments into [contemporary] debates on climate change" (Hirsch et al. 2011: 267). Why anthropology? According to Howe (2015: 239),

> Beyond our ability to detail local responses to specific renewable energy projects or climate change policies, and beyond our ability to express the values and cultural contingencies at work in these (often fraught) political and social domains, … anthropologically informed analysis has a capacity, and even a responsibility, to provide parallels, points of contrast, and polydimensional interpretations of energy transition and climate change mitigation.

Ecological perspectives in the anthropology of the environment and climate change

Anthropology is a diverse field and it incorporates various points of view and theoretical models. As a result, there is no single universally shared anthropological perspective on climate change—or many other topics—and hence the use of "perspectives" in the subheading. In this book, the emphasis is on those perspectives that draw attention to issues of social structure, power, and inequality, as these loom as critical to forces both driving climate change and resisting mitigation efforts despite the increasing vulnerability of large segments of the global population. Two perspectives that have been employed by anthropologist in climate change research are examined below, cultural ecology and critical anthropology (Baer and Singer 2018).

Cultural ecology: anthropologists and the environment

Historically an important anthropological perspective on human/environment relations is known as cultural ecology or, more recently, ecological anthropology. This approach dates to the work of Julian Steward (1902–1972). Steward argued that throughout human history, pre-industrial societies were closely linked to their environments, but he did not accept the previously widely shared theory of environmental determinism which claimed that human culture systems are fully shaped by their environments. Steward recognized the complexity of the environment, and that people interact with the environment, extracting resources from it through their technological system, which includes local knowledge about the environment. For example, in fishing societies this would include where it is best to fish and how to make and use fishing equipment, as well as how to clean and prepare fish for consumption. Culture, in other words, is not narrowly shaped by the environment because technological systems developed or adopted by people living in even quite similar environments can vary considerably. He also drew attention to the patterns of behavior associated with different technological practices (e.g. fishing vs farming). Steward concluded that human cultural systems are shaped through interaction between their existing technoknowledge systems and the environmental factors that directly affect them. In short, people are active players in the making of themselves, their cultural systems, and the environment, but the latter also plays a role in influencing cultural systems (Timmerman 2015).

From the cultural ecological perspective, the environment presents possibilities for resource extractions and sets constraints on what is likely to be undertaken given the costs and benefits of various strategies in a given setting. For example, irrigation agriculture is much more likely to develop in areas with flowing rivers than in arid environments without immediate water sources. Still, in some settings, intensive and expensive hydraulic systems have been adopted to move water to dry regions to support agricultural production. A good example is the mountain terrace construction of pools of water to support wet rice or padi production (a Malaysian word that means rice on a stick, referring to the growth of rice under water). Padi construction and maintenance requires a significant labor investment, and considerable reshaping of the environment, but it has proven successful in several parts of the world.

There is a strong tendency in cultural ecology to define culture as an informational and behavioral system that facilitates a community's adaption to the opportunities and challenges presented by its local environment, although there is recognition that culture can include environmentally maladaptive components as well. The issue from the cultural ecological perspective is not optimal adaption but adequate adaption to allow the maintenance of a cultural system over time and the adequate well-being of the population. Of course, some adjustments to environmental opportunities can be quite productive and allow the development of a surplus. This was the case in pre-contact Hawaii, which developed a hierarchical system of social ranks, including, at the top, regional or island-wide chiefs. Surplus production from fishing, agricultural, and other activities was transferred to the chief. While much of the surplus was redistributed to insure everyone had enough to live on—while affirming the generosity of the chief—some was retained to support the chiefly household and attendants.

As noted in chapter 2, what happens to a surplus, including how it is distributed in society, is a critical issue for this book. In this light, the question can be raised: was the industrial revolution, which enabled a monumental boost in the harnessing and use of physical energy embedded in the environment adaptive or maladaptive, as well as the corollary question; adaptive, or more accurately, advantageous and disadvantageous for whom?

Cultural ecology understands each individual cultural system as having evolved in and adapted to specific local eco-niches, such as savannahs, deserts, arctic tundra, semi-arid conditions, coastal areas, or arboreal or tropical rainforests. As Adger et al. (2003: 170), point out, however, while cultural systems are fundamentally adaptive there may be some groups in society that are more vulnerable to climate change than others. In other words, adaptation is not necessarily based on equity, and, in fact, may occur because of the imposition of power and the oppression of—and extraction of the labor of—lower-status social sectors. Hidden in the concept of adaptation is the issue of advantage: adaption does not mean equitably beneficial adaptation.

According to Milton (2008: 59), the "ecosystem approach developed by ecologists in the 1940s and 1950s, and adopted into anthropology in the 1960s, held no place for an understanding of culture in its narrower sense—people's thoughts, feelings and knowledge about the world." As this statement implies, the framework of cultural ecology did not easily lend itself to asking questions that some anthropologists see as central to the mission of the discipline and to their understanding of culture. These tend to include cognitively rooted questions such as how the conception of the environment relates to the internal conception of society, or how people's attitudes about the world shape their specific engagements with it, or the ways knowledge about the environment are structured within cultural systems, including the evenness (or unevenness) of the dispersal of such information across gender, ethnicity, or other social divisions.

Although Steward's concept of cultural ecology was widely adopted by anthropologists and archaeologists during the mid-twentieth century, it ran into strong criticism for seemingly, to some, as a resurrection of environmental determinism and for failing to address culture as a cognitive system. Nonetheless, it remains a part of the legacy of anthropological understanding and is an influence on modern political ecology. and hence on contemporary anthropology. Today, it finds expression in ecological anthropology, which Orlove (1980: 235) defined as

> the study of the relations among the population dynamics, social organization, and culture of human populations and the environments in which they live … . In many cases, systems of production constitute important links among population dynamics, social organization, culture, and environment. Defined as such, ecological anthropology provides a materialist examination of the range of human activity and thus bears an affinity to other materialistic approaches in the social and biological sciences.

On the issue of climate change, cultural ecologists Sutton and Anderson (2004: xiii) note that "[o]ne of the goals of most cultural ecological work is to use … knowledge in an effort to stem global catastrophe." They state: "deforestation releases massive amounts of greenhouse gases as the trees are burned or allowed to decay. These gases have been a factor in global warming, although fossil fuels are a far more serious cause" (Sutton and Anderson 2004: 298).

During their Arctic Climate Impact Assessment project, Nuttall and co-workers assessed the influence of climate change on subsistence patterns and adaptive strategies of indigenous Arctic peoples, past and present. They maintain that "as the climate changes, the indigenous peoples of the Arctic are facing special challenges and their abilities to harvest wildlife and food resources are already being tested" (Nuttall et al. 2004: 685). In other words, because of climate change environments are not stable and cultural systems must constantly adjust to this flux. Both systems in this process, the physical environment and the cultural system, are dynamic and, as a result, creating multiple opportunities for maladaptation and enhanced vulnerability.

The larger Arctic Climate Impact Assessment project (2004: 92) found that

> Across the Artic, indigenous people are already reporting the effects of climate change. In Canada's Nunavut Territory, Inuit hunters have noticed the thinning of sea ice, a reduction in the numbers of ringed seals in some places, and the appearance of insects and birds not usually found in their region.

In the same vein, Athabaskan people in Alaska and Canada report changes in weather patterns, and both plant and animal life, while the Saami reindeer herders of Norway have experienced changes in wind patterns that have forced them to change their traditional travel routes.

Several anthropologists who use a cultural ecological approach incorporate the concepts of "risk" and "resilience" into their analysis of climate change. Nuttall (2009: 298), for example, in his work on the Inuit, people who are indigenous to Greenland, argues that their culture is characterized by flexibility and ecologically resilient, traits that enable them to "adjust to climate variation and change, to move around, and to see and seize opportunities in the environment." In recent research,

Nuttall (2018) has paid particular attention to the "weather words," as he has found that the terms people use to describe changing weather and sea conditions offer insights into their experience of the effects of climate change on the environment. The Inuit word "*putsineq*," for example, refers to slushy ice and traditionally was most commonly used in the spring as the warming weather diminished the solidity of the ice. Today, however, the word is heard in January and February, reflecting one of the changes wrought by global warming. Words as they used in everyday communication convey meanings that are critical to everyday survival in the Artic and elsewhere. They are, from the perspective of cultural ecology, part of the adaptive process.

Hastrup (2009: 15) also notes that the risks related to climate change are unevenly distributed, leading to "new patterns of regional migration, political unrest, economic vulnerability, shifting resource bases, and a profound sense of risk affecting everyday life in many parts of the world." Under these conditions, she maintains, resilience is not only a question of systemic (social or cultural) adaptation to external factors but also a fundamental component of any working society (Hastrup 2009). Resilience in the face of climate change is a topic of growing concern among anthropologist, as addressed in a series of cases in the next five chapters.

Orlove, along with Agrawal, Lemos, and Ribot created the Initiative on Climate Adaptation Research and Understanding through the Social Sciences (ICARUS), an intentional referencing of the mythical Icarus who was given a pair of wax and feather wings by his father, Daedalus, the great craftsman. Despite his father's cautionary pleadings, Icarus flew too close to the sun, which melted his wings, and he fell into the sea and drowned. Climate change also draws attention to the risks of the heat of the sun and the failure to recognize the risks of technology. In this light, ICARUS was founded to bring together researchers and practitioners to increase social scientific contributions to the understanding and response to climate change (Agrawal et al. 2012). These researchers focus on three primary topics that are informed by cultural ecology: a) theorizing key concepts like vulnerability, adaptation, adaptive capacity, and resilience; b) understanding the causal structures of vulnerability, effects of adaptation, and the empirical referents of both adaptation and vulnerability at various social scales; and c) understanding and informing the formation of climate change adaptation policy. Specifically, the Initiative is concerned with identifying and analyzing in detail concrete human responses to climate change as they are experienced in known social, economic, cultural, and political settings. As Agrawal et al. (2012: 330) state: "Such research can also help document the ways effective adaptation is achieved and the conditions and forms of interventions likely to produce maladaptive responses and outcomes."

In other words, a goal of applied anthropology from the cultural ecological perspective, is the study of local adaptive tactics in order to fashion both acceptable and effective interventions in light of the growing threats of climate change.

McElroy and Townsend (2009), two anthropologists well known for their work in applying ecological models in medical anthropology, view "traditional ecological knowledge" as an adaptive mechanism that enables the limiting of vulnerability to environmental conditions including climate change. They see ecological approaches as asking questions like: how do people survive under varying environmental conditions? What social, and cultural resources do they employ in addressing their perceived health needs? Is a population growing or shrinking, healthy or unhealthy, and how do these features reflect environmental challenges and interactions?

Like Agrawal and colleagues, in her own work, Townsend (2011: 191) argues that the greatest contribution of anthropology to the study of global climate change is likely to be the steady accumulation of local-level, small-scale studies of how human populations have adapted, or failed to adapt, to drastic changes in a changing climate, including quite contrastive changes like the melting of polar ice and rising seas and the spread of the desert's edge into previously arid but non-desert areas. Townsend and Masters (2015), for example, have used a cultural ecology approach in developing a local knowledge and science-based proposal for increasing "ecological and social-ecological resilience in tropical mountain ecosystems experiencing rapid climate change."

However, based on their respective field research projects, Crate and Nuttall (2009: 9) ponder whether the "frames of adaptive capacity and resilience … are sufficient" because the "ability to respond to climate change is severely constrained for many people around the globe." They argue:

> Resilience, both social and ecological, is a crucial aspect of the sustainability of local livelihoods and resource utilization, but we lack sufficient understandings of how societies build adaptive capacity in the face of change. Furthermore, we suspect that environmental and cultural change, far beyond the reach of restoration, is occurring … . Some of us feel we are in an emergency state as field researchers and struggle to design conceptual architecture sturdy enough to withstand the storminess of the intellectual and practical challenges before us.
>
> (Crate and Nuttall 2009: 10–11)

Observes Crate (2009: 147), "we need not be overly confident in our research partners' capacity to adapt." One of the reasons for the threat to resiliency produced by climate change she points out is the potential to cause relocation, which can result in a breakdown of locally situated environmental knowledge:

> [C]limate change is forcing not just community adaptation and resilience, but also relocation of human, animal, and plant populations. Lost with those relocations are the intimate human—environment relationships that not only ground and substantiate indigenous worldviews but also work to maintain and steward local landscapes. In some cases, moves also result in the loss of mythological symbols, meteorological orientation, and even the very totem and mainstay plants and animals that ground a culture.
>
> (Crate 2009: 147)

Wrenched from familiar environments and with social networks disrupted, climate change refugees may suffer a loss of meaning in life and a sense of purpose. One result may be a breakdown of resiliency and a failure to adapt, leading to catastrophe for impacted populations. As this discussion suggests, there are limits to resilience and sociogeographic barriers to climate change adaptation, especially among poorer populations. This point is a shared concern with the critical anthropology of climate change.

These types of cultural ecological studies, based on ethnographic and archeological research on climate change response, represent a dominant segment of the growing literature on the anthropology of climate change. The cultural ecological perspective applied to the anthropology of climate change addresses questions about sociocultural responses to the challenges presented by the climatic chaos of a warming planet. The perspective draws attention to the ways people collectively react and use their cultural systems to try and handle new threats and develop novel behaviors in the face of climate change adversity. But available options for response may be inadequate to cope with radical enviroclimatic change given the multiple expressions of climate change that are occurring at an ever-faster pace. The issue of social inequality is a factor here because of the differential capacity to cope in hierarchical societies, which reflects differences in access to resources.

The critical anthropology of climate and environmental change

As suggested by the last quoted comments by Crate, there is a need for a more critical understanding of climate change in social context that transcends the issue of adaptation. The critical anthropology perspective on climate change is guided by an ecosocial perspective that draws on three theoretical models that come from within and beyond anthropology: 1) world systems theory and its particular application within an ethnographically informed anthropology; 2) political ecology theory with its understanding of the politicized nature of human interaction with the environment; and 3) critical health anthropology and its emphasis on the social determinants of health inequalities.

First, world systems theory, which began with the work of Emmanuel Wallerstein (1974), a historical social scientist, understands capitalism not as the economic system shared by countries that are otherwise diverse and independent but rather as an economic and social system that surpasses national boundaries and ties regions and countries together hierarchically around distinguishing three features: the privatization of the means of production, a market-based distribution of goods and services, and the control of human labor as a commodity that can be bought and sold. These particular features of capitalism create two interlocked social orders. The first involves the hierarchical ordering of relationships among the countries of the world involving a tripartite division into: 1) economically dominant core countries that are mass producers of greenhouse gases; 2) developing but still economically subordinate semi–periphery countries, some of which have already become major greenhouse gas emitters; and 3) periphery countries with relatively weak and potentially unstable governments and local economies focused on extracting and exporting raw materials to core nations, and often being the repository of the waste products of core countries (e.g. electronic devises, car batteries) for local extraction of sellable components and environmental disposal. The second hierarchy involves human labor and the construction of social classes. As anthropologist Eric Wolf (1982: 354) observed, a market economy "creates a fiction that this buying and selling [of labor] is a symmetrical exchange between partners, but in fact the market transaction underwrites asymmetrical relationship between classes." Consequently, in ways that parallel the climate change features of the world economic system, wealthier (i.e. production-owning, labor-buying, and more powerful) classes most benefit from the processes that lead to the emission of greenhouse gases into the atmosphere, as this produces no cost for them, while the poorest classes, because of reigning policies and practices of environmental injustice and limited protective resources, suffer disproportionate harm from climate change.

Adopting world systems theory leads to the asking of questions such as: to what degree do core countries economically require that the periphery remain underdeveloped? How do core countries benefit from climate change denial and uncertainty? Can the world system be changed to be more equitable? In its deployment within anthropology, and in light of the discipline's historic focus, research questions have been directed at the nature of the relationship of macro-level forces and structures and more micro-level social realities and actions, including issues of indigenization of foreign cultural elements, resistance, resilience, and emergent cultural heterogeneity in the face of the homogenizing tendencies of globalism. On the one hand, neoliberal globalization has pushed toward ever-greater degrees of cultural and especially structural uniformities around the world. On the other, indigenization, the reconfiguration of global forms to fit local cultural designs for living, has pushed back in the direction of increased cultural diversity. The clash of these countervailing forces raises the importance of paying close theoretical attention to macro-micro-exchange and its determination.

A complementary process of globalization is localization: the creation and assertion of highly particular, often place-based, identities and communities. For example, young Bakongo men from the Democratic Republic of the Congo (Tamagni 2009), who call themselves Sapeurs (Society for the Advancement of People of Elegance), often compete with one another by trying to acquire the most stylish French and Italian clothes. They wear and care for this finery in social environments of extreme poverty. Research indicates that they do this not to copy wealthy Europeans but rather to accumulate personal prestige and project their self-worth, and, further, to rebel against their marginal place in society, and, indeed, in the world system. Localization often is reflected in patterns of consumption, a traditional mode in which people express their local identities. People use clothing to convey cultural messages, but consumption patterns may communicate very different things, depending on specific cultural and historical influences. Hence at first blush conclusions about homogenization often prove problematic under closer anthropological scrutiny.

The second theoretical model, political ecology theory, is a multidisciplinary perspective that developed out of the study of societies in environmental context, especially the cultural ecology initiative discussed above (e.g. Cole and Wolf 1974, Wolf 1972). The political ecology perspective emphasizes the fundamental importance of the interplay among political, economic and environmental factors in the making of society (Foster 1994, Roberts and Grimes 2002). Political ecology transcends the traditional cultural ecological approach by addressing the role of power in the unequal distribution of the costs and benefits of environmental access and change across class, ethnic, or other social divisions, the ways this unequal distribution reinforces (or, in particular contexts, reduces) social and economic inequalities in society, the political consequences of environmental changes, and the adverse effects of human activities on the environment. Moreover, the political ecological approach focuses on how the actions of more powerful groups within and across societies adversely affect the environment in ways that endanger the well-being of less powerful groups. Robbins (2012: vii) cites climate-influenced Hurricane Katrina as perhaps greater than any other recent environmental event in tearing

> back the veil on the structural inequalities or race and class in the United States, which are physically inscribed on the seascape, implicated in the ecological transformation of the coastal zone, and inseparably linked to the flow of water through the Mississippi delta.

A specifically anthropological approach to political ecology investigates environmental degradation and change by investigating the power relations, economic and social structures, and associated cognitive and value systems that comprise dominant cultural systems and resistances to prevailing hierarchies. As summarized by Harper (2004: 296):

> rather than seeing human societies and cultures as adapting to environmental change, political ecologists tend to view the social impact of environmental change, and the social forces shaping it, as uneven, with certain groups adapting effectively to environmental changes, others failing to effectively adapt, and still others engaging in behaviors that might be adaptive in the short term that, ultimately, are maladaptive for the larger cultural group.

The final theoretical component is critical health anthropology (Baer et al. 2016). This is a theoretical perspective that developed during the 1980s, initially under the title of critical medical anthropology, that focuses attention on the nature and causes of human health, illness, and treatment. During the early years of anthropology's engagement with health issues, explanations within the subdiscipline were framed narrowly with a primary focus on the nature of health-related beliefs and behaviors at the local level in terms of specific ecological conditions, cultural configurations, or psychological factors. While increasing our understanding of local and non-biomedical health models, the original perspectives in the field tended to overlook the wider causes and determinants of human health. Societies were treated as social wholes rather than being seen as linked to a world economic system that in many settings included complex colonial and related histories. Questioning the value of explanations that are limited to accounting for health-related issues in terms of the influence of human personalities, culturally constituted motivations and understandings, or even local ecological relationships, early critical health anthropologists pointed to the importance of understudied "vertical links" that connect the local social group to larger and cross-cutting regional, national, and global processes, including factors like commodification and the capitalist market, the globalization of production and the restructuring of labor, and the spread of biomedicine as a reflection of the penetration of capitalism globally. The critical approach defined health not as a narrow expression of biological states but as access to and control over the basic material and non-material resources that sustain and promote life at a high level of satisfaction.

Since it emerged, critical health anthropology has drawn attention to questions about the social origins of illness, including the ways poverty, discrimination, structural and physical violence, exposure to stress and stigmatization, disease interactions in social context, inequity in healthcare, and anthropogenic environmental degradation shape health. More recently, critical health anthropology has focused more intensely on environmentally mediated inequalities in health, such as the role of polluting industries and the polluting elite in causing disease and creating disparities of health across social classes, genders, or ethnic populations (Baer 2009, Singer 2011).

Integrating components of these three approaches, the critical anthropology of climate change asks questions about the relationship of the capitalist mode of production and planet sustainability, the role of power in the production and release of greenhouse gases and industrial pollution, the social origins and social impact of the climate change denier movement, the unequal distribution climate change health effects, unequal access to climate change knowledge, the contradictions of green capitalism, and local and wider social movements that have emerged in opposition to business-as-usual corporate environmental degradation. In short, the critical anthropology of climate change seeks to develop an integrative understanding of the interface of power and social hierarchy in the anthropogenic making of climate change and other environmental disruptions and their unequal health and social consequences, differential experiences across social groups, and the responses that develop as people struggle to cope with climate change turmoil.

Conventional economic thinking accepts the premise that the global economy must continue to grow and, further, that humans have an inherent need to consume and to acquire things of social and individual value. In the modern world, regardless of whether it be in a developed country, an advanced developing country, or even in more peripheral nations, capitalist hegemonic ideology about human acquisitiveness has diffused broadly and been naturalized as "common-sense thinking" and hence beyond question. Yet, social discomfort and even panic arise in capitalist circles if retail sales slump and the economy begins to stagnate. During times of recession—which continue to occur despite announcements about achieving a recession-proof economy—hope collapses and poor and working people eventually begin to grow uneasy and questioning, even rebellious. Reflecting these concerns, Singer and co-workers (2016) carried out a study of climate change knowledge and concern in an inner-city Latino population in Hartford, CT. Based on interviews with community members, the study identified four themes in their responses: (1) there were a range of ideas among participants about climate change, including some ideas that aligned with the findings of climate science and others that did not; (2) worry and uncertainty about climate change; (3) a shared sense of not knowing enough and strongly wanting to know more about climate change; and (4) feeling excluded from government-sponsored preparation efforts that improve confidence about coping with the future of climate turmoil. Participants, in short, were very concerned about climate change but felt disempowered to make the kinds of broad societal change suggested by the threats of poverty and climate change.

An important lesson of anthropology is that human nature is highly malleable. If we live in a capitalist society, most people around us will be socialized to be highly desirous of acquiring new and presumably better things to make our lives easier, mark our successes, and reward our efforts in life. But under capitalism, our impulses to acquire more are stimulated routinely by massive advertisements campaigns that play out in every penetrable space around us, including all electronic and social media, billboards, gas pumps, bus shelter posters, print advertising, direct mail, posted advertisements on the walls of sports stadiums, on race car drivers' uniforms, through commodity giveaways, through company-promoting philosophic donations, and much more. Advertising has invested vast sums of money to develop literally thousands of ways for a company to channel its message to the consumer. The message of advertising is the creation of various wants and seeming needs that can only be filled through the acquisition and consumption of products.

This development was not the natural evolution of a cultural pattern, but was the product of a profit-driven strategy. In the 1927 words of Paul Mazur, a Wall Street banker working for Lehman Brothers in the 1930s, at one time the fourth-largest investment bank in the United States, "People must be trained to desire, to want new things even before the old had been entirely consumed. We must shape a new mentality in America" (quoted in Lubin 2013). In the new consumer culture, values and behaviors once seen as immoral moved from the periphery to the heart of core capitalist nations. The emphasis shifted from living frugally within one's means to the unmitigated pursuit of personal pleasure and gain, or at least the intense desire to have great material possessions even if this was unachievable. People came to be willing to fall into ever-greater debt in their pursuit of a materially defined and advertisement encouraged "good life." These patterns eventually appeared intrinsic to life itself.

In this kind of society, in analyses stemming from the thought of Italian political economist Antonio Gramsci, people are influenced by a cultural hegemony of motivated consumerism. Cultural hegemony involves the social diffusion through all of the dominant institutions of society of a set of ideas, norms, and values that have their origin in the dominant social class but come to be perceived as natural and inevitable by all classes. But from an anthropological perspective developed through the study of diverse societies in time and location, the question is raised: is consumerism natural, is it an inherent characteristic of human nature? As numerous ethnographic studies of societies not closely tied to the capitalist world system, have shown, people in these societies tend to emphasize sharing and reciprocity rather than the accumulation of material goods or achievement of status through the mere accumulation and retention of material possessions.

Consumer capitalism which had been growing since early in the 21st century really began to take off in the early 1950s, when households in developed societies were flooded with messages, primarily through their new TVs, about new "labor-saving" appliances and devices. These energy-using machines were described as making life easier and as markers of the new leisure life of accomplishment. Other consumables like frozen and prepared foods added to the list of time and labor-saving commodities available to those enculturated to the post-war consumption-oriented era of capitalism. Linked to the ethic of unrelenting consumption was a message of optimism. This included an advertisement-created idealized modern family consisting of a father, mother, son ,and daughter who collectively shared in and enjoyed the newfound comforts of their first track home, the pride and con-venience of a shiny new car, and asserted increased shared family leisure and recreational time. For the first time, minors became the targets of advertising with the promotion of records, record players, radios, magazines, clothing, soft drinks, other teen-oriented products that ultimately, with the development of the internet and mobile phones, would feed the rise of a global youth culture. Throughout the 1950s, corporate advertising expenditures increased to unprecedented levels.

Given it profit-motivated predilection for built-in obsolescence, capitalism encourages people to update older models of all their commodities with newer, better ones. Further, sociologist Zygmunt Bauman (2011: 24) reports that "Europe and the United States spend 17 billion dollars each year on pet food, while according to some experts, just \$19 billion is needed to save the world's population from hunger." Although developed societies constitute the leading cultures of consumption, several rapidly developing societies, such as China and India, are quickly joining the pack of intense consumer nations. Many of the refrigerators, air conditioners, washing machines, televisions, and computers manufactured in China are exported, yet increasing numbers of them stay "at home" and are sold to the members of the new Chinese middle class as well as to the Chinese elites. More-over, travel outside of China has significantly increased and shopping for foreign goods is a prime driver of this trend (Zipser et al. 2016).

Linda Connor argues that climate change constitutes a cultural crisis across societies "that begs critical anthropological analysis" (Connor 2012: 1). She found during interviews with religious believers in the Hunter Valley of New South Wales that almost all of her participants connected climate change "to the threat of an ending, although there was a variety of 'end' scenarios, dominated by humanistic rather than apocalyptic views." Pentecostals, however, tend to deny climate science's assertions about the reality of changing climatic patterned, but, even if climate change is occurring, they have faith the Apocalypse will provide them with an afterlife. For Connor (2012: 12–13), capitalism functions as an artificial "immortality system" in which "consumerism engenders and sustains feelings of pleasure and future security though linking self-identity with values and practices of acquisition, affluence, endless exploitation of nature, novelty, and perpetual renewal." Lost in the embrace of consumer culture is recognition of the dangers of exceeding limits of resource extraction and by-product emission.

Adding to the literature on the critical anthropology of climate change is James Trostle's (2010) identification of a contradiction between the World Bank's historic statements and actions on climate issues. The World Bank is an international financial institution that provides loans to developing countries for capital programs which has a history of pressuring countries to adopt structural adjustment and market-based reforms. Structural adjustment programs have been used by the World Bank and other international lending institutions to promote the kind of market fundamentalism—namely, only a market-driven economy can produce wealth—that comprises the dominant feature of neoliberalism. As Pfeiffer and Chapman (2010) point out, the stories anthropologists bring home from the field indicate intensified immiseration caused by neoliberalism's elimination of public sector services for the poor.

Moreover, as Trostle notes, the World Bank's World Development Report 2010: Development and Climate Change states that efforts must continue to reduce poverty and sustain development, especially because climate change will make this even more difficult, and that addressing climate change is critical because it threatens all countries and especially poor ones. Consequently, economic growth alone is not the answer to resolving climate change. World behavior and public opinion must be changed so that new policies can be developed and implemented at all levels, local, regional, national, and international. Despite these assertions, Trostle notes that many World Bank-sponsored development projects in developing countries, such as large-scale fossil fuel power plants, are contributing to greenhouse gas emissions, and the Bank's 2010 report failed to acknowledge its role in increased emissions. To improve the chances that their voices are heard, Trostle urges anthropologists to learn the language of modeling researchers and adopt methods for crossing conceptual scale. In the years since Trostle's paper was published, a number of anthropologists have followed his advice and some anthropological voices have been heard by quantitative, model-oriented climate scientists. Hastrup (2013: 269) adds:

> While natural scientists have generally taken the lead in the debate on the consequences of climate change, social scientists are increasingly invited to take part in the discussion; it has convincingly been argued that the issue of climate

change is not simply a 'prediction problem' but a more complex question of how great risk society is willing to take on behalf of future generations … .

In his own research on climate-related diarrheal diseases, Trostle and colleagues (Carlton et al. 2014) note that global climate change may increase the total burden of diarrheal diseases on human populations, especially among the poor. These diseases are a leading cause of childhood morbidity and mortality, responsible for approximately 700,000 deaths annually in children under five. To investigate this relationship, these researchers carried out weekly surveillance for diarrhea in 19 villages in Ecuador in order to evaluate whether biophysical and social factors modify vulnerability to heavy rainfall events (defined as 24-hour rainfall exceeding the 90th percentile value in a given seven-day period), a noted feature of climate change. They found a relationship between heavy rainfall events and the incidence of diarrheal disease in their study villages, affirming this significant health risk of climate change for the poor.

Within the social worlds brought into being by global capitalism, there are more than a billion people in the world, sometimes referred to as the bottom billion, who must go without many of their needs met, while at the same time there are many others who consume much more than they need and acquire much more than they can use. As Gardiner (2017) observes with reference to Britain, the expanding home wealth of the rich is connected to the shrinking wealth of other classes:

> The 21st Century rise in multiple property ownership is set against a backdrop of the overall decline in home ownership over the past 15 years … . These twin trends – fewer people with any properties and more with many – underpin the growing concentration of housing assets that is fueling the recent increase in overall wealth inequality.

Not only are high-level consumption patterns creating great social divide, they are draining natural resources and degrading the natural environment through the process of converting them into commodities, including producing greenhouse gas emissions that are driving climate change. Global warming and anthropogenic environmental changes raise the question of how long humanity can continue to expand its population and wide-ranging places of habitation in the late half of the twenty-first century and beyond. Further, contemporary climate change forces us to question whether global capitalism must be surpassed by an alternative economic system if life as we know it on the planet is to be sustainable.

From the critical anthropology perspective, climate change constitutes one of the most important environmental challenges faced by humanity, although in the short run and in local contexts other environmental crises, many of them anthropogenic in origin, may be more immediately pressing. Climate change is of such importance because it has global impact, has multiple adverse expressions, and is related to and entwined with many of the other environmental threats. Some of these other ecocrises facing the planet and its inhabitants include acid rain and acidification of the oceans (which, like greenhouse gas, comes from the burning of fossil fuels), disappearance of wetlands (which exacerbates the flooding caused by climate change), air pollution (which is made more damaging by global heating), salinization of fresh water sources (caused by a drop in rainfall due to climate change), a global potable water crisis (contributed to by climate change), deforestation (enhanced by climate change), and a general loss of biodiversity through extinctions (advanced by climate change).

As noted, the capitalist world system exhibits numerous contradictions, including 1) its emphasis on profit-making, endless economic expansion, and its embrace of the treadmill of production and consumption; 2) the growing socioeconomic gap it creates and maintains between rich and poor both within nation-states and between nation-states; 3) the exhaustion of natural resources and environmental degradation, the most profound form of which is climate change; 4) population growth, which in large part is stimulated by ongoing poverty; and 5) the resource wars carried out by various developed countries in advancing the interests of multinational corporations. Climate change underlines the unsustainability of the capitalist world system and its impact does not occur in a vacuum but rather is significantly magnified by interactions with other ecocrises. For example, as I have noted elsewhere (Singer 2013), the respiratory risks to human health, as exemplified by the global frequency of diseases like asthma around the globe, is a product of the combined effects of anthropogenic air pollution and climate change. An important cause of this increase in respiratory disease is interaction between heavier pollen loads, noxious molds, wildfires, thunderstorms and extreme precipitation events (related to climate warming), and diminished air quality due to industrial, vehicular, chemical, and other sources of air pollution. While various ecocrises are a grave hazard

> because the respiratory system is a primary body nexus for diverse environmental threats to cluster, intermingle, and multiply their adverse impacts (e.g. diesel fuel droplets and bacteria, allergens and infectious agents), there is a second set of threats to respiratory health also being ushered in by global warming.
>
> *(Singer 2013: 98)*

It is inevitable that in the short run humanity must adapt to the changes wrought by global warming. From the perspective of the critical anthropology of climate change, the longer-term issue is that of mitigation (Baer 2008). This entails significantly cutting greenhouse gas emissions in order to ensure the survival of human life as we know it, or better yet, a more equitable form of human life, as well as preserving other species and the biodiversity upon which human life depends. For example, significantly changing the way industries make things would contribute towards mitigating greenhouse gas release. In some cases, simply redesigning a product cannot only improve the product's life span but also lead to a more efficient use of resources, easier recycling, and less pollution during the manufacturing process and life of the product. Modern technical innovations like recycling heat waste and closed-cycle production processes can save both natural resources and money, while also lowering emissions. Remanufacturing and reconditioning, which are both labor-intensive activities, can create new jobs while cutting emissions. However, as noted, the engine driving most manufacturing in the world, certainly almost all large-scale industrial manufacturing, is an economic perspective that promotes continual increases in production. While technical fixes can help, only approaches that alone or in combination significantly lower emissions will be adequate to effectively diminish the risks of global warming.

A parallel argument can be made for the transportation sector. People have been enculturated to embrace a motorized lifestyle, which, while highly profitable for vehicle manufacturers and the energy industry, produces significant air pollution, over a million fatal traffic accidents per year, and greenhouse gas emission. Yet, there is little indication that the global appetite for private vehicular transport is diminishing. Vehicle use in developing countries is increasing, and at the current rate, the total global number of vehicles on the planet is set to triple by 2050. Investment in public transportation and vehicle efficiency, however, is limited. Research suggests that a green, low-carbon transport sector could substantially reduce greenhouse gas emissions but it is not occurring. For it to happen, there would need to be a major shift toward sustainable/renewable low-waste producing fuels, public transportation, and non-motorized transport, as well as improved and empowered city planning to moderate transport needs.

Additionally, there is the problem of waste. The ideal way to manage waste is to produce less of it, and thus minimizing waste must be an integral part of greenhouse gas mitigation. The goals of authentic mitigation programs must be to produce as little waste as possible with the goal building a zero-waste society, recycling or remanufacturing as much as possible, and treating any unavoidable waste in a manner that is the least harmful to the environment and humans. Capitalist production, however, promotes waste (e.g., in packaging, product obsolesce, promotion of novelty) as it both facilitates sales and drives consumer culture.

Since the late 1980s, climate regimes—agreements designed to mitigate climate change—have emerged at the international, regional, provincial, state, or even local levels. Most climate regimes take capitalism for granted as the reigning world economic system. Specifically, climate regimes embrace a set of so-called green capitalist strategies such as greenhouse gas emissions trading schemes, enhanced energy efficiency, use of recycling, and related practices based on the assumption that they can render the world system environmentally sustainable. Various corporations, politicians, policy makers, research scientists, and academics advocate for green capitalism based on the belief that this approach is not only good for the quality of life on the planet but increasingly may be very profitable. Another expression of green capitalism is speculative materialism. Whitmore (2016) cites two imaginative but unsuccessful examples. The first involved a company proposal submitted to the Australia's Carbon Farming Initiative to generate saleable carbon offsets by culling a population of approximately two million wild camels and thereby eliminating their methane emissions. The proposal was rejected. The second example was developed by an entrepreneur–inventor who was searching for investors. This for-profit initiative sought to build numerous buoys to circulate on the open ocean. The buoys would contain passive deep-water pumps that would pull up deep nutrient-rich waters to stimulate plankton growth for carbon sequestration and offset sales. After the failure of the 2009 UN climate conference to make real progress in significantly cutting emissions or implementing a carbon offset scheme, the plan to commodify carbon sequestration technologies was jettisoned.

Historically, corporations have resisted the assertions of environmental activists that they engage in practices that are immediately damaging to the environment while significantly contributing to long-term climate change. However, a growing number of corporations have begun to assert publically that they can achieve sustainable development while reducing their greenhouse gas emissions through technological modernization. A case in point is Tyson Foods, Inc., one of the world's largest producers of meat and poultry. The company has a broad portfolio of products and brands like Tyson, Jimmy Dean, Hillshire Farm, Ball Park, Aidells, and State Fair. Tyson's pollution footprint includes manure from its contract growers' factory farm operations, fertilizer runoff from grain grown to feed the livestock it brings to market as meat, and waste from its processing plants. Tyson historically has been responsible for dumping more toxic pollution by volume into U.S. waters than companies like Exxon and Dow Chemical. A substantial portion of Tyson's discharges are nitrate compounds which can contribute to algal blooms and water dead zones (where little or no life survives), and also constitute a threat to human health (Environment America Research & Policy Center 2016).

At a shareholders' meeting early in 2018, Jay Ford, a representative of the Commonwealth of Virginia's Eastern Shore, asked Tyson to reconsider its plans to construct 250 new chicken houses containing 55,000 birds each to supply broilers to two local plants looking to expand capacity. Ford noted (quoted in Souza 2018):

> The 250 new houses are going to an area that already has 300 houses and the two plants have already racked up considerable violations from regulators that impact the Chesapeake Bay area … . We are asking that Tyson honor its promise to be a good neighbor and take the necessary stewardship steps to protect our water that this community depends upon.

Ford's group asked Tyson Foods to adopt a water stewardship program and require suppliers to follow sustainable practices to ensure good water quality and introduced a shareholder's proposal supporting its position. Tyson's board of directors recommended that shareholders vote against this proposal, and they did.

Despite this event, in recent years Tyson has tried to change its image as a major environmental polluter through the adoption of green capitalist strategies. These changes include initiatives designed to reduce company truck miles, such as installing ultra-light equipment, using direct shipment to customers, and partnering with rail carriers. The company has explored various other ways to reduce emissions, lower fuel consumption, and decrease greenhouse gases while improving the miles per gallon performance of its fleet of company trucks. But Tyson remains committed to continued growth and expansion. As the company announces on its website (Tyson 2018): "Strong operating cash flows, a prudent capital allocation strategy and the financial flexibility to make strategic acquisitions position Tyson Foods to achieve long-term profitable growth." A commitment to never-ending growth and increased profit-making explains the actions of Tyson's board despite its public embrace of sustainability.

Without question, technological innovations, such as increasing use of renewable sources of energy and improving energy efficiency, have a critical role to play in climate change mitigation, but as long as they are wedded to the capitalist imperative of constant economic growth even these measures cannot contain climate change in the long run. Consequently, the critical anthropology of climate change contends that green capitalism faces insurmountable limitations in mitigating climate change.

Thus, climate change obliges us to engage in a serious evaluation of alternatives to global capitalism and its inherent acceptance of unbridled growth. The critical anthropology of climate change has as one of its defining features the analysis of social justice initiatives that attempt to make current societies more socially equitable and environmentally sustainable. Consequently, the critical anthropology of climate change perspective maintains that it is necessary to think outside of the socially allowable box constructed by the capitalist world system by identifying or developing alternatives to global capitalism as the ultimate and vitally needed climate change mitigation approach.

Despite historic espousal in many capitalist nations of individual freedoms, including the freedom of expression, there has often been little acceptance of truly critical thought, as some ideas are delegitimized by not being considered worthy of serious consideration. This mechanism of social control is deeply embedded in the tapestry of capitalist society, finding expression overtly or more covertly across most social institutions. For example, one of the ways researchers have brought to light subtle academic forms of hierarchicalization and legitimation is through the analysis of what is known as the politics of citation (Mott and Cockayne 2016). In this form of discriminatory academic politics, authors tend to be cited based their relative status in a field of study or the stature of their home institutions, as well author gender, ethnicity, and sexual orientation, while texts that question reigning social mythologies about the capitalist world system are ignored through a process of academic snubbing (i.e. rarely being cited). Beyond citation, there is the politics of publication, including processes by which academic manuscripts achieve or fail to achieve publication. The need for academic publication is summed up by the well-known phrase "publish or perish," which is used to describe the constant pressure faced by academics to publish their work. Achieving a solid publishing record matters because it can impact job prospects, promotion, research grants, and fellowships—in short, it can make or break careers. Consequently, there is considerable pressure on academics to avoid truly critical thought.

Nonetheless, the critical anthropology of climate change questions analyses that fail to consider how local patterns connect to the world system and to the distribution and direct and hegemonic roles of power in society locally, regionally, and globally. At the same time, it finds unsatisfactory top-down explanations that over-generalize local variation in interface with the global.

Like critical anthropology generally, the critical anthropology of climate change embraces an applied or activist/scholar stance that entails the merger of theory and social action. Known as praxis or engaged scholarship, this approach maintains that knowledge production and academic teaching are not the only responsibilities of scholars. In a world facing crisis where lives are at stake, mobilizing knowledge in the creation of beneficial social change is also necessary. Like many others involved in the anthropology of climate change, regardless of their orientation, the critical anthropology of climate change promotes collaboration with local communities and other marginalized and subordinated populations and social movements dedicated to fighting global warming. As indicated, the critical anthropology of climate change asserts that there are fundamental contradictions between capitalism and the sustainability of human and other lifeforms. This view is informed by recognition that no social system lasts forever.

A review of the historic records for 74 ancient civilizations by Larry Freeman (2016) found that the average length of time that a civilization lasts is 349.2 years. The capitalist world system is about 600 years old but contains multiple inherent contradictions, including promoting climate and causing environmental degradation, that may forecast it future collapse.

It is for this reason that the critical anthropology of climate change perspective believes that the current world system must be surpassed to ensure the future of humanity and animal and plant life on Earth. There is a need for an alternative global system, one that is committed to meeting people's basic needs, social equity and justice, democracy, biodiversity, and environmental sustainability. Proposals for such an alternative system have had various labels, including global democracy, Earth democracy, economic democracy, eco-anarchism, and eco-socialism. But we are in a time when capitalism is still overtly strong and it is evident that the struggle for alternatives will not be easy. Certainly, the number of anthropologists and other progressive social scientists is too small to lead such struggle against global warming and capitalism. Instead, they must use their skills to form links with anti-systemic movements, including the labor, anti-corporate globalization, social justice, peace, indigenous and ethnic rights, and environmental movements, women's movements, and the growing climate or anti-global warming movement (Baer 2009).

The effort to examine the impact of climate change on humanity and how to mitigate it has to be a broad collaboration that includes both natural and social scientists, public health workers, policy analysts, and humanists and anti-systemic and environmental grassroots movements. Going from the present capitalist world

-system to a different sustainable political economy, however it is defined, will require massive effort, and there are no guarantees that such efforts will succeed. But is there a valid alternative?

In building a critical anthropology of climate change, Lahsen (2005a) carried out ethnographic research on how climate models and atmospheric scientists handle issues of certainty and uncertainty associated with computerized models that seek to project possible global climatic changes emanating from greenhouse gas emissions. She also has written about U.S. climate politics and discussed the role that "conservative and financial elites" play in supporting campaigns to deflect growing concerns among Americans about climate change (Lahsen 2005b), as well as how Northern countries dominate the framing of science that underpins international environmental and climate negotiations (Lahsen 2007). In her commentary (2008) on Crate's seminal article which, as noted earlier, asserts that anthropologists are strategically well situated to interpret the impact of climate change on local populations, communicate information about this process, and even respond to climate change both in the field and at home as advisors to climate policy decision-makers and as advocates for the people they study, Lahsen (2008: 587) perceptively observes:

> To truly enhance our effectiveness and overcome our marginality in scholarship and policy arenas related to global change research, we need to study all types of relevant "locals" and especially those populating institutions of power. That means overcoming our abated but continued aversion to study power brokers such as scientists, government decision makers, industry leaders, journalists, and financial elites, all of whom are much more important in shaping climate change and associated knowledge and policies than are the marginal populations we are accustomed to studying.

More recently, Lahsen (2013) has warned that by promoting an overly idealized understanding of science, social scientists risk increased public vulnerability to climate denier campaigns.

Like Lahsen, David Rojas (2016) has studied scientists who are attempting understand and respond to climate change through collaboration with various partners including industry to develop carbon markets and other modes of privatized environmental management. But these scientists are not actually hopeful that such mitigation schemes will work. Rather, they are burdened with the likelihood of widespread human suffering caused by unchecked global warming. So, Rojas asks, why do these scientists engage in such collaboration? He found that it is because they presume that humanity is entangled in planetary changes that we may have initiated but which now are out of our control and will not be contained by techno-managerialism. While climate scientists would prefer rigorous conservationist regulations, they work with industry to make the best use of ecological potential in light of the unwillingness of government to enact such regulation. Thus, Rojas (2016: 22) quotes one scientist who asserted, "I don't think it is legitimate to criticize [carbon market forestry] because it does not solve capitalism's problems."

In another critical anthropology study, Verity Burgmann and Hans Baer (2012) examined Australian climate politics at three levels, from above, in the middle, and from below. In looking at contemporary Australia, they note that it has thoroughly adopted a consumer culture as described above. In the first part of their book, they assessed climate politics from above, namely the corporations and federal and state governments. These researchers point out that there is a robust public concern about climate change and environmental degradation in Australia, but "from above" they encounter euphemisms, delays, and compromises by both of the two major political parties.

The public also is exposed to deliberate obfuscation of the issues and resistance to developing renewable energy by corporate and industrial interests, as well as being exposed to misrepresentations of climate change in the corporate media. Bergmann and Baer refute the rhetorical claims to disinterested impartiality made by the major political parties, such as the neo-liberal democratic claim to support a free market. Instead of addressing the widespread public concern about environmental damage by investing public funds in renewable energy, both major Australian parties ignore the free market principle and direct public funds into subsidizing the private mining and energy companies. As Connor (2016: 233) points out, the Australian government's 2015 Energy White Paper envisions the country as a "global energy superpower" dominated by fossil fuels well into the future. This pattern reflects the power corporations have in shaping government policy.

In terms of climate politics in the middle, they looked at a range of entities including the Australian Greens, the major environmental non-government organizations, academic research centers, think tanks, public intellectuals, and the trade union movement. Actors in the middle they found frequently reach out to the burgeoning movement from below and participate in ground-level climate movement activities, but also occasionally develop formal and informal input into the very top level of climate politics. For example, these entities can engage in official consultations or off-the-record conversations with relevant ministers or public servants. Finally, in terms of climate politics from below, they investigated the grassroots climate movement including the various local, regional, and nationwide climate movement groups and networks and far-left groups to whom climate change confirms their worst suspicions about global capitalism. Paying attention to grassroots groups is crucial to the authors' sense of the potential for change. They find that the ways people in grassroots politics are able to join forces with entities in the middle to reject the compromises and complicity of federal politics, thereby reclaiming the role of moral and civic leadership on climate change in Australia, indicate that it is possible to fight back effectively against those higher up in the social hierarchy.

Raminder Kaur (2011) is another anthropologist who worked with a critical climate change perspective in her examination of how Indian elites are promoting a nuclear state as a mechanism for responding to climate change. India is not the only country where there is the promotion of nuclear energy as a remedy for climate change. But, as Kaur (2011: 277) comments, "critics continue to dispute the hijacking of environmentalism … and argue that if climate change is the problem, then nuclear power is by no means a solution."

Richard Wilk also alludes to a critical anthropology of climate change understanding in his critique of the notion of individual overconsumption as the cause of climate change. He observes that many consumption choices are made by "governments, regulatory agencies, and businesses" rather than by individuals (Wilk 2009: 266). Anthropology and the other social sciences, he comments, have "provided only fleeting and partial answers to questions of why have human beings become so insatiable" (Wilk 2009: 269). While an anthropology of consumption is certainly undeveloped, this effort must begin with the recognition that global capitalism spends billions of dollars marketing the commodities it produces using communication strategies designed to create a strong sense that people need numerous items to lead full, meaningful, and enjoyable lives. Wilk observes that most non-renewable resources, such as copper, iron, and coal, are still in abundant supply, while various renewable resources, such as timber and fish, are in danger of being depleted due to overconsumption and population growth. He argues, "[t]he most immediate ecological dangers of pollution, extinction, and climate change are due more to waste, poor regulation, and unregulated emission than to the using up of resources" (Wilk 2009: 266). In short, it is those who control resources and shape emission policies and practices—the polluting elites— who are the primary culprits.

Since the release of the 2010 World Development Report, physician-anthropologist and health activist Jim Yong Kim was selected by President Obama to fill the presidency of the World Bank, an organization he once proposed should be abolished. Kim's nomination met with vocal opposition in part because he was the lead co-editor of an anthology titled *Dying for Growth* (Kim et al. 2000) and was lead author on its chapter on the imposition of neo-liberalism on Peru. Consequently, a number of economists within and outside the Bank argue that Kim was anti-growth. In a BBC interview (BBC News 2012), however, he responded to these assertions by stating: "I'm very much for capitalist market-based growth, which will create jobs and at the same time, lift people out of poverty." In the foreword to the World Bank's (2012) report 4°: Turn Down the Heat: Why a 4°C World Must be Avoided, a document which takes the findings of climate science on the impact of climate of changes on the environment and human societies seriously, Kim (2012: ix) emphasized that "The lack of action on climate change not only risks putting prosperity out of reach of millions of people in the developing world, it threatens to roll back decades of sustainable development." From a critical anthropological perspective, however, the notion of sustainable capitalist development is problematic in that it tends to imply the possibility of a complementarity between economic expansion and environmental sustainability.

In a subsequent *Washington Post* editorial titled "Make climate change a priority," Kim affirmed that the World Bank is committed to preventing a climate catastrophe through its $7 billion-plus Climate Investment Fund, which is purportedly "managing forests, spreading solar energy and promoting green expansion for all cities, all with the goal of stopping global warming" (Kim 2013). Kim's perspective was further confirmed in an interview with the Guardian, during which, according to Larry Elliott, Kim claimed that:

> reducing poverty … was impossible without growth, and 90% of new jobs would be created by thriving private sectors. But he said growth on its own was not enough, and governments needed to adopt policies that made growth more inclusive.
>
> *(Elliott 2015)*

At the Climate action Summit in 2016, Kim (2016) further stressed the rising danger of climate change,

> We have no time to waste. Delay is not an option … . We must regain the sense of urgency we all felt on the eve of COP21 [21st yearly session of the Conference of the Parties to the 1992 United Nations Framework Convention on Climate Change]. Inaction means we will not meet our targets set in Paris, and the global temperature will soar above 2 degrees Celsius. That would spell disaster for us, for our children, and for the planet.

Despite his deep and unquestionable concern for effectively addressing the issues of poverty and climate change, Kim appears to be overlooking the increasing number of scholars and activists who are challenging the growth paradigm associated with the capitalist world system, especially in light of the mounting evidence that the fossil fuel-driven treadmill of production and consumption is contributing not only to increasing social inequality around the world but also to the depletion of natural resources and climate/environmental crises. Kim and the World Bank have become proponents of ecological modernization, a perspective popular not only in certain corporate and governmental circles but also among many social scientists. Proponents of ecological modernization embrace the notion that climate change can be sufficiently mitigated through the adoption of various technological innovations, such as greater development of renewable sources of energy, enhanced energy efficiency, expanded use of public transit, adoption of electric cars, and other related "tech-fix" approaches. Thus in his Climate Action Summit 2016 presentation, Kim (2016) praised the city of Rio de Janeiro's implementation of "energy efficient trains to improve services, cutting travel times for poor people living on the city's outskirts, and providing them with access to jobs, schools and health care."

But there is no consideration in the ecological modernist approach as to whether capitalism itself, with its emphasis on constant growth, is compatible with sustainability.

Conclusion

In sum, while the critical anthropology of climate change recognizes along with ecological approaches the importance of the human/environment interface, central to the perspective is a concern with the ways that structures of social inequality and power impact how humans engage and interact with ecological systems and the differential impacts of this engagement across social and national divisions. Of particular importance in the perspective of the critical anthropology of climate change is the role of polluting elites in the production and release of plant-warming greenhouse gas and the ways this process endures because of power of elites and the burdens of social inequality. Moreover, climate change contributes to social inequality and to social suffering among marginalized social groups as it further diminishes their health and well-being.

As discussed in this chapter, the anthropology of climate change has produced alternative perspectives, and with them, differing sets of questions that anthropological researchers bring to their encounter with climate change issues. While alternative perspectives can lead to debate and disagreement, this is not an inherently negative occurrence as even heated discussion can lead to new insights, raise new questions, and result in productive synergies.

References

Adger, W., J. Paavola, S. Huq, and M. Mace (eds). 2003. *Fairness in Adaptation to Climate Change*. Cambridge, MA: MIT Press.

Agrawal, A., M. Lemos, B. Orlove, and J. Ribot. 2012. Cool heads for a hot world: Social sciences under a changing sky. *Global Environmental Change* 22(2): 329–331.

Arctic Climate Impact Assessment. 2004. Impacts of a warming Artic. Cambridge: Cambridge University Press.

Baer, H. 2008. Global warming as a by-product of the capitalist treadmill of production and consumption: The need for an alternative global system. *Australian Journal of Anthropology* 19: 58–62.

Baer, H. 2009. The environmental and health consequences of motor vehicles: A case study in capitalist technology and hegemony and grassroots responses to it. In M. Singer and H. Baer (eds), *Killer Commodities: Public Health and the Corporate Production of Harm*. Walnut Creek, CA: AltaMira Press, pp. 95–118

Baer, H. and M. Singer. 2018. *The Anthropology of Climate Change: An Integrated Critical Perspective*, 2nd edition. Abingdon, UK: Routledge, Earthscan.

Baer, H., M. Singer, D. Long and P. Erickson. 2016. Rebranding our field: Towards an articulation of health anthropology. *Current Anthropology* 57(4): 494–510.

Bauman, Z. 2011. *Collateral Damage: Social Inequalities in a Global Age*. London: Polity.

BBC News. 2012. Jim Yong Kim takes top job at World Bank. www.bbc.co.uk/news/business-17757480.

Burgmann, V. and Baer, H. 2012. *Climate Politics and the Climate Movement in Australia*. Melbourne: Melbourne University Press.

Carlton, E., J. Eisenberg, J. Goldstick, W. Cevallos, J. Trostle and K. Levy. 2014. Heavy rainfall events and diarrhea incidence: The role of social and environmental factors. *American Journal of Epidemiology* 179(3): 344–352

Cole, J. and Wolf, E. 1974. *The Hidden Frontier: Ecology and Ethnicity in an Alpine Valley*. Berkeley, CA: University of California Press.

Connor, L. 2012. Experimental publics: Activist culture and political intelligibility of climate change action in the Hunter Valley, Southeast Australia. *Oceania* 82: 228–249.

Connor, J. 2016. Energy futures, state planning policies and coal mine contests in rural New South Wales. *Energy Policy* 99: 233–241.

Crate, S. 2009. Gone the bull of winter? Contemporary climate change's cultural implications in Northeastern Siberia, Russia. In S. Crate and M. Nuttall (eds), *Anthropology and Climate Change*. Walnut Creek, CA: Left Coast Press, pp. 139–152.

Crate, S. and M. Nuttall (eds). 2009. *Anthropology and Climate Change: From Encounters to Actions*. Walnut Creek, CA: Left Coast Press.

Dove, M. 2014. *The Anthropology of Climate Change: An Historic Reader*. Chichester, UK: John Wiley & Sons.

Elliott, L. 2015. Scrap fossil fuel subsidies now and bring in carbon tax, says World Bank chief. *The Guardian*, April 13. www.theguardian.com/environment/2015/apr/13/fossil-fuel-subsidies-say-burn-more-carbon-world-bank-president.

Environment America Research & Policy Center. 2016. As shareholders mull clean water resolution, new data shows Tyson one of nation's top water polluters. https://environmentamerica.org/news/ame/shareholders-mull-clean-water-resolution-new-data-shows-tyson-one-nations-top-water?_ga=2.206234899.1249530868.1523315005-1506111406.1523315005.

Foster, J. 1994. *The Vulnerable Planet: A Short Economic History of the Environment*. New York: Cornerstone Books.

Freeman, L. 2016. How long did the empires of ancient civilizations last? *Owlcation*. https://owlcation.com/humanities/How-long-do-empires-last.

Gardiner, L. 2017. Homes sweet homes: The rise of multiproperty ownership in Britain. Resolution Foundation. www.resolutionfoundation.org/media/blog/homes-sweet-homes-the-rise-of-multiple-property-ownership-in-britain/.

Harper, J. 2004. Breathless in Houston: A political ecology of health approach to understanding environmental health concerns. *Medical Anthropology* 23: 295–326.

Hastrup, K. 2009. Waterworlds: Framing the question of social relevance. In K. Hastrup (ed.), *The Question of Resilience: Social Responses to Climate Change*. Denmark: Det Kongelige Danske Videnskabernes Selskab, pp. 11–30.

Hastrup, K. 2013. Anthropological contributions to the study of climate: past, present, future. *Wires Climate Change* 4: 269–281.

Hirsch, J., Phillips, S., Labenski, E., Dunford, C. and Peters, T. 2011. Linking climate action to local knowledge and practice: A case study of diverse chicago neighborhoods, In *Environmental Anthropology Today*, Kopina, H. and Shoreman-Ouimet, eds. Philadelphia: Taylor & Frances Group.

Howe, C. 2015. Latin America in the Anthropocene: Energy transitions and climate change mitigations. *Journal of Latin American and Caribbean Anthropology* 20(2): 231–241.

Kaur, R. 2011 A "nuclear renaissance": Climate change and the state of exception. *Australian Journal of Anthropology* 22: 273–277.

Kim, J. 2012. The latest predictions on climate change should shock us into action. *The Guardian*, November 19. www.theguardian.com/global-development/poverty-matters/2012/nov/19/latest-predictions-climate-change-shock-action.

Kim, J. 2013. Make climate change a priority. *Washington Post*, January 25. http://articles.washingtonpost.com/2013-01-24/opinions/36527558_1_global-carbon-dioxide-emissions-climate-change-climate-and-energy.

Kim, J. 2016. Remarks by World Bank Group President Jim Yong Kim at Climate Action Summit 2016. World Bank. www.worldbank.org/en/news/speech/2016/05/05/remarks-world-bank-group-president-jim-yong-kim-climate-action-summit.

J. Kim, J. Millen, A. Irwin, and J. Gershman (eds). 2000. *Dying for Growth: Global Inequality and the Health of the Poor*. Monroe, MA: Common Courage Press.

Lahsen, M. 2005a. Seductive simulations? Uncertainty distribution around climate models. *Social Studies of Science* 35(6): 895–922.

Lahsen, M. 2005b. Technocracy, democracy, and U.S. climate politics: The need for demarcations. *Science, Technology & Human Values* 30(1): 137–169.

Lahsen, M. 2007. Trust through participation? Problems of knowledge in climate decision making. In Mary E. Pettenger (ed.), *The Social Construction of Climate Change: Power, Norms, and Discourses*. Aldershot, UK: Ashgate, pp. 173–196.

Lahsen, M. 2008. Commentary on "Gone the bull of winter? Grappling with the cultural implications of and anthropology's role(s) in global climate change" by Susan A. Crate. *Current Anthropology* 49: 587–588.

Lahsen, M. 2013. Climategate: The role of the social sciences. *Climate Change* 119(3–4): 547–558.

Lubin, G. 2013. Culture. *Business Insider*. www.businessinsider.com/birth-of-consumer-culture-2013-2.

McElroy, A. and T. Townsend. 2009. *Medical Anthropology in Ecological Perspective*, 5th edition. Boulder, CO: Westview Press.

Milton, K. 2008. Climate change and culture theory: The need to understand ourselves. In H. Baer (ed.), *The Impact of Global Warming on the Environment and Human Societies*, pp. 39–52. PASI Research Paper No. 1. School of Philosophy, Anthropology, and Social Inquiry, University of Melbourne.

Mott, C. and Cockayne, D. 2016. Citation matters: Mobilizing the politics of citation toward a practice of "conscientious engagement." *Gender, Place and Culture* 24(7).

Nuttall, M. 2009. Living in a world of movement: Human resilience to environmental instability in Greenland. In S. Crate and M. Nuttall (eds), *Anthropology and Climate Change*. Walnut Creek, CA: Left Coast Press, pp. 292–310.

Nuttall, M. 2018. Artic weather words. *Anthropology News* 59(2): 7–10.

Nuttall, M., F. Berkes, B. Forbes, G. Kofina, T. Vlassova, and G. Wenzel. 2004. Hunting, herding, fishing and gathering: indigenous people and renewable resources. In C. Symon, L. Arris, and B. Heal (eds), *Impacts of a Warming Arctic: Arctic Climate Impact Assessment*. Cambridge: Cambridge University Press, pp. 649–690.

Orlove, B. 1980. Ecological anthropology. *Annual Review of Anthropology* 9: 235–273.

Pfeiffer, J. and R. Chapman. 2010. Anthropological perspectives on structural adjustment and public health. *Annual Review of Anthropology* 39: 149–165.

Robbins, P. 2012. *Political Ecology: A Critical Introduction*. Chichester, UK: John Wiley & Sons.

Roberts, J. and P. Grimes. 2002. World-system theory and the environment: Toward a new synthesis. In R. Dunlap, F. Buttel, P. Dickens, and A. Gijswijt (eds), *Sociological Theory and the Environment: Classical Foundations, Contemporary Insights*. Lanham, MD: Rowman & Littlefield, pp. 167–198.

Rojas, D. 2016. Climate politics in the Anthropocene and environmentalism beyond nature and culture in Brazilian Amazonia. *PoLAR: Political and Legal Anthropology Review* 39(1): 16–32.

Singer, M. 2011. Down cancer alley: The lived experience of health and environmental suffering in Louisiana's chemical corridor. *Medical Anthropology Quarterly* 25: 141–163.

Singer, M. 2013 Respiratory health and ecosyndemics in a time of global warming. *Health Sociology Review* 21(1): 98–111.

Singer, M., J. Hasemann, and A. Raynorm. 2016. "I feel suffocated": Understandings of climate change in an inner city heat island. *Medical Anthropology* 35: 453–463.

Souza, K. 2018. Tyson Foods shareholder meeting includes optimism, protestors. TB&P. https://talkbusiness.net/2018/02/tyson-foods-shareholder-meeting-includes-optimism -protestors/.

Sutton, M. and E. Anderson. 2004. *Introduction to cultural ecology*. Walnut Creek, CA: Alta-Mira Press.

Tamagni, D. 2009. *Gentlemen of Bacongo*. London: Trolley Books.

Timmerman, P. 2015. The ethics of re-embedding economics in the real: Case studies. In P. Brown and P. Timmerman (eds), *Ecological Economics for the Anthropocene: An Emerging Paradigm*. New York: Columbia University Press, pp. 21–65.

Townsend, P. 2011. The ecology of disease and health. In M. Singer and P. Erickson (eds), *A Companion to Medical Anthropology*. Malden, MA: Wiley-Blackwell, pp. 181–195.

Townsend, P. and K. Masters. 2015. Lattice-work corridors for climate change: A conceptual framework for biodiversity conservation and social-ecological resilience in a tropical elevational gradient. *Ecology and Society* 20(2): 1 .

Trostle, J. 2010. Anthropology is missing: On the World Development Report 2010: Development and Climate Change. *Medical Anthropology* 29: 217–225.

Tyson. 2018. Tyson foods unveils new innovations as part of its continued evolution into a modern food company. www.tysonfoods.com/news/news-releases/2018/2/tyson-food s-unveils-new-innovations-part-its-continued-evolution-modern.

Wallerstein, I. 1974. The rise and future demise of the world capitalist system: Concepts for comparative analysis . *Comparative Studies in Society & History* 16(4): 387–415.

Whitmore, J. 2016. What does climate change demand of anthropology? *PoLAR: Political and Legal Anthropology Review* 39(1): 7–15.

Wilk, R. 2009. Consuming ourselves to death: The anthropology of consumer culture and climate change. In Susan A. Crate and Mark Nuttall (eds), *Anthropology and Climate Change*. Walnut Creek, CA: Left Coast Press, pp. 265–275.

Wolf, E. 1982. *Europe and the People Without History*. Berkeley, CA: University of California Press.

Wolf, E. 1972. Ownership and political ecology. *Anthropological Quarterly* 45(3): 201–205.

World Bank. 2012. Turn down the heat: Why a 4°C warmer world must be avoided. World Bank, Washington, DC.

Zipser, D., Y. Chen, and F. Gong. 2016. Here comes the modern Chinese consumer. McKinsey & Company. www.mckinsey.com/industries/retail/our-insights/here-com es-the-modern-chinese-consumer.

6

CHANGING WORLD OF THE INDIGENOUS ALASKAN YUPIK AND IÑUPIAT PEOPLES

Indigenous people in changing Alaska

The Eskimo, as they came to be called by European arrivals in the New World, are part of a group of indigenous peoples who inhabit the northern circumpolar region running from eastern Siberia in Russia, across Alaska, Canada, and Greenland. The term Eskimo, by which they are still popularly known outside of their communities, means "a person who laces a snowshoe." It was the name used for them by the Algonquin Native American people who were their southern neighbors. French fur traders who encountered the Algonquin, adopted the word but transliterated it as Esquimau, which came, in English, to be Eskimo. Even the term Inuit, which is now replacing Eskimo in Canada, is problematic for the indigenous people of Alaska because of language and some cultural differences among the northern dwellers across their wide range. In Alaska, the term Eskimo is still commonly used by indigenous people because it includes both the non-Inuit Yupik and Iñupiat peoples. Complicating matters further, the aboriginal peoples of Canada and Greenland see Eskimo as a pejorative term, preferring Inuit as a self-reference. The word Yup'ik comes from the indigenous term *yuk*, meaning person, while *pik* means real (i.e. real people). Iñupiat, another language and cultural grouping in the north, also means real people. In addition to traditional languages, English is general spoken by the indigenous people of Alaska because, in boarding schools, children were punished for speaking their own languages.

With such a wide dispersal across very challenging natural Arctic conditions, the indigenous northern peoples developed highly successful cultures closely attuned to their local environments, including extensive environmental knowledge and understanding of the making and use of human and dog-powered technologies derived from local resources. These they have used to produce tools, transport themselves, make clothing, build protective structures, and even produce art.

Women's household tools included a fan-shaped slate knife, stone seal-oil lamps, and skin-sewing implements made from stone, bone, and walrus ivory. Men's tools were for hunting and included various types of spear, harpoons, snow goggles, ice canes, and bows and arrows. The skins of birds, fish, marine mammals, and land animals were used to make clothing. The clothes of hunters were designed to be insulated and waterproof (Alaska Humanities Forum 2017a).

Traditionally, most northern groups were semi-sedentary, depending on the location where they lived. Some of the groups, especially those in the interior, moved from site to site following herds of caribou, while others, living along the coast, spent a considerable amount of time in permanent communities such as Barrow, but they too moved at certain times of the year to fishing camps or game-hunting areas. At times in the past, small groups of northern peoples no doubt suffered from breakdowns in their access to wild food sources as a result of natural forces. But most of the time in most locations people were well nourished and ate a nutritionally balanced diet. Their wild food menu provided all of the essential nutrients, including vitamins, minerals, protein, and energy-rich polyunsaturated fatty acids, when prepared and consumed using traditional patterns (Draper 1977).

Their dwellings ranged from semi-subterranean shelters dug into the earth and covered by driftwood, packed dirt and the skins of harvested animals to summer tents of animal hides. Homes were occupied by nuclear families but might include extended kin members. Children were seen as the reincarnation of a recently deceased relative. As Hippler (1974: 453) noted, "Eskimo values stressed cooperation, avoidance of aggression, subordination of oneself to others, honesty, openness, [and] sharing of goods … ." Nevertheless, interpersonal conflicts and violence were not unknown.

Anthropologist Marshall Sahlins (1968) introduced the term original affluent society to refer to hunter/gatherers like the indigenous people of Alaska. Swimming against the tide that viewed forager type societies as living near the brink of survival and often on the edge of starvation, Sahlins reviewed various newer studies and used them to support the argument that they did not suffer from deprivation but instead lived in a kind of society in which all the people's wants were relatively easily satisfied much of the time. He termed this affluence because they could get what they needed, but this included desiring little and meeting their needs with what is readily available in the environment. It is affluence without abundance, but, if needs and desires are met, it is affluence nonetheless. Their mode of production requires some degree of mobility, as game moves and migrates and plant resources become available in new locations throughout the season. Mobility limits the amount of possessions possible, as large items cannot be moved, which minimizes acquisitiveness and surplus. People in many locations were dispersed much of the year in small settlements and seasonal camps that contained extended families or small groups of families. Through their detailed and subtle knowledge of their environment, foragers may live meagerly by outside standards but are able to turn unreliable and shifting natural resources into a rich subsistence base. In this way, they are able to provide for themselves efficiently without spending all of their time acquiring food. There is time for dance, songs, storytelling, courting, healing rituals, and other aspects of cultural systems.

The resources they relied upon and their muscle-based technology were constraints on population growth. The U.S. Census Bureau (2000) estimated the Yupik and Iñupiat peoples to number approximately 24,000 in Alaska in 2001, but the population has grown since then. And life has changed in many ways for the indigenous Yupik and Iñupiat peoples of Alaska since the territory was acquired from the Russian Empire in 1867 and became a state in 1959. The Americans chose Alaska, an Aleut name, for their vast new territory. American settlers, who believed there were riches to be had in Alaska, rushed there. Shortly after Congress approved the treaty to purchase Alaska, more than 30 ships sailed from San Francisco carrying fortune seekers. The great Klondike gold strike in 1896 brought in multiple new waves of fortune hunters. Others came to exploit the seal fur trade. The harvested skins were transported in great numbers to London to be dressed and prepared for sale on the global markets of the world economic system.

Between 1890 and 1900 the population of Alaska almost doubled to about 63,000 people. Most came north with intentions of striking it rich and then going home. But some came to think of Alaska as their new home and stayed. In the late 1950s, oil was found on the northern end of Kenai Peninsula and in Cook Inlet. Then in 1967, the largest oil field in North America was discovered at Prudhoe Bay (Alaska Humanities Forum 2017b). The territory and eventual state was changing rapidly and so too the lives of the indigenous peoples.

Indigenous settlements and climate change

There are over a dozen native communities in Alaska that are directly and currently feeling the ravages of climate change. Exemplary of their struggles, the lives of the people living in the largely indigenously populated small city of Barrow (or Utqiagvik) and the indigenous villages of Newtok, Kivalina, and Shishmaref are examined in this chapter.

No roads lead to the isolated community of Barrow, America's northernmost settlement with a population 4,500 people. Getting there requires flying in or, if sea ice conditions allow, going by ship. In town, Barrow's residents use cars or four-wheel-drive ATVs, but they turn to snowmobiles to hunt caribou, moose, or other game. In 2010, journalist and novelist Bob Reiss arrived on a U.S. Coast Guard transport plane to learn about people's experience of the impact of climate change locally. Looking down through a small airplane window, he saw below a triangular-shaped town that clasped the edge of land lying at the junction of the Chukchi and Beaufort seas. The town was constructed of small wooden homes built on pilings to keep them from melting the permafrost on which they stood. If, because of climate change, the permafrost melts, their houses will sink and the community will collapse. He also could glimpse a scattering of vehicles, fish-drying racks, and small boats. Besides dwellings, there was a supermarket and a new hospital going up near some office buildings. Further to the north, along a coast road, there stood a number of Quonset huts on a repurposed World War II-era U.S. Navy base. The huts had become home to a changing array of scientists studying various aspects of climate change and Reiss stayed in one of them during his time in Barrow. Ultimately, he would write a book entitled *The Coming Storm: Extreme Weather and Our Terrifying Future*. Notes Reiss (2010),

> I had come to Barrow to learn about ice and climate change from Eskimo elders and hunters and from scientists. For two weeks I'd been visiting northern Alaska coastal villages as a guest of the Coast Guard, and what I'd heard was disturbing. Each year the sea ice was getting thinner and arriving later … . River banks—without enough ice to shore them up—were eroding, filling the waterways with silt. When hunters went out after moose, their boats increasingly ran aground in flats. 'It's harder to find food,' I heard again and again.

Among those Reiss interviewed was Edward Itta, then the mayor of North Slope Borough, the most northerly county that encompassing Barrow, who told him (Reiss 2010): "Barrow is ground zero for climate-change science … . We worry that climate change is shrinking the sea ice and we don't know how that will affect the animals that depend on it."

His words echo those of indigenous Alaska hunter John Goodwin, a long-time seeker of the bearded seal, a marine mammal prized among local peoples for its meat, oil, and hide. The largest of Alaska's ice seals, the bearded seal uses sea ice to rest and to give birth to its offspring. After the long cold winter, when the sea ice breaks into floes, there's an opportunity for hunters like Goodwin to steer his boat between ice floes, shoot and butcher seals, and bring their catch home. But the window of opportunity shuts quickly because the seals soon migrate north through the Bering Strait. Climate change is disrupting this pattern. A hunting season that used to last several weeks is now ending early and ice that formerly froze 1.5 meters or more thick is far thinner and more fragile. As the weather warms, the ice melts quickly, and the seals move on, leaving the local hunters with far less to show for their efforts. Says Goodwin, "As soon as the sun comes out, it starts melting, or we have a heavy rain … . Basically, it's the rain that deteriorates the ice real quick. We don't have enough time to hunt" (quoted in Joling 2015).

Another marine mammal of importance to indigenous Alaskans is the bowhead whale, a species named for its substantial bony skull that enable it to break through ice to breathe. Living up to 200 years, full-size adults can weigh up to 100 tons. Bowheads are a rich source of vitamins A and C. The whale's biannual migrations between the Bering Sea and the Eastern Beaufort Sea carry them past Barrow each fall and spring. According to Edward Itta,

> The whale is central to our culture … . The warmer ocean and currents will markedly shorten our spring whaling season … . The impacts are around us

already. We need more baseline science so we can measure these impacts over time.

(Quoted in Reiss 2010)

This has led indigenous whalers to team up with researchers to tag bowheads with radio devices. The study is designed to learn how the whales forage and how their food sources are organized in the ecosystem. If warming seas cause the whales' preferred foods to move, the whales could follow—with graves consequences for local people who depend on bowheads for food and other resources.

Like Barrow, the tiny village of Newtok near Alaska's western coast is not accessible by road, but it also has no running water or sewage pipes. The community has a population of over 400 people living in about 60 households. Notably, Newtok is even closer to the frontlines of climate change than Barrow as buildings have been sliding into the Ninglick River for several years. Like a snake, the Ninglick River coils around Newtok on three sides before emptying into the Bering Sea. It has been steadily eating away at the land. Coastal storms and thawing permafrost have further worn away the land on which Newtok is built. About 70 feet of land a year erodes away between the river and the village, putting the community's buildings, some of which are on stilts, ever closer to the threatening water's edge (Waldholtz 2017). Almost all indigenous Alaskan villages are located along rivers and sea coasts, thus almost all are facing similar peril as Newtok. In fact, over the last 50 years the Alaska has warmed at more than twice the rate of the rest of the United States. Now the long-frozen permafrost is melting.

The people of Newtok have tried to get the federal government to declare the growing impacts of climate change an official disaster. Villagers need disaster relief to help them relocate to a safer place. Says local representative Romy Cadiente, "We just need to get out of there … [f]or the safety of the 450 people there." Cadiente met with state officials about moving the village, which includes a school that was erected in 1958 by the Bureau of Indian Affairs. A new village site called Mertarvik has been selected that is nine miles away from the current community, and several houses have been constructed. The new site is on the top of a high ridge of dark volcanic rock on the other side of the river on Nelson Island. But there is not enough money in the community to move everyone: the Army Corps of Engineers estimates it will take between $80 million and $130 million to relocate key infrastructure. Newtok has already lost its barge landing, sewage lagoon, and landfill. As river water flows in and land sinks, the community expects to lose its source of drinking water, its school, and airport within a few years. Cadiente says that Newtok has run out of other options. The Federal Emergency Management Agency has pushed communities to plan for climate change, but the federal government lacks policies to handle issues like relocation. If federal aid to relocate the whole village together is not received, Newtok residents could be forced as climate refugees to scatter on an individual household basis, with some moving as far away as Anchorage. But George Carl, the village council vice president, emphasizes that it is not just buildings that are at stake, but the community's culture, its Yup'ik (or Iñupiaq) language, and its traditional identity. Stresses Carl, "Being born an Eskimo from that village, you know, that's my life … . Place me to another village or city, it's not for me" (quoted in Waldholtz 2017).

Kivalina village, with a an Inupiat Eskimo population of about 400 people, was built on the southern end of a 7.5 mile-long barrier island located between the Chukchi Sea and a lagoon at the mouth of the Kivalina River. It is located 1,000 miles northwest of Anchorage. There are no restaurants in the village, no libraries, no doctors or dentists, and no fitness centers. People buy food at a place called the Native Store, the only shop in Kivalina except for a candy store in the front room of a family's home. In fact, the Native Store is not native at all but is owned by a Seattle-based company and almost everything it stocks is made by Kraft or PepsiCo. The prices for items like lunch meat, bread, and soda are astoundingly high.

The closest town, Noatak, is 50 miles away. To travel there for basketball tournaments, young people from Kivalina ride snowmobiles or all-terrain vehicles over the tundra. When the government built a school in the village early in the twentieth century, people were forced to send their children or face punishment. The children were penalized for speaking their native Inupiat language in school. Children who grew up in that era became hesitant as parents to speak Inupiat to their children. But one Inupiat word everyone still regularly uses is *tammaq*, to lose or to get lost. People in Kivalina have lost many things, both big and small, and now they may lose their home (Knafo 2015).

The village is about two square miles in size and it is increasing threatened by violent ocean storms, flooding, and erosion beneath the homes of community members. The looming threat from climate change has been traumatic (Waldholtz 2017). Sea ice that previous provided protection from harsh winter storms has stopped forming early enough in the fall to prevent rising waters and storm surges from reaching the Kivalina's shores. The undependable and patchy sea ice increases the difficulty and danger of winter travel and hunting. But the problems are not only coming from the coast; the permafrost is thawing as a result of higher temperatures, the Wulik River is now washing away large hunks of its streambank, and an increase in river sediment is threatening the community's water supply. Moreover, the underground ice cellars, called *siġluaqs,* that traditionally provided a year-round freezer for whale, seal, and caribou meat are melting at unexpected times. Some cellars have collapsed because of erosion, while others have been pushed to the margins of safety and are vulnerable to further warming. People have noticed that cellars located nearest to the water are especially warming and, sometimes, filling with water. They have also observed that warmer air and soil temperatures have lengthened the time it takes to freeze stored meat and maktak [blubber]. This loss is complicated by two other challenges that have arisen with traditional food sources: animals are more scarce and harder to find, and hunting them is more difficult because of the unstable and riskier environment. The people of Kivalina have not caught a bowhead whale since 1994, for example. There was a time when they could reasonably expect to land a whale every three or four years (Knafo 2015). Despite the long drought, hope springs eternal and each year the whale hunters keep trying to land a bowhead. But the failure to do so is not their only food-related problem. Additionally, diminishing numbers of fish in the Wulik River, alterations in caribou migration routes, reduced availability of berries and wild vegetable, and the inability to hunt other sea mammals due to loss of sea ice have generated considerable worry about food security in the community. During parts of the year, a growing number of families are facing periods of hunger.

Heavier snowstorms have resulted in an increase in the number of injuries related to snow clearing. Anxiety is building about the future. The future weighs heavily on the community. As expressed by Russel Adams, Sr., a lifelong resident of Kivalina, "When people start talking about climate change, it really scares me … The sea ice used to be twelve feet thick, and there was just one lead [fractures in the ice]. Now it is four feet thick and there are many leads" (quoted in U.S. Climate Resilience Toolkit 2017). Another resident, Joe Swan, Sr. explains "The ice used to push migrating whales in close. That was why we could hunt them. But now the ice is too thin; they can go anywhere" (quoted in U.S. Climate Resilience Toolkit 2017). Global warming seems to be challenging the community on all sides and in multiple ways.

As a result, in 2008, the village government of Kivalina and the federally recognized tribe, the Alaska Native Village of Kivalina, sued ExxonMobil, Shell Oil, as well as seven other oil companies, 14 power companies, and one coal company, arguing that the release of great quantities of greenhouse gases by these energy giants was causing global warming and threatening their community's existence. Kivalina asserted in its complaint that the energy industry conspired to suppress the awareness of the link between greenhouse gas emissions and climate change through the use of "front groups, fake citizens organizations and bogus scientific bodies," like those described in chapters 3 and 4 (quoted in Schwartz 2010). The lawsuit put the cost of relocating the community to a safer place at $400 million. The suit was dismissed, however, by the U.S. district court on the grounds that regulating greenhouse emissions was a political rather than a legal issue and one that needed to be settled by the federal government. The decision came at a time when the science of climate change and its causes was well developed. Instead of recognizing the right of people to live in healthy environments and finding against the elite polluters who despoil the land, air, and water, the court, in effect, found that people are not entitled to compensation when corporations engage in activities that destroy their homes, their health, and cultural ways of life (Luber and Lemery 2015).

Many in the community recognize that they must relocate to safer ground. In 2000, they agreed on a nearby site, called Kiniktuuraq, for relocation. Assessment by the U.S. Army Corps of Engineers, however, determined that Kiniktuuraq could also be prey to climate change impacts in time. This has led to the search for a new home site. Meanwhile, the community has initiated efforts to buy them some time. Several ways to protect the beach have been tested but none have worked. One costly effort that had been completed was destroyed in a large storm leading to worse erosion than before. In 2010, the Army Corps completed a rock retaining wall. Installation of this large structure shrunk the size of Kivalina but offered the community at least ten years to make a relocation decision. Because of the encroaching sea and the protective wall, space for housing has become scarce in the community, resulting in overcrowding and deteriorated sanitation. Household sewage must be hauled to four disposal bunkers located at sites throughout the community. Residents transport their solid waste to a landfill located just over a mile from town, but this poses a contamination threat to fisheries during storms. Additionally, the dump site lacks a perimeter fence and attracts wild animals, including bears. To overcome this problem, a charcoal-based sanitation system that uses pyrolysis is being designed to turn human and solid waste into a source of sustainable energy.

The Climate Foundation, which won a Bill & Melinda Gates Foundation "Reinvent the Toilet Challenge" grant is partnering with Kivalina leaders and a group of social artists to help in developing an innovative waste management technology and with relocation efforts. In recent years, the people of Kivalina have developed relations with diverse federal, state, regional, and local partners in the development of relocation plans.

At times of the year, people are trapped on the shrinking island as there is no way to leave on foot or by vehicle during a storm and transportation by boat or plane in storm conditions would be highly risky. Consequently, the community is developing plans for an evacuation road. In 2012, the village of Kivalina voted to seek permission to build a new school seven miles inland, on a hill called Kisimi-giiqtuq, a site that appears to have stable soils and be better protected from ocean storms. In 2015, the community began considering changing the evacuation road project into a relocation project linked to the Kisimigiiqtuq site. Residents have also engaged several non-profit organizations as well as the international community in seeking support for their relocation project. The group Re-Locate received a $500,000 ArtPlace grant to fund a village-based planning hub for Kivalina, which will be housed in the village's community center. Planned projects included a living archive, drawings and large-scale models of Kivalina's traditional territory, sanitation technology demonstration projects, and an artists-in-residence initiative. While president, Barack Obama recommended a budget of $400 million be approved to relocate Alaskan villages like Kivalina, Congress refused to approve it (Robinson 2017).

All of these efforts by the community reflect an agentive approach to confronting the pressing climate change challenge. While deeply worried, to the point of some people developing anxiety disorders, they have remained empowered to help themselves deal with a massive problem that is not of their own making but which they must endure. Social suffering has increased, food insecurity looms, and threats to health multiply, but the people of Kivalina have demonstrated considerable resilience, including the ability to network and develop allies in their struggle.

Similar woes are faced by the comparatively well-publicized village of Shishmaref, which is located near the Bering Strait in the far west of Alaska. The community sits on Sarichef Island, which like Kivalina is also a barrier reef island in the

Chukchi Sea. The island is a quarter of a mile wide and two and a half miles long. It has a population of about 700 people living in 142 households (U.S. Census Bureau 2010). Shishmaref is a traditional Inupiaq village. Shishmaref Airport, which has one asphalt runway, is the only direct connection between the island town and the rest of Alaska. The community has attracted international attention because of its precarious position in a time of global warming.

Like other indigenous communities in northern Alaska, the people of the island are hunters, with their primary food sources bearded seals, other seals, walrus, dall sheep, fish, birds such as ducks, geese, and ptarmigan, caribou, musk ox, and moose. They also gather berries like the cloudberry, blueberries, and blackberries, as well as the roots and shoots of various plants in season. The village gained a reputation for producing high-quality seal oil and fermented meat, which are traded for other items. The people of Shishmaref are also known for their art work, especially carvings by men of old or fossilized whalebone, which are sought after by native art galleries. Island artists also use other medium including walrus ivory, sealskin, and whale baleen. Common subjects of whalebone carving are masks, animals, and people engaged in traditional activities such as hunting, fishing, drumming, and dancing. Women artists are known for their leather dolls and ornaments. Native art brokers buy up their artwork and crafts, which eventually sells for three or four times what the artist is paid.

Consequently, these sources of income do not allow many conveniences. Few people have running water inside their homes. They must buy water that arrives by barge during the summer, and they collect freshwater ice from the mainland to melt for drinking at other times of the year. Their diets have been influenced by imported foods like dried ramen noodles, frozen burritos, and Spam sold at the two grocery stores. Without running water, few people have a flush toilet. Instead, they use buckets fitted with toilet seats, and then bag up the waste for dumping at a sewage lagoon. Trash gets hauled to a landfill at the island's south end and is burned.

Due to warming temperatures, Shishmaref is being threatened by unusually strong storm surges that are causing flooding and erosion of the shoreline at a rate of about ten feet each year. Without an early build-up of protective shoreline pack ice, Shishmaref has become ever more vulnerable to erosion during storms that occur in October and December. A number of buildings have tumbled into the sea. Threatened with such loss, some people have had to move their homes away from the sea, only to find in time that the shrinking island has put them once more near the water. Esau Sinnok, a 19-year old community member, posted a statement on his blog in 2016 saying that the community has "lost 2,500 to 3,000 feet of land to coastal erosion" over the past 35 years. As a result, he wrote, his family has moved 13 times in 15 years, "from one end of the island to the other because of this loss of land" (quoted in Kennedy 2016).

The adverse impacts of climate change in Shishmaref include melting permafrost, a rise in sea level, and a delay in the freeze-up of the Bering Sea. This delayed freezing and the thinner ice also limit the hunting of traditional game animals like as seals. This loss has forced community member to become more dependent on highly processed Western foods that are shipped in to the community at great cost. It is estimated that as a result of erosion, the village site will be lost to the sea in about fifteen years. Says Sinnok, "It's crazy to know that your only home will soon be underwater if the federal government doesn't do anything to help you out" (quoted in Kennedy 2016). Sinnok feels the loss deeply, fears the harm done to the cultural tradition he was raised in, and hopes the community will decide to move to safer ground off of the island:

> [O]ur unique community of Shishmaref will soon die out because we have our unique dialect of Inupiat Eskimo language, our unique Eskimo dancing, our unique gospel singing translated in Inupiat. All that will soon die out if we do not move as a community.
>
> *(Quoted in Kennedy 2016)*

But some people do not want to move away from the island. Tribal coordinator Jane Stevenson, for example, told a reporter that she is inclined toward remaining at the current site because it is closer to subsistence foods that people rely on for much of their diet. Howard Weyiouanna, the town's mayor, believes that staying at the current location would be the most cost-effective given the steep expense of moving the community. Annie Wyiouanna adds, "You are taking away our identity … . That's like a punch in the gut. That's who we are—we are tied to this land and the sea." She adds that she is worried that Trump is president: "He doesn't believe climate change is real … . And I see that and think it's scary" (quoted in Hughes 2017). Many people here blame human-caused climate change for pushing erosion of the island and worry that Trump's decision to pull out of the Paris climate agreement will only make matters worse for those on the frontlines of climate change.

The site where the community might relocate is about twenty miles away on the mainland. It is surrounded by the 2.5 million-acre Bering Land Bridge National Reserve, which means the federal government's permission would be needed to construct roads to the new site and to develop a quarry for foundation materials. Says Lorraine Jungers, "I wish we didn't have to move … . This is our whole life right here. I can't picture us anywhere else" (quoted in Hughes 2017).

The issue of moving has been under discussion for years. Residents have voted multiple times to relocate to the mainland and several community members have testified about their plight before Congress. One representative from Shishmaref even attended the Paris climate talks in 2015. Still, not much has changed really and the clock is ticking on the island's future.

Climate turmoil, politics, and the displacement of indigenous communities and cultures

As the environment changes due to human activity, the indigenous people want policies enacted to protect their culture. A report issued by the Inuit Circumpolar

Council-Alaska in 2015, which advocates for the Yupik and Iñupiat coast villages across Alaska, calls for new measures that protect traditional food and the Arctic environment that produces it. "When we say food security, it has to do with the health of all of it," said Carolina Behe, the organization's indigenous knowledge and science adviser (quoted in Joling 2015). More than 90 percent of the food purchased with cash in Alaska comes in from elsewhere and a reliable food supply in more urban communities such as Anchorage means affordable prices and uninterrupted service on groceries shipped north by barge or jet. For the Yupik and Iñupiat peoples who have survived for thousands of years in one of the harshest climates on Earth, food is the connection between the past and today's culture. Food is not just a means of survival, it is central to identity. Over millennia, the ways of hunting of caribou and seals, the techniques of finding and gathering of salmonberries, and the knowledge of how to process, store, and prepare each food source were incorporated into the art, storytelling, dance, drumming, and language of the community and shared with new generations. "Our traditional foods are much more than calories or nutrients; they are a lifeline throughout our culture and reflect the health of the entire Arctic ecosystem," the report's authors stated (quote in Joling 2015).

As changes began to be directly experienced, indigenous leaders began to talk about the importance of food at public forums. Their understanding of the meaning of food differed from that of people in academia or the government, who emphasized nutritional value and purchasing power. At a meeting several years ago, someone asked whether local people were looking forward to increased shipping because it would allow more food to arrive from the outside. But Behe said, "Our people were saying the exact opposite: We're really concerned about these ships because they're going to disrupt our hunting, the noise is disrupting the animals, the pollutants, and that's a threat to food security" (quoted in Joling 2015).

The report, which was based on visits to 15 villages, urged Arctic policy decisions be made through the lens of food. Indigenous leaders want baseline data collected on the Arctic ecosystem using both science and indigenous knowledge. A scientist researching salmon might look first at the population dynamics of the fish. An elder, by contrast, might taste the water, look at streamside vegetation, check fish scales, and gauge the texture of the meat to determine the health and well-being of the salmon. People are causing change in the Arctic as a result of greenhouse gases or pollution, stresses Behe, and they must take responsibility for actions affecting the Yupik and Iñupiat: "The people causing the pollution have to have more responsibility and have to be expected to change their behavior, as opposed to expecting Inuit to change theirs" (quote in Joling 2015).

Numerous studies show that summer sea ice in the Arctic region is shrinking. The tundra is a massive watery wilderness. Below it is the permafrost, the layer of frozen earth that begins about two feet beneath the surface and goes down, in North Alaska, some 2,000 feet. Globally, permafrost holds an estimated 400 gigatons of methane, one of the greenhouse gases that is hastening the earth's warming.

As the permafrost thaws—which it has begun to do—lakes can drain away and the thawed soil can release billions of tons of methane into the atmosphere, fueling climate change in a dangerous feedback loop (Reiss 2010). The dangerous feature of such loops is that once they get started they feed themselves independent of new human inputs. But, of course, new anthropogenic inputs in the form of greenhouse gas and black carbon release continue, speeding the destruction of indigenous communities in Alaska and poorer communities everywhere.

Joel Clement, a scientist, was director of the Office of Policy Analysis at the U.S. Interior Department until July 2017. At the Interior Department he helped endangered communities in Alaska prepare for and adapt to a changing climate. Then with Trump's election, he was reassigned to the accounting office that collects royalty checks from energy companies. But he is not an accountant. A few days after his reassignment, Trump's interior secretary Ryan Zinke testified before Congress that he would use reassignments as part of effort to eliminate employees. In Clement's view, Zeke expects people to quit in response to undesirable transfers. He saw colleagues being relocated across the country, at taxpayer expense, to serve in jobs equally as ill fitting as the one he was given. He believes he was

> retaliated against for speaking out publicly about the dangers that climate change poses to Alaska Native communities. During the months preceding my reassignment, I raised the issue with White House officials, senior Interior officials and the international community, most recently at a U.N. conference in June. It is clear to me that the administration was so uncomfortable with this work, and my disclosures, that I was reassigned with the intent to coerce me into leaving the federal government.
>
> *(Clement 2017)*

The costs to Clement, however, are far smaller than those now faced by indigenous Alaskan communities:

> The Alaska Native villages of Kivalina, Shishmaref and Shaktoolik are perilously close to melting into the Arctic Ocean. In a region that is warming twice as fast as the rest of the planet, the land upon which citizens' homes and schools stand is newly vulnerable to storms, floods and waves. As permafrost melts and protective sea ice recedes, these Alaska Native villages are one superstorm from being washed away, displacing hundreds of Americans and potentially costing lives. The members of these communities could soon become refugees in their own country.
>
> *(Clement 2017)*

When Scott Pruitt, head of the Environmental Protection Agency in the Trump administration, announced that global warming may be a positive change, he was clearly not thinking of the indigenous populations of the 49th state in the

American union. As this chapter has shown, climate change is already causing harm to the lives, homes, communities, and livelihoods of Alaska's original peoples. As environmental anthropologist Dana Graef (2018) comments, "global inequality is one of the greatest tensions at the heart of climate change."

References

Alaska Humanities Forum. 2017a. Yup'ik and Cup'ik. Alaska Native Heritage Center. www.akhistorycourse.org/alaskas-cultures/alaska-native-heritage-center/yupik-and-cupik.

Alaska Humanities Forum. 2017b. Population and settlements. Alaska Native Heritage Center. www.akhistorycourse.org/americas-territory/population-and-settlements.

Clement, J. 2017. I'm a scientist: I'm blowing the whistle on the Trump administration. *Washington Post*, July 19. www.washingtonpost.com/opinions/im-a-scientist-the-trump-administration-reassigned-me-for-speaking-up-about-climate-change/2017/07/19/389b8dce-6b12-11e7-9c15-177740635e83_story.html?utm_term=.2b053b162f10&wpisrc=nl_most&wpmm=1.

Draper, H. 1977. The aboriginal Eskimo diet in modern perspective. *American Anthrpologist* 79(2): 309–316.

Graef, D. 2018. Glacial melting isn't someone else's problem. *Sapiens*, February 28. www.sapiens.org/column/the-climate-report/cotacachi-glacial-melting/.

Hippler, A. 1974. The North Alaska Eskimos: A culture and personality perspective. *American Ethnologist* 1(3): 449–469.

Hughes, T. 2017. Residents on remote Alaska island fear climate change will doom way of life. *USA Today, June 2.* www.usatoday.com/story/news/nation/2017/06/02/alaska-island-fear-climate-change-dooms-town/102398636/.

Joling, D. 2015. Climate change threatens traditional Inuit food supply in Alaska. *The Globe and Mail.* www.theglobeandmail.com/life/climate-change-threatens-traditional-inuit-food-supply-in-alaska/article27952759/.

Kennedy, M. 2016. Alaska village decides to relocate. New England Public Radio (NPR). www.npr.org/sections/thetwo-way/2016/08/18/490519540/threatened-by-rising-seas-an-alaskan-village-decides-to-relocate.

Knafo, S. 2015. The last whale hunt for a vanishing Alaskan village. *Men's Journal.* www.mensjournal.com/features/articles/the-last-whale-hunt-for-a-vanishing-village-kivalina-alaska-w443825.

Luber, G. and J. Lemery 2015. *Global Climate Change and Human Health: From Science to Practice.* San Francisco: Jossey-Bass.

Reiss, B. 2010. Barrow, Alaska: Ground zero for climate change. *Smithsonian Magazine* (March). www.smithsonianmag.com/science-nature/barrow-alaska-ground-zero-for-climate-change.smithonian.

Robinson, M. 2017. This remote Alaskan village could disappear under water within 10 years: Here's what life is like there. *Business Insider.* www.businessinsider.com/what-life-is-like-in-kivalina-alaska-2017-9/#kivalina-is-no-ordinary-small-town-1.

Sahlins, M. 1968. Notes on the original affluent society. In R. Lee and I. DeVore (eds), *Man the Hunter.* New York: Aldine Publishing Company, pp. 85–89.

Schwartz, J. 2010. Courts as battlefields in climate fights. *New York Times*, January 27. www.nytimes.com/2010/01/27/business/energy-environment/27lawsuits.html.

U. S. Census Bureau. 2000. Table 1: American Indian and Alaska native alone and alone or in combination population by tribe for the United States: 2000. www.census.gov/population/cen2000/phc-t18/tab001.pdf.

U.S. Census Bureau. 2010. Shishmaref city, Alaska. *American Fact Finder.* https://factfinder. census.gov/faces/nav/jsf/pages/community_facts.xhtml?src=bkmk.

U.S. Climate Resilience Toolkit. 2017. Relocatig Kivalina. https://toolkit.climate.gov/ca se-studies/relocating-kivalina.

Waldholtz, R. 2017. Alaskan village, citing climate change, seeks disaster relief in order to relocate. New England Public Radio (NPR). www.npr.org/2017/01/10/509176361/ala skan-village-citing-climate-change-seeks-disaster-relief-in-order-to-relocate.

7

WATER VULNERABILITY AND SOCIAL EQUITY IN ECUADOR

Glaciers, water, land, and poverty in Ecuador

There are approximately 198,000 glaciers in the world, although there are another 200,000 smaller glacierets or snowpacks. Together, they cover 0.5 percent of Earth's surface. Forty-four percent of glacierized areas are in arctic regions. But glaciers are melting and losing mass everywhere. Climate scientists believe that by the year 2100 about half of all glaciers will be gone, barring extensive mitigation efforts. This loss will have devastating consequences for the lives of millions of people who rely on normal summer melt from glaciers to provide freshwater, and would dramatically increase the flash flood hazards produced by glacier recession (Davies 2017). One of the places these risks are mounting is Ecuador (Painter 2010).

Even though the Republic of Ecuador is on the equator – a fact celebrated in the country's name – 17 of its mountains in the Andes have peaks that extend above the regional snowline and support more than a hundred small glaciers. The total area of glaciers on the 17 mountains is 37.5 square miles (Jordan and Hastenrath 1999).

Ecuador has a population of over 13.6 million people, many of whom are extremely vulnerable to a changing climate. Vulnerability, however, varies considerably across ethnic and class lines. Indigenous citizens are mostly (96.4%) highland Quichuas who live in the valleys of the Sierra region (Gerlach 2003). Poverty rates are disproportionately higher among indigenous groups, reaching 87 percent among all Quichuas and 96 percent among those living in the rural highlands. For non-indigenous people, the poverty rate is 61 percent. Poverty is notably higher in rural areas where people have only limited access to healthcare, education, and sanitation resources. In recent decades there has been significant migration to the cities, increasing the level of urban poverty. Least vulnerable are the super-rich elite whose wealth is dependent on oil and commodities exports. Many people, close to two million, left the country between 1998 and 2003 because of worsening economic conditions under a regime of neoliberal economics (Smith 2017). In the analysis of Hidalgo et al. (2017),

> Permissive governmental policies for expanding water-intensive crops have helped large agricultural companies accumulate water rights. These expansion processes compete for water and land with small local-Indigenous farmers, degenerate local ecosystems, undermine local food security, and profoundly alter existing modes of production and income distribution … .

Attitudes toward indigenous Ecuadorians and even mixed-ancestry mestizo often reflect timeworn stereotypes devoid of real familiarity with the objects of opprobrium. The worst of these sentiments were found in a study of first-year university students in Guayaquil and Quito. Felipe, a 19-year old responded to the question "are you mestizo?" by saying he was not mestizo because

> Indians (*Indios*) are brutes, less than an animal, left abandoned by their children, who are only a source of income which is why they have so many … . The Indian who has overcome his origins, besides being educated, is an Indian who bathes.

Ximena, aged 16, another student, insisted, "I am not mestiza because I am white; I have nothing Indian in me and I am from a good family" (quoted in Meisch 1992: 69).

Melting glaciers and community response

Climate patterns in Ecuador vary due to the effects of altitude and coastal factors. One of the three climate zones is the highlands of the Andes. Equatorial climates do not have a seasonal cycle akin to higher latitudes, rather the climate of Ecuador has a wet season and a dry season, though each of these varies by geographical location. People living in the Andes depend on glaciers for their water, especially during the dry season, but grave threats are now looming. Several peaks, including Cotacachi, Corazon, and Sincholagua, have already lost all of their snow cover (Burke et al. 2011).

Indeed, the growing risk from climate change in Ecuador is expressed in the fact that the country has lost 30 percent of its snowcaps in recent decades. If global warming continues at its current rate, in 70 years they will disappear completely. Those below 16,500 feet will be gone far sooner. One of these fast-melting glaciers in Ecuador is the Antisana, which reaches an altitude of 18,880 feet. Antisana, is located just 40 miles west of the Amazon, which contributes to it being one of the world's dampest mountains. In the last 50 years the glacier has lost more than a third of its original surface area. This shrinkage is of critical importance because

Antisana is one of the main sources of fresh water in Ecuador's capital city of Quito, providing its two million people with about one-third of their water (Cuenca High Life 2015).

A sign of the changes going on is that it now rains at higher elevations. Because of the changing climate, the line at which precipitation falls as snow has moved up the mountain to approximately 16,500 feet. Now in an area that was covered by glacier as recently as the year 2000 there is an alpine lake about a mile wide. Reflecting the fragility of the ecosystem, the lake is filled with melted glacier ice. In fact, Antisana was home to the largest ice cap in all of Ecuador. But 40 percent of that ice cover has already melted and the remaining glacier's average thickness is shrinking between 14 and 35 inches a year. Moreover, the pace of the shrinkage has been accelerating since the 1970s. Like Antisana, the sur-rounding *páramo*—a delicate, high-altitude, spongy grassland with an unusual ability to absorb, store, and gradually release water—is a fundamental water resource for Quito (Tegel 2012).

Another Ecuadorian mountain, the Cayambe volcano, sits on the Equator and is the third-highest mountain in all the Americas at 17,159 feet. Thirty years ago there was a 9.8 thousand long, 195-foot thick slide of ice hanging off the peak, but now there is only bare, black rock because of glacier melt. A whole valley that once was filled with ice is now mostly devoid of it and the end of the glacier, which used to stretch miles down the mountain, is 1,800 feet higher than it was three decades ago. Most of the 20 glaciers on Cayambe are in full retreat. The consensus among Ecuadorian scientists is that nearly 40 percent of Cayambe's ice mass has been lost over the last generation, with nearly 10 percent in the last 15 years (Vidal 2010). In the short run, glacier melt on Cayambe may not be a great problem because the extra meltwater from the shrinking icecap is compensating for the lack of rain, another impact of climate change. But this offers only time-limited relief. Ultimately, the melting of the Andean cryosphere (iceworld) will diminish urban water supplies and put at enhanced risk some of the poorest people in the world who are dependent on the rivers fed by the spring meltwater flowing off of mountains like Cayambe. The small farmers, or campesinos, of Cayambe have over several generations been steadily nudged up the mountain by the acreage-hungry wealthy landowners. This push has forced them on to the high pasture areas where they farm small plots on the rocky hillsides and graze their small animal herds. The farmers use ox-drawn plows, wooden hoes, and digging sticks, planting their seeds by hand. But the cattle grazing and ploughing have seriously degraded the fragile land and led to conflicts. In the dry season the pasture areas are completely drying up. Climate change, which has intensified and, as noted, caused less rain to fall, is further complicating tensions over water.

From the indigenous perspective, Earth is regarded as a "supernatural symbol of procreation, fecundity, protector of the weak, the infirm and is propitiated accordingly" (Cáceres 1993). Land provides the fundamental framework within which community and family relations and values are expressed. Moreover, in the words of one Quichua man, "Kimsacocha is [the embodiment of] Mother Earth.

Just like the veins that we have in our body, so does the Pachamama [Mother Earth]. Instead of blood, her [veins] are filled with water" (quoted in Velásquez 2015a). But access to water and the most fertile land is not equitably distributed. Rather it is a product of both historical and contemporary distribution patterns of resources in a context of encroachments by the elite. This means that water security for the wealthy is gained by creating water insecurity for the poor, reflecting prevailing social power relations. Water grabbing by mining interests, hydropower companies, energy corporations, and cut-flower exporters is also expanding.

Ethnographic examination of the demise of an Andes glacier

In their ethnographic fieldwork, Robert Rhoades and colleagues explored local perceptions and social impacts of climate change as expressed by glacial retreat on Cotacachi, the highest of the northernmost grouping of volcanic peaks in the Ecuadorian Andes. Cotacachi is among the first Andean mountains over the last half-century to completely lose its glacier due to climate change. The glacier was 20,000 years old, dating to the Great Ice Age. Over a relatively short period of time the glacier lake that was a primary water source for mountain communities started shrinking at a rate of about three feet a year, and local rivers and springs began to dry up as well. The result was growing strain over water between indigenous communities and wealthy landlords.

The mountain the glacier was on is characterized by sharp altitude gradients topped, in the past, by a cap of permanent snow. The various gradients are best suited to different crops like corn, grains, tubers, and at the highest levels, by pasture for domestic animals. As with other indigenous areas of the Andes, agriculture is the main productive activity, although many young men seek work in nearby towns or in Quito. In the lower zones, the floriculture and agro-industrial greenhouse industries have taken hold.

Indigenous Cotacacheños view their mountain in feminine terms as a mother, with a body and head, on whose broad "skirt" they live. As Rhoades and co-workers (2008: 219) discovered:

> Local people described Cotacachi as constantly interacting with other features in the landscape and told of her intimate sexual relations with Tayta [father] Imbabura, a volcano located directly across the valley to the east. She has relations with her human inhabitants as well, expressing anger and disappointment with them and at times interfering in the life of the community, especially when social conflict and behavior meet with her disapproval … .

Cotacachi is a frequent theme in community folklore, including tales of volcanic eruptions, landslides, earthquakes and other disasters. One community narrative focuses on the time when Tayta Imbabura and Cotacachi fell in love. At the time, Cotacachi was a beautiful young girl and the owner of a large hacienda. By contrast, Tayta Imbabura was an aging womanizer who had grown weary of chasing Cayambe and Tungurahua, the names of other glaciated peaks, and decided to remain with Cotacachi. Together they had a child, which bears the name of a smaller volcano mountain called Yana Urcu. But Imbabura became ill and wrapped his head with a white cloth. This, people say, is the reason why Imbabura is covered by snow in winter.

As part of their work, Rhoades and co-workers organized workshops with residents from several villages in order to understand their perceptions of the climate change and glacial retreat. Whereas "[e]lderly people and those from more remote villages believed that [glacial retreat] was due to Cotacachi's punishment ... younger people with formal education and contacts with local nongovernment organizations pinpointed global climate change" (Rhoades et al. 2008: 221). Regardless of varying perceptions of climate change and glacier retreat, these events have been a source of disorientation for Cotacacheños because in the past Cotacachi always supplied abundant water for subsistence farming and the needs of daily life. Now, in addition to the loss of the glacier, people stressed that rainfall has decreased and become irregular in its timing. Some people said that the rain was "playing" with them and making life more difficult. Farmers complained that it is hard to know when to prepare their land for planting. A female farmer's comments were typical of those made by others:

> It doesn't rain as much anymore. It seems the weather is changing so that there is only a drizzle today. It used to be more abundant. The climate seems to be playing. The rains were harder and longer. Today the clouds are polluted and there are only strong winds and everything is dry.
>
> (Quoted in Rhoades et al. 2008: 221.

Added one woman, "What I remember of Cotacachi is that it had more snow that came down to near the road to Intag" (quoted in Rhoades et al. 2008: 222). Finally, a farmer from Morales Chupa stated that today Cotacachi is "black" compared with the "white" of Cotapaxi and Chimborazo:

> I remember that Cotacachi had snow in the past, but in contrast it has hardly any. These days what we see is black. We used to climb to the páramo and observe that there was snow, but now there is none. What I remember of the mountain is that it had snow and looked white. The whole corridor of Cotacachi now looks black.
>
> (Quoted in Rhoades et al. 2008: 222)

In their own conception of their local world, memory has a strong presence. People still think of Cotacachi's peak as snow-capped, a culturally and spiritually meaningful framing of reality that resists what their own eyes tell them and represents, perhaps, an undying hope for a return to better times. This hope is reflected in people praying for rain and through water ceremonies, or food offerings that are buried on the mountain to give back to the land the products that people need from "Mother Earth."

The disappearance of the Cotacachi glacier, a feature that always in the past dominated their landscape, is a totally new and strange experience for mountain residents. Life is now less secure, more precarious, and people feel more vulnerable. How far their traditional knowledge, technologies, and skills will take them in the struggle with their upended world is uncertain. Rhoades, an anthropologist who values the insights and complexities of local knowledge, was forced by his experience in the Andes to "rethink the adaptive capacity of traditional knowledge in the face of global warming" (Rhoades 2007: 39). Rhoades (2007: 48) found that although Cotacachi is sacred to people and traditionally a powerful force in their lives,

> people sense she is dying. The shamans of Cotacachi feel their own powers diminishing and this too is symbolic of a people in social decay. They believe the fate of the mountain will be the fate of the people.

Adding to the reasons to share Rhoades' concern is experimental research (Tito et al. 2017) indicating that climate change is having adverse impact on two dietary staples of highland diets—potatoes and corn. According to Kenneth Feeley, a tropical biologist at the University of Miami, "If farmers ignore climate change and keep farming the same fields they always have, we find it's going to be disastrous for these crops" (quoted in Catanoso 2017). The research team, led by biologist Richard Tito, who is himself a native Quechuan, found that, with a temperature increase as small as between 2.3°F and 4.7°F, nearly all of their experimentally planted corn plants died when they were grown at the same elevations as previous years and generations. The plants were either eaten by birds or overwhelmed by pests. When the same type of plant was grown at a higher elevation in order to remain within the temperature zone to which the corn was adapted, the lesser quality and lower nutrients of the high elevation soil had a significant adverse impact. Plants survived with fewer pests, but the size of the total harvest and its quality were diminished. Corn production declined by 21–29 percent in response to new soil conditions. The impact on potatoes was even worse. Potatoes are already grown at the highest farmable elevations, so it is often not possible to migrate up the mountain to a higher level. With the same expected temperature increases due to climate change, the potato plants survived attacks by novel pests, but the tuber production was heavily deformed and lost all market value. With both crops, the researchers only used local fertilizers like manure and no pesticides were applied because rural farmers cannot afford them. Weed control was done by hand, as is typical among rural highland farmers.

The implications of the experimental study were highlighted by Kenneth Feely:

> It's always important to stress that climate change is having and going to have real impacts on lots of people through food... And what we found is that

relatively small changes in temperature can have a huge effect on the liveli-hoods and health of millions of people … . If people can't live in these rural areas because of reduced food production, they will move to the cities and you will have more urban slums.

(Quoted in Catanoso 2017)

In light of the multiple threats of climate change, Rhoades and his co-workers emphasized the need for collaborative research to understanding what is happened to people who have historically relied on glacier melt-off. They assert that "[o]nly with a strong interdisciplinary approach that involves the participation of the people directly affected can we hope to achieve solutions to what may become major disruptions of ancient cultures deeply rooted in glacier-fed mountain land-scapes" (Rhoades et al. 2008: 225).

Mining and water: enhancing the ecocrisis of climate change

In 2009, indigenous small farmers in highland Ecuador publically challenged a proposed government water law by holding public rituals to honor their water-shed, Kimsacocha, as the embodiment of the Pachamama, Mother Earth. They denounced the proposed law because it gave mine companies the rights to mineral extraction in communal watershed areas. The protesters asserted that human and nonhuman spiritual entities are interconnected and that the Ecuadoran state should designate communal watersheds as no-mining zones to defend their right to life (Velásquez 2017). Campesinos, indigenous people, and environmentalists banded together in the "defense of life" coalition in opposition to the law, feeling that it would reduce peoples' ability to manage and access vital water resources. The law permitted contentious mining projects in critical watersheds while increasing state control over autonomously managed communal water systems. Water as life became the protestors' rallying cry, drawing attention to the complex inter-rela-tionships between people and the environment. As one highland woman expressed it: "water is the blood of our life, water flows through our veins, without water, there is no life. Without [agricultural] production, there is no life" (quoted in Velásquez 2015a). Observes Velásquez (2015b): "The turn towards the language of indigenous environmentalism—a simultaneous global and local construction—provided farmers with a new way of imagining their watershed and participating in a globalized environmental movement."

   This case exemplifies one of the social challenges faced by the indigenous people of the Ecuadoran Andes that intertwine with and exacerbate the risks they face from climate change. This kind of conflict continues. In August 2016, in the Río Blanco area of the highlands, local people set up a tent at the entrance of the Chinese-owned Junefield mining company's base camp. Their goal was to stop the initiation of mining for copper and gold in the fragile páramos in southern Ecua-dor. For two months they occupied the site in an atmosphere of growing tension between them and the miners. Then in early October, tensions boiled over.

Members of the local community say that for 24 hours they were under unrelenting harassment by mining company's private guards, as well as the police, who officially were in the area with the goal of preventing such clashes. Says Rubén Cortés, a farmer who explained the community's fundamentally dependence on their crops in the area: "We sow, we eat it ourselves, and we can't sell it because it's difficult to transport … . The water comes from the mountain, and right now it's drying out. Seventy percent is already dry …" (quoted in Puertas 2017).

These events are unfolding at a decisive moment for the Río Blanco mining project. A source of controversy for a decade due to its location in the páramos, critics worry about the project's potential effects on the water sources that supply rivers in the region. This controversy has continued to grow, as the dual effects of mining and climate change put local farmers in a dangerous bind.

The danger of flowers

Flowers in Western societies have become a cultural symbol of love, caring, and sympathy. This linkage of love and flowers in a global market economy has fueled the growth of a $30 billion cut-flower industry. Only one third of cut flowers sold in the U.S., for example, are grown locally. Highland areas of Ecuador and Columbia account for more than half of the flowers sold in U.S. In the Cayambe Valley in highland Ecuador, volcanic soils, snowmelt from the Andes, and 12 hours a day of sunshine year-round produce large, full roses. Since these ideal growing conditions were discovered by international investors in the 1980s, rose exports from Ecuador have skyrocketed, transforming the country's rose industry into the fourth largest in the world. Two-thirds of Ecuador's roses—about 500 million a year—are exported to the United States. The flowers are tended to, cut, packaged, and shipped by almost 200,000 workers in these and other developing countries. But the vast share of the wealth generated by this industry does not flow to its predominantly female work force, many of whom are from small farmer families, it goes to multinational corporations. Generally, the workers receive low wages and few if any benefits, work unpaid overtime, and face dismissal for pregnancy. Third-party contractors shuffle workers from plantation to plantation, avoiding payment of social security and inhibiting union organizing. Industrial floriculture for export tends to displace crops grown for local consumption. Further, the industry requires large quantities of local water that is then not available for food growing. Also, flowers are a pesticide-intensive crop; flowers carry up to 50 times the amount of pesticides allowed on food crops. Reports from environmental and labor watchdog groups have suggested that U.S. and foreign workers are overexposed to harmful chemicals each year as producers race to deliver their product to the waiting marketplace. Pesticide-related health problems are well documented among floriculture workers. Notes Wehner (2003), who investigated the industry as a journalist, "almost everyone in town, it seems, has a tale of miscarriages, skin rashes, and babies born with birth defects." The USDA tests for pests on imported crops, but not for pesticides, and this promotes heavy pesticide use in an industry anguish to get fresh flowers into the lucrative U.S. market. Comments Wehner (2003):

> The equatorial sun beats down on the clear plastic roof of a greenhouse in the Cayambe Valley of Ecuador. Despite the suffocating heat, the workers inside move at a frantic pace. In two weeks it will be Valentine's Day, and every rose in sight will be for sale in the United States … . The flowers have already been treated with chemicals to kill insects and mildew; now they are dunked in preservatives to keep them from rotting during their journey through U.S. Customs. After being wrapped in cellophane and boxed, the flowers are chilled and flown overnight to Miami. By the time they reach florists and supermarkets across the country, a rose that cost less than 17 cents to produce in Ecuador will sell for as much as $8.

Under these oppressive conditions, anger and rebelliousness boiled to the surface among the Quechua small farmers. Ultimately, their growing consciousness of the politics of indigeneity and the campesino communal sense of belonging on the land by historic right exploded. As Meisch (1992: 58) explains, the Quechua have joined other indigenous groups because of their shared interest in fighting for the issues of vital interest to them:

> the fundamental problem is scarcity of land, which has provoked indigenous migration to the cities where [they] are subjected to the worst kind of employment; where we are badly treated and badly remunerated … . Right behind land is access to water because the land is frequently useless without irrigation … . The demand for genuine land reform, however the details are worked out, is the glue that binds the [country-wide] indigenous movement.

Expressing these concerns, several thousand indigenous people living on the mountain who had grown weary of the domination of their lives by the elite took matters directly into their own hands. In a sudden and swift social uprising, they drove the cattle of the rich farmers down the mountain, limited the numbers of their own animals allowed on the páramo, cleaned out and re-established miles of old water channels, some dug by their ancestors, and banned the burning of the land by community members. Water supplies to all small farmers soon increased by about 10 percent, showing that sustainable farming strategies can combat some of the effects of climate change. They also decided to dig channels to bring water around from the mountain from the east side, which receives more rain. These farmers linked climate change and domination by the super-wealthy as a dangerous combination causing their poverty and social suffering. They did not respond passively, but rather, reflecting a modern tradition of resistance that can be dated at least as far back as the 1930s, agentively took responsibility for adapting to climate change on their own without waiting for help from the state or international organizations. Uninfluenced by the popular media image of the passive, docile indigenous peasant, people organized for action. Inequality and neocolonialism caused climate change, they concluded, so eliminating these was their pathway to fighting the effects of a warming planet. There is a catch however, if the glaciers on Cayambe melt away the campesinos will face catastrophe despite their courage and best communal efforts. Climate change is a global issue and while communities can make a difference, a few thousand committed small farmers cannot overcome climate change on their own.

The range of experience of Ecuadoran indigenous small farmers

Research has shown that highland rural communities vary by location and other factors such the size of the area they live in, soil quality, and their history of relations with outsiders, including wealthy landowners. Communities in which these variables are similar tend to share the ability to access resources from the environment, cultural definitions of well-being, and types of economic activities. For most households, access to land (for both growing crops and animal husbandry), water, and credit is constrained, producing a historic cycle of marginalization and scarcity. This economic challenge pushes small farmers during hard times to replace traditional cultivation strategies, which have proven to be sustainable, with more intensive techniques that heighten the risk of soil exhaustion and erosion. Traditional crops include corn, barley, and potatoes, the staple food sources of the highlands. Other crops people grow include onions, beans, quinua, lentils, and several native tubers. Crop rotation is used to limit soil depletion. Farm work is primarily household-based but can include labor exchanges with extended family members or other community members when needed. Households that do not have access to pasture cannot keep domestic animals and the resources they provide, including meat, wool, and cheese. Families that can still maintain pigs and chickens in areas adjacent to their homes. Guinea pigs are raised inside people's homes and used both as a food and as ritual items during religious ceremonies. In their communities, there are often no public services. Local water systems, however, are commonly built by community members and may include pipelines to a tap in front of each house in a settlement. Traditionally, houses were of a type known as *chozas,* which had dirt floors, adobe walls, and straw roofs. Over time, these are being replaced by buildings constructed of cement blocks, with metal roofs.

In times of hardship—for example, when the rains do not fall—people have learned to supplement their subsistence farming and small animal husbandry with several sources of income, including having a family member migrate temporarily to the city or to jobs in, for example, the cut-flower industry, with the intention of sending remittances back home, taking on piecework when available from labor-seeking industries, and making or selling handicrafts such as ponchos, shawls, and skirts woven on hand looms using home-spun wool. When possible, cash crops are grown and sold as well. Families also adjust by reducing their expenditures on clothing, community religious fiestas, and food. The food threat, which tends to occur during the dry season, is explained by a small farmer from the Ayora, Cayambe area, this way:

> When there is no money, we eat what we have. My daughter stays at her cousin's during the summer vacations. Then we would spend less on food and eat only in the morning and in the afternoon. As we like to say 'the hunger passes, the money stays… .' The summer has a great influence, we have less food, we have the risk of not paying our credits. Even migration increases, people are prepared to leave their animals and go to the city to get a job.
>
> *(Quoted in Rothmayer 2016)*

Despite these efforts, malnutrition rates in rural Ecuador remain an issue.

Based on fieldwork in several high altitude villages, Hentschel and co-workers (1996) describe the case of Angel, a 31-year old farmer, and his 29-year old wife Maria. The couple had four small children at the time of the interview. They lived in a cement block house with a tile roof. They got water from the faucet in front of their home but lacked electricity or a latrine. Meals were usually cooked in a fireplace but the family owned a small gas stove. They also possessed a treadle sewing machine and an old bicycle, but this was the extent of their purchased possessions. Angel was given a small plot of land by his father on which the family grew corn, potatoes, beans, chochos (a leguminous bean), lentils, quinua, barley, onions, and native tubers, in rotating cycles of planting across crop alternatives. Most of what they grew was directly consumed by the family, but in good years they could sometimes sell some of their harvest for extra income. In addition, the family had three cows, three pigs, four rabbits, and six guinea pigs, all of which might be sold as needed to cover the costs of emergencies like illnesses or crop loss. Yet even the sale of surplus crops and animals did not earn the family enough to cover its expenses. For this reason, Angel traveled to the capital city of Quito for two weeks each year seeking employment as a mason. Some years he found no work in the city and returned home empty-handed, having lost even the money needed to get him to the capital. Other years he arrived back home with as much as $30 for his toil. Maria too sought seek outside work and found a job taking care of the crops and animals of a wealthy man from a nearby town. But as the children arrived, she had to end this relationship to focus on raising the children and tending to her own family's crops and animals. Women traditionally have played a key role in agricultural production in indigenous communities in the Andes, and children too play an increasing role as they grow up. Women and children tend to be the ones who gather firewood, cook meals, and clean the family home. Women also participate in *mingas*, which a communal work parties and in labor exchanges with extended kin. Angel's family does not directly provision all of the food it consumes but buys some imported foods, including rice, noodles, salt, vegetable shortening, and oats, from a store in town. They rarely are able to consume meat, milk, fresh vegetables, or fruit. Over time, with rising prices, their economic situation worsened, putting greater pressure on Angel to spend more time in city labor.

Sometimes, with outside help, things can improve, at least in the short run. Rosa María is a farmer who works a small plot of land with her family in the high altitudes of Cayambe. Like other members of her community, she is forced to deal with a rapidly changing climate. In the past, when rains failed to come, it limited how much food she and her family could consume. Decrease in production meant she had to decide between selling what she could grow for income and consumption for herself and her family. Climate change is making these failures of the rains more frequent (World Food Program 2016). To assist families like Rosa's, the World Food Program constructed a reservoir and people are using the water to grow lupini beans. Grown in the high altitudes of Cayambe, the white lupini bean is a legume rich in vegetable protein, calcium, and fiber. The community decided to plant seeds of this plant since they knew how to cultivate it. Rosa also knows how to prepare this protein-rich plant using recipes passed down through generations in her family. Once cooked, Rosa Maria also is able to sell the bean dish in the local markets, creating a source of income. Says Rosa, "We have made sacrifices, but we also have our reward" (quoted in World Food Program 2016). The longer-term impact of continued global heating, however, has the grave potential to steal away Rosa's reward. This is the troubling reality for the people living high in the mountains of Ecuador.

References

Burke, E., N. Goldenson, T., Moon, and S. Po-Chedlet. 2011. Climate and climate change in Ecuador: An overview. https://atmos.washington.edu/~pochedls/docs/ecuador_climate.pdf.

Cáceres, G. 1993. Mujer andina: Condiciones de vida y participcion. Central Ecuatoriana de Servicios Agrícolas, Quito, Ecuador.

Catanoso, J. 2017. Global climate change increasing risk of crop yield losses and food insecurity in the tropical Andes. *Mongabay.* https://news.mongabay.com/2017/11/global-climate-change-increasing-risk-of-crop-yield-losses-and-food-insecurity-in-the-tropical-andes/.

Cuenca High Life. 2015. Ecuador has lost 30 percent of its glaciers in 30 years due to climate change, scientists say: It could be a blessing in the case of the Cotopaxi volcano. https://cuencahighlife.com/ecuador-has-lost-30-percent-of-its-glaciers-in-50-years-says-organization-that-studies-andean-climate-change/.

Davies, B. 2017. Mapping the world's glaciers. *Antarctic Glaciers.org.* www.antarcticglaciers.org/glaciers-and-climate/glacier-recession/mapping-worlds-glaciers/.

Gerlach, A. 2003. *Indians, Oil and Politics: A Recent History of Ecuador.* Wilmington, DE: Scholarly Resource Books.

Hentschel, J., W. Waters, and A. Webb. 1996. Rural poverty in Ecuador: A qualitative assessment. Policy Research Working Paper 1576. World Bank. http://documents.worldbank.org/curated/en/328351468751759646/pdf/multi0page.pdf.

Hidalgo, J., R. Boelens, and J. Vos, 2017. De-colonizing water: Dispossession, water insecurity, and Indigenous claims for resources, authority, and territory. *Water History* 9: 67–85.

Jordan, E. and S. Hastenrath. 1999. Glaciers of Ecuador. U.S. Geological Survey. https://pubs.usgs.gov/pp/p1386i/ecuador/intro.html.

Meisch, L. 1992. We will not dance on the tomb of our grandparents: 500 years of resistance in Ecuador. *Latin American Anthropology Review* 4(2): 55–74.

Painter, J. 2010. Scientists investigate Ecuador's receding glaciers. BBC News. http://news.bbc.co.uk/2/hi/americas/8629527.stm.

Puertas, M. 2017. Water sources under threat from mining in Ecuador's mountains. *Mongabay*. https://news.mongabay.com/2017/11/water-sources-under-threat-from-mining-in-ecuadors-mountains/.

Rhoades, R. 2007. Disappearance of the glacier on Mama Cotacachi: Ethnoecological research and climate change in the Ecuadorian Andes. *Pirineos* 163: 37–50.

Rhoades, R., Rios, X., and J. Ochoa. 2008. Mama Cotacachi: History, local perceptions, and social impacts of climate change and glacier retreat in Ecuadorian Andes. In B. Orlove, E. Wiegandt, and B. Luckman (eds), *Darkening Peaks: Glacier Retreat, Science, and Society*. Berkeley, CA: University of California Press, pp. 216–225.

Rothmayer, J. 2016. An ethnographically inspired study of farming families and food practices in the Northern Highlands of Ecuador. Department of Social Sciences, Wageningen University. http://edepot.wur.nl/395589.

Smith, L. 2017. Statement of Chairman Lamar Smithe (R-Texas): Climate science: Assumptions, policy implications, and the scientific method. Committee on Science, Space and Technology. https://science.house.gov/sites/republicans.science.house.gov/files/documents/HHRG-115-SY-WState-S000583-20170329_0.pdf.

Tegel, S. 2012. El Salvador in battle against tide of climate change. *The Independent*, September 17. www.independent.co.uk/environment/climate-change/el-salvador-in-battle-against-tide-of-climate-change-8145210.html.

Tito, R., H. Vasconcelos, and K. Feeley, 2017. Global climate change increases risk of crop yield losses and food insecurity in the tropical Andes. *Global Change Biology*. DOI: 10.1111/gcb.13959.

Velásquez, T. 2015a. Defending life in Ecuadorian resource politics. North American Congress in Latin America (NACLA). https://nacla.org/news/2015/06/01/defending-life-ecuadorian-resource-politics.

Velásquez, T. 2015b. Defending life in Ecuadorian resource politics. Rights and Resources. https://rightsandresources.org/en/blog/defending-life-in-ecuadorian-resource-politics/#.Ws1jcy7wbm4.

Velásquez, T. 2017. Tracing the political life of Kimsacocha: Conflicts over water and mining in Ecuador's Southern Andes. *Latin American Perspectives* DOI: 10.1177/0094582X17726088.

Vidal, J. 2010. Glacial retreat: Ecuador's ticking environmental time bomb. *The Guardian*, September 22. www.theguardian.com/global-development/poverty-matters/2010/sep/22/ecuador-water-climate-change-vidal.

Wehner, R. 2003. Deflowering Ecuador. *Mother Jones* (January/February). www.motherjones.com/politics/2002/01/deflowering-ecuador/#.

World Food Program. 2016. Adapting to climate change and ensuring food security in the highlands of Ecuador. www.wfp.org/stories/adapting-climate-change-and-ensuring-food-security-highlands-ecuador.

8

ON THE BOTTOM RUNG OF A LOW-LYING NATION

Social ranking and climate change in Bangladesh

On the risky frontlines of climate change

Bangladeshi anthropologist, Siddiqur Rahman (2010), is struck by the irony that over time Bangladesh is likely to be one of the worst victims of climate change but is one of the countries least responsible for causing global warming and the turmoil it brings:

> Bangladesh's greenhouse gas emissions rate is one of the lowest in the world, both in the aggregate and in per capita terms. The per capita emission of CO_2 in Bangladesh is a mere 0.2 tons, compared with an average of six tons in the industrial world. However, because of its location in the tropics, Bangladesh is geographically exposed to a multitude of adverse impacts of climate change, a problem compounded by the country's low adaptive capacity (due to its extreme poverty).

Ati Rahman (no relation), the executive director of Bangladesh's Center for Advanced Studies and the country's top climate scientist, has a radical solution for this conundrum. Calling it "a matter of global justice," he proposes that Bangladeshis forced from their homes by climate change "should have the right to move to the countries from which all of these greenhouse gases are coming. Millions should be able to go to the United States," an idea, of course, that flies in the face of the harshly anti-immigrant, climate change-denying stance of the Trump administration (quoted in Harris 2014). Ati Rahman's proposal reflects the concept of "differentiated responsibility" adopted at the Rio Earth Summit in 1992. Parties to that convention established that the industrialized nations—those that had produced the lion's share of greenhouse gas emissions—should take the lead in combating climate change and responding to its impacts. The emergence of the concept of differentiated responsibility signaled recognition both that industrialized nations were the source of most global warming emissions and that their wealth was intimately linked to the economic activities that produced those emissions (Shue 1999).

Siddiqur Rahman (2010) does not see a brighter future for his country without dramatic mitigation and internationally supported adaptation efforts. As the temperature on the planet goes up, seas rise, and storms and storm surges intensify, he knows that there will be an increase in salinity and waterlogging in the coastal zones of Bangladesh. Salinity is deadly for most food crops, and food crops are the main sustenance for poorer Bangladeshis in rural areas. Already, he notes, the north-central, east, and central floodplains are impacted by frequent and prolonged flooding, greater water depth, and land erosion. The northwest drought-prone area of the country, however, is dealing with a scarcity of water, low rainfall, higher temperatures, more heatwaves, and sudden storms, all of which are linked to global warming. The people of Bangladesh, he stresses, face different types of risk: rising sea level will decrease 17 percent of the total land mass of the country and 13 percent of cultivated land, affecting 35 million people in 19 coastal districts. The frequency of cyclones will increase as seawater warms. Sea level rise and the intrusion of seawater into the coastal areas will increase the salinity of the soil and likely reduce fresh water by 20 percent. Food production loss will be further driven by expanded river erosion. The already weak health sector will be overburdened as the diseases of climate change mount and food insecurity continues to rise.

The impact of climate change, he argues, is clear. It is increasing people's vulnerability to poverty and social deprivation, already existing burdens of life for many people. Moreover, populations of indigenous people in several areas of the country, people whose rights are poorly protected, are likely have the least physical and social capital to allow them to adapt to the adverse effects of climate change. Climate change, explains Rahman, adds to existing challenges endured by indigenous peoples, including political and economic marginalization and land and resource encroachments by more powerful social groups and other entities (Rahman 2010). As anthropologist Jim Wilce (2004: 359) indicates,

> Risk generates anxiety. Whether or not we invoke psychological constructs like anxiety in explaining the fact, people try to extend human control into threatening or uncontrolled domains. It may well be that that which is out of control provokes such a quest in and of itself, not because it poses an immediate threat but simply because it might do so.

In short, as the impacts of climate change unfold, the people of Bangladesh face not only physical but also psychological risks. Under threat is not only their livelihoods but also their culture and all they hold meaningful—and having meaning in life is fundamental to human well-being.

Bangladesh is the eighth most populous nation in the world. People living there identify closely with their language, Bengali, and the geography of their homeland.

The dominant religion is Sunni Islam, although there is a Shia Islam minority and a small Hindu population. Indigenous Chakma and other tribal peoples live in the Chittagong Hill area in southeastern Bangladesh. Most people live in the fertile Bengal delta as farmers. In rural areas, the smallest social unit in a village is the family, which is usually made up of extended kin traced through the male line. The individual nuclear family is often submerged in this larger social unit. Patrilineal kin ties extend to larger grouping based on real, fictional, or assumed relationships. People and their close kin community participate in a voluntary religious and mutual benefit association known as a *shomaj* or *milat*. Shomajs maintain the extended kin group's mosque and support its mullah. Village disputes and other legal disputes are settled by an informal council of shomaj elders. Factional competition among shomaj elders is often a core dynamic of community social and political interaction. Nearby groups of homes, buildings that were traditionally constructed of thatched bamboo but are increasing made of brick, are called *paras*, and each has its own unique and meaningful name. Several paras constitute a *mauza*, which is the basic revenue and census survey unit in each village (Heitzman and Worden 1989).

Although farming has traditionally been seen as one of the most desirable ways of life, by the 1980s parents began encouraging their children to move from the increasingly overcrowded countryside to seek more secure employment in towns and cities or even abroad. Older ways of life based on traditional sources of prestige, such as landholding, having distinguished lineage, and maintaining religious piety, started to be replaced by having a modern education, achieving a higher income, and securing regularly paying work. Despite the ensuring migration, rural poverty continued to increase as the population grew.

Exemplary of changing conditions is the poor, rather remote village of Achingaon in Manikganj district in central Bangladesh. A community with a population of 310, all Bengali Muslims, it was studied by Rao and Hossain (2012: 418), who note:

> Thirty-five percent of the households have very small land-holdings (less than one acre), and 48 percent are landless. Although previously many worked on their own farms and as agricultural labor, less than a third of men are now actively engaged in cultivation … . Women largely work within their homestead. In the past 15 to 20 years, with the rapid expansion of employment opportunities in the Export Processing Zones … and overseas, especially to the Gulf countries, a shift is visible in people's employment choices. Nearly 27 percent of men are now migrant, working in the garment factories and welding workshops in the city or work as unskilled laborers abroad.

By 2017, about 36 percent of the population lived in cities (World Factbook 2017) and Dhaka had grown into a populous megacity. As a result of continued labor migration and faster modes of communication, Dhaka is no longer feared by villagers as a distant, unknown and threatening place, although it is not necessarily seen as welcoming or a good place to live. Migration and adaptation to the new urban environment is not a straightforward or simple endeavor. It necessitates the acquisition of new life skills, such as the ability to negotiate with bosses, landlords, and other strangers by individuals who are used to face-to-face daily involvement primarily with kin. Further, it entails learning the insider languages of particular work environments, adjusting to new food patterns, and adopting a new lifestyle in many ways different from the one experienced in the rural setting; these changes include both adapting existing skills as well as acquiring new ones.

Some people are successful in this transition. Kamran, now a middle-aged man, came to Dhaka from Achingaon at age 15.

> In 1979 my cousin advised me to learn welding in Dhaka. I worked as a "helper" for three years, receiving only food and accommodation, and no salary. I slept on the shop floor with three other apprentices, observing the master's activities, learning the skill and the trade from him, and talking and sharing with each other. In 1982, I moved to another welding shop for taka [the currency of Bangladeh] 290 monthly. By then, I was known as a good welder, so I switched shops to increase my earnings and also learn the more difficult aspects of welding work.
>
> *(Quoted in Rao and Hossain 2012: 420)*

Eventually, in 2003, Kamran was able to acquire his own welding shop where he employed ten workers. He assisted at least 25 boys from Achingaon to learn welding. Kamran hopes to retire in Achingaon, where he built a new masonry house. He remains a respected man in the village. Although he came from a poor family and never completed his primary education, in the village he is called engineer, which makes him feel very proud.

But most, more recent, climate-driven migrants to Dhaka do not share Kamran's success. Typical is Parul Akter who was forced to flee her rural home with her family to escape floodwaters. The shack she shares with her husband and four children lies on the edge of the sprawling Korail slum, which is next to a lake. When it rains, dank water sloshes into their shelter. Only the bed, which they raised up on bricks, stays dry. "This room is all we have, so we need to stay here no matter what happens," said Akter (quoted in McPherson 2015). As Parul Akter and her family discovered, Dhaka's urban periphery has evolved as rings of concentrated urban poverty. Most of the new migrants to the city are forced to try to find shelter in the peripheries because housing costs are lower. At the same time, the poor already living in the city center are being forced to the periphery because of the demand by wealthier groups for land for urban development. The new urban poor living in the peripheries are economically marginalized as they are excluded from the formal sectors of the economy and must try to make a living in the undependable informal economy. They are also marginalized in terms of access to health and other services in the city. Victims of circumstances they did not create, the urban poor are seen as disruptive, unproductive, and even a threat and are often treated by the police and other sectors of social control institutions as criminals (Hossain 2013). One place where some migrants do find work is the garment industry, a labor-intensive field that mass-produces goods, including rapidly changing "fast fashions" for export to Western markets. It is an industry with a tainted record with regard to worker' rights and well-being. In 2013, a five-story garment factory collapsed killing more than 1,000 workers and injuring 2,500 more. Even though cracks had been discovered in the building, garment workers were ordered to return to work, which they did just as the building collapsed.

Employment in the garment industry is not a sure thing. After Cyclone Aila destroyed his village of Dakope, Bablu Gazi and his wife Shirin Aktar worked with other community members to rebuild the raised bank along the river washed away by the storm surge. They also rebuilt their hut, determined to continue to try to make a go of it in Dakope. The first year their harvest, though small, was sufficient to squeak by on. But the soil was becoming increasingly infertile because of the salt-water intrusion. Plots of land that in the past could support three harvests a year could now only produce one, and some previously productive plots were now barren. Struggling with food insecurity and hunger for two years, the couple finally gave up and moved to Chittagong, hoping that Aktar could find garment industry work and Gazi could find day-laborer employment. Indeed, Gazi quickly found work digging foundations for new buildings. But headaches and other health problems made it impossible for Aktar to work in a garment factory. The couple longs to return to Dakope. Gazi says, "I don't want to stay here too long … . If we can save some money, then we will go back. I'll work on a piece of land and try to make it fertile again" (quoted in Harris 2014). Many of his neighbors packed together in a slum of Chittagong feel the same way; none of them want to be in the city, but the extent of the salinization in Dakope and the wider area likely makes Gazi's dream an unfulfillable reality.

Another industry some migrants fleeing the impacts of climate change find employment in is the tanneries. A hundred and fifty tanneries operate in Dhaka's Hazaribagh district. The factories use toxic chemicals to work animal hides for the country's lucrative export leather industry while dumping at least 21,000 cubic feet of untreated wastewater daily into the waters of one of the of the world's most crowded cities. The tanneries export shoes, handbags, suitcases, and belts to 70 countries worldwide, including China, South Korea, Japan, Italy, Germany, Spain, and the United States. While wealthy shoppers can find these goods at local malls at prices none of the workers who made them could ever afford, what tannery workers do get along with their small income is a panoply of health problems. An investigation by Human Rights Watch (2012: 8) found that

> Past and present tannery workers described and displayed a range of health conditions including prematurely aged, discolored, itchy, peeling, acid-burned, and rash-covered skin; fingers corroded to stumps; aches, dizziness, and nausea; and disfigured or amputated limbs.

Moreover, many children work 12 or even 14 hours a day in the tanneries.

Despite what awaits many of them in the crowded city, adverse climate events continually push people toward Dhaka and other cities. In 2007, for example, a tropical cyclone made landfall and caused one of the worst natural disasters in Bangladesh. Cyclone Sidor formed in the central Bay of Bengal, and quickly strengthened to develop sustained winds of 160 mph, making it a Category 5-equivalent tropical cyclone on the Saffir-Simpson Scale. This is the highest ranking for storm wind speed. More frequent and stronger cyclones caused by climate change push walls of water 50 to 60 miles up the Delta's rivers, inundating villages. In the case of Sidor, it is estimated that the storm caused between 5,000 and 10,000 deaths. After Sidor, a huge number of migrants moved to the city. Akther, for example, who migrated to the capital with his family, commented, "We lost our house, land, cattle and we were unable to manage our livelihood there after Sidor. Now we are alright here as we are working in the factories" (quoted in Hossain 2013: 372).

Based on their fieldwork in Bangladesh, Rao and Hossain (2012: 415) indicate:

> The export-oriented garments industry and overseas migrants' remittances comprise 20 percent of Bangladesh's GDP ... . Employment in the factories, and in manual jobs overseas, involves adjusting to harsh working environments, long working hours at low wages, cheating, harassment, and lack of security.

Talking of the harshness of life for a rural migrant in the city, one man, who like many others is unemployed, told Rao and Hossain:

> I feel disappointed, as I am unemployed. There is no respect here for an unemployed person. While people do respect those who are educated, it is difficult to get a good job after passing grade ten. I will go abroad as I can do any kind of work to earn there.
>
> *(Quoted in Rao and Hossain 2012: 417)*

Another man, Rashid, moved to an urban slum in Dhaka with his family because of the impacts of climate change. Rashid lost his land because of river erosion and felt his only real option was to migrate to the city. He says, "I never wanted to move here but I had no other option to choose. When my land was destroyed by the river, what I can do there. I have learnt [how to pull a] rickshaw to [support] my family here" (quoted in Hossain 2013: 372). Like Rashid, a massive number of people fleeing the effects of climate change are headed to the decrepit urban slums located on Dhaka's peripheries. Residents eke out a living as rickshaw drivers, street sweepers, and domestic workers. Many say they miss the countryside where they could grew their own food (McPherson 2015). The places where they now live are seen as having no value or even purpose by wealthier classes. These areas have, in effect, become the dumping grounds of the urban poor in the new age of surplus humanity. Life and labour in the urban peripheries reveals their poverty and marginality. The experience of poverty and [street] violence for the migrants living in the peripheries … [embodies] the very opposite to their expectations and aspirations.

(Hossain 2013: 380)

Climate scientist Ati Rahman and his research group carried out several surveys in the poor areas of the capital and used these to estimate that as many as 1.5 million of the five million slum dwellers in Dhaka moved from villages near the Bay of Bengal.

Ironically, even Dhaka, which is low-lying relative to sea level, is prone to flooding. The city is also running dry. About 90 percent of its water supply comes from ground reserves, which are being depleted by almost ten feet a year. The expectable result is chronic shortages during the summer months. Poor people in particular are not getting enough to drink. Moreover, the city is slowly sinking.

Areas of high risk from climate change and other anthropogenic stressors

As is evident from the prior discussion, Bangladesh is one of the most vulnerable countries to climate change, especially from rising oceans but also from extreme weather. The struggling nation has a 435-mile long coastline that is threaded by a vast network of rivers draining the huge flow of the Ganges-Brahmaputra-Meghna system. These three rivers come together in Bangladesh upstream from the Bay of Bengal. The mega-river discharges on the Bangladesh coastline and is heavily laden with sediments, giving rise to a highly dynamic estuary. The low topography and general flatness of the land creates a strong backwash effect, with significant seasonal variation in the interaction between brackish waters and freshwater. Freshwater dominates during the monsoon and the salt water penetrates further inland during the dry season (Agrawala and Ota 2003). Increased sea levels under climate change result in saline intrusion further upstream into the river system. The whole process is likely to lead to increased salinization and flood risks for coastal areas.

Linked to the problem of coastal flooding is the potential impact of climate change on the Sundarbans, which span southwestern Bangladesh and the adjoining coast in the Indian state of West Bengal. Comprising an area of over 6,000 square miles, the Sundarbans represent the largest contiguous mangrove forest ecosystem in the world. With roots like spider legs planted both in the water and on land, mangroves constitute unique ecoenvironments that "foster relations that blur boundaries between land and sea, animate and inanimate, nature and society" (Vaugh 2017: 262). The saturated mud flat of the typical mangrove is a hostile environment for typical plants, because (like rainforests) the soil has very low levels of oxygen and toxic levels of sulfides. Ocean water generally has 33–38 parts of salt per thousand, but evaporation of water from mangrove mud results in much higher salt concentrations, which plants must cope with. All species that inhabit the outer (ocean-facing) portion of the mangrove swamp are halophytes. These are plants that are adapted to saline soils and often grow as if on stilts (keeping only the roots in the water). Some mangrove plant species can tolerate soils more than double the salinity of ocean water. Plant species that are less resistant to salt damage grow on the landward side, where high tides reach only infrequently, or along riverbanks (called estuarine mangroves) where freshwater mingles with sea water due to tidal influences. Mangroves serve as breeding and nursing grounds for marine fish, shellfish, and other species. They help stabilize shorelines and reduce the devastating impact of ocean storms and surges, and, through their root systems, they limit erosion. Climatically, they are to the coasts what wetlands are to land areas: they function as storm buffers and flood inhibitors. They are also sources of food, medicine, fuel, and building materials for local human communities. Additionally, they play a role in the sequestration of CO^2 and thus help regulate climate.

The Sundarbans is a biodiverse zone that is home to the Bengal tiger and 425 other animal species. The area provides livelihood for about 3.5 million inhabitants within and around the forest boundary. Industrial development in the region and the opening up of access to trade, however, increased the demand for forest resources, especially timber. The growing barge traffic and lax environmental enforcement by the government and the fossil fuel industries' drive for profits have led to a number of oil spills, which harm this critical ecosystem on which so many depend.

On December 9, 2014, for example, a wrecked tanker released approximately 94,000 gallons of heavy fuel oil directly into the Shela River, which runs through the Sundarbans. The incident reflects the fact that the Sundarbans coastal waters have significant oil tanker traffic. In 2015, a capsized cargo vessel, the *Jabalenoor*, leaked 200 tons of potash fertilizer into the Sundarbans' Bhola River, southeast of the earlier oil spill (Alexander 2015).

Another threat to the Sundarbans is commercial saltwater shrimp (prawn) farming. The desire for quick profits by the industry has led to the adoption of destructive production methods of export-oriented industrial aquaculture. Vast tracts of mangrove forests have been cleared to make way for the establishment of pond-based coastal shrimp farming facilities. Ironically, industrial shrimp aquaculture requires clean water, but the way it is practiced leads to severe water pollution. The often unrestricted use of chemical inputs, such as antibiotics, pesticides, and water additives, when combined with the build-up on pond bottoms of unconsumed shrimp food and feces, has led to epidemic shrimp diseases and pond closures and desertion. The end product is a ruined, poisoned, and—barring considerable cost and restoration effort—unusable area that no longer serves any of the critical functions offered by mangroves. The lucrative earnings of shrimp culture development in any local area are short-lived, while the real costs in terms of consequent environmental damage and social disruption are long term. So many of the outer island mangroves have been destroyed that storm surges caused by cyclones now move much further inland, causing further destruction and loss of life.

The climate change impacts threatening the Sundarbans magnify the adverse consequences of these other anthropogenic ecosystem stressors. These impacts include increased intensity of river flow and associated erosion due to extreme weather, while the rise in sea level leads to flooding and salinization of land, including areas used to grow crops or raise freshwater shrimp. Since the composition of vegetation has a strong influence on the distribution of forest animal species, climate change is beginning to affect the long-term sustainability of the ecosystem. It is believed to be unlikely that forest species will have sufficient time or room, given inland settlements, to migrate in response to these changes. Loss of animal species will have negative rebound effects including on local communities.

Sirajul Islam once lived in Kolbari village across the river from the Sundarbans with his wife and four children. He had one acre of land, which he used to raise freshwater galda shrimp (*Macrobrachium rosenbergii*) for sale. Then in 2009 a severe storm, Cyclone Aila, hit his region and Kolbari village was flooded, along with Islam's acre of land. The most devastating part of the storm was a near ten-foot wall of water that roared through local villages at mid-afternoon. Aila was responsible for about 350 deaths in Bangladesh and India and more than one million people were left homeless. Islam and his family fled temporarily to Shyamnagar, a town nine miles away, where for four months he made $4–5 a day driving a rented motorbike for hire. When the floodwater finally subsided, Islam returned home but found that his field was too salty for galda shrimp. He also found that village buildings were flattened and there was no longer fresh water to drink. So in 2011 the family moved, like so many others, to Dhaka. Comments Islam, "The cyclone had broken my economical backbone by destroying everything … If there had not been such a big cyclone, I would not have moved to Dhaka" (quoted in Darby 2017). In his small Dhaka home, Islam displayed a set of deer antlers, a trophy from hunting in the Sundarbans. Besides raising shrimp in Kolbari village, he caught and sold fish and crabs in the Sundarbans and gathered honey from beehives in the mangroves. The family's income was supplemented by the wages earned by his eldest daughter, who worked in a garment factory in Chittagong, a large port city on the southeastern coast of Bangladesh. Now that life is gone.

One resident of the area who has fought to remain despite the punishing cyclone is Jahanara Khatun. She was at home with her husband, parents, and four children when Aila arrived. Their mud and bamboo hut quickly was washed away. Unable to save their belongings, Khatun put her smallest child on her back and the family fought their way through the surging flood. They made it to a road that was above the raging water, but her parents were swept away. Pushed by the rushing water, her father and mother were eventually able to grab a tree. They clung tightly to the tree for hours waiting for the water to calm down. Then they swam to a hut that was still standing and climbed on to the roof. The family was reunited the next day, but the night on the road had been harrowing because of the many snakes also seeking higher ground. The rain continued to fall and they drank what they could capture. Rescue workers arrived several days later with bottled water, food, and other supplies. But the event damaged her husband's health. To pay for treatment and the cost of rebuilding her hut, the family borrowed money from a loan shark. In exchange for the loan, Khatun and her three older children, 10–15 years in age, agreed to work in a brickmaking factory for seven months. Her husband died four years later. Khatun was able to build a new bamboo home, but it is below sea level behind a slumping bank that was built to hold back the river. Her time is spent gathering cow dung to use as fertilizer on a small vegetable garden. But the salinity of the soil allows only marginal rewards for her labor. Nevertheless, she wants to hold out as this is home. Battling global warming, however, is not a fight one destitute woman can win (Harris 2014).

Some people from the Kolbari village area did not flee to Dhaka but rather crossed illegally into India hoping to find a livelihood. This was the case with the two younger sisters of Zainab Begum, a 40-year old woman from Gabura village. Gabura was devastated by Aila. As in Kolbari, not a single house was left standing. The levee that was supposed to keep the river out failed in this and then trapped a layer of salty water on the land for three years. During this time Begum lived in a makeshift house on the embankment; others with more resources left the area permanently. Eventually, the government helped the village rebuild, including constructing a cyclone shelter. But land that had previously good for growing one rice crop a year was now too salty for rice. Some people turned to saltwater shrimp farming. The risks attached to entering India, Begum's sisters found, are significant. One of them got caught by border guards and they beat and detained her for a week before she could bribe her way out. Now her sisters and their families work as waste pickers in Tamil Nadu, a southern Indian state. Waste pickers comb the mounds of trash discarded by a city in search of recyclable items that can be sold to dealers. The work is not just dirty, it is dangerous, and the rewards are usually small, providing only a marginal existence. All members of families must scour the trash, even children, to make enough money to live on. Scrap building materials found in the trash piles are used to fashion shelters. But life can be precarious and storms can cause deadly trash slides.

Disappearing islands

Among the first climate change refugees in Bangladesh are the people of Bhola Island. Located at the mouth of the Ganges delta area, 250 miles from the capital, Bangladesh's largest island, Bhola, is home to 1.6 million people. Due to rising sea levels, the island is half as large as it was in the 1960s. For this reason, Bhola is one of the places that has been dubbed "ground zero" for climate change. Jalil Mia, who now lives in Dhaka, used to reside on Bhopa. Recalling the night when a storm flooded and destroyed his home, forcing him and his family to flee, he stated, "Luckily we survived that night as we went to take shelter at a cyclone centre. But my house and all the furniture and even the utensils—everything was washed away" (quoted in Roy 2009). Now Jalil, who was once a farmer, lives in a slum in the capital with his family. He works unloading boats on the Buriganga River. His two daughters are going to school. But his son Palash, a 13-year-old, had to take a job at a glass factory in the old part of the city to help support the family.

Other populated islands in the Bay of Bengal are also facing the threat of rising seas and more intense storms. People from Kutubdia island moved their community to a site called Cox's Bazar on the mainland. They call their neighborhood Kutubdia Para (Kutubdia village). "We did not want to forget our island. So we named our village after it," explained an older man who made the move but who like his neighbors still clings to his memories of home (quoted in Roy 2009). The population of what the government of Bangladesh refers to as "immediately threatened" islands, or "*chars*" as they are known in the country, is over four million (Glennon 2017). What happened on Kutubdia island increasingly appears to be in microcosm the disaster facing the millions of Bangladeshis who live on its disappearing islands (Wright 2017).

Poverty and climate change preparedness

In order to better understand the complex relationship between environmental risk, poverty, and vulnerability in the context of climate change, Brouwer and colleagues (2007) interviewed almost 700 floodplain delta residents, mostly middle-aged men who were heads of household, living without flood protection along the River Meghna in southeast Bangladesh. At the time of their study, over 400,000 people lived in the area, most of them farmers. Almost three-quarters of the land was being used for farming, with rice being the main crop but wheat, vegetables, pulses, oil seeds, and corn also grown. The main objective was to investigate the complex relationship between poverty and social and economic vulnerability in a concrete case. Annual monsoon rainfall causes excessive flows in the rivers and flooding of the area almost every year. The floods damage houses, agricultural crops, and local transportation and other infrastructure. In recent years, however, the area has suffered from devastating flooding far beyond what was seen in the past. This enhanced wave of intense storms is attributed to climate change.

A quarter of the participants identified flooding as the main problem they faced, followed by bad roads (23%), unemployment (20%), and lack of electricity (17%). Almost half of the population (46%) reported that each year they suffer from diarrhea during the rainy season. The mean annual flood damage costs are almost $200 per household or about 20 percent of average household income. The researchers found that people who live in villages that are closer to the river have lower income levels. Also, they discovered a significant negative relationship between distance from the river and equity of income distribution. Villages located further away from the river had more equal income among residents. Another finding was that people with lower incomes suffer greater water inundation levels and more exposure to flood risks. Participants who owned more land suffer lower inundation levels than those with less land. At the community level, greater income inequality is associated with higher costs from flood damage.

These finding confirm the hypothesis (Adger 2000) that vulnerability is determined, among other things, by income inequality. The assumption behind this hypothesis is that inequality is linked to the extent to which resources are allocated communally. Communities with more equitable distribution of wealth are more likely to spend their resources on collective projects such as flood protection than if most resources are concentrated in the hands of a small, comparatively wealthy sector of the population. Higher levels of income equality tend to promote more cohesive communities whose members are able collectively to support each other in preventing and responding to threat.

Flood damage costs can be controlled somewhat by actions aimed at preventing, avoiding, or alleviating the physical and socioeconomic impacts of flooding. One such coping mechanism is income diversification. Households living further away from the river not only have more income, they also have significantly more income streams. The researchers also found that 86 percent of the floodplain residents were not using any preventive measures to limit flood damage. This, people explained, was for several reasons; most importantly they lacked the financial means needed to protect themselves against flooding, followed by not knowing which type of measures to take, and the fatalistic belief that flooding is a natural process that cannot be prevented. Those participants who build elevated structures to protect them from flooding have significantly higher incomes and reap the reward of suffering significantly lower costs from flood damage. In sum, this research confirms that there is a positive relationship between environmental risk, poverty, and vulnerability. While this is true during regular annual flooding, depending on the level of the storm surge involved it may be doubly true with the more intense storms being ushered in by global warming.

Climate refugees

Bangladesh's high vulnerability to rising sea levels exists because it has so many people (25% of its population) living in low-lying coastal zones. Globally, the number of people living in low-elevation coastal zones, as well as the number of people exposed to flooding from "1 in 100 years" storm surge events, is highest in China, India, Indonesia, Viet Nam, and Bangladesh (Neumann et al. 2015). Some climate scientists predict that by the year 2030 as many as 20 million people in Bangladesh will be climate refugees. As noted, many such refugees are already moving into the densely crowded slums of the capital, Dhaka, which is itself facing grave fresh water problems because of the pollution of nearby rivers.

Currently, there is no international law to protect the rights of these people, even though they are among an estimated 25 million climate refugees in the world according the Environmental Justice Foundation. The United Nations High Commissioner for Refugees, also known as the UN Refugee Agency, does not recognize climate or environment refugees and hence they are not counted or able to receive refugee assistance. This roadblock occurs because climate and environmental refugees were not included under the UN's 1951 Refugee Convention, which tended to focus on people who were displaced because of persecution, conflict, and war, nor were they included in subsequent additions to international refugee laws. In recent years there has been a push to amend the Convention to allow for environmental displacement, but this has been resisted by those who want to keep the conflict focus, as this source alone continues to produce enormous numbers of refugees in critical need of assistance. There are also conceptual problems. For example, to qualify as a refugee under the 1951 Convention it is necessary to have a "well-founded fear of persecution," but it is unclear who might be considered an agent of persecution in climate-related displacement. It is also uncertain how the indiscriminate nature of climate-related causes of displacement could be reconciled with a legal definition of persecution.

As a result, climate change refugees literally fall through the cracks of international refugee policies. As the Environmental Justice Foundation (EJF) (2014: 5) stresses,

> there is a deficit of adequate legal and policy frameworks governing climate-induced displacement at the international level. [This deficit is referred] to a 'protection gap' to indicate the lack of satisfactory measures addressing the various adaptation, disaster risk reduction, humanitarian assistance and legal protection needs of climate refugees … . [T]he term 'climate refugee' underscores the human rights dimension of climate change and also successfully reflects the reality that a form of refugeehood – the experience of involuntarily leaving one's home due to persecution – is an inherent feature of the globally unequal distribution of responsibility for climate change, which has systematically marginalised the world's most vulnerable communities.

EJF employs the term "climate-induced displacement" to refer to a variety of situations in which environmental hazards and processes of change related to global warming can reasonably be said to have contributed to the dislodgment of people from an area for any period of time, without actually implying direct or exclusive causality. In some cases, such as displacement from small island nations, climate refugees may be rendered stateless individuals. Climate change, in short, has the (well demonstrated) capacity to destroy people's homes, take away all their possessions, rob them of a livelihood, tear them loose from their supportive social networks, displace them to areas culturally different from their prior experience, subject them to marginalization in their new location, render them stateless, and cause death and injury. And yet, for those industries that produce greenhouse gases in massive quantities, making all this suffering possible, the issue of culpability is lost in legal systems designed to sustain social inequality. This is the problem with legal frameworks: someone makes the rules and enjoys the benefits of engaging in harm-causing, but profit-making, activities without fear of punishment and others endure the adverse aspects of their enforcement. This bedrock, but often denied, truth was creatively expressed by Brant Parker and Johnny Hart in an oft-cited classic daily newspaper cartoon strip, *The Wizard of Id*. The strip is set in a rundown and oppressed kingdom called "Id" with a tyrannical monarch who refers to his subjects as "Idiots". In a 1964 edition of the cartoon, the king urges his subjects to follow the golden rule. When someone asks, "What's that?," the peasants shout out, "Whoever has the gold makes the rules." As Nobel prize-winning French poet, novelist, and journalist, Anatole France (1894: 118), whimsically pointed out, in its majestic equality, "the law … forbids rich and poor alike to sleep under bridges, beg in the streets, and steal loaves of bread." Of course, such laws are only ever enforced against the poor because the rich are not forced to sleep under bridges, beg for food, or steal loaves of bread. The wealthy, however, are not held legally accountable for the lack of housing that causes people to sleep under bridges, and the lack of jobs that force people to beg or steal food.

References

Adger, W. 2000. Institutional adaptation to environmental risk under the transition in Vietnam. *Annals of the Association of American Geographers* 90(4): 738–758.

Agrawala, S. and T. Ota. 2003. *Development and Climate Change in Bangladesh: Focus on Coastal Flooding and the Sundarbans*. Paris: Organisation for Economic Co-operation and Development.

Alexander, C. 2015. After oil spill, unique mangrove forest faces more threats. *National Geographic*. https://news.nationalgeographic.com/2015/05/150507-sundarbans-india-bangladesh-oil-spill-royal-bengal-tiger-irrawaddy-dolphin-bay-of-bengal/.

Brouwer, R., S. Akter, L. Brander, and E. Haque. 2007. Socioeconomic vulnerability and adaptation to environmental risk: A case study of climate change and flooding in Bangladesh. *Risk Analysis* 27(2): 313–326.

Darby, M. 2017. What will become of Bangladesh's climate migrants? *Climate Home News*. www.climatechangenews.com/2017/08/14/will-become-bangladeshs-climate-migrants/.

Environmental Justice Foundation (EJF). 2014. Falling through the cracks: A briefing on climate change, displacement and international governance frameworks. London: EJF.

France, A. 1894. *The Red Lily*. Paris: Maison Mazarin.

Glennon, R. 2017. The unfolding tragedy of climate change in Bangladesh. *Scientific American*. https://blogs.scientificamerican.com/guest-blog/the-unfolding-tragedy-of-climate-change-in-bangladesh/.

Harris, G. 2014. Borrowing time on disappearing land. *New York Times*, March 29. www.nytimes.com/2014/03/29/world/asia/facing-rising-seas-bangladesh-confronts-the-consequences-of-climate-change.html?_r=0.

Heitzman, J. and R. Worden 1989. *Bangladesh: A Country Study*. Washington, DC: Department of the Army.

Hossain, S. 2013. Migration, urbanization and poverty in Dhaka, Bangladesh. *Journal of the Asiatic Society of Bangladesh* 58(2): 369–382.

Human Rights Watch. 2012. *Toxic Tanneries: The Health Repercussions of Bangladesh's Hazaribagh Leather*. New York: Human Rights Watch.

McPherson, P. 2015. Dhaka: The city where climate refugees are already a reality. *The Guardian*, December 1. www.theguardian.com/cities/2015/dec/01/dhaka-city-climate-refugees-reality.

Neumann, B., A. Vafeidis, J. Zimmerman, and R. Nichols. 2015. Future coastal population growth and exposure to sea-level rise and coastal flooding: A global assessment. *PLOS One* 10(6): e0131375.

Rahman, S. 2010. Climate change and human rights in Bangladesh. *Anthropology News* 51 (1): 30–31.

Rao, N. and M. Hossain 2012 "I want to be respected": Migration, mobility, and the construction of alternate educational discourses in rural Bangladesh. *Anthropology & Education* 43 (4): 415–428.

Roy, P. 2009. Climate refugees of the future. *International Institute for Environment and Development*. www.iied.org/climate-refugees-future.

Shue, H. 1999. Global environment and international inequality. *International Affairs* 75: 531–545.

Vaugh, S. 2017. Disappearing mangroves: The epistemic politics of climate adaptation in Guyana. *Cultural Anthropology* 32(2): 242–268.

Wilce, J. 2004. Madness, fear, and control in Bangladesh: Clashing bodies of power/ knowledge. *Medical Anthropology Quarterly* 18(3): 357–375.

World Factbook. 2017. Bangladesh. www.cia.gov/library/publications/the-world-factbook/ geos/bg.html.

Wright, P. 2017. Bangladesh's rising seas, erosion robs climate change refugees of everything, again and again. The Weather Channel. https://weather.com/science/environm ent/news/2017-11-10-bangladesh-climate-change-victims/.

9

HAITI

A legacy of colonialism, a future of climate change

Troubled past, a damaged land

While Haiti has a rich and colorful history on the Caribbean island of Hispaniola, which it shares with the Dominican Republic, the country has long been shaped by external political and economic domination, enormous poverty, and intense vulnerability. Its population is almost completely descended from nearly half a million African slaves, who were brutally imported to toil for their French masters but rose up and won their independence in 1804. To force the French out and put an end to the culture of slavery, Haitian rebels had to burn the island's economic assets, including a thousand sugar and coffee plantations that would have provided an economic foundation after the Revolution. Nonetheless, their victory made Haiti the second country in the Americas, after the U.S., to free itself of colonial rule. But unlike the U.S., Haiti was forced to pay France an indemnity of 80 million gold francs for the loss of its most lucrative colony. Overtly, this blood money was intended to repay former French plantation owners for the property they lost in the revolution, and, in turn, France agreed to recognize Haiti's independence, although it took 21 years for this recognition to occur. Other countries that participated in the global slave trade responded to Haiti's achievement by isolating Haiti. The new nation's motivation for paying the gold was fear of re-invasion by France, which was probably a real possibility. When France picked up the first gold payment in Haiti, it sent 12 well-armed warships to affirm its prowess. It took until 1947 for Haiti to finally pay off the interest on the debt to France. The steep reparation began the economic downfall of Haiti and its troubled history of poverty and suffering.

The French plantations had another lasting effect on the islanders: they began a process of deforestation and significant mountain erosion. French lumber companies selected desired tree species, especially old-growth mahogany, and cut them down for shipment to France. This process even continued after independence to raise money to pay the French debt. Rapid deforestation of Haiti was also spurred on during the colonial period when coffee growing was introduced in 1730. Upland forests were cleared and within 50 years a quarter of the colony's land was planted in coffee. The system of plantation monoculture without crop rotation and the planting of indigo, tobacco, and sugarcane between the rows of coffee plants exhausted soil of its nutrients and contributed to rapid erosion (Paskett and Pholoctete, 1990). A policy of concentrating land ownership implemented during U.S. occupation of Haiti, from 1915 to 1934, led to large areas of woodland being cut down for plantation expansion. Additionally, the U.S. saddled Haiti with a dynastic dictatorial family that drained the country of wealth. The Duvalier dictatorships between 1957 and 1986 adopted a program of terror to create a docile, low-paid labor force for export assembly production for the global market.

Following colonial rule, land remained unequally distributed among the Haitian people, and peasant farmers were only allowed access to marginal slopes between 650 and 1,900 feet above the fertile plains and below the zones of continued coffee production by wealthy Haitian landowners. Small farmers planted a combination of New World crops introduced during the colonial period (Murray 1991). Hillside soils, subject to deforestation, were particularly susceptible to erosion when they were cleared for farming and hit by intense storms. Lacking other sources of fuel for cooking, farmers slowly cut down most remaining trees. Urban demand for charcoal and fuel wood further stressed the environment and its ability to hold back flooding waters from rainstorms. Gully erosion is widespread, especially along rural roads and paths. A Haitian saying that expresses the problem of erosion is: "The mountains have grown old. You can see their bones poking through their skin" (quoted in McClintock 2003). With unemployment estimated at 70 percent, trees are a highly sought after commodity. Haiti is now the most deforested country in the Caribbean. Consequently, it is estimated that Haiti loses around 25,000–37,000 acres of once-fertile land to erosion every year.

Poverty and inequality in Haiti

Haitian poverty and inequality statistics are striking. Over 75 percent of the population lives in poverty, of which 55 percent is mired in extreme poverty, living on less than two dollars a day. A mere 10 percent of the population owns 68 percent of the wealth of the country. Haiti has the highest wealth inequality in the western hemisphere, a legacy of colonialism, U.S. intervention, and neoliberal economics imposed on the debt-ridden country. Engle (2016: 55) notes the consequences of neoliberalism for Haiti's urban workers:

> In terms of economic development, strategies to create jobs through export processing zones for assembly industries have been a 'manifest failure' intended to exploit Haiti's 'ultracheap labour.' This approach has contributed to environmental degradation, reduction of land needed for agriculture,

increasing numbers of people living in miserable conditions in vast urban informal settlements – and with jobs that, for the most part, fail to pay workers a living wage.

Poverty is especially high in rural areas where 82 percent of the population is impoverished, 77 percent of which is in extreme poverty. Two-thirds of the rural population cannot read or write and many people do not even hold their own birth certificate. Unemployment is about 40 percent (Charles 2012). Levels of poverty in Haiti are generally assessed as the most severe in the western hemisphere. Globally, Haiti ranks 163 out of 185 of countries on the UN's Human Development Index (United Nations Development Programme 2016), a summary measure of average achievement in three key dimensions of human development: health/longevity, education, and income. Haiti ranks poorly on all of these measures.

Poverty significantly affects health. In rural areas in particular, people lack access to basic health care services due to poverty. Haiti has some of the worst health statistics in the western hemisphere. While life expectancy in the U.S., just 800 miles northwest of Haiti, is 76 years, in Haiti it is 61 years. The probability of living to 65 in Haiti is 34 percent; in the U.S. it is 77 percent. Infant mortality is 54 per 1,000 live births in Haiti compared to six per 1,000 live births in the U.S. (NationMaster 2015).

Lack of access health care in Haiti is not only an issue of cost but also the result of a shortage of doctors and facilities (Larson et al. 2015). Rosseel and co-workers (2010) reported there were only 25 doctors available per 100,000 people in Haiti in 2009, compared to 230 doctors per 100,000 people in the U.S. The scarcity of medical equipment and supplies in Haiti hospitals contributes to medical response shortages, putting its population at greater risks of acquiring diseases. The U.S. has four times more hospital beds per 1,000 people than Haiti (NationMaster 2015). Additionally, in terms of water and sanitation infrastructure, Haiti is the most underserved country in the western hemisphere. Only 69 percent of the population has access to an improved water source; 17 percent had access to improved sanitation facilities in 2010. This level of coverage is far below the regional average of 80 percent for Latin America and the Caribbean (Gelting et al. 2013). Lack of water and sanitation services contribute to the severity and rapid spread of infectious disease, such as the deadly cholera epidemic that broke out in 2010 and killed over 8,000 people. Research by Mazzeo (2009) found that according to hospital data, the three most common diseases affecting rural populations diagnosed between 1996 and 2001 were parasitic infections (20% of patients), malaria (18%), and respiratory illnesses (13%). The country's total annual expenditure on health per capita is a mere $131 (World Health Organization 2015).

Food insecurity is a long-standing and pressing problem in Haiti. It is estimated that Haiti suffers from one of the heaviest burdens of hunger and malnutrition in the western hemisphere, with 40 percent of households having one or more members who are undernourished and 30 percent of children showing symptoms of chronic malnutrition. In 2012, the rates of these symptoms were striking: the proportion of stunted children under five years of age was 21.9 percent; wasting levels were 5.1 percent; and the percentage of underweight children was 11.4 percent. Stunting reflects a child's failure to thrive. It is irreversible. It develops when a child endures chronic malnutrition early in life. It often begins in the womb when a mother, who herself is malnourished, does not get enough nutritious food to support her baby's growth and development. Wasting, or thinness, usually indicates a recent and severe process of weight loss, often associated with acute starvation and possibly severe disease. Overall, approximately 50 percent of Haiti's population is undernourished (USAID 2017).

The lived experience of food insecurity and hunger is expressed by two individuals interviewed by Engle:

> When we can get it we eat meat; also rice, beans, plantains, corn, sweet potatoes, avocadoes, oranges. We get them from our gardens and the market. We eat 2–3 times per day, or once per day when things are tight. Sometimes we go to bed without having eaten, we wake up, make coffee, and have nothing else all day. Or a good Samaritan comes and brings some food for us, we cook a meal and go to bed. Sometimes we don't have salt or oil, so we just boil whatever it is, take some greens from the bushes, and eat them. We can't buy on credit, because we won't have money to repay it.
>
> *(Quoted in Engle 2016: 98)*

> [I]f you have 1,000 [Haitian] dollars, you will be holding only a little plastic bag to carry what you purchased. 100 [Haitian] dollars cannot buy a good pair of sandals. Life has become very hard for us.
>
> *(Quoted in Engle 2016: 98)*

A perfect storm of events, including bad weather, poor harvests, and rising oil prices led to skyrocketing grain prices across the globe and triggered a global food crisis in 2008. The rise in staple food prices brought about snapping point in Haiti and led to a series of food riots. Haiti's growing dependence on foreign food imports and the jump in food prices caused households to further cut their food purchases, which has led to growing hunger, especially among the poor. Ultimately, despite initial inaction, the government began to subsidize the cost of rice, which diminished popular unrest (Mazzeo 2009).

Storms and climate change

Historically, hurricanes and other severe storms have proven to be especially disastrous in Haiti. Unrelenting rains and savage winds, which comprise hurricanes, produce devastating mudslides and sustained flooding. In the wake of such intense climatic events, thousands of inhabitants must cope with severely damaged (or completely destroyed) homes, deteriorated living conditions, lack of clean water and food, and increased health risks from injury and infectious disease. Storms aggravate the already poor level of health in Haiti people, especially among those who are already undernourished, and further damage the already frail health care and transportation systems as well as food production.

With climate change, hurricanes and tropical storms are becoming more frequent and unpredictable. In 2008, the summer before the nation was struck by a deadly earthquake, Haiti endured four tropical storms in a row. Its fourth largest city, Gonaives, was inundated with water for months. Gonaives is on a floodplain, one of the biggest watersheds in the country. Deforestation results in water running down the river and creating massive flooding. Catholic Relief Services (2008), which brought food aid to Gonaives during the flooding, reported:

> In places like flood-prone Haiti with its mountainous terrain and deforestation, it's not the size of the storm, it's how long it stays and how much rainfall it brings that dictates the severity of a storm's devastation. We're very impressed by the huge hurricane, but the slow-moving storm does the most damage.

In 2012, heavy rain, intense wind and flooding caused by Hurricane Sandy led to the death of 54 people, while damaging or completely destroying thousands of houses and infrastructure like roads and bridges, and caused extensive crop damage (USAID 2013). This scenario played out again in 2014 when heavy rains fell on northern Haiti; in 2015 when Cité Soleil and other areas were hit by heavy rainfall; in 2016 when Hurricane Matthew with its 145mph winds and torrential rains killed 872 people, destroyed more than 3,200 homes, displaced 15,000 people, ruined plantations, and drowned livestock; and in 2017 when powerful hurricanes Irma and Maria brought heavy rainfall and caused floods and landslides (ReliefWeb 2015–2017). Based on its history, and rising seas in the Caribbean, the UK-based risk analyst firm Maplecroft (2011) rated Haiti in 2011 among the seven countries in the world that are most vulnerable to the damaging effects of climate change.

As Hurricane Irma was headed to Haiti, Nadeige Jean, a 35-year-old mother of three who sold fruit the market in the capital city of Port-au-Prince expressed the gnawing dilemma of many Haitians caught in the trap between extreme weather and poverty:

> I guess we are worried, but we are already living in another hurricane, Hurricane Misery… How much worse can our lives get? … So they say I should board up my house? With what? Wood? Who's going to pay? With what money will I buy it? Ha! I don't even have a tin roof. If the winds come, I can't do anything but hope to live.
>
> *(Quoted in Falola and Wootson 2017)*

Added Edwitch Gabriel, a hairdresser: "I don't have words to describe this. We go from one crisis to another. I am speechless" (quoted in Falola and Wootson 2017).

Intervention efforts

Haiti has been called the "Republic of NGOs" (nongovernment organizations). Stemming from the limited capacity of the Haitian government and the country's weak national institutions, NGOs have stepped in to play a very prominent role, equivalent to "a quasi-privatization of the state" (Ramachandran 2012). Literally, thousands of aid organizations operate in Haiti, accountable to no one but their boards of directors and donors. Charities and NGOs have become the main source of foreign relief because of the immense instability in Haitian politics. NGOs are seen as more stable than the government and can be held more accountable to international donors than the government. International nonprofit organizations also bring in much-needed expertise and a stream of funding to the country. Yet this situation is fraught. The dominance of international NGOs has created a parallel state, one that is more powerful than the government itself. NGOs in Haiti have built an alternative infrastructure for the provision of social services, creating little incentive for the government to develop its capacity to deliver services. Asks Doucet (2011):

> Why has the international community excluded Haitians from the process of allocating aid funds? A recent AP investigation revealed that of every $100 of Haiti reconstruction contracts awarded by the American government, $98.40 returned to American companies, suggesting that non-Haitian companies and organizations have much to gain from the relief effort. Haiti's reconstruction, like almost everything else in that country, has been privatized, outsourced, or taken over by foreign NGOs.

Coordination among NGOs is limited, as is any form of monitoring, and competition occurs. NGOs follow their own agendas and set their own priorities, largely excluding the Haitian government and civil society from the decision-making process. Each NGO, on its website and in donor mailings, celebrates the achievements of its own local interventions while the scaling up of interventions is limited. As Klarreich and Polman (2012) indicate,

> the money that did reach Haiti has often failed to seed projects that truly respond to Haitians' needs. The problem is not exactly that funds were wasted or even stolen, though that has sometimes been the case. Rather, much of the relief wasn't spent on what was most needed.

Relief workers affiliated with the NGOs are often young and idealistic but not very aware of Haiti, its needs, and its culture. They also often lack the skills to learn the Haitian point of view or the patience to do so.

Léogâne is a coastal commune port town located about 18 miles west of the Haitian capital. Joseph Philippe is a technical coordinator of the Municipal Civil Protection Committee of Léogâne. Léogâne lies at the intersection of three rivers.

NGOs were not willing to work on shoring up the riverbank and creating a sustainable drainage system to avoid flooding, according to Philippe (Klarreich and Polman 2012). Although badly needed, it was simply not part of the established intervention plan of any of the NGOs, it was not what they were fundraising to accomplish. Ultimately, the Canadian Center for International Studies and Cooperation helped reinforce the riverbanks with rocks, reducing the flood risk by only about 15 percent. According to Philippe,

> The irony is that all the projects that the NGOs did put money into will get washed away in the floods that will come. The NGOs will continue to finance projects in underdeveloped countries in an underdeveloped ways … . Our priorities are not the same as theirs, but theirs are executed.
>
> *(Quoted in Klarreich and Polman 2012)*

One of the final insults is that it is the NGO donors who decide not only where and how the money will be used but also when it is no longer needed; this tends to occur without Haitian input.

In one of the poorest parts of urban Haiti, and one of the worst slum areas in the western hemisphere, is a squalid community in Port-au-Prince known as Cité Soleil, which the U.N. once labeled "the most dangerous place on earth." It is a site of over-crowded and suffocatingly hot makeshift tin structures, muddy and garbage-strewn pathways, malnutrition and overt starvation, and disease, misery, and death. It also is home to many Haitians. The most impoverished people in Cité Soleil have resorted to preparing what some call "mud cakes" (commonly composed of dirt, cooking oil, and salt) in order to satisfy their hunger while food prices sky-rocket. In Cité Soleil, children carry water, run daily errands, help with productive work by making things to be sold in the marketplace or along busy streets, wash dishes and clothing, prepare meals, care for other, younger, children, and, as a consequence of living in a land that is at the bottom of the global economy, forage through the frequent mounds of rain-drenched garbage in desperate search for bits of food, or anything else of immediate utility or sales value.

In 2008, I participated in a community-based assessment of some of the development projects implemented in Cité Soleil. Based on an extensive door-to-door survey with several thousand community residents, we assessed three projects: the building of basketball courts for children's recreation, the construction of a public market place, and the laying of roads. We found that residents were unhappy about all three projects and reported they had had no input in the process. The problem with the basketball courts is that the game is not popular, soccer is the game of choice; the newly built "public market" remained empty because merchants and customers felt that the area it was built in was dangerous; the problems that emerged once roads were built included the flooding of roadside homes and the demolition of homes in the path of the road. These three top-down projects illustrate what comes of failing to involve recipient communities in intervention initiatives.

For all the disappointments of NGO work in Haiti, there are instances of NGOs that successfully collaborate with Haitians to meet their needs. One example is the work of Partners in Health (2017), an organization founded by two physician/anthropologists. Over the last three decades, Partners in Health has initiated clinics and hospitals at 12 sites across the Central Plateau of Haiti and the lower Artibonite, two of the country's poorest regions. Today, Partners is the largest NGO health care provider in Haiti, serving an area of 4.5 million people with a staff of more than 5,700. Unlike other NGOs, it seeks to work with and help strengthen government oversight of public healthcare. Among Partners' successes is 1.6 million patient visits, provision of educational assistance to 9,400 children, delivery of prenatal care to 30,000 pregnant women, and 1,700 patients started on treatment for tuberculosis.

The organization opened a University Hospital in Mirebalais, a 200,000-square foot, 300-bed teaching hospital that offers a level of care never before available at a public facility in Haiti. At a time when the country desperately needs skilled professionals, Partners is able to provide high-quality, patient-centered education for doctors and nurses. Partners pioneered the use of community health workers in Haiti to deliver health care to people living with chronic diseases such as HIV and tuberculosis. In 1998, it launched the world's first program to provide free, comprehensive HIV care and treatment in an impoverished setting.

It is the philosophy of Partners that to effectively treat someone living with HIV, tuberculosis, or any number of other diseases, it is vital to address some of the root causes, most of which, in Haiti, are related to poverty. This has led Partners to support numerous schools, hundreds of small farms, and housing and water projects throughout the region to encourage education, economic development, and proper sanitation.

Small-scale local projects with a long-term commitment to Haiti have also had some success. The Organization for the Rehabilitation of the Environment (ORE) (2016) is a non-profit NGO, established in Haiti in 1985 to improve environmental, agricultural, and economic conditions in rural Haiti by promoting high-revenue tree crops, improved seeds, and marketing programs. As a local program operating for over 25 years in Haiti, ORE has been able to continually assess the needs of the local population where it works and adapt its interventions accordingly. Where it works in the south of Haiti, ORE has assisted farmers plant fruit-bearing trees like mango, avocados, and citrus for local uses and sales and for the export market. The approach gives farmers trees that make more money every year than their value as wood. Perhaps hundreds of millions of dollars have been spent on reforestation in Haiti, without bearing this simple fact in mind—hence the widespread failure of so many programs. But when a few million was used to fund ORE's program of commercial tree crops, the result improved incomes by local standards and an improved and more stabilized environment.

With the continued rise of the ocean water of the Caribbean and intensification of hurricanes, Haiti, with its denuded hills, continues to be highly vulnerable to climate change. Social inequality, inscribed into Haiti social organization since before the revolution, ensures that some people are in a particularly precarious situation. Haiti's vulnerability to climate change is in large part defined by socio-economic factors that interact with, and exacerbate, the physical impacts of anthropogenic climate change. Participatory initiatives, however, do show promise.

References

Catholic Relief Services. 2008. Storms turn Haiti's roads into rivers. https://reliefweb.int/report/haiti/storms-turn-haitis-roads-rivers.

Charles, J. 2012. Haiti and the issue of extreme poverty. *Tribune Business News*. https://search-proquest-com.ezproxy.lib.uconn.edu/docview/1149666979?accountid=14518&rfr_id=info%3Axri%2Fsid%3Aprimo.

Doucet, 2011. The Nation: NGOs have hailed Haiti. NPR. www.npr.org/2011/01/13/132884795/the-nation-how-ngos-have-failed-haiti.

Engle, J. 2016. Stories of tragedy, trust and transformation? Learning from participatory community development experience in post-earthquake Haiti. Doctoral dissertation. McGill University.

Falola, A. and Wootson, C. 2017. Haiti has already been devastated by natural disasters. Now it's bracing for Irma. *Washington Post*, September 7. www.washingtonpost.com/news/worldviews/wp/2017/09/07/haiti-has-already-been-devastated-by-natural-disasters-now-its-bracing-for-irma/?utm_term=.abf662bf7da5.

Gelting, R., K. Bliss, M., Patrick, G. Lockhart, and T. Handzel. 2013. Water, sanitation and hygiene in Haiti: Past, present, and future. *American Journal of Tropical Medical Hygiene* 89 (4): 665–670.

United Nations Development Programme. 2016. *Human Development Report 2016*. http://hdr.undp.org/sites/default/files/2016_human_development_report.pdf.

Klarreich, K. and L. Polman. 2012. The NGO Republic of Haiti. *The Nation*, October 31. www.thenation.com/article/ngo-republic-haiti/.

Larson, E., Nadas, M., Louis-Charles, C., Gideon, M., Gaetchen, P., Trouillot, M., and Curry, C. 2015. Expanding medical and nursing educational experiences in Haiti: A partnership in learning. *Annals of Global Health* 81(1), 160.

Maplecroft. 2011. Risk calculators and dashboards. https://maplecroft.com/about/news/ccvi.html.

Mazzeo, J. 2009. Laviché: Haiti's vulnerability to the global food crisis. *Napa Bulletin* 32: 115–129.

McClintock, N. 2003. Agroforestry and sustainable resource conservation in Haiti: A case study. http://works.bepress.com/nathan_mcclintock.

Murray, G. 1991. The tree gardens of Haiti: From extraction to domestication. In D. Challinor and M. Frondorf (eds), *Social Forestry: Communal and Private Management Strategies Compared*. Washington, DC: Johns Hopkins University Press, pp. 35–44.

NationMaster. 2015. Country vs country: Haiti and United States compared: Health stats. www.nationmaster.com/country-info/compare/Haiti/United-States/Health.

Organization for the Rehabilitation of the Environment. 2016. Commercial fruit trees generate income and protect the environment. www.oreworld.org/trees.htm.

Partners in Health. 2017. Haiti. www.pih.org/country/haiti.

Paskett, C. and C.-E. Pholoctete. 1990. Soil conservation in Haiti. *Journal of Soil and Water* 45(4): 457–459.

Ramachandran, V. 2012. Is Haiti doomed to be the Republic of NGOs? *Huffington Post*. www.huffingtonpost.com/vijaya-ramachandran/haiti-relief-ngos_b_1194923.html.

ReliefWeb. 2015–2017. Haiti floods. https://reliefweb.int/disaster/fl-2015-000037-hti;https://reliefweb.int/disaster/fl-2016-000019-hti;https://reliefweb.int/disaster/fl-2017-000043-hti.

Rosseel, P., M. Trelles, S. Guilavogui, N. Ford, and K. Chu. 2010. Ten years of experience training non-physician anesthesia providers in Haiti. *World Journal of Surgery* 34(3): 453–458.

USAID (United States Agency for International Development). 2013. Haiti: Hurricane Sandy. www.usaid.gov/sites/default/files/documents/1866/02.15.13%20-%20Haiti%20Hurricane%20Sandy%20Fact%20Sheet.pdf.

USAID (United States Agency for International Development). 2017. Agriculture and food security: Haiti. www.usaid.gov/haiti/agriculture-and-food-security.

World Health Organization. 2015. Haiti. www.who.int/countries/hti/en/.

10

MALI

Climate change, desertification, and food insecurity

Climate change and a riskier environment

Although Mali produces very low levels of greenhouse gas emissions compared to the world average, the increasing temperatures ushered in by anthropogenic change are altering its environment. Diallo Deidia Kattra, a former minister for employment and vocational training in the Malian government, stresses, "We are the forgotten ones, although we suffer every day from climate change" (quoted in St. Fleur 2015). A primary factor in this alteration is a rising rate of evapotranspiration, the process involving plant absorption of water through the roots and its release into the atmosphere as vapor through pores in plant leaves. Enhanced evapotranspiration in Mali is leading to drier soil conditions, and it is occurring at a time when the human demand for water due to population increase is rising. The pressure to secure water can easily trigger human conflict by dropping levels of food production and raising levels of food insecurity, famine, survival migration, and other threats to life. On the issue of conflict, although disputed by some, Burke and co-workers (2009) presented a paper entitled "Warming increases the risk of civil war in Africa" to the U.S. National Academy of Sciences in which they argue that temperature rises in Africa have coincided with significant measurable increases in the likelihood of war. The issue of climate change-triggered migration is also complex as people often have multiple reasons for relocation. As Jane McAdam, an Australian law professor who studies migration, asserts, "Climate change on its own doesn't force people to move but it amplifies pre-existing vulnerabilities." People relocate "when life becomes increasingly intolerable" (quoted in Sengupta 2016).

While it remains difficult to estimate exactly the effects of climate change on the important informal economy in Mali, a set of activities that play a vital role in the livelihoods of many Malians, it is clear that already vulnerable poor rural groups are being particularly impacted by climate change. At the same time, Malians have always had to manage an unpredictable climate and, as will be described, have developed various coping strategies to deal with climatic challenges.

The climate trials in Mali are real and pressing. Since 1975, average temperatures in the country have increased by more than 1.4 degrees Fahrenheit. As assessed by USAID (2012),

> This transition to an even warmer climate could reduce crop harvests and pasture availability, amplifying the impact of droughts … . Mali is becoming significantly hotter. Time series of air temperature data … indicate that the magnitude of recent warming is large and unprecedented … .

The menace of anthropogenic climate change in Mali is not a future looming event, the adverse effects are already occurring—and climate trends suggest they will continue to mount, with dangerous consequences for the people, especially those that are already the most vulnerable.

Food insecurity and famine in the Republic of Mali

Once the site of several pre-colonial empires, including the ancient city-state of Timbuktu, Mali is a landlocked arid country in West Africa, with a mostly Muslim population of 18 million people (United Nations Department of Economic and Social Affairs 2017). At its height in the mid-fourteenth century, the Mali Empire comprised a confederation of three states, Mali, Memo, and Wagadou. Its emperor ruled over 400 cities, towns, and villages. Gold and control over the trans-Saharan caravan trade were the main sources of the empire's wealth.

Most of what we know about this period in Malian history comes from the writings of Muslim scholars such as Ibn Battuta (1304–1368) and Ibn Khaldun (1332–1406). Ibn Battuta traveled by caravan from Sijilmasa, Morocco to Timbuktu, recording his observations along the way. Ibn Khaldun recorded the royal genealogy of the Malian Empire and took notes on the empire's oral history and traditions. Throughout West Africa, oral history was preserved and passed down by griots, individuals who served as repositories of community history and customs and played a major role in maintaining community cultural consciousness, and the practice continues in many places. But this sharing does not tend to extend beyond the community level. There is a weak sense of both national unity and national identity among the citizenry of Mali. People tend to be locally focused, especially in rural areas.

In 1828, René Caillié became the first European to visit Timbuktu. Having grand expectations of the fabled city, he disappointedly reported that it was but a small, provincial town with "nothing but a mass of ill-looking houses, built of earth" (quoted in Coutros 2017). This dour description may have contributed to the subsequent development within European perspectives on sub-Saharan Africa of a paternalistic and elitist stance. During the second half of the nineteenth century, sub-Saharan Africa came to be seen in Europe as a region that lacked a history worth knowing and its people as having made no significant social, political, or technological advances. The people of Mali, like others around the world subject to colonial control, became "people without history" (Wolf 1982). This European perspective was not just an expression of ignorance of the region's deep history or even a case of disappointed romanticism. Rather, it was politically convenient in that it justified a colonial campaign organized around the official goal of bringing European "civilization" to the backward people of Africa, which, in practice, involved extracting wealth from sub-Saharan Africa for European development, including the wealth gained through African enslavement. By 1894, Timbuktu was formally incorporated into the French Empire, with long-term consequences for the city and the region.

Spatially, much of Mali falls within the ecoclimatic and biogeographic zone that stretches all the way across the African continent between the Sahara desert to the north and the savannas and rain forests to the south. This semi-arid zone is known historically as the Sahel, a name derived from the Arabic word for shore, which in this case was used metaphorically to refer to the southern edge of the vast, sandy Sahara.

Since gaining independence from France in 1960, Mali has followed a fractured course, suffering droughts, rebellions, a coup, over 20 years of military dictatorship, civil war, and survival-driven mass migrations. Today, Mali is one of the poorest countries in the world. Mali's limited economy is primarily based on agriculture (especially cotton, rice, millet, corn, vegetables) and fishing, but despite this significantly food-centered economic system, food insecurity is a growing problem.

Mali scores extremely low on established measures of economic and social development. The country ranks near the bottom, 182 out of 187, on the United Nations Human Development Index (HDI). The HDI is a composite measure based on three dimensions: life expectancy, education, and standard of living. The harshness of life for many Malians is reflected in life expectancy levels—51 years for men and 53 years for women (CIA Factbook 2017). Additionally, Mali's infant, child, and maternal mortality rates are among the highest in sub-Saharan Africa. On average, adults attend only two years of school. The gross national income per capita in 2011 was only $610. Consequently, poverty levels are high, with 43.6 percent of the population living below the national poverty line. "In practical terms this means that very few people have electricity, running water, telephones, or cars. They don't have favorite clothes and favorite foods. They wear what they have and eat what is available," comments Halloway (2011: 2), based on her extended time in a village in Mali. The Human Development Index can be used as a proxy for the adaptive capacity of people in Mali in response to the changes occurring because of the continued increase in planetary temperatures and associated extreme wealth events. While experience and local knowledge are critical resources, the ability of most Malians to respond to climate change is comparatively limited.

Three-quarters of Mali's population relies on agriculture for their food and income. The majority are subsistence farmers, focused on growing enough to feed their families. These small farmers are dependent on raising rainfed crops on small plots of land. Irrigated lands represent only about 3 percent of the total national cropland and are confined to areas along the Niger River in the south (USAID 2012).

Agricultural production is inadequate to feed Mali's growing population. The country faces falling levels of cereal production (19% lower than in 2012/2013) and inadequate water supply for agriculture and livestock production (Food and Agriculture Organization 2017). As a result, it is likely that over a quarter of the country's population is undernourished, and this situation has not improved for years. The Food and Agriculture Organization (2017) estimates that approximately 970,000 people in the country are severely food insecure and over 2.3 million people are moderately food insecure. It is believed this number will jump, especially in rural areas, with an additional 1,130,000 people falling below the poverty line by 2050 (Pedercini et al. 2012).

The perceptions of Malians about their changing environment are seen in a study by Ebi and co-workers (2011) in the village of Zignasso, in the southwest Sikasso region of the country. This is a rice and potato growing area. The farmers explained that the span of the rainy season for rice had decreased while moisture stress had gone up. They also reported decreasing yields of potatoes, even with the use of fertilizer and improved farming techniques. In the experience of the villagers, over the past three decades crop yields had decreased by a third. In the past, they were able to plow twice before sowing. But the farmers know that times have changed. Now they plow once immediately after the first rain and sow after the next rain. And they plow lightly to increase the retention of moisture. But yields continue to fall. Fatoumata Diarra, who lives in the village of Massantola in western Mali, also laments the deteriorating availability of water, "The problem of water is critical, which is why gardening, which was always our favorite activity, is almost impossible to achieve" (quoted in Baumwoll and Egan 2017).

The changes perceived by Malians are multiple. Sali Samake from Tamala in southwest Mali observes, "Times have changed ... . In the past, the arrival of migratory birds like the heron was known as the deadline to start sowing. Now farmers risk failing when they rely on those references" (quoted in Diarra 2015). Migrating birds still visit the area but their arrival no longer coincides with the rainfall that is needed to sow the season's crops. These fall later and later in the year, making life unpredictable and failure more likely.

In many parts of Mali, an enduring problem for small farmers is "maintaining a full granary through the seasons of fluctuating rainfall" (Lewis 1981: 55), a challenge that has intensified over time. The vulnerability of many Malians to food insecurity and famine continues to grow as processes of climate change unfold in the twenty-first century. Food insecurity refers to situations in which people lack sustainable physical or economic access to enough safe, nutritious, and socially acceptable food to sustain a healthy and productive life. Food insecurity can be chronic, limited to certain seasons, or temporary. A markedly risky season for food insecurity runs from January to May. This is a hot, dry period during which people may be forced to sell off assets because food reserves begin to drop. Malians call it the *soudure* or hungry season.

The lived experience of food insecurity is painful. Exemplary of this experience is a small farmer named Moussa Doumbia, a father of nine from the village of Mafélé who began growing cotton several decades ago. His farm is about five acres in size and on average produces 1,100–1,750 pounds of cotton a year. But with the money he gets from selling his crop Moussa is barely able to feed his children. He said, "Sometimes, the young ones cry because they're so hungry … . I become very angry when I'm not able to get enough food for my family. All the time, I feel sad" (quoted in Daly 2010). When two of his youngest children contracted malaria, Moussa couldn't afford to buy medicine. He added, "That made me very afraid. It makes me feel ashamed because I am the chief of the family but I am not able to protect them. In our culture, this is unacceptable" (quoted in Daly 2010). Another, somewhat different, story comes from Bori Bokoum, a 21-year old man from a village in the Mopti region of Mali. Bori had endured one bad harvest after another. The land was too dry and he could not grow enough rice and millet to allow a sustainable way of life. Eventually he gave up and tried his hand at selling watches in the nearest market town. He then moved to a job on a farm in Côte d'Ivoire, but he hoped one day to make it to Europe and to a life free of a constant sense of vulnerability (Sengupta 2016).

The nutritional consequences of food insecurity are significant and include protein energy malnutrition, anemia, and vitamin and mineral deficiencies. Famines are defined as extreme health events in which populations lack adequate access to food, contributing to widespread malnutrition and death. Predisposition to famine does not occur suddenly; rather, it builds up over several months or more as the proportion of the population that is famine-prone grows. Adds Adams (1993: 41):

> The famine process is characterized as a collapse in an individual's ability to legally command food through the disposal of productive resources or endowments (land, labour, assets) and exchange in the form of trade and production. Overlooked in this analysis of individual entitlement failure vis à vis food in the market economy, is the parallel collapse of social structures which sustain important non-market sources of food in much of the developing world … .

Because the malnourished suffer from encumbered and weakened immune systems, many of the deaths during a famine are due to the spread of infectious diseases. Small children in particular become vulnerable to common diseases like gastrointestinal infections. By definition, famines have three primary features: 1) a minimum of 20 percent of households face extreme food deficits, with limited or no ability to respond effectively; 2) at least 30 percent of children are acutely malnourished with perilous weight for height ratios; and 3) mortality rates that exceed two people per 10,000 population a day (U.N. News 2011).

The role of climate change in food insecurity and famine

The Sahel is an area that is highly vulnerable to significant climate variability of the sort characteristic of the present era with its ever-rising planetary temperatures. Evidence of this vulnerability was seen during the latter part of the last century in a series of severe droughts that devastated farmers' and pastoralists' livelihoods, brought famine and death, and forced mass migration. Famine and displacement on a massive scale occurred in the Sahel during the period from 1968 to 1974 and again in the early and mid-1980s. The cause was drought and the casualties were high: at least 100,000 people died, while 750,000 were forced into needing emergency food aid (Ayeni et al. 2000). During the summer of 2010, drought struck parts of the Sahel again. Crops failed and famine soon followed. Over 300,000 people faced starvation, and over a million more confronted food insecurity. There also were rising incidences of diarrhea, gastroenteritis, and respiratory diseases. While not the only factor implicated in the crisis, climate change was found to be a contributory element.

Two years later drought hit once more. Millions of people in the western Sahel—including those in Mali—faced a severe food crisis that led to over a million children under five years of age at severe risk of acute malnutrition. A number of factors contributed to the emergency including low and erratic rainfall and a resultant poor harvest. The dire conditions on the ground were magnified by armed conflict occurring in Mali that forced thousands of refugees to flee into neighboring countries. As Samberg (2017) emphasizes, conflict and climate are not unrelated: "Conflict-torn communities are more vulnerable to climate-related disasters, and crop or livestock failure due to climate can contribute to social unrest."

As this account of recent food-related crises in the Sahel indicates, a primary driver of suffering and death has been climate change. Mali's average annual rainfall has decreased by 30 percent since 1998. As a result, Mali is experiencing a "climate zone shift" that will usher in impactful, even catastrophic changes. In climate models that forecast to 2030, the worst-case scenario is a rainfall decrease of 10 percent and a rise in average temperatures of 1.8 degrees Fahrenheit (Steward 2013).

Epule et al. (2014) point out that there are

> four main causes of the Sahelian droughts …: sea surface temperature changes, vegetation and land degradation, dust feedbacks and human–induced climate change. However, human–induced climate change is seen as the major drought-determining factor because it controls sea surface temperatures, dust feedbacks and vegetation degradation.

This conclusion is supported by paleoclimate records that indicate that mega-drought episodes occurred in the region during periods of significant surges of iceberg melt and sea level rise. Several computer-modeling studies suggest a close correspondence between the weakening of monsoons in West African and the release of fresh water into the ocean because of ice sheet melting due to planetary warming. These studies raise questions about whether such episodes will occur during this century "in response to a massive freshwater discharge triggered by a significant ice sheet destabilization or surface melting and, if so, what would be the related environmental and human impacts in the Sahel area" (DeFrance et al. 2017: 6533). If they do, for the people of Mali the consequences would be catastrophic.

A core element in the growing climate-related vulnerability of the people of Mali is desertification, the process whereby fertile land deteriorates into an area that is too dry to support human life or its food sources. Desertification, an enemy of food production, is a barrier to the development needed to raise poor households to improved social, economic, and health levels. In particularly fragile ecosystems like those found in various parts of Mali, desertification will be irreversible as rising temperatures diminish rainfall. Moreover, desertification has been found to be a self-accelerating process that drives the desert edge across previously productive spaces.

In Mali, as in other countries of the Sahel, the Sahara desert is creeping southward at the rate of about thirty miles a year (Holthuijzen and Maximillian 2011). Various factors are propelling this process, including human activities like the overgrazing of livestock. When animals overgraze they eat the roots and destroy plants structures, preventing regeneration. Dead plants cannot hold soil in place, making it liable to being blown away by forceful Saharan winds, which results in erosion. Recurrent drought also drives desertification. The climate change-influenced droughts faced by Mali in recent years combine with overgrazing to extend the desert. Without water, even plants that are not overgrazed die off, accelerating the desertification process. The result, as noted by the documentary filmmaker Bruce Cockburn (1993), who shot the film *Rivers of Sand in Mali*, was a rapidly changing landscape: "We found farmland turning to dust. We watched the buses fill up every day with people heading south to escape the encroaching desert." Remembering how the landscape around the city of Timbuktu has changed under drying conditions and acknowledging the dusty dunes impinging on the northern border of the city, a local butcher commented:

> We are not proud of killing a camel and this one was young. But there are not enough cattle at this time of year, because of the [lack of] rain. There used to be grazing all year round. Until the … drought, there were even trees here.
>
> *(Quoted in Smith 2014)*

Another example of the impact of desertification is Arauane a village located in an arid area known as Azauad. In the past, the village environment was an oasis. With the spread of the desert, sand buried the local mosque up to its minaret. In the early 1990s, Arauane was surrounded on three sides by sand dunes 65 feet high. The sand blown from the dunes slowly buried the village. People continued to live in Arauane but their homes were underground. This adaptation to desertification demonstrates the flexibility people can display in the face of an increasingly hazardous environment. But there are limits to resilience, and climate change threatens to surpass those limits (SakhaliaNet 2014).

Stephenson and Stephenson (2016: 305) argue that contemporary research indicates that people tend to develop effective environment management regimes based on local knowledge. They raise this point to counter earlier assertions that local people are to blame for desertification. Calling this assignment of blame the "desertification narrative," they argue that its origin lies in prevailing

> sociocultural attitudes toward environmental change. These include the political marginality of dry land populations and colonial attitudes to development, which attributed African environmental change to poor land management and population pressures (effectively a neo-Malthusian argument). This reasoning also overlooked local people's extensive ecological knowledge concerning dynamic geomorphological processes.

There is, in short, debate about the role of local practices in desertification, but what is not in doubt is the critical role played by climate change.

Surviving in a warming world: responding to the threat of climate change in Mali

Without doubt, the most visible coping mechanisms adopted by rural agricultural populations facing famine due to climate-related disasters is migration. The disruption to food production caused by climate change has contributed to the growing number of refugees and internally displaced persons in the world. Estimates are that the number of people forced to leave their homes doubled between 2007 and 2016 (Samberg 2017). While migration is risky and refugees tend to have comparatively poor health, the most underprivileged people, those with the fewest resources, may be trapped and unable to flee despite the even graver risk of staying in place.

Water is everything in Mali, but farmers and pastoralists in Mali have a long history of dealing with drought and have developed a body of cultural knowledge about their environment and coping strategies. In terms of agricultural strategies for dealing with a precarious environment, research with Malian small farmers indicates that they employ a variety of approaches, including the use of early-ripening crop varieties, the dispersal of planted areas across different locations, and staggered planting to help spread production risks over time. Income-generating activities intended to develop a small monetary surplus to fall back on during hard times include planting a market garden of salable crops, engaging in small craft production, collecting wild foods, intercropping grains and legumes, and investing in livestock. Additionally, small farmers in Mali rely on kinship and other social relationships to provide assistance in times of need. This net of social connections is founded on a moral economy of sharing, social obligation, and mutual aid (Adams 1993). What small farmers cannot count on is assistance from the government in times of severest need, nor can they depend on the capitalist market system. As Adams (1993: 49) explains. based on her research in seven villages in central Mali:

> Despite the existence of a countrywide early-warning system, government food aid did not reach any of the households surveyed in 1988, many of whom went hungry. While the current orthodoxy expects the market to take the place of the state, it too has a flimsy institutional foundation.

In short, in times of crisis, smaller farmers in Mali can count on their own skills and local knowledge, and they can usually expect some help from members of their social and kin networks. The weakness of the Malian state structure is reflected in its inability to dependably fulfill its responsibilities to citizens as well as its inability to project power through a strong presence, a situation that increases the likelihood of challenges by rival armed groups. The country is characterized by ungoverned spaces where the national government has little influence. This unstable situation came to a head in 2012 when a rebellion occurred in the north of the country, leading to a coup d'etat and the loss to rebel forces of the northern two-thirds of the state, a crisis that was eventually brought to an end by French military intervention, although new problems arose in 2015 and continue today.

In other words, household and social network reliance are the primary resources available to Malian small farmers. Research by Cekan (1993) in five agropastoral villages in northern Mali illuminates the role of local knowledge and techniques as mechanisms for coping with the vagaries of climate. His study was designed to enhance understanding of how people respond to the increasing probability of famine in a time of climate change. Interviews with household heads found that productive activities were diversifying and that many households relied more than previously on the annual migration of able-bodied members in search of paid labor. He also found that faith was an important emotional resource for people. In response to the question, "What will you do avoid hunger or famine next year," people frequently responded, "Pray to Allah." In fact, during the twenty-first century there was a rise in the number of Muslims in Mali taking part in religious rituals in the hope of stopping the desertification of the Sahel and return their world to the temperate conditions of past years (Bell 2014).

Cekan (1993) proposed a continuum of strategies adopted by Malian small farmers. At one end of the continuum are emergency behaviors during famines, such as cutting back food consumption to one meal of millet or less per day, eating the leaves of baobab trees, and the sale of productive resources like plows or female cattle. The latter are drastic measures that make it hard for people to bounce back and return to pre-crisis levels of household production. More toward the center of the continuum are coping strategies adopted in response to pressing but not yet crisis-level events. These approaches, which include cutting and selling firewood and selling family jewelry, allow survival but do not promote growth and development. At the other end of the continuum are diversification activities. These are adopted during non-crisis periods to develop assets and involve behaviors such as investing in livestock and intercropping fields. Also included here are the sale of labor, handicraft production, and wild food gathering.

Helping poor farmers in Mali cope with climate change

Faced with mounting challenges, small farmers in Mali have demonstrated a willingness to learn about new approaches and an openness to participating in programs introduced by various international non-government organizations to increase their capacity to respond to a changing environment. These projects are often local and time limited and few have been scaled up for broad impact.

One of these climate change response projects was initiated in 2009 by the World Food Programme and Catholic Relief Services (CRS). It involved introducing new crop varieties and agricultural techniques suited to Mali's dry conditions. Peter Shapland, a CRS agriculture expert, found that small farmers are aware of intercropping, rotation, microdosing, and composting as climate-smart agriculture techniques. He also found that it was "not difficult to get farmers to adopt these practices, because they see the results of their neighbors and once they learn more they are eager to apply the techniques themselves" (quoted in Roby 2017). For example, Tansa Tessougue, who has grown millet and cowpeas (a sandy soil legume) for 15 years said that she uses microdosing—a process in which small quantities of fertilizer are mixed with seeds during planting to provide adequate growing conditions in poor soil—and that this inexpensive technique has more than doubled her harvest output while preserving the environment from heavy fertilizer use. She commented, "Without these techniques, I produced five sacks [0.5 tons] per harvest, now I can get up to 12 or 18 sacks [1.2–1.8 tons]" (quoted in Roby 2017). This increase has allowed her to sell about 80 percent of her crops.

Other introduced techniques include 1) building compost heaps around planting areas to improve soil quality, help with retaining moisture, and limiting pests; 2) intercropping species, such as planting several rows of millet followed by several rows of cowpeas in a continual pattern, a technique that slows the spread of parasitic weeds; and 3) crop rotation.

The Mali National Directorate of Agriculture has collaborated with United Nations Development Program (UNDP) to empower women to mitigate the social and economic consequences of climate change. In Massantola, located in western Mali, just north of the capital, Bamako, the project has supported a local women's cooperative to clear a plot for gardening and provide access to water. With help from the project, cooperative members built a fence to protect several solar panels and a well run by solar power. The women sold the vegetables they harvested and used part of the money for the cooperative's development fund and another part to feed their families. Additionally, the UNDP supported training for women's collectives in Mali to enhance the skills of women on sustainable agriculture and land management practices. The program also supplied seeds and tools, and provided funds to build alternative income generating activities for local communities (United Development Fund 2016).

The Food and Agricultural Organization of the United Nations (FAO) (2017) developed a "produce more with less" approach in its intervention projects. By promoting sustainable intensification of agriculture, the FAO model was intended to boost income while improving the environment as well as health in rural communities. The approach found expression, in part, through the implementation of farmer field schools designed to raise resilience by equipping small farmers with new knowledge and skills needed to adapt to a changing climate. Entitled "Integrating climate resilience into agricultural production for food security in rural areas of Mali," the four-year project was launched in 2011. The project uses a variety of participatory and non-formal educational approaches.

As with many development schemes, there is little evaluative information available on these Malian projects, so what the enduring impact might be is unclear. Non-government agencies tend to be better at telling what they have done than how they have done, including whether any short-term improvements continue once the project ends. Certainly, some interventions are successful at the local level, but they are rarely scaled up to wider areas in order to make a real difference to the struggle of small farmers in Mali with global warming. It appears that Malians welcome new approaches, but their ability to sustain them under the crushing weight of poverty and an ever-drier environment raises fundamental questions about what types of intervention are appropriate. Participatory models that build on existing local knowledge, broad implementation, clear lines of coordination and communication, and ongoing evaluation and adjustment would seem vital to meaningful intervention in response to climate change.

References

Adams, A. 1993. Food insecurity in Mali: Exploring the role of moral economy. *IDS Bulletin* 24(4): 41–51.

Ayeni, B., Ballance, M.Chenje, T.Chiuta, D.Nightingale, E.Laisi et al. 2000. Africa Environment outlook: Past, present and future perspectives. United Nations Environmental Programme, Nairobi.

Bauman, Z. 2011. *Collateral Damage: Social Inequalities in a Global Age*. London: Polity.

Baumwoll, J. and A. Egan 2017. Supporting Mali's women to adapt to climate change. United Nations Development Program. https://stories.undp.org/supporting-malis-women-to-adapt-to-climate-change.

Bell, D. 2014. Understanding a 'broken world': Islam, ritual, and climate change in Mali, West Africa. *Journal for the Study of Religion, Nature and Cuture* 8(3): 287–306.

Burke, M., E. Miguel, S. Satyanath, J. Dykema, and D. Lobell. 2009. Warming increases the risk of civil war in Africa. *Proceedings of the National Academy of Sciences* 106(46): 10670–20674.

Cekan, J. 1993. Famine coping strategies in Central Mali. *GeoJournal* 30(2): 147–151.

CIA World Factbook, Mali. 2017. www.cia.gov/library/publications/resources/the-world-factbook/geos/ml.html.

Cockburn, B. 1993Rivers of sand interactive. http://kensingtontv.com/go/riverofsand/indextop.html.

Coutros, P. 2017. Digging into the myth of Timbuktu. *Sapiens*. www.sapiens.org/column/off-the-map/timbuktu-archaeology/?utm_source=SAPIENS.org+Subscribers&utm_campaign=4ddb92ed39-Email+Blast+11.3.2017&utm_medium=email&utm_term=0_18b7e41cd8-4ddb92ed39-227262425.

Daly, E. 2010. The desperate plight of Africa's cotton farmers. *The Guardian*www.theguardian.com/world/2010/nov/14/mali-cotton-farmer-fair-trade.

Defrance, D., G. Ramstein, S. Charbit, M. Vrac, A. Famien, and B. Sultan. 2017. Consequences of rapid ice sheet melting on the Sahelian population vulnerability. *PNAS* 114 (25): 6533–6538.

Diarra, S. 2015. How Mali's women are central to adapting to climate change. World Economic Forum. www.weforum.org/agenda/2015/09/how-malis-women-are-central-to-adpating-to-climate-change/.

Ebi, K., J. Padgham, M. Doumbia, A. Kergna, J. Smith, T. Butt, and B. McCarl. 2011. Smallholders adaptation to climate change in Mali. *Climate Change* 108: 423.

Epule, E., C. Peng, L. Lepage, and Z. Chen. 2014. The causes, effects and challenges of Sahelian droughts: A critical review. *Regional Environmental Change* 14(1): 145–156.

Food and Agricultural Organization of the United Nations. 2017. Integrating climate resilience into agricultural production for food security in rural areas of Mali. www.fao.org/agriculture/ippm/projects/mali/gcp-mli-033-ldf/en/.

Halloway, K. 2011. *Monique and the Mango Rains*. Long Grove, IL: OneWorld.

Holthuijzen, W. and J. Maximillian. 2011. Dry, hot, and brutal: Desertification in the Sahel of Mali. *Journal of Sustainable Development in Africa* 13(7): 245–268.

Lewis, J. 1981. Domestic labor intensity and the incorporation of Malian peasant farmers into local descent groups. *American Ethnologist* 8(1): 53–73.

Pedercini, M., H. Kanamaru, and S. Derwisch. 2012. Potential impacts of climate change on food security in Mali. Natural Resources Management and Environment Department, FAO, Rome.

Roby, C. 2017. Mali smallholder farmers see benefits of smart climate agriculture technologies. *Devex*. www.devex.com/news/mali-smallholder-farmers-see-benefits-of-smart-climate-agriculture-technologies-90493.

SakhaliaNet. 2014. Sahara territory: Mali ethnography. http://freevst.x10.mx/sahara/mali%20ethnography.htm.

Samberg, L. 2017. World hunger is increasing thanks to wars and climate change. *The Conversation*. https://theconversation.com/world-hunger-is-increasing-thanks-to-wars-and-climate-change-84506?utm_medium=email&utm_campaign=Latest%20from%20The%20Conversation%20for%20October%2017%202017%20-%2085847118&utm_content=Latest%.

Sengupta, S. 2016. Heat, hunger and war force Africans onto a 'road on fire.' *New York Times*, December 15. www.nytimes.com/interactive/2016/12/15/world/africa/agadez-climate-change.html?rref=collection%2Ftimestopic%2FMali&action=click&contentCollection=world&region=stream&module=stream_unit&version=latest&contentPlacement=8&pgtype=collection&_r=0.

Smith, A. 2014. Life in Timbuktu: How the ancient city of gold is slowly turning to dust. *The Guardian*, September 16. www.theguardian.com/cities/2014/sep/16/-sp-life-timbuktu-mali-ancient-city-gold-slowly-turning-to-dust.

St. Fleur, N. 2015. Mali grapples with adapting to climate change. *New York Times*, December 2. www.nytimes.com/interactive/projects/cp/climate/2015-paris-climate-talks.

Stephenson, E. and P. Stephenson. 2016. The political ecology of cause and blame: Environmental health inequities of colonialism, globalism and climate change. In M. Singer (ed.), *A Companion to the Anthropology of Environmental Health*. Walden, MA: John Wiley & Sons, pp. 302–324.

Stewart, D. 2013. *What is Next for Mali? The Roots of Conflict and Challenges to Stability*. Carlisle, PA: Strategic Studies Institute and U.S. Army War College Press.

United Development Fund. 2016. Supporting Mali's women to adapt to climate change. https://stories.undp.org/supporting-malis-women-to-adapt-to-climate-change.

United Nations Department of Economic and Social Affairs. 2017. Mali, in *National Accounts Statistics: Main Aggregates and Detailed Tables*. New York: United Nations.

U.N. News. 2011. When a food security crisis becomes a famine. https://news.un.org/en/story/2011/07/382342-when-food-security-crisis-becomes-famine.

USAID (United States Agency for International Development). 2012. A climate trend analysis of Mali. https://pubs.usgs.gov/fs/2012/3105/fs2012-3105.pdf.

Wolf, E. 1982. *Europe and the People without History*. Berkeley, CA: University of California Press.

11

THE CONSEQUENTIAL INTERSECTION OF SOCIAL INEQUALITY AND CLIMATE CHANGE

Health, coping, and community organizing

From individual, to global, to planetary health

As Maslin (2015) emphasizes, "Climate change is one of the few scientific theories that makes us examine the whole basis of modern society." The rising potential for drastic adverse impact of climate change should sound a clarion call for a new era of planetary health, respect for human rights and dignity, and the promotion of social well-being based on principles of eco-equity and social and economic equality.

Based on a review of the science, the University College London Commission concluded that climate change is the biggest threat to human health in the twenty-first century. Health has entered a new epoch in which environmental factors, under adverse human influence, must become a central public health, biomedicine, health science, and public policy focus worldwide. This recognition sparked the planetary health initiative, spearheaded by *The Lancet*, the leading journal of medicine in the United Kingdom, which is motivated by acceptance of the fundamental need for collective achievement of a world "that nourishes and sustains the diversity of life with which we coexist and on which we depend" (Horton 2014). This forward-looking development has significant implications for the anthropology of climate change and health.

Emergence of planetary health, "a nascent concept focused on the interdependence of human health, animal health, and the health of the environment" (Panorama 2017: 3), has been suggested as constituting a fifth stage in the historic evolution of the modern population health paradigm (Singer 2014). This mode of thinking about health as more than an individual-level condition—which has been the prevailing orientation of biomedicine—and even more than a strictly human-level condition is, has its roots in local public health efforts, especially in Europe during the nineteenth century, transitioned to tropical medicine as a consequence of the colonial encounter with the infectious diseases of tropical environments, grew during the post-World War II period into international health with the expansion of multinational health initiatives like the World Health Organization, and during the 1990s emerged as global health, a reflection of the consolidation of a global neoliberal economy and global communication systems, combined with recognition that risks to health transcend borders and require multilateral responses. The shift to a planetary health understanding as a further advance in population health thinking was driven by the awareness that not only are human communities worldwide now multiply linked together by flows of commodities, ideas, people, money, and health-related influences from vectors to medicines, but the health and well-being of human communities are multiply linked to the environment and to other species. As aptly stated in the planetary health manifesto: "Our patterns of overconsumption are unsustainable and will ultimately cause the collapse of our civilization. The harms we continue to inflict on our planetary systems are a threat to our very existence as a species" (Horton et al. 2014: 847). In short, a planetary health perspective reveals the fundamental ways in which human beings are not just agents of environmental change but also vulnerable objects of that change.

Through their ability to harness ever more powerful levels of energy, produce prodigious quantities of toxic waste, and rapidly increase their population size, humans have acquired the dangerous ability to overtax "planetary boundaries" and "trigger abrupt or irreversible environmental changes that would be deleterious or even catastrophic ..." (Rockström et al. 2009). We stand on the precipice of conditions that "can be called, without hyperbole, threatened apocalypse" (Foster et al. 2010: 109).

Pivotal to the incipient planetary health movement is a commitment to equity in a world of unjust societies and unequal relations among societies. As articulated in the planetary health manifesto: "The discipline of public health is critical to this vision because of its values of social justice and fairness for all, and its focus on the collective actions of interdependent and empowered peoples and their communities" (Horton et al. 2014: 847). The evidence on anthropogenic climate change demonstrates the consequences of inequity. The U.S., with just 4 percent of the world's population, produces 25 per cent of emitted greenhouse gases. It releases more greenhouse gases than most of the developing countries in Asia, Latin America, and Asia combined (Lindsay 2001: 228). The average U.S. citizen accounts for as much greenhouse gas production as nine Chinese, 18 Indians, and 90 Bangladeshis, but even more alarming, a U.S. citizen on average pollutes more than 500 citizens of Ethiopia, Chad, Zaire, Afghanistan, Mail, Cambodia, or Burandi (Roberts and Parks 2007: 146). Generally, as described in prior chapters, the least developed countries, which produce comparatively low levels of greenhouse gas emissions, have the most to lose from global warming because they have fewer assets to use in adapting to its negative health and social impacts. Translated into stark moral and palpably human terms, anthropogenic climate change can be assessed as a form of social murder, a term introduced by Frederick Engels in 1845 to characterize the impact of the corporate-owning class on the health and survival of poor and working people. Chernomas and Hudson (2009) employed this term more recently to label contemporary corporate policies designed to maximize the accumulation of private profit while socializing associated risks and costs. Corporate externalization involves two components: 1) shifting significant production costs, such as those inherent in the release of greenhouse gases, onto government and also onto the kind of less powerful communities commonly studied by anthropologists; and 2) underplaying or denying responsibility for adverse outcome of such practices. In an insightful quip about the nature of capitalism and the alleged corrective benefits of the invisible hand of the market economy (articulated in Adam Smith's *The Wealth of Nations*), a climate-conscious character in one of science fiction writer Kim Stanley Robinson's (2015: 646) books remarks, " the invisible hand never picks up the check."

The theme of social murder in the context of anthropogenic climate change was emphasized by Mohamed Nasheed (2012), the deposed activist president of the Maldives, a cluster of low-lying islands: "If we can't stop the seas rising, if you allow for a 2-degree rise in temperature, you are actually agreeing to kill us."

The anthropology of climate change and health, now grappling with the transition to a global health perspective, is challenged again to consider the implications of planetary health in a time of global warming. At the theoretical level, this entails assessing the pathways through which all health issues everywhere are shaped by a human-impacted environment undergoing advancing degradation driven by the productivist/consumerist ethic that both dominates the world economic system and sustains vast social and health inequality. At the practical level, this requires urgent consideration of ethnographically informed pathways to sustainability that counter the march towards environmentally triggered disease and social collapse. This kind of work represents an important contribution anthropology can make toward addressing the dangers of climate change, namely revealing and explicating the interconnected social causes of climate change and social inequality.

Lived experience of climate change

Another important contribution of anthropology is investing and bringing to light the lived and culturally meaningful experience of climate change impacts, especially the experiences of those whose voices are rarely heard beyond the local level and whose ability to produce change is hampered by powerful social groups who benefit from this kind of silencing. Comments anthropologist Arjun Shankar (2016), "It is an understood fact that privilege and silence are strongly correlated." In light of this pattern, the lived experience of climate change—especially among the poor and other marginalized groups grappling already with the harsh realities of warming— constitutes a crucial missing link in our knowledge about global warming (Abbott and Wilson 2015).

Underlying this approach, from an anthropological perspective, is the role of culture in the shaping of experience and the role of experience in the shaping of culture. While older anthropological understandings tended to essentialize cultural systems (e.g. the unique culture of the Nuer, the Trobriand Islanders, the people of highland Burma), by seeing them as determinate, bounded, and homogeneous, newer conceptions emphasize fluidity, constructed processually through interaction and internally contested. Today, anthropologists tend to see culture as a resource people draw on to understand their world and to act in meaningful ways within it. Culture in this sense is not a trait list of values and norms, nor is it a straitjacket that narrowly confines action; rather it is a community process in which both sharing and nonsharing occur, as does negotiation and conflict about the best course of action or the most accurate interpretation of events. Culture allows our actions, our relationships, the environment and, for many, the spiritual realm to make sense to us.

There is an additional wrinkle in the contemporary anthropology understanding of culture. While cultural groups in the past were never socially isolated from their neighbors, from the sweeping forces of regional history, or, for hundreds of years, from the global reach of European colonialism, today, all people—including all of the groups discussed in this book—live in a globalizing world. There have been vast changes in the original populations, such as the peasant farmers of the Andes or those facing desertification in Mali, that have been of historic concern to the discipline. Today, a traditionally somewhat isolated, semi-nomadic, rainforest-dwelling horticulturalist and foraging group like the Waorani people of Ecuador now wears western clothes, prays in Christian churches, trades for soccer balls and packaged noodles, and must contend with the encroachments of multinational oil companies, logging companies, and the global epidemic diseases brought to them by outsiders. As a result, the Waorani cannot fairly be studied any longer as a remote people with a distinct and unique culture, however great the need for "lost tribes" has long been in the Western imaginary. While they have not lost key components of their traditional lifestyle, the Waorani are citizens of far broader social and economic worlds than in the past, as signaled by events like their public march in 2005 on the Ecuadoran Congress chanting "We don't want more drilling in our land. We don't want to disappear. We want our rights to be respected" (Survival International 2005). In this assertion of identity politics, the Waorani echo other groups around the world that have begun to formulate their concerns in a common, globally circulating language of human rights. Consequently, the issue has been raised about the restructuring capacity and fast-paced nature of globalization and the consequent demise of cultural diversity. Various observers have noted the potential source of such loss: multinational corporations, whose reach is seemingly limitless (and endlessly restless), promote the development of a consumerist culture and the thirst for manufactured commodities in the far-flung corners of the world. At the same time, global electronic communication promotes the rapid global flow of ideas and understandings, values and lifestyles, primarily of Western origin, that imperially overrun local traditions and lead arguably to the homogenization of human social life and the emergence of a global monoculture. The Waorani, the Eskimo, the Biloxi-Chitimacha-Choctaw, and all of the other diverse groups "tribal" and otherwise that have been studied by anthropologists must be re-imagined as local actors on a shifting global stage characterized by global forces of homogenization and local processes of indigenization (borrowing and integrating outside cultural elements) and resistance to the sense of being swallowed up by globalization.

As revealed among the indigenous people in Alaska, one form that resistance is taking involves traditional food. While, because of globalization, Eskimos buy and consume imported packed food, a loss of traditional foods, due to changing climate, feels like far more than a dietary alteration but rather is experienced as a loss of identity and personhood. In the case of the high mountain dwellers on Cotacachi mountain in Ecuador, the peak is still snow-capped, a culturally and spiritually framing of the world that struggles against the image of a snowless peak before their eyes. But people hold fast to the hope that the snow will come back and they will enjoy a return to better times. This optimism is expressed through praying for rain and, notably, through traditional offerings in which parcels of food are buried on the mountain to give back to the land the products that people receive from Mother Earth. A similar concern about traditional food and medicine is found among the Pointe-au-Chien Indian community located at the other end of the exposed road from the Isle de Jean Charles discussed in chapter 1. The Pointe-au-Chien too are facing devastating loss of their traditional lands because of rising seas and extreme storms. Before their lands slipped below the waves, tribal members fed themselves well, especially on seafood caught in the Gulf. But cheap imported shrimp has driven the market price below the sum indigenous fishers would need to spend on boat fuel and ice. People also raised livestock, trapped marsh hens, planted an array of fruits and vegetables, gathered indigenous plants like wild celery and parsley, hunted for turtles and alligators, and gathered medicinal plants from the now vanishing land. As the tribe was forced to move away from food self-reliance, family diets have shifted toward store-bought processed food. According to Shirell Parfait-Dardar, "We're on the front lines and it's going to spread … we can help make a difference. We have to consider what we're leaving behind for the next seven generations" (quoted in Yeoman 2017).

Beyond food tastes, people develop cultural understanding of the environment, such as the rich imagery of living on the skirts of Mother Earth of the people of Cotacachi. For the small farmers of Bangladesh, working the land has special cultural meaning. Even if they have been forced by climate change to flee to the city, many long to return to the world they knew, living close to the land, working with the soil to produce their family's sustenance, using their hard-won cultural knowledge of the environment to live a meaningful life.

With this kind of understanding of the importance of culture in a time of global warming, David Lipset (2017) studied the relationship of masculinity and the culture of rising sea levels among the Murik, a lagoon-dwelling, coastal people in Papua New Guinea. His project adds depth to the anthropological approach to climate change research. The Murik practice subsistence aquatic foraging using the lagoons to harvest fish and shellfish. But in 2007, as sea levels were rising, very high tides significantly eroded the narrow beaches on which the central Murik villages stand, leaving a shoreline just barely dividing the lakes from the ocean and affirming the vulnerability of coastal and small island ecosystems.

Living next to the ocean and long familiar with bad storms, the Murik developed a cultural understanding of harsh weather events. In Murik cosmology, society consists of human-spirits and ancestor-spirits that both possess canoe-bodies through which they act or travel. Both kinds of spirits wear sacred ornaments that legitimize their use of a hereditary magic called *timiit* that empowers them to succeed as members of society. Timiit spells influence many aspects of life, but they can also change the weather, create a tsunami, or raise sea levels to destroy beaches. People have differing views of their future. Some feel the risk from the ocean is critical and the future uncertain. In one Murik village, for example, a place where all the coconut palms had been washed out to sea, Lipset spoke to a small group of men about their situation. A middle-aged man summed up the group's sentiment: "The sea is killing us … . Now the distance between the sea and the lakes is very small … . We don't know what will happen. We will drift like logs" (quoted in Lipset 2017: 8).

Although everyone interviewed agreed that the tides of 2017 were the highest in their lifetimes, opinion regarding their meaning, and therefore what to do in response to them, was divided. Some people viewed the tides as signifiers of "nature" in a time on the edge of a catastrophe caused by global warming. The rival perspective was informed by timiit beliefs in magical explanations of weather events, which suggested using magical solutions to remove the risks the tides posed. Simultaneously, uncertainty and mistrust were widespread: most people were unsure about the causes of the high tides and either wanted to ignore them or just did not know what the future might hold. Whatever their view, most men and women of all ages were reluctant to move and leave behind their established villages.

As this discussion suggests, in times of rapid change, the ability of culture to allow people to experience a stable world where things happen for generally explicable reasons and the threat of chaos is kept at bay may weaken. The Murik are clearly struggling with this dilemma, and fissures have opened in people's understandings of what is going on with the tides. Various alternatives are possible, but, given the likelihood of more crushing tides, rapid cultural transformation and even relocation may be in store for the Murik.

Based on an array of anthropological, other ethnographic, and journalistic sources, as well as various case studies like the one involving the Murik above, an effort has been made in this book to bring together the diverse insider-articulated experiences of those being hit hardest by climate change and show how they are coping with painful circumstances over which they have little control. Central to this presentation is the interconnection between the effects of climate change and the consequences of social, economic, health, and other inequality. This approach reflects common themes in anthropology about the contribution the discipline can make in the study of climate change. For example, one articulation of anthropology's role in the climate crisis was presented by Barnes et al. (2013). These anthropologists identified three core contributions. The first draws nuanced attention to the local cultural values and structures of political relation that shape the production and interpretation of climate change knowledge and also influence responses to climate and environmental changes. The second is an awareness of the historical context that underpins contemporary climate debates. The last stems from anthropology's broad, holistic view of society and environment, which highlights the multiple and complex cultural, social, political, and economic changes that unfold in human society that always shape the impact of environmental change and may have more influence in shaping cascades of events than the actual physical transformation brought by global warming.

Interacting ecocrises

As Noyes et al. (2009: 971) point out, "climate change coupled with air pollutant exposures may have potentially serious adverse consequences for human health in urban and polluted regions." Moreover, as an experiment by Dreschslet-Parks, as well as the work of many other epidemiologists and laboratory scientists (Mauderly and Samet 2009), indicates, interaction among pollutants is especially risky. I have suggested the term "pluralea interactions" (derived from the Latin words *plur*, meaning many, and *alea*, meaning hazards) to refer to the growing number of health-related interactions that are occurring not just among anthropogenic contaminants but across the full panoply of environmental degradations in our increasingly human-dominated environment (Singer 2009). Exemplary of this phenomenon is that in addition to the problems that indigenous farmers face in relation to water availability in the Andes, they must simultaneously contend with water grabbing in the parámos by mining interests, hydropower companies, energy corporations, and cut-flower exporters. Similarly, the people of the Sundarbans of Bangladesh struggle not only with the effects of climate change but also with ocean tanker spills of toxic materials and the damaging effects of commercial salt-water shrimp farming.

As Spratt and Sutton (2008: xi) stress, global climate change constitutes only the exposed "tip of [a] broader global-sustainability iceberg" that includes a litany of environmental degradations that are now "converging rapidly in a manner not previously experienced." At the same time that climate change is disrupting the planet's geophysical feedback mechanisms that sustain inhabitable environments, Earth is also beset by multiple other ecocrises set in motion by human socioeconomic activities (Smil 2008). Ecocrisis interactions are increasingly putting humans and other species at risk of catastrophic outcomes (Rees 2003). Consequently, rather than framing the various environmental disasters we face as standalone threats, which is the conventional but narrow outlook that facilitates delayed and fragmented mitigation efforts as well as denialism, a focus on how the negative human impacts on the environment interact and enhance their effects raises questions about the extinction of species, populations, and ways of life.

Illustratively, one of the major difficulties facing scientists working to document the planetary effects of global warming involves establishing which of the many changes across physical and biological systems—including the disappearance of glaciers, melting permafrost, warming of the oceans, drying up of lakes, coastal erosion, species movement to higher latitudes and altitudes, changes in patterns of bird migrations, shifts of plankton and fish from cold- to warm-adapted communities, and the spread of vectors of infectious disease—are the direct consequence of anthropocentric greenhouse gas release and which have other causes (Parry et al. 2007). As Rosenzweig (2008) affirms, "Separating the influence of human-caused temperature increases from natural climate variations or other confounding factors, such as land-use changes or pollution is a real challenge." As this statement indicates, the focus of such analyses commonly is on single-cause understandings. Yet, in the contemporary world, climate change does not occur alone, it occurs in interaction with other ecocrises, often with even more harmful effects than would otherwise be the case.

One of the most useful contributions anthropology can make to the study of pluralea phenomenon, in addition to calling attention to their growing importance in planetary health, is the careful on-the-ground analysis, very likely often as members of multidisciplinary teams, of the nature of local and regional ecocrisis interactions, their social determinants, and community responses to these adverse events. Additionally, given the grave nature of the issues involved, the tremendous disparities in the distribution of the human consequences of pluralea phenomena, the inequalities in the distribution of political and economic power that underlies anthropogenic environmental changes, and the growing emergence of local and social movements for change, there is a need for an engaged anthropology to apply its insights in mitigation efforts.

Coping

Dealing with the effects of climate change can be conceived as unfolding along a continuum, with context- and location-specific local responses at one end and introduced organizational assistance programs at the other. In the middle are participatory programs that, to varying degrees, are structured around community input and involvement, and perhaps even community decision-making about the types of interventions to be implemented. In each of the case studies, varied indigenous ecologically adapted climate change coping mechanisms have been discussed, such as use of early ripening crop varieties, dispersion of planted areas to different locations, and staggered seed planting to help spread production risks over time among farmers facing desertification in Mali. Several income-generating activities, which, if successful, allow people to bank a small monetary surplus during hard times, were also described. A somewhat similar set of climate coping strategies—including planting rice earlier than in the past, switching to drought-resistant rice or flood-resistant rice (depending on location), tree planting, and seeking supplemental wage labor—have been reported by Sujakhu et al. (2016)

based on research in the Melamchi Valley of Nepal. Research among small farmers in Limpopo Province, South Africa, shows that they too have developed culture-based mechanisms of adaptation to the increasingly harsh weather conditions threatening their communities and subsistence agricultural production. These mechanisms emerge from people's indigenous knowledge of the seasons, soil fertility and texture, and crop variations. But climate change has taken a cultural toll. People report that because of harsh weather conditions they have had to give up consumption of traditional fruits and vegetables, brewing of traditional beer, production of traditional crop and livestock species, celebration of the first-fruit rituals, communal labor groups, and hunting and fishing (Rankoana 2016). Culture loss due to climate change remains an understudied issue but it was evident in discussion of food, attachment to place, connection with the activities of ancestors, and the loss of social networks among climate refugees in the case study chapters.

Research by climate scientists indicates that East Africa is experiencing warmer temperatures and will face a 5–20 percent increase in rainfall during the wet season and a 5–10 percent decrease in rainfall during the dry season by 2050 (Hulme et al. 2001). It is expected that these changes will occur in the form of sporadic and unpredictable weather events. Increased precipitation may come in a few very intense rainstorms that cause sudden erosion and water management problems. A number of studies have examined coping among small farmers in East Africa. A consistent observation is that East Africa is already experiencing increased temperature and decreased rainfall across all its agro-ecological zones (Gbegbelegbe et al. 2017).

Riziki Shemdoe (2011) of the Institute of Human Settlements Studies, for example, investigated effective indigenous climate change adaptation strategies among subsistence farmers in two different agro-ecological zones in Tanzania. All of the 400 respondents in his study confirmed climate change was a significant factor in their respective areas. The several indicators of climate change included prolonged drought, unpredictable rainfall, food shortages, poor pasture regeneration, and emerging human and animal diseases. About 45 percent of the respondents in each zone indicated that drought was the main factor contributing to food shortages. Participants reported that they depended on subsistence farming and livestock, both of which they said had been adversely affected by the unpredictable amount of rain and unreliable rainfall patterns. In each area, residents developed a range of coping strategies, including terracing the land to hold in water, tree planting, well drilling, digging of water reserves, mixed cropping, adoption of drought-resistant crops, and crop diversification. Farmers also used a traditional form of food preservation called *vihenge*, a storage structure for shelled corn made of bricks or twigs and plastered with mud or cow dung. People also reported that they changed their living and working behaviors, such as reducing cattle grazing near water sources or reducing the number of meals eaten per day. While these approaches were proving effective at the time of the study, temperatures have risen since then and, like local coping strategies everywhere, their long-term sustainability in prevention food insecurity and hunger is open to question.

When asked how the government could help them in dealing with climate change, "teaching environmental education" was ranked first in both communities. Otherwise the two communities differed in ranking their needs but both mentioned water source conservation. Both communities thought that village meetings were the best venue for government interventions. As this suggests, participatory efforts involving communities in a traditional gathering to address specific community-identified needs emerges as a principle for organized climate change coping interventions.

Not all introduced climate change coping strategies find ready acceptance among their target audiences. In Zimbabwe, the government has tried to promote a water-conserving form of farming known as "no till" or "zero tillage." This involves not plowing one's field and instead planting seeds directly into the ground without disturbing the soil. Additionally, the approach includes leaving the by-product from earlier harvests, like the stalks and leaves of corn, on the ground to hold in moisture and add nutrients to the soil, building soil fertility while limiting soil erosion. Preparation for no-till farming begins in the dry season when farmers dig small holes on their plots of land. They put a small portion of fertilizer or manure into each hole, and once the rains come, they plant their seeds. One small farmer who has adopted the method is Elizabeth Runema, a 67-year old woman from Guruvem, which is among Zimbabwe's driest districts. Runema explains:

> I used to rely on other people's cattle for draught power, and I never got to harvest on time … . I always failed to benefit from the first rains because those with draught power would still be busy and could only lend me their livestock and equipment when they had finished plowing their own fields… These days, I use zero-tillage, and I am getting much more yield than I ever used to get when I used to rely on other people's draught power … .
>
> (Quoted in No-Till Farmer 2011)

Despite the benefits touted by some adopters, the method encountered problems. In some areas where soils are sandy, farmers who tried no-till farming saw no improvements compared to farmers who ploughed their land. Additionally, notes Phillimon Ngirazi, an agricultural extension officer, "Changing minds that crop production is possible without ploughing has been difficult" (quoted in Bafana 2017). People want to see real evidence that the method works before giving up an approach to farming they learned from their parents and have practiced all of their lives. The growing pressures and disruptions of global warming prepare people for change, but knowing which changes to make is not a simple process.

Another approach implemented in East Africa is called Landcare (Mogoi et al. 2009). This community-based and government-supported approach to the sustainable management and use of agricultural natural resources was first implemented in East Africa in Uganda with a focus on capacity building among small farmers. The initiative seeks to enhance local ownership of natural resource management strategies by emphasizing the need for collective action, partnership, and sustainable methods in light of climate change. Some of the programs implemented through Landcare include the formation of farmer groups and farmer educational field schools that address issues like soil erosion, water pollution, deforestation, siltation (the build-up of fine mineral particles in water), ownership of land, and low productivity.

Because the specific impacts of climate are local, influenced by geography, river systems, among other environmental features, and by the structure of social relations and extent of social inequality, interventions must be grassroots and community based. The experience of Landcare staff is that while their projects are smaller scale and have not been scaled up to and developed into a broadly implementable model(s), communities that are provided with the kind of farm-related technologies that they see as useful, when coupled with participatory capacity building and empowerment initiatives, can build resilience to climate change. Moreover, "indigenous knowledge could be integrated into short and long-term adaptation strategies, and may be an important component of environmental conservation at the local level" (Kangalawe et al. 2011: 222).

Can there be a just and sustainable future?

In essence, while I have discussed many issues in this book, from the nature and causes of climate change, climate change denial, and social inequality, to the enhancing interaction of climate change with other anthropogenic ecocrises, to the many and varied local experiences, impacts, and responses to the adverse impacts of contemporary and future climate turmoil, the ultimate question, as always in discussing a grave and threatening problem, is what can be done about it. Is it possible to overcome ever-growing levels of human suffering, biodegradation and loss of biodiversity, the triggering of negative feedback, and our belated efforts to forcefully fight against climate change?

Some anthropologists have optimistically envisioned a sustainable future (Bodley 2014). Bodley's upbeat vision of an ecologically stable planetary society entails the development of a world system that has been referred to as democratic eco-socialism (Baer et al. 2013) or what world systems theorists Boswell and Chase-Dunn (2000) call global democracy. In other words, these ideas about a pathway to both sustainability and social equality stem from a belief that the current world system based on the capitalist mode of production cannot achieve either of the desired goals regarding the planet and human relations on it. The inability of the capitalist world system to achieve these goals stems from the inherent nature of this mode of production and the ways that it fosters the accumulation of wealth and power in few hands. Labor in capitalism is unavoidably hierarchically structured, as most people must sell their capacity to do work as a commodity on the market, where it is bought by those with the means to do so. Moreover, relations among nations are hierarchically ordered, in Wallerstein's model, into core, semi-periphery, and periphery nations. These structures are the foundations of global inequalities, which also extend to gender, ethnicity, sexual orientation, and other dimensions of human diversity. For example, factory workers in Haiti, mostly women, Paul Farmer (2005) reports, were being paid 28 cents per hour sewing Pocahontas pajamas in 2005; meanwhile, Michael Eisner, the U.S.-based chief executive officer of the Walt Disney Company, which commissioned the work, was being compensated at a rate of $97,000 an hour.

Those with great wealth acquire great power to protect and extend their riches, often at the expense of others, hence the emergence of polluting elites who drive global warming and other ecocrises by treating the environment in which we all live as a waste bin for their toxic and heat-blanketing emissions. Thus, Uruguayan scholar and author Eduardo Galeano (1991) referred to the exercise of power by the super-rich elite as the terrorism of money.

In considering responses to the unsustainability of capitalism, struggling for a global democratic organizational structure that prioritized social equity and planetary health appears as a reasonable direction for combating the entwined twin threat of inequality and global warming. To date, democratic eco-socialism remains a vision, but one in this age of multiple mounting ecocrises that merits thoughtful consideration. Included as elements of democratic eco-socialism are: 1) an economy oriented to meeting basic social needs, namely adequate food, clothing, shelter, recreation, the arts, and healthful conditions and resources; 2) a high degree of social equality and social fairness; 3) public ownership of productive forces; 4) representative and participatory democracy; and 5) environmental sustainability (Baer and Singer 2018). Ultimately, to succeed in light of opposition from those who most benefit from the world as it is, the shift to democratic eco-socialism in any country would have to be part of a global process.

The transition toward a democratic eco-socialist world system is not of course guaranteed and will require tremendous collective effort. But the first steps in this process are already underway as movements for justice and struggles against climate change spread around the world. Elements of these efforts can be seen in: 1) the demand for the implementation of emissions taxes at the site of production that include efforts to protect low-income people; 2) the rapid and spreading adoption of renewable energy sources and the creation of green jobs; 3) the anti-car movement and its demand for sustainable public transportation and travel where possible; 4) reforestation efforts and growing concern with sustainable food production 5) resistance to the capitalist culture of endless consumption; and 6) the exploration of sustainable settlement patterns and local communities (Baer 2018). These transitional steps suggest a direction for shifting human societies toward democratic eco-socialism and a safe climate.

Anti-systemic movements will no doubt have to play an instrumental role in building the political will that will enable the world to shift to an alternative world system organized around social justice and environmental sustainability. Given the failure to date of established international and national climate regimes in adequately containing the climate crisis, efforts to create a global climate governance process will have to build from below. For this to occur, the climate justice movement will need firm alliances with other progressive social movements, including the anti-corporate globalization or global justice movement. As Michael Hardt and Antonio Negri (2009: 94–95) assert, "only movements from below" possess the "capacity to construct a consciousness of renewal and transformation"— one that "emerges from the working classes and multitudes that autonomously and creatively propose anti-modern and anticapitalist hopes and dreams."

Going from the present capitalist world system, which has and continues to generate anthropogenic climate change, to an alternative global political economy, however it is defined, will require untold effort, but it is fair to ask: do we really have any other meaningful choice if we seek to avoid the downward spiral leading to the destruction of large sectors of humanity and life as we currently know it on Earth? We must also ask if global capitalism has any serious potential to become socially just or environmentally sustainable? Or must humanity move to new mode of economic, sociality and environmental interaction, whatever we may call it? Wallerstein's (2007: 328) answers to these queries is clear:

> I do not believe that our historical system is going to last much longer, for I consider it to be in a terminal structural crisis, a chaotic transition to some other system (or systems). I therefore believe that it could be possible to overcome the self-destructive patterns of global environmental change into which the world has fallen and establish alternative patterns. I emphasize however my firm assessment that the outcome of this transition is inherently uncertain and unpredictable.

Anthropologists and other social scientists have roles to play in this transition based on their on-the-ground research and familiarity with lifeways around the world and their analyses of social, political, and economic organization. By providing their skills and insights, the discipline can make a contribution to a achieving the transition to a more democratic and sustainable stage in the history of human societies on Earth. Needless to say, this seems a worthy goal for a field of study which, though born of colonialism, is intimately familiar with global poverty and social inequality, has studied the painful consequences of neoliberalism, and is now beginning to confront the social processes and relationships that drive climate change and people's responses to it.

In the aftermath of Trump's withdrawal from the Paris Climate Agreement, celebrated theoretical physicist, cosmologist, and Director of Research at the Centre for Theoretical Cosmology at the University of Cambridge, Stephen Hawking (quoted in Galeon and Norman 2017) asserted:.

> We are close to the tipping point where global warming becomes irreversible. Trump's action could push the Earth over the brink, to become like Venus, with a temperature of two hundred and fifty degrees, and raining sulphuric acid … . Climate change is one of the great dangers we face, and it's one we can prevent if we act now. By denying the evidence for climate change, and pulling out of the Paris Climate Agreement, Donald Trump will cause

avoidable environmental damage to our beautiful planet, endangering the natural world, for us and our children.

While this assessment is in keeping with the arguments made in this book, Hawking's proposed solution, the dispersal of human populations to other planets, is not. Such a technological initiative, if it were possible, would be enormously expensive, generate its own increase in greenhouse gases, and not address the issue of social inequality. Hence, the critical anthropology of climate change emphasizes the need for global warming mitigation, planetary sustainability, and social equity. Achieving these—something only possible through organized public action—is fundamental!

References

Abbott, D. and G. Wilson. 2015. *The Lived Experience of Climate Change: Knowledge, Science and Public Action.* Cham, Switzerland: Springer International Publishing.

Baer, H. 2008. Global warming as a by-product of the capitalist treadmill of production and consumption: The need for an alternative global system. *Australian Journal of Anthropology* 19: 58–62.

Baer, H. and M. Singer. 2018. *The Anthropology of Climate Change: An Integrated Critical Perspective*, 2nd edition. Abingdon, UK: Routledge, Earthscan.

Baer, H., Singer, M. and Susser, I. 2013. *Medical Anthropology and the World System. A Critical Perspective.* Santa Barbara, CA: Praeger.

Bafana, B. 2017. Faced with more drought, Zimbabwe's farmers hang up their ploughs. Thomas Reuters Foundation. http://news.trust.org/item/20170609001146-bphxi/.

Barnes, J., M. Dove, M. Lahsen, A. Mathews, P. McElwee, F. McIntosh et al. 2013. Contribution of anthropology to the study of climate change. *Nature Climate Change* 3: 541–544.

Bodley, J. 2014. *Anthropology and Contemporary Human Problems.* Lanham, MD: AltaMira Press.

Boswell, T. and C. Chase-Dunn. 2000. *The Spiral of Capitalism and Socialism.* Boulder, CO: Lynne Rienner.

Chernomas, R. and I. Hudson. 2009. Social murder: The long-term effects of conservative economic policy. *International Journal of Health Services* 39(1): 107–121.

Farmer, P. 2005. *Pathologies of power: Health, Human Rights, and the New War on the Poor.* Berkeley, CA: University of California Press

Foster, J., B. Clark, and R. York. 2010. *The Ecological Rift: Capitalism's War on the Earth.* New York: Monthly Review Press.

Galeano, E. 1991. Professional life/3, as cited in Paul Farmer, 2005, *Pathologies of Power: Health, Human Rights, and the New War on the Poor.* Berkeley, CA: University of California Press.

Gbegbelegbe, S., J. Serem, C. Stirling, F. Kyazze, M. Radney, and M. Misiko. 2017. Smallholder farmers in eastern Africa and climate change: A review of risks and adaptation options with implications for future adaptation programmes. *Climate Development* 10(4). DOI: 10.1080/17565529.2017.1374236.

Galeon, D. and A. Norman. 2017. Stephen Hawking: We are close to the tipping point where global warming becomes irreversible. *Futurism.* https://futurism.com/stephen-hawking-we-are-close-to-the-tipping-point-where-global-warming-becomes-irreversible/.

Hardt, M. and A. Negri. 2009. *Commonwealth*. Cambridge, MA: Harvard University Press.

Horton, R. 2014Reimagining the meaning of health. *The Lancet* 384: 218.

Hulme, M., D. Doherty, T. Ngara, M. New, and D. Lister. 2001. African climate change:1900–2100. *Climate Research* 17: 145–168.

Kangalawe, R., S. Mwakalila, and P. Masolwa. 2011. Climate change impacts, local knowledge and coping strategies in the Great Ruaha River catchment area, Tanzania. *Natural Resources* 2: 212–223.

Lindsay, J. 2001. Global warming heats up. *Brooking Review* (Fall): 26–29.

Lipset, D. 2017. Masculinity and the culture of rising sea-levels in a mangrove lagoon in Papua New Guinea. *Maritime Studies* 16: 2.

Maslin, M. 2015. How does the IPCC know climate change is happening? *ULC Lancet Commission*. http://blogs.ucl.ac.uk/lancet-commission/.

Mauderly, J. and J. Samet. 2009. Is there evidence for synergy among air pollutants in causing health effects? *Environmental Health Perspective* 117(1): 1–6.

Mogoi, J., K. Masuki, J. Tanul, and J. Mutua. 2009. Beyond coping mechanisms: Adaptation of communities to climate change through landcare in East Africa. Paper presented at the 4th Biennial National Landcare Conference held in Limpopo, RSA. www.worldagrofor estry.org/downloads.

Nasheed, M. 2012. Coup in Maldives: Adviser to ousted Pres. Mohamed Nasheed speaks out from hiding as arrest sought. *Democracy Now*. www.democracynow.org/2012/2/9/ coup_in_maldives_adviser_to_ousted.

No-Till Farmer. 2011. Zimbabwe farmers discover no-Till. www.no-tillfarmer.com/articles/ 932-zimbabwe-farmers-discover-no-till.

Noyes, P., M. McElwee, H. Miller, B. Clark, L. Van Tiem, K. Walcott et al. 2009. The toxicology of climate change: Environmental contaminants in a warming world. *Environment International* 35(6): 971–986.

Panorama. 2017. Planetary health 101: Information and resources. Panorama Perspectives: Conversations on Planetary Health. https://assets.rockefellerfoundation.org/app/uploads/ 20170919100156/Planetary-Health-101-Information-and-Resources.pdf.

Parry, M., O. Canziani, J. Palutikof, P. van der Linden, and C. Hanson (eds). 2007. Impacts, adaption and vulnerability: Contributions of Working Group II to the Fourth Assessment Report of the Intergovernmental Panel on Climate Change. Cambridge: Cambridge University Press.

Rankoana, S. 2016. Perceptions of climate change and the potential for adaptation in a rural community in Limpopo Province, South Africa. *Sustainability* 8: 672.

Rees, M. 2003. *Our Final Hour: A Scientist's Warning: How Terror, Error, and Environmental Disaster Threaten Humankind's Future in this Century—On Earth and Beyond*. New York: Basic Books.

Roberts, T. and B. Parks. 2007. *A Climate of Injustice: Global Inequality, North-South Politics, and Climate Policy*. Cambridge, MA: MIT Press.

Robinson, K. 2015. *Green Earth*. New York: Del Rey.

Rockström, J., K. Steffen, A. Noone, H. Persson, F. Chapin III et al. 2009. Planetary boundaries: Exploring the safe operating space for humanity. *Ecology and Society* 14(2): 32.

Rosenzweig, C. 2008. Warming climate is changing life on global scale. Goddard Institute for Space Studies. www.giss.nasa.gov/research/briefs.

Shankar, A. 2016. Silence and privilege renegotiated. *Cultural Anthropology*. https://culanth. org/fieldsights/1001-silence-and-privilege-renegotiated.

Shemdoe, R. 2011. Tracking effective indigenous adaptation strategies on impacts of climate variability on food security and health of subsistence farmers in Tanzania.: African Technological Policy Studies Network, Nairobi, Kenya.

Singer, M. 2009. Beyond global warming: interacting ecocrises and the critical anthropology of health. Anthropology Quarterly82(3): 795–820.

Singer, M. 2014. Climate change and planetary health. *Somatosphere*, September 8. http://somatosphere.net/2014/09/climate-change-and-planetary-health.html.it.

Smil, V. 2008. *Global Catastrophes and Trends: The Next Fifty Years*. Cambridge, MA: MIT Press.

Spratt, D. and P. Sutton 2008. *Climate Code Red: The Case for Emergency Action*. Melbourne, Australia: Scribe.

Sujakhu, N., S. Ranjitkar, R. Niraula, B. Pokharel, D. Schmidt-Vogt, and J. Xu. 2016. Farmers' perceptions of and adaptations to changing climate in the Melamchi Valley of Nepal. *Mountain Research and Development* 36(1): 15–30.

Survival International. 2005. Waorani indians march against oil drilling. www.survivalinternational.org/news/864.

Wallerstein, I. 2007. The ecology and the economy: What is rational? In A. Hornborg, J. McNeill, and M. Martinez-Alier (eds), *Rethinking Environmental History: World-System History and Global Environmental Change*. Lanham, MD: AltaMira Press, pp. 379–389.

Yeoman, B. 2017. Reclaiming native ground sapiens. *Sapiens*. The Conversation. www.sapiens.org/culture/louisiana-native-americans-climate-change/.

INDEX